MW01598702

DAY BY DAY IN PRAYER

Day by Day
in
PRAYER

Edited By
IVAN STEEDS

PRECIOUS SEED PUBLICATIONS

© Copyright Precious Seed Publications
P.O. Box 8, Neath, West Glamorgan, UK SA11 1QB

First Published December 1997

ISBN 1 871642 11 6

This is the fifth book in the Day by Day series.
The others are:
  Day by Day through the Old Testament
  Day of Day through the New Testament
  Day by Day in the Psalms
  Day by Day – Moments with the Master

Printed and bound by Redwood Books Ltd., Trowbridge

Contents

Acknowledgements

This latest publication in the Day by Day series of books takes the number of titles available to five. Over the years we have been made aware of their popularity with Christian readers, not only because of a continuing demand for them, but also because of the expressions of appreciation that are brought to our notice. These come from many quarters. We are deeply thankful to God for granting us a unique opportunity to serve Him in helping to meet the needs of His people. With such thoughts in mind we now publish Day by Day in Prayer, and it is our hope that it will be seen as a worthy addition to the earlier books, and be as well received.

A number of people have contributed towards the production of this book, and the committee of *Precious Seed* would wish to acknowledge the extent of their participation, with grateful thanks for all that has been done.

The written ministry accompanying the suggested readings from Scripture has been provided by brethren whose record of service among assemblies of God's people recommends them for this particular task. All were already busy in the Lord's work, yet they willingly accepted this extra burden, appreciating the value that attaches to such an extension of their ministry as comes through publication of this book. Particular thanks should be expressed to Malcolm Horlock for his helpful support since the project was first considered and, latterly, for his painstaking assistance in the onerous task of proof-reading. Roy Hill's expert help in planning and directing production of this volume has proved invaluable, as has the attentive, dedicated efforts of Derek Hill in supervising the typesetting. The beautiful pictures shown on the front and back covers were provided by Professor Alan Linton, who also wrote helpful, descriptive captions for each of them.

Our prayers go with *Day by Day in Prayer*, that it may prove to be a help and a blessing to all its readers.

On behalf of the *Precious Seed* Committee

Ivan Steeds

November 1997

Contributors and their Contributions

John Riddle	*Broxbourne*	Jan. 1 - 15
Roy Hill	*Pensford*	Jan. 16 - 31
Eric Parmenter	*Ilminster*	Feb. 1 - 14
Paul Young	*Maesteg*	Feb. 15 - 29
Howard Barnes	*Bromborough*	Mar. 1 - 15
Arthur Shearman	*Worcester*	Mar. 16 - 31
Cyril Cann	*Glastonbury*	April 1 - 14
Dennis Clapham	*Leicester*	April 15 - 17
Ivan Steeds	*Bristol*	April 18 - May 2
John Mitchell	*Cardiff*	May 3 - 18
Bernard Osborne	*Cardiff*	May 19 - 31
Ken Rudge	*St. Austell*	June 1 - 15
Howard Coles	*Coleford*	June 16 - 30
David Newell	*Glasgow*	July 1 - 14
Michael Browne	*Bath*	July 15 - 29
Alan Gamble	*Glasgow*	July 30 - Aug. 10
Brian Charles	*Appledore*	Aug. 11 - 27
David Gilliland	*Craigavon*	Aug. 28 - Sept. 12
Jim Flanigan	*Moneyrea*	Sept. 13 - 29
Tony Renshaw	*Manchester*	Sept. 30 - Oct. 15
Stephen Essery	*Tycroes*	Oct. 16 - Nov. 1
Peter Scammell	*Cwmbran*	Nov. 2 - 17
Colin Lacey	*Stourbridge*	Nov. 18 - Dec. 1
Malcolm Horlock	*Cardiff*	Dec. 2 - 16
Jim Baker	*Jim Baker*	Dec. 17 - 31

INTRODUCTION

In life we accept that there are certain elements that are essential to our physical survival—our breathing, eating and drinking, taking exercise, resting—these are the basic necessities of life, and deprivation of any one of them must lead to a deterioration in the quality, or even loss, of life. Again, we all know that the adoption of a proper, recommended life-style leads to a good condition of general health, and physical fitness. It is so for 'born again' Christians in their new way of life! They too must realize there are other vital elements that cannot be neglected, and proper practices that must be followed in aspiring towards a healthy spiritual life-style. Let it be said that although we are already possessors of eternal life through Jesus Christ our Lord, true fulfilment in life can only be achieved to the degree that we seek to 'lay hold on eternal life' i.e. reach out to grasp, and to enjoy that which is 'ours for the taking'.

In any compiled list of elements deemed essential for our spiritual survival or, better, our spiritual health and vigour, prayer must rank high in priority. Prayer has been described as 'the Christian's vital breath, the Christian's native air'. It is our 'lifeline'; on earth it is our link with heaven. It is our means of communication with God—He is our Father, and we are His needy children, entirely dependent on Him.

Although it might present us with some difficulty to attempt to define in exact terms what constitutes prayer, nevertheless it is true to say that we all have some appreciation of what it is. This is not because we have at any time undergone a process of education, or programme of induction in prayer, but because we have prayed from the very beginning of our new life in Christ. 'Oh happy day that fixed my choice on Thee, my Saviour and my God', we sing, looking back to that 'happy day' when we cried to God for mercy and forgiveness. We know that on that happy day He heard our cry, although we need no reminding of the imperfect and inarticulate manner in which we expressed faith and trust in the One who died that we might live. Nevertheless, we are assured that He heard us and we were gloriously saved! That initial cry might be likened to the first cry of the newly-born infant—it was proof of life, establishing that link between child and parent whereby the needs of the one, expressed in such inadequate fashion, are fully appreciated and met by the care of the other. So we cried out to God and were heard—we prayed, and knew immediately and instinctively something of the nature and value of prayer.

No one needs to take lessons in praying, neither is prayer reserved for only the gifted, for there is no spiritual gift that comes under this heading. Prayer is for every child of God, and is a spiritual exercise in which we all may address our God who is spirit through the promptings of the Holy Spirit. It is thus that we pray in the Spirit, and such a holy occupation provides the means whereby we may rise to greater heights of spiritual experience through increased fellowship with God, our Father. Prayer is a form of service *to God* and it is essential in our service *for God*. Prayer is protective, and prevents our lapsing into sin. Prayer is the indication in our lives of our dependence upon God, and through it we express our own inadequacies and claim the sufficiency of God's provision for us. Prayer is a tacit admission of our own helplessness, and an acknowledgement of almighty God's willingness to help. Prayer should not be a tactic of last resort in times of trouble but a practice of daily, hourly, momently seeking God's help in every circumstance of life. We should 'pray without ceasing'.

PRAYER IN THE OLD TESTAMENT

From Genesis to Revelation the Bible presents us with a record of men and women praying to God, and of God responding to their prayers. What is indicated from the beginning is that the prayer of the suppliant was heavily dependent upon the suppliant's conception of God. The very act of calling upon Him in such a way demonstrated an assumption that He was available to them, and capable of hearing their cry. Wherever the situation, and whatever the circumstances, there was belief that God was sufficiently interested in the welfare of men that He would personally intervene to help where help was required. Each and every intervention by God reinforced this belief, and assisted in the compilation of a record of His mercy, might and majesty. Each revelation of God brought greater realization of His character, and His requirements of man: to some extent this influenced both the pattern and the practice of prayer. The establishment of a covenant relationship between Israel and God contained within it the idea of full, continuous lines of communication established between God and His earthly people, as He maintained them in the midst of surrounding nations. His special care for them encouraged their appeal for His help in times of difficulty and danger. Many of the psalms illustrate this development, and indicate that, in part, Old Testament prayer was made up of petitions, supplications, and protestations that invite God to pour out judgement upon the ungodly. However, there are inclusions of thanksgiving, and praise for help given by God, as well as ascriptions of worshipful praise rendered to God with reference to His person and His works. Again, in the Old Testament there are occasions recorded of prayerful intercession, as for example Moses' prayers of appeal to God on behalf of sinning Israel. The prophets had a prayerful relationship with God, regularly seeking His face and looking for guidance as to the messages He would have them deliver to His people.

PRAYER IN THE NEW TESTAMENT

The full-orbed revelation of God in the person of His Son introduced us to a deeper understanding of prayer. In His life our Lord set an example of prayer and continually raised the issue of prayer in His teaching. We note the manner in which He prayed, the frequency of His praying, and in what situations He resorted to prayer. We hear the statements He made and the enlightening parables He told concerning prayer—we learn of God's desire that His people should so speak to Him in every circumstance of life, and of the certainty of His response. At the request of His disciples our Lord gave an example of prayer, the so-called 'Lord's Prayer', saying, 'After this manner therefore pray ye'.

The Son revealed that prayer was to be addressed to the Father, and we see this as a reflection of the new relationship between God and man created by Christ's redemptive work upon the cross. Prayer would be offered in the name of Christ; this was not intended to be a simple and repetitive form of words attached to our prayers on each occasion of prayer, but rather an acknowledgement in prayer of the part played by Christ in the matter of our communication with God. To pray in that name should cause us to seek to emulate the manner of Christ's praying. In life He demonstrated total submission to His Father's will, and this was reflected in His prayers and His acceptance that God's will must be done. Prayer would be prompted by the Holy Spirit of God, and in our praying we would become aware of His leading and help.

The Acts of the Apostles tells us how much the early Christians followed our Lord's example and teachings concerning prayer. They believed in prayer, and so in prayer they turned to God in every situation that arose, proving again and again that God hears and answers prayer. They learned the value of corporate prayer and demonstrated the extent to which prayer should figure in the life of the local church if the church is to serve God effectively in its locality.

The teachings of the later books of the New Testament build upon the teachings of our Lord regarding prayer, emphasizing the value, indeed the necessity, of prayer. We are enlightened as to the means whereby we can pray, through the constant ministry of our Great High Priest. The New Testament ends with heartfelt prayer, 'Even so, come, Lord Jesus'.

Prayer is essential ...

For engagement with God. It is by this means that we communicate directly with Him. God encourages us to do so, and at all times.

For empowerment from God. As God is the source of all our power, prayer is the channel by which power is directed to us.

For enlargement through God. Our spiritual development depends upon the extent to which we bring before God the deepest desires of our hearts, that He may respond to us out of His heart of love. To pray out of need brings answers to our prayers—but more than that, it brings about changes in us!

For enrichment by God. God's heavenly blessings are sought and realized through prayer. The alternative is spiritual poverty!

For enjoyment with God. Prayer is delightful. When at prayer, we are enabled to sit under His shadow with great delight. Sorrow can be turned to joy through prayer.

For enlightenment in God. Our spiritual perception is improved by praying. When we are perplexed, or undecided, we receive guidance from God through prayer.

For encouragement from God. Spirits are uplifted, and hope is restored through prayer.

For entrustment to God. Whatever the burden, whatever the care, we can with confidence 'take it to the Lord in prayer'.

Essentials to prayer

Our Eligibility. As beloved children, we can bring our petitions and praises to God, our Father, crying 'Abba, Father'.

Our Enthusiasm. We should 'give ourselves continually to prayer'.

Our Entreaty. Out of our need we cry to God, and our prayers must express the intensity of our feelings and desires.

Our Enquiry. In the manner of His Son, we should seek for God's guidance that His will might be done in our lives—this should be our first recourse in any situation of difficulty, as well as in the routine events of life.

Our Endurance. 'Men ought always to pray, and not faint' ... 'praying always with all prayer and supplication in the Spirit, and watching thereunto with all perseverance and supplication for all saints'.

Our Effectiveness. 'Elijah was a man subject to like passions as we are', and in his time the 'effectual fervent prayer' of this righteous man availed much. We can prove that even today 'prayer changes things'!

Our Exactness. We need to make specific requests in our prayers, and to concentrate upon particular matters wherein we seek God's help.

Our Expectancy. We must ask in faith, and thereafter wait for God's response.

Essentially, praying is ...

Asking, that we may receive.

Thanking, for what we have received.

Praising God for all that He is to us.

Confessing our sins. 'He is faithful and just to forgive us our sins, and to cleanse us from all unrighteousness'.

Interceding on behalf of others.

This introduction has been written without the inclusion of references from scripture to justify the general statements that have been made. The reason for this is simple—the 366 suggested readings from Scripture that follow more than adequately support all that has been written here. These readings focus on the prayers that God has seen fit to record for us, on incidents where prayer was involved, and on various references to prayer. The believer who takes time daily to read and meditate upon these portions will find enormous help from them, and gain a greater understanding of prayer. If, as a result, the reader's prayer-life is stimulated and enhanced, then the whole intention for this book will have been realized.

January 1st
Genesis 4. 26

CALL UPON THE NAME OF THE LORD

At the very beginning men prayed, calling on the name of the Lord, and others followed in their steps. Abraham 'called on the name of the Lord' after building the altar between Bethel and Hai, Gen. 12. 8. He did so again in the same place after his return from Egypt, and yet again at Beer-sheba, 13. 4; 21. 33. Isaac followed his father's excellent practice in this way when he was at Beer-sheba, 26. 25. The psalmist cried, 'Lord, I have called *daily* upon thee, I have stretched out my hands unto thee', Ps. 88. 9. Perhaps *we* 'began ... to call upon the name of the Lord', but, alas, it is no longer a daily habit.

Many other things which we now know so well began at this time. See Genesis 4. 17-24. It was *then*, in the world of Cain, that men began 'to call upon the name of the Lord'. The streams of human activity which began in those far-off years have now reached flood tide. Industry, commerce, business, music, and so many other things can buy us, body, mind and soul, if we allow them to do so. How necessary for *us* 'to call upon the name of the Lord'!

But look again. God was at work in the world of Cain. 'And to Seth, to him also there was born a son; and he called his name Enos'. We watch another story unfold. Seth, Enos, Cainan, Mahalaleel, Jared, Enoch, Methuselah, Lamech, Noah; Luke chapter 2 traces the ancestry of the Lord Jesus back to these men. How wonderful! God was preparing the way for the advent of His beloved Son! It is the story of His love for *us*! It means that we gladly 'call upon the name of the Lord' with thanksgiving and praise.

Enos means 'mortal' or 'frail'. MATTHEW HENRY calls it, 'that general name for all men, which bespeaks the weakness, frailty, and misery, of man's state'. The apostle Paul felt this keenly, and 'besought the Lord thrice'. It was all to no avail, or so it seemed. But there was an answer: 'He said unto me, My grace is sufficient for thee: for my strength is made perfect in weakness', 2 Cor. 12. 8-9. As a true son of Enos, Paul called upon the Lord, and found divine strength.

Have you begun 'to call on the name of the Lord'? Then continue to do so. But with your petitions for divine help in difficult days, do not forget to say with wonder, 'Thanks be unto God for his unspeakable gift', 2 Cor. 9. 15.

January 2nd

Genesis 12. 7-8

TWO ALTARS

In all, Abraham built four altars, and the first two are in Genesis 12. 7-8. Abraham built altars, Isaac dug wells, and Jacob erected pillars. *We* should do all three. Men and women of faith, Heb. 11. 9, must worship like Abraham, find refreshment like Isaac, and salute the faithfulness of God like Jacob.

'And the Lord appeared unto Abram, and said, Unto thy seed will I give this land: and *there* builded he an altar unto the Lord, who appeared unto him'. His first altar was built in the *plain* of Moreh, with the telling observation, 'And the Canaanite was then in the land'. C H MACKINTOSH reminds us that 'there, too, he finds the Lord'. How often we too feel the power of 'the Canaanite', and the life of faith looks decidedly uncertain. It is then, like the disciples on Galilee, that we hear our beloved Saviour's voice, 'Be of good cheer: it is I; be not afraid', Matt. 14. 27. In thankfulness, we build an altar.

'And he removed from thence unto a *mountain* on the east of Bethel, and pitched his tent, having Bethel on the west, and Hai on the east; and *there* he builded an altar unto the Lord, and called upon the name of the Lord'. Mountains are so often places of communion with God. The Lord Jesus, 'when he had sent the multitude away ... went up into a mountain apart to pray', Matt. 14. 23. A mountain frees us from the distractions of the busy world below, and gives us perspectives that are impossible on the plain. But those rewards are not won without time, effort and discipline.

Abraham looked west, and saw Bethel. He looked east, and saw Hai. In one direction, the 'house of God'. In the other, 'the heap', which is strongly suggestive of ruins. Between the house of God, and the heap of ruins, an altar! *We* should bow in worship as we consider the work of the Lord Jesus, who has delivered us from eternal ruin, enabling as to say, 'I will dwell in the house of the Lord for ever', Ps. 23. 6. Like Abraham we too must call 'on the name of the Lord', first to give thanks that in infinite love He has given us an *eternal home*, John 14. 2, and then to pray and intercede for our fellow men and women who stand in jeopardy of eternal banishment from His presence.

January 3rd

Genesis 15. 2-3

THE PRAYER OF A DEJECTED MAN

We are all people of fluctuating moods, and it is helpful to remember that great men and women of God in the Bible were cast in exactly the same mould. Even Abraham, that man of outstanding faith, was not exempt. After his refusal of any reward from the king of Sodom, 'the word of the Lord came unto Abram in a vision, saying, Fear not: I am thy shield, and thy exceeding great reward'. The elation of victory over Chedorlaomer and his colleagues had evidently given place to depression. Was he disconsolate because Lot had failed to learn the lesson, and returned to Sodom? God knew all about the feelings of His servant, and reminds him of His interest and care; '*I* am *thy* shield, and *thy* exceeding great reward'. It is reassuring to notice that this is in the present tense.

But there was only one reward that was dear to Abraham's heart, and God's promise to be his 'exceeding great reward' did not seem to provide the answer. We can catch the discontent in his voice as he answers, 'Lord God, what wilt thou give me, seeing I go childless, and the steward of my house is this Eliezer of Damascus?'. Abraham was evidently a very disappointed man. God had apparently failed him, and the prospect of Eliezer's succession did not seem an adequate fulfilment of the promise, 'In thee shall all families of the earth be blessed'.

We hesitate to criticize Abraham, for there must be very few of God's people, if any, who have not questioned His ways in their lives. In fact, we have grounds to commend Abraham, for he did tell God exactly what was in his heart. The psalmist set us all a good example when he wrote, 'In my distress I called upon the Lord, and cried unto my God', Ps. 18. 6.

What kind of answer can we expect when we tell God about our disappointments and shattered dreams? Abraham discovered that 'the Lord is gracious, and full of compassion; slow to anger, and of great mercy', Ps. 148. 8. There was no recrimination. God graciously reaffirmed His promise to Abraham; 'He that shall come forth out of thine own bowels, shall be thine heir'. There was no more complaint, for Abraham 'believed in the Lord'. *We* must remember that our God 'cannot lie', Titus 2. 2. His promises are 'yea' and 'Amen', 2 Cor. 1. 20.

January 4th

Genesis 16. 1-16

GOD SHALL HEAR

Hagar would never forget the kindness and mercy of God. She was told to call her son Ishmael, 'because the Lord hath heard thy affliction', v. 11. His name means 'God shall hear'. So often in our own experience, the mention of a name, or a place, or a date, reminds us of God's help and blessing in the past, and we turn to God with renewed thanksgiving.

Genesis 16 does not paint a glowing picture of Abraham, Sarah or Hagar. 'Abram hearkened to the voice of Sarai', without any apparent reference to God in the matter, and seemed quite unwilling to intervene when relationships between Hagar and Sarah became decidedly unpleasant. Sarah evidently blamed God for her barrenness, and 'dealt hardly' with Hagar when it became evident that the Egyptian slave girl was to bear Abraham's child. Hagar was not slow in showing her contempt for her barren mistress, and soon paid dearly for her arrogance. It all began with failure to seek 'counsel at the mouth of the Lord', Josh. 9. 14. But none of us is in a position to point the finger at Abraham. How often *we* fail to 'take it to the Lord in prayer'.

At this point in the narrative, we meet, for the first time in Scripture, 'the angel of the Lord'. There can be no doubt at all that 'the angel of the Lord' is a divine Person. Who else could say, 'I will multiply thy seed exceedingly, that it shall not be numbered for multitude'? It is most significant, therefore, that 'the angel of the Lord' should first appear to a despised and mis-used slave girl! He comes to help a poor young woman in need. There is a remarkable parallel in the New Testament, for the risen Lord Jesus appeared first, not to Peter, James or John, but to grief-stricken Mary Magdalene, Mark 16. 9. The parallel is not quite so remarkable, however, when we remember that 'the angel of the Lord' can be none other than the Lord Jesus Christ Himself!

Centuries later, the apostle Paul wrote about the presence of the Lord when he, like Hagar, was left alone; 'At my first answer no man stood with me, but all men forsook me ... notwithstanding the Lord stood with me, and strengthened me', 2 Tim. 4. 16-17. For Hagar, 'the fountain in the way to Shur', became 'Beer-lahai-roi', meaning, 'The well of Him that liveth and seeth me'. He still sees, and He still delivers.

January 5th
Genesis 17. 18-27

O THAT ISHMAEL MIGHT LIVE BEFORE THEE

The psalmist tells us that 'as for God, his way is perfect', Ps. 18. 30, but we cannot always see the perfection of His plan for *our* lives. Sometimes we have to exclaim, 'Verily thou art a God that hidest thyself, O God of Israel, the Saviour', Isa. 45. 15, and this only serves to emphasize that 'we walk by faith, not by sight', 2 Cor. 5. 7.

Abraham did not doubt the promise of God that 'in thee shall all the families of the earth be blessed', and had been assured that 'he that shall come forth out of thine own bowels shall be thine heir', Gen. 15. 1-4. But Sarah was barren, and since, in any case, she had not been named as the mother of the promised heir, the birth of Ishmael seemed the logical answer to God's promise. It was thirteen years later (compare Genesis 16. 16 with 17. 1) that God told Abraham that a son would be born to Sarah, and emphasized it by repetition, 'I will bless *her* ... and *she* shall be a mother of nations ... *Sarah thy wife* shall bear thee a son ... But my covenant will I establish with Isaac, which *Sarah* shall bear unto thee', vv. 16, 19, 21. After all those long and painful years, Abraham could now see God's perfect will! He saw it on earth and in time: *we* may have to wait until heaven and eternity.

But the narrative does suggest that Abraham still had some difficulty in accepting that Ishmael was not the promised heir; 'And Abraham said unto God, O that *Ishmael* might live before thee!'. After all, 'shall a child be born unto him that is an hundred years old? and shall Sarah, that is ninety years old, bear?'. But God was gracious to his elderly servant, and there was no recrimination when the promise was reiterated, 'And God said, Nay, but Sarah thy wife *shall* bear thee a son', v. 19 RV.

There is another way of looking at Abraham's prayer, 'O that Ishmael might live before thee!'. He had just received a wonderful promise from God. Against all odds, Sarah was to bear a son, and in his joy, Abraham could have completely overlooked the welfare of Ishmael. But there was no selfishness in Abraham. There was none in the Lord Jesus: He was the perfect example of the exhortation, 'Look not every man on his own things, but every man also on the things of others', Phil. 2. 4-8. There should be no selfishness in our prayers either.

Genesis 18. 23-33

WILT THOU ALSO DESTROY THE RIGHTEOUS?

We could describe the story of Abraham and Lot, his nephew, as an exercise in brotherly relations. In Genesis 13. 8, Abraham *deferred* to his brother. In Genesis 14. 4, Abraham *delivered* his brother. In Genesis 18. 23-33, Abraham *interceded* for his brother.

Genesis 18 helps us to understand why Abraham's intercession was so effective. *Firstly*, we should notice the *intimacy of his communion with God*. Abraham is called 'the Friend of God' in James 2. 23, citing 2 Chronicles 20. 7 and Isaiah 41. 8, and this close relationship becomes apparent when God says, 'Shall I hide from Abraham that thing which I do … ?', v. 17. The Lord Jesus said, 'Henceforth I call you not servants; for the servant knoweth not what his lord doeth: but I have called you friends; for all things that I have heard of my Father I have made known unto you', John 15. 15. *Secondly*, we should notice the *integrity of his life before God*. 'For I know him, that he will command his children and his household after him, and they will keep the way of the Lord, to do justice and judgement', v. 19. God knew that Abraham could be trusted to use his influence properly. The apostle John reminds us that 'whatsoever we ask, we receive of him, because we keep his commandments, and do those things which are pleasing in his sight', 1 John 3. 22. *Thirdly*, we should notice the *implicitness of his faith in God*. 'That be far from thee to do after this manner, to slay the righteous with the wicked: and that the righteous should be as the wicked, that be far from thee: Shall not the Judge of all the earth do right?', v. 25. In perplexing circumstances, we can exclaim with Paul, 'Wherefore, sirs, be of good cheer: for *I believe God*, that it shall be even as it was told me', Acts 27. 25. *Fourthly*, we should notice the *importunity of his prayer to God*. This is so clear from verses 23-32. Like Epaphras centuries later, he 'laboured fervently' in prayer.

We see the effectiveness of Abraham's intercession, for 'it came to pass, when God destroyed the cities of the plain, that God remembered Abraham, and sent Lot out of the midst of the overthrow', Gen. 19. 29. In other words, 'the effectual fervent prayer of a righteous man availeth much', Jas. 5. 16. How effective are our prayers? Do we really expect results?

January 7th

Genesis 20.17-18

ABRAHAM AT GERAR

It has been well said that if we fail to learn from our mistakes, we will almost certainly repeat them! Abraham is a case in point, and events at Gerar prove that like Elijah, he was 'a man subject to like passions as we are', Jas. 5. 17. This wasn't the first time that Abraham described Sarah as his sister (see Gen. 12. 10-20), and on both occasions he was reprimanded for his deception. After all, a half-truth is just as bad as a downright lie. *We* must be known for 'sound speech, that cannot be condemned', Titus 2. 8.

Whilst it is not surprising that God exonerated Abimelech from all blame in the circumstances, it *is* surprising that He does not censure Abraham. It is, however, remarkable that it was in response to the intercession of Abraham that God 'healed Abimelech, and his wife, and his maidservants; and they bare children'. We might have expected Abimelech to have prayed for Abraham! But God makes no reference to Abraham's weakness when speaking to Abimelech; 'Now therefore restore the man his wife; for he is a prophet, and he *shall* pray for thee, and thou *shalt* live'. This teaches us at least two important lessons:

Firstly, that *personal failure does not alter our standing before God*, The book of Numbers records the murmuring of Israel in the wilderness, but it also tells us that God 'hath not beheld iniquity in Jacob, neither hath he seen perverseness in Israel', Num. 23. 21. Like Joshua, our 'filthy garments' have been taken away, and we have been clothed with a 'change of raiment', Zech. 3. 1-6. But this does not mean that we are free to do as we please. Personal failure affects our *communion* with God. It is significant that at Gerar, God communicated with Abimelech, not Abraham, 'in a dream by night'. *Secondly*, that *personal failure does not mean the end of effective prayer*. In fact, God *expected* Abraham to pray for Abimelech, and pledged to answer his prayer! The psalmist fully understood God's provision for restoration; 'If thou, Lord, shouldest mark iniquities, O Lord, who shall stand. *But there is forgiveness with thee*, that thou mightest be feared'. God is gracious, and as with the psalmist, once our failure has been confessed, He will continue to hear and answer our prayers, Ps. 130. 3-5.

January 8th

Genesis 22. 1-14

HERE I AM

Genesis 22 proves that Abraham was 'a vessel unto honour, sanctified, and meet for the master's use, and prepared unto every good work'. When God spoke to him, he was ready to hear, and ready to act. 'And it came to pass after these things that God did tempt Abraham, and said unto him, Abraham: and he said, Behold, *here I am*', v. 1. In Genesis 21. 23-24, Abraham had sworn to deal kindly with *another man's son*. Now he is told to sacrifice *his own son*. Whatever his mental turmoil, we see only his 'obedience of faith', for he 'rose up early in the morning ... and went unto the place of which God had told him'. He was persuaded that 'the Judge of all the earth' would 'do right', Gen. 18. 25, even if this meant raising Isaac from the dead, Heb. 11. 19.

If *we* are prepared to say, with Abraham, 'here I am', we must also be prepared to be tried and tested. Devotion to God often involves the sacrifice of things that we dearly love, and sometimes the sacrifice of precious relationships. How much are we prepared to sacrifice for God? If we have any reservations or hesitancy, remember that God 'spared not his own Son, but delivered him up for us all', Rom. 8. 32.

But then God spoke to Abraham again: 'And the angel of the Lord called unto him out of heaven, and said, Abraham, Abraham: and he said, *Here am I*', v. 11. Once more, Abraham stood ready to hear, and ready to act. Three days before, he had received a *command*, but now he receives *commendation*. 'Now I know that thou fearest God, seeing thou hast not withheld thy son, thine only son, from me'. Obedience brought rich blessing. If Abraham had not said 'here I am' in verse 1 and submitted to the will of God, he would not have had the opportunity to say 'here am I' in verse 11, and receive the blessing of God.

Centuries later, God censured His people for their empty ordinances, and urged them to practise true godliness, with the promise, 'then shalt thou call, and the Lord shall answer; thou shalt cry, and he shall say, *Here I am*', Isa. 58. 9. If *we* are prepared to say to God, 'here I am', and make ourselves available to Him, He will say to *us*, 'here *I* am', and make Himself available to us. 'Draw nigh to God, and he will draw nigh to you', Jas. 4. 8.

January 9th
Genesis 24. 12-14
SEND ME GOOD SPEED THIS DAY

Abraham's servant, Eliezer, was an honoured member of the household. He is called Abraham's 'eldest servant', and 'ruled over all that he had', v. 2. At one time, it seemed that he would inherit his master's estate, but God had other plans. We do not know if Eliezer ever seriously expected to succeed his master, and prefer to think that he gladly participated in 'the great feast the same day that Isaac was weaned', Gen. 21. 8. After all, we are very impoverished in spirit if we fail to rejoice in God's blessing on other people.

Eliezer, now intent on finding a bride for his master's son, arrived outside the city of Nahor, 'at the time of the evening', and we might have expected him to look for lodgings for the night. But he had other priorities, and these could not be achieved without divine help and guidance. Listen to his prayer: 'O Lord God of my master Abraham, I pray thee, send me good speed this day, and shew kindness unto my master Abraham'. Eliezer thought only of his master, in the same way that we should make it our grand ambition to bring joy and pleasure to our beloved Lord.

It is worth noticing that there wasn't a great deal left of that particular day, and Eliezer must have prayed with some urgency. We so easily rely on our own judgement when time is short, and decisions have to be made. Eliezer was evidently a man of proven wisdom and discernment who had earned the complete confidence of his master. But he did not trust in his long experience. He acted in the spirit of Proverbs 3. 5-6, 'Trust in the Lord with all thine heart; and lean not unto thine own understanding. In all thy ways acknowledge him, and he shall direct thy paths'.

Unlike the religious leaders in our Lord's day, Matt. 6. 5, there was nothing ostentatious about Eliezer. Listen to him again as he recounts, over the evening meal, events at the well: 'And before I had done *speaking in mine heart*, behold, Rebekah came forth with her pitcher on her shoulder', v. 45. No human ears heard his prayer, but 'the eyes of the Lord are upon the righteous, and *his ears are open unto their prayers*', 1 Pet. 3. 12. We are not surprised that God answered the prayer of this unselfish and humble servant, and gave him 'good speed this day'. We can expect similar help if we pray in the same way.

January 10th

Genesis 25. 20-26

ISAAC INTREATED THE LORD FOR HIS WIFE

We can have every confidence in the promises of God. After all, if a promise is only as good as the person who makes it, it follows that the promises of God must be thoroughly reliable. The apostle Paul refers to the 'hope of eternal life, which God, *that cannot lie*, promised before the world began'. Bible promises are completely trustworthy, not only because it is God who makes them, but because it is Christ who fulfils them; 'For all the promises of God in him are yea, and in him Amen', 2 Cor. 1. 20. Prayer will be a lifeless routine if we do not really believe that God intends to fulfil His promises, and is fully able to do so.

God made it clear to Abraham that 'in Isaac shall thy seed be called', Gen. 21. 12. But there had been times when it was far from easy to see the fulfilment of His promise in Genesis 17. 7. Even Abraham, that great man of faith, exclaimed, 'Lord God, what wilt thou give me, seeing I go childless', Gen. 15. 2, and now Isaac faces the same problem; 'And Isaac intreated the Lord for his wife, because she was barren'.

Whilst we cannot doubt the earnestness and intensity of Isaac's prayer, it was certainly not a bitter complaint. The Hebrew scholar GESENIUS explains that the word 'intreat' means 'to pray as a suppliant', and adds, 'the prayers of the godly being compared to incense'. What a beautiful way in which to approach God! Isaac prayed with a worshipful spirit. Like us at times, he found difficulty with God's timetable, but this did not rob him of adoration for God. All are obliged to say, 'As for God, his way is perfect', Ps. 18. 30. God must have found great pleasure in the way that Isaac handled the delay and disappointment in his life, especially as he had to wait twenty years before his prayers were answered, vv. 20, 26. Perhaps we too have waited many long years for answers to prayer.

But God 'that cannot lie' did hear the prayers of Isaac; 'And the Lord was intreated of him, and Rebekah his wife conceived'. Centuries later, in similar circumstances, God assured Zacharias that his prayer was heard, even though an answer seemed impossible, Luke 1. 5-13. Don't ever lose confidence in God.

January 11th

Genesis 32. 9-12

I AM NOT WORTHY ... DELIVER ME I PRAY THEE

Genesis 32 describes a momentous day in the life of Jacob. After leaving Laban in the *morning*, 31. 55, he was met by angels, 32. 2. During the *day*, he learnt that another 'host' was coming to meet him, v. 6, but his encounter with angels did little to reassure him that 'the angel of the Lord encampeth round about them that fear him, and delivereth them', Ps. 34. 7. In the face of apparent danger, Jacob planned, prayed, and went on planning! At *night*, having sent his family ahead, he was 'left alone; and there wrestled a man with him until the breaking of the day', v. 24. Jacob gained 'power with God', not because he wrestled the man to the ground, but because he clung to him! The apostle Paul sums it up with the words, 'When I am weak, then am I strong', 2 Cor. 12. 10.

There are three component parts to Jacob's prayer in verses 9-12. (i) *He claimed the promises of God.* First of all, he cited God's promise of *personal preservation*, v. 9. Then, he cited God's promise of *national preservation*, v. 11. God delights to honour His promises, and we must never forget to claim them. (ii) *He confessed his unworthiness to God.* 'I am *not worthy* of the least of all thy mercies, and of all the truth, which thou hast shewed unto thy servant'. Jacob certainly speaks for *us* here! The more we contemplate 'the kindness and love of God our Saviour', Titus 3. 4, the more we exclaim, '*I* am not worthy'. (iii) *He cried for deliverance to God.* 'Deliver me, I pray thee, from the hand of my brother'. We scan the previous chapters in vain for evidence of Jacob's prayer-life. Immediate danger certainly concentrates the mind! F B MEYER says: 'Is not this the key to God's dealings with us all? He brings us into sore straits; He shuts us up in a corner; He causes the walls and ceiling and floor of our room to draw together, as if to crush us. At such moments there is only one resource left. It is Himself'.

But was Jacob whole-hearted? It almost seems as if Jacob's prayer just briefly interrupted his planning. He does not seem to have learned the lesson of 1 Peter 5. 7, 'Casting all you care upon him, for he careth for you'. Have we learned that lesson?

27

January 12th

Genesis 39, 1-6, 21-23

THE LORD WAS WITH JOSEPH

It has been said that the brightest and best steel comes through the hottest furnace. The early life of Joseph was certainly spent in the furnace of affliction, and it was just when circumstances seemed to improve that he found himself under still greater pressure. Promotion and prosperity in Potiphar's house exposed him to sore temptation when 'his master's wife cast her eyes upon Joseph', Gen. 39. 7. But he was faithful to his master, and faithful to God; 'thou art his *wife*: how then can I do this great wickedness, and sin against *God*', Gen. 39. 9. His faithfulness meant that he did not lose his purity or his character.

Joseph had to contend with false accusation, false evidence, and false imprisonment. Consider his position. (i) He had tried to be good. But with what result? His moral integrity had earned him an indefinite prison sentence. (ii) He had begun to rise. But only to end up worse than before. But whilst Joseph's circumstances were sufficient to break the spirit of most men, he triumphed over them. Potiphar's house and the prison must have been worlds apart, but Joseph was as diligent and trustworthy in serving 'the keeper of the prison', Gen. 39. 22-23, as he was in the service of the 'captain of the guard', vv. 2-6. We do not have to look far for the secret of Joseph's consistency. In Potiphar's house, '*the Lord was with Joseph*', and what is more, 'his master *saw* that the Lord was with Joseph', vv. 2-3. In the prison, '*the Lord was with Joseph*, and shewed him mercy, and gave him favour in the sight of the keeper of the prison'. He proved the reality of the promise in Isaiah 43. 2, 'When thou passest through the waters, I will be with thee'.

Joseph's imprisonment secured at least two beneficial results for him. (i) It became the means of greater promotion than was ever possible in Potiphar's house. (ii) It was preparation for future responsibility. His uncongenial circumstances were all part of divine training. 'He sent a man before them, even Joseph, who was sold for a servant: whose feet they hurt with fetters: he was laid in iron: until the time that his word came: the word of the Lord tried (tested) him', Ps. 105. 17-19. God makes no mistakes. He is with us in the trials of life, and also directs those trials for our highest good, and His greater glory.

January 13th

Genesis 49. 22-26

MADE STRONG

'The archers have sorely grieved him, and shot at him, and hated him: but his bow abode in strength, and the arms of his hands were *made strong* by the hands of the mighty God of Jacob'. If all we knew about Joseph was contained in the dying words of Jacob, we would conclude that with God's help, he had triumphed in a battle against tremendous odds. And that is exactly what *had* happened! Jacob knew that his beloved son had been cruelly treated. Joseph had been 'sorely grieved' by his own brethren, and by unjust imprisonment in Egypt. Genesis 42. 21 makes it clear how deeply Joseph felt the cruelty of his brethren.

But whilst 'the archers' had 'sorely grieved' Joseph, they had not prevailed. It might have been a different story if he had stood alone in the battle, but 'the Mighty One of Jacob' was with him. The old patriarch draws a beautiful picture, which F B MEYER describes for us in his inimitable way: 'There stands the weak child in whose slender arms there are no muscles strong enough to draw the string or bend the bow, which he vainly tries to use. They resist his utmost endeavours. Evidently he has neither might nor strength. But now see, on his weak hands there are laid other hands, mighty hands that wove the tapestry of the heavens, and that hold in their hollows the depths of the seas; one of these is placed where the left hand holds the bow; the other where the right hand plucks the string. And now with what ease those thin hands wield the bow'.

Centuries later, the apostle Paul was 'sorely grieved' and, once again, it was his own brethren who had 'shot at him.' He writes to Timothy, 'This thou knowest, that all they which are in Asia be turned away from me', 2 Tim. 1. 15. 'At my first answer no man stood with me, but all men forsook me', 4. 16. But there were 'mighty' hands to help him too; 'Notwithstanding the Lord stood with me, and *strengthened* me', 4. 17. Those same hands reach out to us. The 'archers' are still busy, and they use 'fiery darts.' We hold the battle-bow with weak and trembling hands, only to hear the blessed Saviour say, 'My grace is sufficient for thee: for my *strength* is made perfect in weakness', 2 Cor. 12. 9. Christ will enable us to do 'all things', Phil. 4. 13.

January 14th

Exodus 2. 23-25

THEIR CRY CAME UP UNTO GOD

The children of Israel settled down well in Egypt, Exod. 1. 7. But Egypt was not Canaan, and God never intended His people to remain there. When the time came for them to return to the land of divine promise, God took steps to ensure that His people had no wish to remain in the land of the Pharaohs. Their adversity and hardship at the hands of the 'new king over Egypt' was no quirk of fate. Psalm 105 makes it clear that God 'turned their heart to hate his people, to deal subtilly with his servants', vv. 23-25. He sometimes reminds *us* rather sharply that 'here we have no continuing city, but we seek one to come', Heb. 13. 14. Present trials remind us of our heavenly rest.

The suffering of God's people in Egypt did not mean that He was unmindful and heedless of their sorry plight. 'Their cry came up unto God by reason of the bondage', and four things followed. (i) 'And God *heard* their groaning'. The apostle Peter, writing to suffering Christians, reminded them that 'the eyes of the Lord are over the righteous, and his ears are open unto their prayers', 1 Pet. 3. 12. We must not forget, however, that Peter is speaking about the prayers of the '*righteous*', and that 'if I regard iniquity in my heart, the Lord will *not* hear me', Ps. 66. 18. (ii) 'And God *remembered* his covenant with Abraham, with Isaac, and with Jacob'. Moses later cited their deliverance from Egypt when reminding Israel that 'the Lord thy God, he is God, the faithful God, which keepeth covenant and mercy with them that love him', Deut. 7. 9. God honoured His covenant with the fathers then, and He will honour every one of His promises to us now. We can confidently exclaim, 'there hath not failed one word of all his good promise', 1 Kings 8. 56, and this will become abundantly clear in that 'morning without clouds'. (iii) 'And God *looked* upon the children of Israel'. No detail of their suffering escaped His gaze. Like Job, we can say, 'he knoweth the way that I take'. (iv) 'And God *had respect* unto them', meaning that He cared for them. David wrote about this in Psalm 103, 'Like as a father pitieth his children, so the Lord pitieth them that fear him. For he knoweth our frame; he remembereth that we are dust'. We can cast all our care upon Him, 1 Pet. 5. 7.

January 15th

Exodus 3. 1-12

WHO AM I THAT I SHOULD GO?

When God called Moses 'out of the midst of the bush', he replied, *'Here am I'*, v. 4. With these simple words, Moses responded to God's call. Centuries later, Isaiah 'heard the voice of the Lord, saying, Whom shall I send, and who will go for us?', and replied, *'Here am I, send me'*, Isa. 6. 8. Still more centuries later, the Lord spoke to Ananias in a vision, and he replied, 'Behold, *I am here, Lord'*, Acts 9. 10. *Our* lives will lack divine direction if we are not 'a vessel unto honour, sanctified, and meet for the master's use, and *prepared* unto every good work', 2 Tim. 2. 21. Young Samuel was told to say, 'Speak, Lord; for thy servant heareth', and whilst it would be rather churlish of us to condemn the boy because he only said, 'Speak; for thy servant heareth', 1 Sam. 3. 9-10, we must always say, 'What saith my *Lord* unto his servant?' Josh. 5. 14.

When God commissioned Moses to lead His people out of Egypt, he replied, *'Who am I?'*, v. 11. In the first place, he questioned his ability to face Pharaoh: 'Who am I, that I should go unto Pharaoh?'. In the second place, he questioned his ability to lead Israel: 'And that I should bring forth the children of Israel out of Egypt?'. It is, of course, quite wrong for any servant of God to 'think more highly of himself than he ought to think', Rom. 12. 3. On the other hand, it is equally wrong to question the will of God, and to make our limitations an excuse for failure to serve Him. When God calls us to serve Him, He always makes available the necessary resources, and Moses was no exception. The command, 'Come now therefore, and I will *send* thee', v. 10, was accompanied by the promise, 'Certainly, I will be *with* thee', v. 12. The Lord Jesus commissioned His disciples in the same way: 'Go ye therefore, and teach all nations, baptizing them in the name of the Father, and of the Son, and of the Holy Ghost: teaching them to observe all things whatsoever I have commanded you: and, lo, I am with you alway, even unto the end of the world. Amen'. Like Moses, we all feel our weakness, whether in leadership or in any area of service, but like Moses, we are all promised divine strength. Let us listen again to the voice of our beloved Lord as He says, 'My grace is sufficient for thee: for my strength is made perfect in weakness', 2 Cor. 12. 9.

January 16th

Exodus 3. 13-18

BEHOLD ... WHAT SHALL I SAY?

Moses had decided that that he would indeed go to deliver the people of God out of bondage in Egypt. Having made the decision, he soon found, however, that there were still many concerns. Some of the people may not want to be delivered while others would question his authority and qualifications. Moses well understood the challenges he would face. He felt that he would be cross-examined and his experience and personal knowledge of God would be explored. He could say, 'the God of your fathers hath sent me', but they would ask for more details, e.g. 'What is his name?'.

Wisely, he went to God and put his concerns clearly, 'What shall I say unto them?'. It is good to be open with God regarding our worries and concerns. An unexpressed concern is often a great debilitator while failure to address it only seems to make it grow larger.

Moses had seen the character of God in the burning bush. He had experienced His holiness, and was aware that God had seen and heard and was intent on delivering His people from the bondage of Egypt. God had shared with Moses details of the land they would go to and of the nations who were to be driven out of it. God had declared, 'I am coming down', but now He added, 'I will send you!'. Thus, Moses was to be God's representative and he was anxious that all God's authority and knowledge should be available to him.

God said to Moses, 'I AM THAT I AM', and instructed him to say, 'I AM hath sent me unto you'. This is God's great name, indicative of His sovereignty and sufficient in itself to demand reverence and obedience. How great the names of God and His Christ are! We should use them more for our own reassurance and for confession to those around us. Now God assures Moses that the people will listen to him and details the steps to be taken subsequently. Moses was to identify himself to the elders, go to the king of Egypt and seek permission for the people to leave for three days' journey into the wilderness to sacrifice to the Lord God.

Moses' prayer had been limited, 'What shall I say?', yet God's response was what to say, whom to see, where to go and how to handle disappointment. When we freely admit our ignorance of God's will and our part in it we discover that God will unfold more than ever we thought to ask, for every step in the future is known to Him.

January 17th
Exodus 4. 10-17

SEND BY THE HAND OF HIM WHOM THOU WILT SEND

Moses has second thoughts! He is anxious that the people might simply not believe him. Would oral testimony alone be enough to convince the sceptics? In great mercy God understands His reluctant servant's plight and arms him with three convincing signs. *Firstly*, his rod turns into a serpent; *secondly*, his hand becomes leprous; and *thirdly*, water from the river becomes blood. These were not simply one-off phenomena but repeatable signs to convince the people. It is true that while some may not be convinced by oral testimony alone they will be convinced by an appreciation of the power of God in a person's life.

However, in spite of this support Moses' nerve fails and he indicates that while all these signs are fine as 'back-up' his vital problem is one of communication. He deeply felt his lack of eloquence and this had not changed. How often we look for circumstances to change for the better rather than rely on God to see us through them. Moses, on this suspect premise, tries to avoid the responsibility and God is angry. It is He who can teach him; it is He who gives eloquence; it is He who convicts hearts.

Moses suggests someone else be sent. While he appreciated the needs of the people and the demands of God, he would be grateful if someone else would take on the responsibility. Some are faced with this today, a lack of self-confidence, an evident need, no one else to help, not even an Aaron. We need to pray for those in small assemblies who, feeling inadequate, have responsibility thrust upon them.

Nevertheless, God is merciful to His servant. He says, 'I will teach thee'. Furthermore, He offers practical help in providing Aaron to assist him. He is to become Moses' spokesman.

Thus, we see that God surrounded Moses with every support he could possibly need. We must understand that God's purpose will always be worked out. If He chooses someone for His work He will equip and support him in every way, and demonstrate His power to him.

Be heartened—'if God be for us, who can be against us?'.

Exodus 5. 10-23

LORD ... WHY IS IT THAT THOU HAST SENT ME?

The first request to Pharoah to let the people go to worship is rebuffed angrily. The king accuses the people of being idle—in his view they should be too busy to worship, which of course today is still a ploy of Satan. Pharoah devises a plan to make the people work harder. He demands that the same number of bricks be made each day but the workers must now find their own straw. This made the task virtually impossible yet the officers drove the people on in a fruitless attempt to please Pharoah.

The people complain to Pharoah but are spurned. Thus, they vent their anger on Moses and Aaron—men who had promised much but failed to deliver. Wisely, Moses and Aaron took the complaint to God. However, rather than representing God to the people and offering them comfort and counsel they chose to identify themselves with the complaint. They demand to know why God has evil intreated the people—of course He hadn't, it was Pharoah. Moses explicitly blames God, 'The people are treated evilly and thou hast not delivered them'. Finally, Moses gets to the point that is really bothering him, 'Why hast thou sent me?'.

The complaint of the people can readily be understood. Since Moses had announced the great plan for deliverance from Egypt, things had gone from bad to worse. The people were forced to work harder and were physically beaten when they were unable to produce the same number of bricks as before. Furthermore, Pharoah was angry and an impasse had been reached. Prospects were grim and some people would soon die. Didn't God care?

Sometimes we may find ourselves in similar circumstances when there appears to be no way out. We blame ourselves, or others; we are tempted even to blame God and to question whether His call to service is worth all the hassle—why not let some other person do it? Lessons, however, have to be learned. Don't expect miracles, though they may happen. Don't expect instant answers, though they are sometimes provided even before the request is made. Don't expect things to get better, they may temporarily get worse. We must be like Moses, who, even though the problem seemed intractable he took it to the Lord. Already, God was at work behind the scenes.

January 19th

Exodus 9. 27-35

AND MOSES ... SPREAD ABROAD HIS HANDS

Many plagues had tormented the Egyptians as Pharoah constantly refused to bend to the will of God—flies, frogs, the river turned to blood. Now God tells Moses to stretch his rod toward heaven and He will send thunder, hail and fire to smite all who did not fear the Lord. This was a 'very grievous' plague. Men and animals died, all the crops were destroyed and all the trees were broken, except of course in Goshen where the Israelites dwelt. How amazing to see the power of God at work in the elements of nature and how glad we are that we are preserved from such calamities. Yet, we must pray for those who are so stricken and often lose all, as but for the grace of God so would we.

Pharoah sent for Moses and Aaron and confessed his own and his people's wickedness. He promised that if the hail and thunder stopped the people could go to worship God. Moses was sceptical of this turn of events, anticipating the usual faithlessness of Pharoah once the pressure was off. However, he promised he would intreat the Lord, and that as soon as he lifted up his hands to the Lord the hail and thunder would cease. When he did so, the hail and thunder stopped immediately. Predictably, however, Pharoah changed his mind and hardened his heart against the Lord.

There are interesting lessons here. The king and his people were suffering, and deservedly so, but there was apparent contrition. Though we may be suspicious of people's motives, we should still pray for them and their circumstances. Though we may feel they are unreliable and self-centred, they should be on our prayer list.

So, Moses, in keeping with God's will goes out of the city and spreads his hands abroad unto the Lord, and the plague is stayed. Here was a public demonstration of the power of God; here a declaration that Moses spoke for Him; here an act of mercy towards suffering Egyptians who were not directly involved as well as to the one who was, Pharoah himself.

Once again Pharoah reneges. Nonetheless, through Moses' prayer many had been blessed, God had been shown to be in control, the position of Moses and Aaron had been strengthened, and the people of God reassured. Let us pray in difficult circumstances and, even if the desired end is not achieved, many will be blessed, not least ourselves.

THEY WERE SORE AFRAID AND CRIED UNTO THE LORD

There must have been tremendous excitement among the people. They had given the Egyptians the slip and at last were well on their way out of Egypt. They were leaving behind the pressures and constraints of slavery while the freedom and opportunities of the Promised Land beckoned. Keen to obey the Lord and His servant Moses they were surprised at the instruction to turn off the direct route they had anticipated. Then they discovered that the new path led to a 'dead end'. They were hemmed in by the Red Sea in front and marshlands on either side. They were literally 'entangled in the land'; the wilderness had shut them in.

Back in Egypt Pharoah questioned the wisdom of his decision to let them go. He gathered together his chariots, his horsemen and footsoldiers and with this massive show of strength pursued his erstwhile slaves. As the Egyptians came near the Israelites' camp the people saw them and panicked.

Many cries for help and salvation went up to the Lord; all seemed lost, but they reckoned without the power of their God! Then Moses commanded, 'Fear not, stand still, and see the salvation of the Lord'. 'The Lord shall fight for you', he added. Moses believed that if they stood still the Lord would fight the Egyptians on the shore and His people would be free to cross the Red Sea.

However, God had in mind an even greater deliverance. He said to Moses, 'Speak unto the children of Israel that they go forward'. From running away, to standing still, to going forward! They did, and as the Red Sea appeared nearer, the angel of God 'removed and went behind them', as did the pillar of cloud. It was 'darkness to them' (the Egyptians) and 'light to these' (the Israelites). All night a wind blew and it opened up a path through the Sea. The people passed over without loss, while their pursuers 'assaying to do were drowned'. What a God was theirs! What a God is ours!

When the way ahead is unclear and the circumstances threatening, when all appears lost, stand still, go forward, hold your peace—the Lord will fight for you. You will be surprised at His power and delighted at His salvation.

January 21st

Exodus 15. 23-26

MOSES CRIED ... THE LORD SHOWED HIM A TREE

Following their miraculous escape through the Red Sea from the hands of the pursuing Egyptians, the Israelites journeyed into the wilderness for three days. They found no water so they kept going till they came to Marah, so called because of the bitter taste the minerals gave to its water. After such an escape this turned out to be a 'bitter' disappointment. The people murmured and grumbled against Moses with the question, 'What shall we drink?'.

Clearly, there was a major problem and Moses handled it the only way he knew how—he cried unto the Lord. We are told that 'the Lord showed him a tree'. It is not just simply that the Lord identified a tree, but also, because of the meaning of the word 'show', He instructed him in the use of this tree in the purposes of God. This tree, or bush, had to be cast into the water and on so doing Moses found that the water became drinkable. The properties of the tree overcame the bitterness of the water.

Many of the Lord's people experience bitter waters. They may have hoped for better, but there are disappointments, frustrations and failures in Christian experience. If these are allowed to develop they will destroy life and testimony. The only way to find relief is to cry to the Lord and the answer will be found in the tree. As gold speaks of the deity of Christ so wood speaks of His humanity. A study of His life will show that disappointments, failure and disloyalty of others surrounded Him. Yet, these never dislodged Him from His intent to do His Father's will. It never changed His love and sympathy. His determination to carry on was manifest.

The tree would also remind us of the cross where great waters swept over His soul. A proper understanding of the cross will help us to overcome the bitter aspects of life and make them not only bearable, but profitable. The Israelites found the waters sweet. In fact the bitterness was still there but the grace of God ensured it was overcome—where sin abounded grace did much more abound.

Our prayer should be that the sweetness of Christ in our lives will enable us to hold up in its trials and make them profitable to us, and eventually to others.

January 22nd

Exodus 22. 22-23

ANY WIDOW, OR FATHERLESS CHILD

At this point in the book of Exodus, God is laying down regulations for the guidance of His people to govern their behaviour in the wilderness. The first regulations are to do with altars, and directions are given for worship and modesty to go hand in hand. These are followed with regulations concerning slaves, quarrels, injuries, robberies, spiritism and bestiality. Finally there are regulations to do with protection for the underprivileged—strangers, widows, orphans and the poor.

The basic thing the Israelites had to remember was that at one time they had been vulnerable themselves. In Egypt they were slaves and that experience should affect their behaviour towards the weak in society.

Widows, and widowers, have a special place in God's affections. They have had to endure the pain of a broken relationship and have known sorrow and tears in the loss of their loved ones. The world, and the believers, may sympathise, but after a time their sympathy is called to go out to others and the bereaved are forgotten. God, however, keeps them right at the forefront of His thoughts and, when they have occasion to call on Him, He instantly moves for their protection and blessing. The Israelites are warned in the direst terms against afflicting such. God says, 'I will kill you', and the offender's family will be visited with the same judgement.

Many, today, are in sorrow because of the loss of a loved one. Such, as well as other disadvantaged, should be at the top of our prayer lists. We must never treat them brusquely, nor unkindly—we were once disadvantaged ourselves and rebellious too, yet God loved us with everlasting love. Widows and orphans can be of great value to an assembly of God's people. They have God's ear ahead of everyone else, and whatever they pray for, 'if they cry at all unto me, I will surely hear their cry'. Many an assembly and many an individual has been preserved by a widow's prayers.

So, in turn, we who are blessed by a continuing relationship with our partner in marriage should pray for widows and orphans, yet an even more blessed thing is that they might pray for us.

Exodus 32. 9-14

AND MOSES SAID ... LORD, REMEMBER

Moses had gone up into the mount to commune with God. He was rather longer than expected and the people feared he may have died. Consequently, they persuaded Aaron to authorise the collection of gold in order to build an object to worship—a golden calf. Once the gold was melted down and the calf made, they celebrated at an inaugural ceremony, much to God's displeasure.

Meanwhile, up on the mountain God shared with Moses His thoughts about what had happened. He described the people to Moses as 'thy people which thou broughtest out of the land of Egypt'. He tells Moses precisely what they had done; and underlines their stubbornness by their recurring failure to respond to His leading. God tells Moses that He will destroy the people but honour His promise to Moses himself; indeed He would expand it by making *him* into a great nation.

The anger that Moses felt was reserved for the people, but before God he argues against this proposal, while rejecting glory for himself. He asks, 'Why?'. He reminds God that they are indeed God's own people and that it was He who had brought them out of bondage. He also indicates that such an act would give the Egyptians grounds for rejoicing at the ultimate failure of the great escape. He pleads with God to be faithful to His promises.

These people had made life difficult for Moses and had rebelled against him, yet he is selfless in his approach. God had saved them—so why destroy them? Why give the enemies of God occasion to rejoice? God, Moses claims, must be consistent with His promises to generations of His people in earlier years.

We are told that God repented of the evil. This is not to say, however, that He changed His mind, nor indeed that He had regretted something He had intended to do, but simply that He embarked on a different course of action to that He had earlier suggested as a possibility. We note that our prayers do not alter God's purpose, but help, in fact, to facilitate it. Here Moses reflects the character of his God and in our prayers we should do the same. We need to know where God stands on a matter, to see it as He sees it, and pray earnestly that, despite failure, God's original purpose should be worked out. It will be.

January 24th

Exodus 32. 30-35

AND MOSES ... SAID ... IF THOU WILT FORGIVE THEIR SIN

In the general rebellion against God in the making of the golden calf the sons of Levi had no part. To them now falls the execution of discipline as Moses sends them out to slay the people. A total of 3,000 are slain—a tragedy, yet a demonstration of the mercy of God in that not all Israel perished, as they deserved. However, all would yet suffer loss.

The next day, after mature reflection, Moses announces that he will seek to make atonement for the sins of the people. He approaches God in confession, 'This people have sinned a great sin', and he proceeds to lay the matter out before God in some detail, 'They have made them gods of gold'. He first appeals to God to forgive—some action has already been taken, 3,000 have died, but is that sufficient to appease an angry God? Moses adds, 'and if not, blot me, I pray thee, out of thy book which thou hast written'. Here, again, we see the selflessness of the man of God. He would prefer punishment for himself, indeed even to perish, rather than for God's people to miss out entering into and enjoying the blessings of the Promised Land. God, however, reiterates that sinners must bear their own punishment and be blotted out of His book. He gives Moses renewed instructions, 'Go to the place of which I have spoken; mine Angel shall go before thee: nevertheless in the day when I visit I will visit their sin upon them'.

Here we may learn lessons from the actions of Moses. Firstly, we must bring discipline into our own lives and into the assembly of God's people. In addition to discipline taken by men, God will also visit in discipline Himself. Discipline now does not cancel out loss in the future. In this sad case the entire generation was not allowed to enter the Promised Land as a result of their sin. We need to remember that sin and unfaithfulness is offensive to God. We need to identify ourselves with the sin and the punishment. Sin causes heartache for everyone touched by it and destroys lives and debilitates service for the Lord. We must judge it first in ourselves and only then in others. All this is best achieved on our knees in prayer, and in humility. We must not be smug when others fall, for perhaps but for the grace of God there go we.

January 25th

Exodus 33. 7-17

I PRAY THEE ... SHOW ME NOW THY WAY

In the early verses of this chapter it is clear that the people were showing an inclination to repent of the evil they had done. They did not put on their ornaments—a recognized outward sign of inward sorrow. In view of this God responds in a gracious way and sets about rebuilding the bridges between His people and Himself.

Due to the fact that the camp had been defiled with the sin of the golden calf incident, Moses took the 'tent of meeting' and pitched it outside the camp. As he did so every man stood in the door of his own tent to see what would happen. As Moses entered the tent a marvellous and reassuring thing took place— 'the cloudy pillar descended, and stood at the door of the tabernacle, and the Lord talked with Moses'. Whereas, before, God had been in the midst of His people, now He was only to be found outside the camp. The people stood and worshipped afar off. God was still available to them but their sin meant that He was no longer in their midst. Nevertheless, through Moses they still had access.

God and Moses spoke face to face, i.e., in close communion. Moses, frustrated with the people, and impatient with God, says, 'Show me now thy way'. He wanted to know exactly where he was going, who was going with him, and when they would reach the Promised Land. And he wanted to know now! Away with faith—sight is better! We can sympathize with Moses in this prayer but we need to learn from the way in which God answers it.

God responds to Moses' prayer in two ways. He will not describe the future in detail but He does say, 'My presence shall go with thee, and I will give thee rest'. Moses recognizes these two promises and appreciates too that if the Lord goes with them they will be a unique and separated people.

Often to us our future is obscure or dark. We have many problems and we wish we knew precisely what is going to happen. Our concern should not be for tomorrow—God will take care of that, and of us too. We know that His presence will go with us and that in all our doubts and fears we have the promise of His fellowship and power. He knows the future, and we are glad! This knowledge and experience brings peace.

41

January 26th

Exodus 33. 18-23

I BESEECH THEE, SHOW ME THY GLORY

In communion with God in prayer Moses had been assured of God's continuing presence and of the rest which that brings. The steps ahead will still be unclear but with his hand in God's all will be well. Emboldened by this promise, and enjoying this closeness to God, 'thou hast found grace in my sight, and I know thee by name', Moses now prays, 'Show me thy glory'. What he wanted was not only to see the majesty of God but to understand Him fully. The primary meaning of the word 'glory' is width, breadth, or possibly, height. What Moses was after was an understanding of the dimensions of God, or the 'weight' of God.

We know that God is without limitation and that He cannot be fully known. It is impossible to look on the effulgence of His glory; it is impossible, except in His Son, to understand in measure who He is and what He does. God responds to the desire of His servant to know all by allowing him to know more. To Moses He promises to demonstrate His glory in His goodness, so that it will be possible to comprehend Him, at least in part.

No man can see God and live. While we cannot know Him fully He is nevertheless anxious that we should make progress in divine things. God says to Moses in a beautiful phrase, 'There is a place by me, and thou shalt stand upon a rock'. There is a place even nearer to God than perhaps we are presently experiencing. That place is in the enjoyment of full fellowship with His Son, the Rock of our salvation. In the cleft of the rock, covered and sheltered by the hand of God, we can be acutely aware of His presence as He passes by.

From time to time He may remove His hand and we have the opportunity to glimpse something of His goodness and glory—but to understand more fully we must wait for eternity.

Like Moses we too need to make progress in our knowledge of God. We may do so much more easily than Moses as we can look upon the Son who has made the Father manifest. Glory is not just an attribute of God, it is the outworking of His goodness through us. 'Show me thy glory ... I will make all my goodness pass before thee'. May that be our experience too.

January 27th

Exodus 34. 1-9

I PRAY THEE, GO AMONG US

Arrangements are made by God for the replacement of the broken tables of the law. Moses is instructed to hew out two tables of stone and to carry them up the mountain where, says God, 'I will write ... the words'. Interestingly, later, God tells Moses, 'Write thou these words', thus picturing how the Bible was inspired by God, yet written by men. Moses is told to go alone to God at the top of the mountain. These are perhaps the circumstances best suited to prayer, in God's presence, and alone with Him.

As Moses, early in the morning, ascended the mountain, 'the Lord descended in the cloud, and stood with him there'. The Lord passed by before him and thus the promise of chapter 33, 'I will make all my goodness pass before thee', is fulfilled. What is His goodness and His glory? It is described by God to Moses in the following terms, 'the Lord God, merciful and gracious, longsuffering, and abundant in goodness and truth'. In this we see the kind of God Moses knew and He is ours too. He is a God who will show mercy even unto the thousandth generation of His people. At every opporunity He delights in blessing those who belong to Him, and in forgiving their iniquity, transgression and sin. He is, however, also described as One who will by no means clear the guilty.

On seeing this goodness of the Lord God, Moses bows his head in awe and reverence, and worships. The glory of God demands worship and we too delight to worship as He reveals Himself to us. Moses now prays, 'I pray thee, go among us; for it is a stiffnecked people'. Moses was only too well aware of the sins and stubbornness of the people. He had seen compelling evidence of this ever since they left Egypt, yet He realizes that this God is precisely what the people need—merciful, gracious, longsuffering and abundant in goodness and truth.

We, too, knowing the frailties and stubbornness of our own lives, desire the presence of such a God. One who is not quick to mark iniquity but One who through His Son will bless us and lead us on to better things. Today, we pray this prayer of Moses, 'I pray thee, go among us'. When God is present in the midst of His people then they go forward with Him, make progress, and spiritual blessings ensue. May our God lead us on in His goodness.

THE SKIN OF HIS FACE SHONE

Moses was with the Lord in the mountain for forty days and forty nights. The number 'forty' in scripture is very significant, and of its eight main occurrences, this is the second. It usually indicates trial, or probation, or renewed rule. During these forty days Moses ate nothing, neither did he drink, which is quite remarkable, and at this time God wrote His law on the two replacement stones.

When Moses came down from the mountain his face shone. This phenomenon was the result of time spent in the presence of the Lord. Even for us today, communion with Him means that while we see His glory, so too will His glory be seen in us. The more time given to prayer and meditation the more like the Lord Jesus we become. Yet, we must not allow such heavenly experience to spoil us by becoming proud. Moses was unaware that his face was shining. Spiritual men and women do not get carried away with a sense of their own importance, but are often surprised when others see in them the character of the Lord.

The glory shining from Moses' face was of such intensity that the people could not look on him. It was necessary for him to cover his face with a veil. There was, of course, no need for the veil when he was speaking with God. Paul, in 2 Corinthians 3, points out that another reason for the wearing of the veil was to conceal from the people the fact that the glory was gradually, yet perceptibly fading, whereas the glories of the Lord Jesus and of the new covenant never fade.

In order to be able to display the glories of the Lord consistently we must be focused and consistent in our prayer life. Only constant renewal will keep us close to Him and able to represent Him here on earth. There is no sadder sight than that of fading glory, where better days and happier times are remembered.

We, therefore, ought to continue in prayer and not allow ourselves to be deflected from it even by the legitimate things of life. That His glory should be seen in us is a great privilege and will have the effect of encouraging others to follow our example, thus to enjoy His glory and to persevere in prayer. Prayer will keep us humble and fit us better to deal with all aspects of life.

January 29th

Numbers 9. 6-14

STAND STILL

Moses had come down from the mountain armed with the law of God for the guidance of His people. It was evident that he was God's man as his face still shone from being in the intimate presence of God. There is in Moses' words a remembrance of the instructions for keeping the Passover, and specifically that all were to celebrate it on the fourteenth day of the first month. All the rites and ceremonies were to be observed in detail.

However, there were 'certain men' who on that day were defiled, through no fault of their own, as they had come in contact with 'the dead body of a man'. These men were concerned because of their exclusion from the day of celebration and petitioned Moses and Aaron about it. There was apparently no precedent for this case. The exclusion, made by God Himself, must stand, though it seemed unreasonable that those with desire to worship should 'accidentally' be unable to do so. Moses was not able to decide what to do and wisely took the problem to the Lord. This is the best thing to do with all problems—through prayer ask God to grant us the ability to interpret correctly, and properly apply, what scripture has to say on any particular matter that concerns us.

God's response was a great relief to all. Certainly, on the appointed day they could not participate, but such should have an opportunity to 'offer an offering' on the fourteenth day of the *second month*, provided that all the ceremonies of the occasion were observed in detail. While they would miss out on fellowship on the original day, opportunity was provided to offer to the Lord so that He, and they, should have their portion.

Not only was the specific request answered for this group for this year, but direction was given that this would hold good every year. Also to be included in such arrangements when the people had settled in the land were those who were 'in a journey afar off'. The request had brought a much fuller answer than had been expected. We will also discover that when we take a simple question to the Lord we receive rather more than we ask or think. So, when circumstances seem unreasonable, we may find that there is a way that the Lord will show us. Even when His word seems clear let us check with Him that we understand it aright.

January 30th
Numbers 10. 35-36

RISE UP, LORD ... RETURN, O LORD

The time had now come to move on. There was now to be, at last, a forward movement of the people of God. As they moved off, the pillar of cloud was upon them—an evident token of God's presence with them. When the ark set forward, Moses prayed, 'Rise up, Lord, and let thine enemies be scattered', and when it rested, he said, 'Return, O Lord, unto the many thousands of Israel'.

At this point, Moses' father-in-law refused an invitation to accompany them and decided to return to his own people. He could have been of great help but apparently had no wish to be involved in this forward movement, even as many today share such reluctance. As it was not possible to stay in the same place, he went back! What a privilege it is to be among the Lord's people when, under divine guidance, they move forward. Moses' first request on this occasion was that the presence of God would be seen in reassuring power. When we enter unknown territory, without our loved ones, or friends upon whom we relied in the past, let us pray that we might have the strength to go forward looking only to Him.

Some of the Lord's people are debilitated by grief, the loss of loved ones, or the unfaithfulness of some close to them. They need not stay in that situation. They must pray for help, and move forward in the knowledge that the Lord is still with them. During this forward movement, occasions for rest were very necessary. At these times, Moses prayed, 'Return, O Lord'. This was a prayer for His presence to be felt individually and corporately. Even as the company moved forward, individual time with the Lord was very important. Such experiences are precious and as we enjoy seasons of rest we feel closer to Him. Not just involved in the activity and excitement of a forward movement, but also resting when He rests, and having time for worship as well as service.

Let us pray, as did Moses, for the things that will help us through—a sense of His presence and an appreciation of His return. So armed, the people of God as individuals, as churches, and in general, can have the confidence to move forward. He delights to demonstrate His power to us and we delight in the promise of His presence here and now, as well as in His promise, 'I will come again'. We happily respond, 'Even so, come Lord Jesus'.

Numbers 11. 1-3

MOSES PRAYED ... THE FIRE WAS QUENCHED

As the people moved on, however, all was not well. They complained. The basis of their complaint comes out later in the chapter. They were missing the good things of Egypt and had become disenchanted with the trials of the journey. The Promised Land seemed as far off as it had ever been.

The Lord was angry with them and sent fire throughout the camp, even to the uttermost parts, and consumed many. Alas, in a forward movement there will always be those who look back and complain about their personal problems and remember the settled days before the venture of faith started. Such a complaining spirit is debilitating to those around, frustrating to those who lead and inexcusable to the Lord. There is not much others can do about it, but He can, and does. Here, punishment was swift and fatal. God was angry—lives were lost. His anger was justified. Moses believed the action that God was taking was right, nevertheless he prayed for the people.

'The effectual fervent prayer of a righteous man availeth much'; Moses' prayer was promptly answered, 'When Moses prayed ... the fire was quenched'. When the Lord's people are suffering, perhaps even deservedly so, the Lord is ready to pardon, forgive and deliver. Praying for the relief of such is very likely prayer in line with His purpose, and, as such, will be answered. We need to pray for the hungry, the sick, the injured and the emotionally crushed among our fellow believers and among those in the world, whether or not their situation is a result of their own rash or careless actions. Our God delights to demonstrate His care and His power, and our prayer may well act as the trigger to set in motion His plans for deliverance.

Alas, it was not long before there were even more complaints. This displeased Moses and angered God. Moses felt he could no longer lead the people—he found the task too daunting. Nevertheless, in great patience, the Lord made specific arrangements to help him, so that the work of God should continue. We need to learn not to complain, nor to abuse the Lord's servants orally, but instead to commit one another to the Lord in prayer. He has the power and the will to support and lead His people through their trials.

February 1st

Numbers 11. 10-15

I AM NOT ABLE

Whatever hardships had arisen in the encampment of Israel, Moses does not identify them. Irritations experienced by Israel in the wilderness resulted in murmuring. The people of Israel murmured in their unbelief and ingratitude. How soon in the life of a believer do such sins arise!

The Murmuring of the People

The sin of unbelief soon manifested itself as the people began to doubt the promises of God. This led on to the sin of ingratitude—the people forgot how favoured they were and the many benefits coming their way. Jehovah heard the murmuring of His people and sent fire into one end of the camp. In response to the appeal of the people, Moses prayed; the fire abated. Out of fear over this experience the people called that part of the camp 'burning'. Very soon after the event, another murmuring rumbled through the camp. The diet of manna which God miraculously sent down into the camp every morning, feeding two million people, was the cause for Israel's second complaint. The Israelites overlooked the fact that food for such a multitude was a miraculous provision from the stores of heaven. In their ingratitude they presumed to tell God that in taste His provision was nothing like to the fish, cucumbers, leeks, onions, and garlic. Israel added to their sin of unbelief the sin of base ingratitude. Failing to appreciate the sweet bread from heaven, they wanted some of the sharp and sour food of Egypt.

The Despair of Moses

The murmuring of the masses drove Moses to despair. He opened his heart to the Lord and asked why the Lord had brought him into such a dilemma. Do I have to nurse this kind of child? Where can I get this food to give all these people? I cannot bear this load alone; it is too heavy for me. Take my life; do not let me undergo such ordeal. There was an immediate response, an offer of help by Jehovah to alleviate the despair of Moses under the load. The Lord is just the same today, whether we are leaders or one of the people. He is still willing to step into situations that may face us. He willingly responds with a similar offer of help, when in our despair we pray, 'Lord, I am not able to bear all this ... alone'.

February 2nd

Numbers 12. 1-13

O GOD, I BESEECH THEE

Temptation to sin is no respecter of persons, and now it struck at Aaron and Miriam. In this instance it was envy. Moses was the supreme leader, called by God to this high responsibility. Miriam, sister to Moses, was a prophetess. Aaron, Moses brother, as High Priest was the spiritual head of the people. Miriam's jealousy appeared the stronger, and she no doubt instigated the rebellion. There were degrees of guilt involved in this dual rebellion. Both were party to the same sin, 'Miriam and Aaron spake against Moses', v. 1.

The Accusation

The complaint against Moses was double-barrelled. They first suggested he had committed a questionable act in marrying a Cushite woman. Next they suggested that Moses was not the sole representative for God. 'And they said, Hath the Lord indeed spoken only by Moses? hath he not spoken also by us? And the Lord heard', v. 2. How will Moses react? He refrained from taking any action. He would not make an issue of it; but the Lord heard the unjust accusation against His servant. God who heard what they said, sprang into action. 'He spoke suddenly unto Moses', v. 4.

The Trial

God acting as prosecutor and judge presented His case with three points. (1) I revealed Myself to prophets by visions and dreams. (2) I reveal Myself to my servant Moses mouth to mouth; that is, openly and not in dark speeches. (3) Why were you not afraid to speak against My servant Moses? This implied they were guilty and brought on the punishment of Jehovah. He was angry with both Aaron and Miriam. The judgement inflicted on Miriam caused Aaron to confess their foolishness and cry out in his remorse, 'We have sinned', and make his plea to Moses, 'Let her not be as one dead'. Envy is not only foolish, but in the sight of God it is hideous like leprosy.

The Intercession

Moses, the injured party, with Godlike grace prayed to the Lord, 'Heal her now, O God, I beseech thee', v. 13. God responded and restored Miriam, but not until she paid for her sin of haughtiness and envy by the humiliation of being 'shut up without the camp'. We too can pray in the same spirit of meekness, when sometimes others foolishly and falsely speak against us.

February 3rd
Numbers 14. 1-5, 13-18

LET THE POWER OF MY LORD BE GREAT

Under the strain of his distress over the people's sinful ways, Moses implored God not to let the heathen have excuse for denying his great omnipotent power.

The Sin of Rejection

Israel looked on their situation in the wilderness as hopeless. The people thought the sword will devour us, our wives, and our little ones. Wailing by day and weeping by night, they vented their feelings on Moses and Aaron. They said, 'Better to die a natural death in the wilderness' and 'Let us make a captain and return to Egypt', v. 4. The unbelieving words of this self-sufficient people were a vote of no confidence in the promises of God. Jehovah's intervention in redemption was meaningless to them. In blatant unbelief they refused to believe God was offering them a good land, with help to get them into it.

The People's Appeal

Moses, Aaron, Joshua and Caleb knew that the nation had sealed its doom by voting to make a return to Egypt. Moses and Aaron fell on their faces. Joshua and Caleb rent their clothes, and made a last appeal to the people. The appeal went unheeded. The people, worked up into a frenzy, called for their stoning to death. The glory of the Lord appeared. God, provoked beyond the limit of His forbearance, declared He would slay the rebellious people. He would disinherit them and make of Moses a greater and mightier nation.

Moses' Appeal

The moment was critical. Moses appealed to God. The nations will misinterpret His actions. They knew God was dwelling in the midst of the people. To destroy them would be an admission He was not able to bring these people into the land. Moses prayed that they have no excuse for denying God's omnipotence. Then he implored God to manifest His power, 'Let the power of my Lord be great'. His power to judge iniquity was already in evidence. Moses interceded for a show of Jehovah's great power to forgive, 'Pardon I beseech thee, the iniquity of this people'. What a tremendous privilege prayer is. To plead with God for Him to display His great power to pardon and forgive His people's sin. Prayer in these circumstances expresses how we value each other even in times of failure.

February 4th

Numbers 14. 19-25

ACCORDING TO THY MERCY

Jehovah's answer to the prayer of Moses does not refer to the first of Moses' appeals. The concerns Moses had, that if Jehovah carries out His promise to destroy the people will in some way damaged His reputation in the eyes of the heathen, did not concern God. The Lord will never sacrifice His righteousness and justice for a reputation. If His glory is to fill the whole earth, His justice cannot be withheld.

The Prayer for Pardon

Moses had a large appreciation of the greatness and glory of God. He knew the Lord is long-suffering, and of great mercy, forgiving iniquity and transgression, and not at all clearing the guilty. He knew the Lord visited iniquity, even to the third and fourth generations, v. 18. His confidence in the Lord was undiminished even in the face of unbelieving rebellion. Out of his personal knowledge of Jehovah he cried, 'Pardon, I beseech thee, the iniquity of this people according unto the greatness of thy mercy'. Moses owned it was not the first time forgiveness had come to God's people. God forgave them repeatedly since leaving Egypt. Now he asked God to pardon them again for He knew with God there was no finality in forgiveness.

Pardon Granted

God responded to the appeal of Moses and gave him a full answer, saying, 'I have pardoned'. Because My glory is going to fill the earth, My justice must act. These people have tempted Me ten times, and have not hearkened to My voice! The first announcement of judgement was death and disinheritance. Now because of their unbelief, all aged twenty years and over at the first census would forfeit the land. Only Caleb, because he followed the Lord fully, and Joshua would enter the land, vv. 24, 30.

Fulfilment of Judgement

The Lord told Moses and Aaron what judgement was coming upon the people. Unmistakable evidence that God will fulfil His word was at hand. The Lord struck dead with the plague those spies who brought up an evil report to the congregation. The people mourned greatly, but mourning would not redeem them now. They confessed, but gone was the hour for confession. Moses intercession resulted in divine pardon being granted, but justice would come upon the instigators of the murmuring.

Numbers 16. 1-7, 15

RESPECT NOT THEIR OFFERING

The most critical event in Israel's wilderness years was the rebellion of Korah and his company against Moses and Aaron. Korah, three Reubenites and two hundred and fifty nobles stirred up sedition and challenged God's leaders in their divinely appointed positions. The challenge was really against God. Moses made this very clear when he said, 'Thou and all thy company are gathered together against the Lord'.

The Challenge

Korah and his band charged Moses and Aaron with retaining their top positions when there was no need of their leadership. They accused the leaders of taking too much upon them. Their argument, based on a pious sounding logic said, 'All the congregation are holy, every one of them; and is not the Lord among us?'. They reasoned that the two leaders were redundant. Korah did not wish to dissolve the offices of these two, but to replace them. This is a strategy applied still where carnal individuals want position. It is not spiritual leadership they want, but a mistaken idea of power over the people.

Moses' Response

Moses recognized the situation called for wisdom. He would let God reveal His mind in the matter. 'The Lord will show who are his and who is holy', v. 5. The time had come for a public demonstration. God would identify whom He would have to serve Him. Jehovah would show who were His holy servants. Moses revealed that the real root of Korah's trouble was he wanted the priesthood. They disregarded their service as Levites. They did not consider their position a high calling, or a ministry to God's people. Dathan and Abiram foolishly charged Moses with failure. They said he had taken the people away from Egypt, but he had not fulfilled his promise to bring them into Canaan. They also accused him of making himself a ruler over everybody. This false charge made Moses very wroth. In his righteous anger he prayed, 'Lord, Respect not thou their offering', v. 15. Prayer in this instance took on a different character. It was the prayer of righteous anger caused through the jealousy and envy of some of God's servants, who despised the service for which He had called and equipped them.

February 6th

Numbers 21. 5-9

AND MOSES PRAYED

Sin and death

Murmuring and discouragement, those adverse elements, were in evidence. The children of Israel had left Mount Hor and were intending to compass the land of Edom. They had no bread or water and they loathed the manna. In their foolhardiness they spoke against God and against Moses. For their sin judgement fell, and a scourge of fiery serpents attacked the camp, fatally biting many of the people. God reiterates His unchanging truth that sin brings judgement. Although they had with them the presence of God, that did not give them licence to sin. Confession of sin and the faithful intercessory praying of Moses again caused God to set up a condition of deliverance for the people.

Salvation and life

God, in response to Moses' intercession, instructed him to make a brass, fiery-looking serpent and set it high on a standard. The object chosen by God corresponded to the deadly serpents that He sent among the people. It was cold and lifeless, to represent what God was able to do for the Israelite—take away the fatal sting and render it harmless. When a live serpent bit an Israelite he escaped death by looking upon the brazen serpent. Its efficacy reached out to everyone who would look upon it. Observe the importance of Moses' intercession. It came at a critical time in the experience of the Israelites. Without the people's confession and Moses' intercession, the people's individual faith and march would have ended here. Moses' prayer made God's grace active in granting this miraculous deliverance from the very judgement for sin which God Himself was bringing. At the same time, only the person who looked up at the representative symbol experienced deliverance. Christ, set up publicly on the standard of a cross, was a visible sign to all people of the guilt He was bearing. He died as representative of the race of sinners, but salvation only comes to those who look up to Him in faith. Moses' intercession played a vital role in the deliverance of the stricken Israelites; so our intercession for lost sinners plays an important role in their salvation. Will you pray earnestly for God to send the power down for the conviction and conversion of souls?

Numbers 27. 1-11

BROUGHT THEIR CAUSE BEFORE THE LORD

Zelophehad, the son of Hepher, of the families of Manasseh, had five daughters but no sons. Since the father died without leaving a male heir, the family name would normally cease to exist because there was no inheritance of land. The daughters of Zelophehad came to Moses. They requested an inheritance of land in the name of their father that his name might be perpetuated in future generations.

The Law of Inheritance

There was no procedure legislated for in Israel to cover a case such as this. There was no law of inheritance for these daughters. Why would they want a claim to their father's inheritance? Because there was a justifiable pride in the family, and they wanted to perpetuate the name, worth and heritage of the family. They wished also to preserve the dignity of the woman as an integral part of the family. Spiritual women today will have a similar exercise in the context of the Christian heritage. There is provision for us to hand on to future generations our Christian heritage, but for Zelophehad's daughters there was no provision made in the law of God for them to obtain a part in the inheritance of their father! So they came before Moses and the priest and the princes and the whole congregation by the door of the tabernacle, and made known their exercise regarding the inheritance. The daughters' question was composite, 'Why should the name of our father be done away from among his family?'. In their concern for the family name, they came to Moses and said, 'Give unto us … a possession among the brethren of our father'.

Brought before the Lord

It was this concern for the family name that caused Moses to bring their cause before the Lord. The Lord answered that the daughters had a just claim to the inheritance of their father. Then for like future situations God enlarged the laws of inheritance, so that the name and heritage of the family perpetuated itself, not being easily dissolved. We can make prayer to God concerning our sons that they will grow up as spiritual plants and our daughters be as polished stones. Paul had a similar prayerful desire for Timothy to pass on to 'faithful men' the things committed to him; that is, the heritage of apostolic teaching.

February 8th
Numbers 27. 15-17

SET A MAN OVER

Moses had failed to sanctify God before the eyes of the children of Israel. The result was he, with Aaron, forfeited the privilege of entering Canaan with his people. Instructed by God, he ascended the mountain of Abarim that formed a tableland, to a point called Mount Nebo that he might have a sight of the Promised Land before his death. It was breathtaking, and perhaps the greatest emotional experience Moses had in his lifetime. There was no expression of the excitement that must have filled His heart at what God was showing him of all the lands that formed the people's inheritance. That God did not allow him to lead the people into the Promised Land did not fill Moses with self pity or mourning. Typical of this selfless man, his immediate concern was for the people of God, that they be not as sheep that have no shepherd. Moses was different to Hezekiah who said, 'Is it not good, if peace and truth be in my days?', 2 Kgs. 20. 19. He was content to go to his rest in good days, but there was no concern for the future of God's people. Moses first concern was for his people. He spoke to the Lord about their future. He said, 'Let the Lord, the God of the spirits of all flesh, set a man over the congregation, which may go out before them ... lead them out ... and bring them in' to the land. God chose Joshua, a man in whom the Spirit dwelt. Moses a mature man of God, still in prime physical condition, would have dearly loved to be there when his people finally crossed the Jordan into the land of Canaan. There must have been a tinge of disappointment in his heart, yet Moses unflinchingly obeyed Jehovah to the very end. He went to his rest, knowing the congregation of the Lord would be not as sheep which have no shepherd. God heard the prayer of His servant, and instructed him concerning Joshua. Moses, before going to his reward, inaugurated the younger man whom God had chosen into his new responsibility of leadership. If all leaders of God's people had the same exercise to pray for those who could be future leaders among the saints, what a boon it would be for the people of God! Like Moses they can then go to their reward, knowing the people are not left as sheep without a shepherd.

Deuteronomy 3. 23-29

LET ME GO OVER

Moses wanted to see the good land beyond Jordan. His great longing was to plant his feet upon the proper inheritance of Israel. He urges the Lord to let him go over, but God could not grant him his request. Not believing God's clear instructions he had spoken unadvisedly with his lips at the waters of Meribah: by his actions God was not sanctified in the eyes of the people. Now by solemn and irreversible enactment of divine government, God prohibits His servant from crossing over Jordan.

The Meekness of Moses

Gathering the assembly, Moses rehearses in their ears how the Lord was 'wroth' with him, and refused to hear his request, saying, 'speak no more unto me of this matter'. All this was morally necessary for the people. It was on their account God denied Moses his greatest longing. Do we find it hard to confess we have made a mistake because we want to retain our reputation? Moses stands before the whole congregation and confesses his mistake and, bowing to the governmental dealings of God, he steps down from his elevated position, and throws his mantle over the shoulders of his successor. Joshua is encouraged by Moses to discharge his duties which he must resign.

The Moral Greatness of Moses

Moses humbled himself under the mighty hand of God, and accepted the discipline imposed on him. We do well to ponder why God could not grant the request of his servant. Moses spoke 'unadvisedly with his lips'. With Aaron he failed to glorify God in the presence of the people. God said 'Ye have rebelled against me', Num. 27. 14. It is a serious matter to rebel against the word of God. Moses was refused entrance into the Promised Land for neglecting the word of the Lord. He had received a plain commandment, and by that commandment his conduct must be governed. He disobeyed—and now no matter how great his desire, or how earnest his pleadings with Jehovah, his disobedience cost him entrance into the land. Here is a solemn lesson for every child of God. Disobedience hinders God granting our requests. Grace elevated Moses to become the leader of His people. Government deprived him of 'going over to see the good land'.

February 10th

Deuteronomy 4. 1-7

WE CALL UPON HIM

The nearness of God was a distinct privilege of Israel. They were His people and He was their God. As a result they could **in everything call upon Him**. If that was true for Israel, how much more so for God's people today! In everything we too can call upon Him.

God's Nearness

The emphasis in the passage is upon God's nearness to His people. In the light of God having come near to them, Moses exhorts Israel to remember three things. Wisdom, understanding and calling upon God, centres in hearing and doing the statutes and ordinances which he had taught them. He calls for attentive hearing to what they had been taught. It was vital to Israel for them to value and obey the word of God, putting into practice in its entirety all they had learned. Moses commanded they were not to add to, nor take from, the word of God. They were not to tamper with divine truth under any circumstances.

God's Intervention

Israel are directed back to God's intervention in the past. Their personal preservation at Baal-Peor was linked with their cleaving 'unto the Lord their God'. To them, the sober message of Baal-Peor was *fidelity to God preserves life*. Failure and sin left twenty-four thousand empty places in the families of Israel. Moses further impresses upon the people that if obedience to God's word was paramount in the wilderness, it will be so when they enter the land of promise.

God's Principles

The principles of God never alter. They may be expanded with further revelation but not altered. For Israel, wisdom, understanding and calling upon God, who had come near to them, resulted from 'hearkening and doing the statutes and judgements'. Those same principles continue in their application today. The Christian has the privilege of knowing that God has drawn near, but to 'call upon Him in everything' makes the same demands upon us as upon Israel. God's word in its entirety is not to be tampered with, but obeyed and acted upon.

February 11th

Deuteronomy 9. 11-20

I PRAYED FOR AARON

Moses had been on the mount forty days and forty nights receiving from Jehovah the tablets of the covenant. Down in the valley the people, under the charge of Aaron and Hur, lost sight of one who had gone up on high. They gave themselves over to idolatry and made a golden calf and worshipped it. Aaron, charged with responsibility for the people, failed miserably. He joined in their infidelity and helped forward their idolatry.

The Anger of the Lord

Jehovah's anger was so great that He would destroy the people whom He loved, and blot out their name from under heaven because they were a 'stiff-necked people'. Little did they know how appallingly near they were to ruin and disaster. The danger of forgetting Christ, at God's right hand making intercession for us, is very real for God's people today.

The Intercession of Moses

For forty days and nights Moses fell down before the Lord interceding for them. He will turn away the wrath of God lest He should destroy the people, Ps. 106. 23. He pleaded with God for the people, God's inheritance, whom He had redeemed. Confessing their stubbornness, wickedness and sin, he powerfully pleaded with God to fulfil His promise and bring them into 'the land'. He wanted the glory of God and the pardon of Israel. There were two things Moses could not endure—reproach heaped upon the name of the Lord, and Israel's destruction. It reminds us of the unceasing, active intercession for us by Christ our Great High Priest.

The Salvation of Aaron

'I prayed for Aaron also.' Moses met Aaron's failure with intercession. Moses was righteously angry with Aaron, but instead of writing him off in his anger, he interceded for him. When priestly persons fail, a ministry of prayer and intercession, not harsh criticism, will meet the situation. It is beautiful to read, 'The Lord hearkened unto me at that time'. It was not the first time Moses had stood between the Lord and the people. He had prevailed before and he prevailed with God again.

February 12th

Deuteronomy 26. 5-15

BLESS THY PEOPLE

To have the blessing of God is the overwhelming desire of the people of Israel. Yet the people freely acknowledged, 'A Syrian ready to perish' was their father. God found them toiling in the brick-kilns of Egypt, beneath the cruel lash of Pharaoh's taskmasters.

We Cried unto The Lord

Their cry of helplessness went up to the throne. It brought Jehovah down to see their affliction and to deliver them. In response, the people came with baskets full of the fruit of the Jehovah's land, and they worshipped before the Lord their God. An ever increasing appreciation of our deliverance will bring us before God with hearts filled with love and lips full of praise.

Bringing the Tithes

According to the commandment of God, they brought the tithes of their increase, and gave to the Levite, the stranger, the fatherless and the widow, 'that they may eat ... and be filled'. With all the commandments of God fulfilled, the people prayed, 'Look down from thy holy habitation, from heaven, and bless thy people'. The blessing of God is not just dependent on Israel worshipping. It demanded also meeting the needs of others. God has not changed His mind over the passage of time. The order of worship, active benevolence and divine blessing still holds today.

Moral Qualifications for Blessing

'Let us offer the sacrifice of praise to God continually, that is, the fruit of our lips giving thanks to his name. But to do good and to communicate forget not: for with such sacrifices God is well pleased', Heb. 13. 15-16. Praising God and active benevolence always go together. To have lips full of praise, and at the same time hearts shut up to a person in need, disqualifies us morally from asking God to look down and bless us. *We look up* to God and offer the sacrifice of praise. *We look out* at a needy world and do good. *We look in* and seek by God's grace to keep ourselves unspotted from the world. Then we have the moral right to pray for, and expect, God to look down from heaven and bless us.

February 13th

Deuteronomy 32. 1-4

ASCRIBE GREATNESS TO GOD

Moses summoned heaven and earth to hearken to this magnificent song. He is going to publish abroad the great name of Jehovah, in view of which, there is a call to, 'ascribe ... greatness unto our God'.

The Name of God

Jehovah's name stands forever. There is no power of earth or hell that can countervail divine purpose or hinder the shining out of divine glory. The opening notes of Moses' song are most comforting. God is the Rock. He abides in unshakeable strength for His people. His works are perfect, without a single flaw. This is like dew upon the thirsty soul. 'All his ways are judgement; a God of truth, and without iniquity, just and right is he'. However, the people of God may fail, they have to do with One who abides faithful. Sometimes He takes the rod of discipline and uses it upon His people as well as the nations. He cannot tolerate evil. God is no respecter of persons. None can deny the goodness, kindness, faithfulness and tender mercy of the Most High. When God planned the settlements of the great national territories, all was in direct reference to Israel. Canaan lies at the centre of God's geography. Jehovah's portion is in His people and Jacob is the lot of His inheritance.

The Greatness of God

God's love, goodness and patience to Israel, in spite of their falling into every kind of sin, inspired its people to ascribe greatness to their God. He is ineffable in holiness, infinite in wisdom, mysterious in trinity, boundless in His attributes of omnipotence, omniscience and omnipresence. His eternal supremacy and redeeming grace call upon the hearts of all who know Him to, 'ascribe ... greatness unto our God'. God chose us in Christ before the foundation of the world, and made us sons by adoption, and placed us in the Beloved. He has also redeemed us and forgiven all our sins. In the riches of His grace God has linked us with Christ eternally as His Body, setting us in the place of highest dignity. Christ in His love for us will bring us to the nearest place of affection as His Bride. How can we not 'ascribe greatness to our God'?

February 14th

Deuteronomy 33. 1-7

BE THOU AN HELP

The last words of Moses are words of blessing for the people in covenant relation with Jehovah. They trace out divine counsel and the abundant goodness of God. Recounting the movements of Jehovah, Moses reflects upon His judicial manifestations at Sinai and Paran.

The Safety of the Saints

Moses reveals the heart of God toward Israel, 'Yea, he loved the people'. What precious truth is here. In spite of all their failures, God loved His people. Nothing they could do would alter His love for them. God is greater than their failures, He loved them with an everlasting love. Israel's security lies in the next statement, 'all his saints are in his hand'. The same is true of believers today. 'None shall pluck them out of my Father's hand'. Such is our eternal security. Sitting at His feet, Israel received God's words. Every word proceeding out of the mouth of the Lord is more precious than gold and silver and sweeter than honey and the honeycomb. Mary of Bethany is the New Testament example. She sat at the Lord's feet and heard His word.

The Blessing of the Tribes

Against the background of Jehovah's love, Moses blesses the tribes of Israel. After the blessing of Reuben, Moses blesses Judah, saying, 'Hear, Lord, the voice of Judah'. Prayer was characteristic of this tribe. Achsah, Jabez and David who prayed, all belonged to Judah. David prayed, 'This poor man cried, and the Lord heard him, and saved him', Ps. 34. 6. Later, David's greater Son, the Lion of the tribe of Judah, prayed. He offered up, in dark Gethsemane, 'prayers and supplications with strong crying and tears … and was heard in that he feared'. Judah's blessing included being heard by God. Another feature of the blessing was, 'be thou an help to him from his enemies'. Judah's history reveals that this tribe was foremost in warfare. Judah was the tribe that captured old Jerusalem, and went on to conquer numerous enemies. The book of Judges declares, 'and the Lord was with Judah'. Christians characterized by prayer have this confidence; God hears their prayers, and will give help in the battle against wicked spirits in heavenly places.

February 15th

Joshua 5. 13-15

THE PLACE ... IS HOLY

Having crossed the river Jordan, the people of Israel now faced a prolonged war to conquer the Promised Land. This meant that enormous responsibilities fell upon the shoulders of Joshua, their God-ordained leader. No doubt these lay heavily upon him as he scouted about in the region of the city of Jericho, and plotted Israel's assault upon that first major obstacle of the campaign.

So it was that Joshua met God 'by (or near) Jericho', and learnt that the city would fall, not through Joshua's planning but because of his obedience. Here Joshua came to recognize who was in command, for God revealed Himself as 'a man ... with his sword drawn in his hand'. Immediately Joshua questioned Him as to whose side He might be on, implying a sort of alliance, with Joshua in commanding role. However, here was the 'captain of the host' and Joshua recognized his superior and bowed before Him in genuine reverence of heart and mind.

True prayer is an encounter with God, and involves recognition of the superiority of the Lord, and the acknowledgement that God is great and we are utterly dependent upon Him. Joshua came to realize this truth, and so the responsibility for the campaign rested less on him and supremely upon the Lord.

We notice that this encounter was two-way and Joshua asked the question, 'What saith my lord unto his servant?'. Do we seek directives from the Lord as we come to Him in prayer? God's answer was to emphasize His holiness. This is one of the great themes of Scripture, with holiness being the one attribute which God would have His people remember Him by more than any other. So like Moses before him, Exod. 3. 5, Joshua took off his shoes and realized that to stand in the presence of God was to stand on holy ground.

Reverence, holiness and obedience are vital characteristics when we approach God in prayer. All that is defiled by contact with this sinful world should be removed, and then we can begin to know the power and victory of believing prayer.

SANCTIFY YOURSELVES

The nation of Israel was now in crisis. The euphoria of victory at Jericho had given way to the despair of defeat at the hands of the tiny community of Ai. Israel's soldiers had retreated in fearful disarray, and thirty-six had been killed. Israel's shocked reaction was not due to the size of the defeat but to its unexpectedness.

Joshua had shown remarkable self-confidence before attacking Ai and had failed to consult with God. If, at that point, he had prayed then the sin would have been discovered and they would not have experienced defeat. However, in the aftermath of defeat he now seeks the Lord. So often we can be like that in failing to seek God's will, and then cry out to Him when things go wrong.

Joshua's approach in prayer was so genuine. Firstly, it was a prolonged time, 'until the eventide', 7. 6. Secondly, it was corporate, as the nation's elders joined him to seek the face of God. Thirdly, they expressed their distress in a public way, by ripping their clothes, putting dust in their hair and lying on the ground. So we see a serious and determined approach to discern the underlying cause for the defeat.

Joshua was certainly concerned for the dishonour which had come upon the name of God. If God had allowed this then it would mean that He had forsaken His people and their future was most precarious. In the light of Israel's defeat the armies of Canaan would be emboldened, and Israel would be defeated and destroyed. Joshua could not make sense of what had happened, even wishing they had stayed on the safer, eastern side of Jordan. By implication he rebuked God and laid the blame for defeat at His door.

In response to prayer, God turned Joshua's thoughts away from the defeat and confronted him with the underlying moral reason for it. The fault was firmly Israel's and there was need for national consecration, with the transgressor identified and punished, before victory could again be experienced.

FAILURE TO PRAY

Israel's victories over the cities of Jericho and Ai produced contrasting reactions amongst the remaining inhabitants of the land. Most of the nations hardened in their opposition to the invaders, and became more organized by uniting into a confederacy, 9. 1-2. However, the four-fold group of Gibeonite cities, v. 17, decided to make terms with Israel in an attempt to stave off the inevitability of destruction.

The Gibeonites were motivated by fear as they were well aware of the greatness of the God of Israel. They recognized that God had destroyed the Egyptians, the Amorites on the east of Jordan, 9. 9-10, and the inhabitants of Jericho and Ai, 9. 3, and that they were next on Israel's invasion path. Instead of military opposition, they chose the path of guile and deceit. They sent a delegation to Joshua with old food, wineskins and clothing to give the impression that they had travelled a great distance.

Joshua questioned the delegation, but was deceived into making a treaty with them. The Gibeonites approached humbly, but with lies and flattery. In humility they sought servanthood, with lies they claimed to have come a great distance and through flattery they praised the great God of Israel. The result was that Joshua did not ask any probing questions but accepted it all at face value. Yet Joshua's great failure was in not consulting God. He did not pray about the matter. Neither he nor the leaders of Israel, 'asked ... counsel at the mouth of the Lord', 9. 14.

The treaty was sealed with an oath, but the deceit was soon discovered. However, such an agreement was sacred and could not be annulled, and the Gibeonites were made slaves to the people of Israel. Failure to pray can cause us to commit actions which we cannot retract as Christians. We may regret what we did but we live with the consequences. The hymn writer spoke the truth when he wrote, 'O what peace we often forfeit! O what needless pain we bear! All because we do not carry everything to God in prayer'.

THE SUN STOOD STILL

In response to Joshua's prayer, the Lord enabled Israel to achieve a spectacular victory. God's miraculous intervention coupled with the energy of Joshua and his army made the day of victory so memorable that 'there was no day like that before it or after it', 10. 14. It was cherished in the national memory and recorded in the 'book of Jasher', 10. 13. That book is now lost and was never part of Holy Scripture.

The newly-formed treaty between Israel and the Gibeonites was the immediate cause of this battle. The king of Jerusalem was so thoroughly alarmed to find that the area to the north of his kingdom was in league with the invaders, that he joined with four other kings to attack the strategic city of Gibeon. The Gibeonites sent requests for help to Joshua and he responded promptly and effectively.

However, Joshua only moved into action after receiving the divine promise of victory, 10. 8. Such assurance did not stop him doing his best and using his skill and energy as a commander. He moved his army into position through a night-time march, surprising the enemy and routing them. Israel was greatly helped as the Lord intervened in two ways; firstly, with hailstones which killed many of the enemies, 10. 11, and secondly, by responding to Joshua's prayer and making the sun stand still, 10. 13.

Many have tried to explain this phenomenon of the sun standing still, while others have tried to discount it altogether. It was certainly a spectacular event which defies any scientific explanation, and that is the essential nature of a miracle. A miracle works outside the laws of nature and even works against them. Such a miracle, by its very nature, can only be performed by almighty God who transcends His creation. Such a miracle was the result of prayer, and a great victory was gained for Israel. Thus the Lord had listened to the voice Joshua, had fought for Israel and had delivered their enemies into their hands, 10. 14, 19.

February 19th

Judges 1. 1-2

DIVINE PROMISE

In many ways death is a great watershed, and this is especially so with the death of a strong and powerful leader. Joshua's death is more fully recorded in Judges 2. 8-9, but is mentioned in our reading as a sort of general introduction to the book of Judges. The death of Joshua is significant for while he was alive Israel was essentially victorious, but after his death Israel was in decline. Joshua's leadership is highlighted in the book of Joshua and is an account of the successful invasion of the Promised Land. The events following his death are recorded in the book of Judges, and cover a period which has been called 'the dark ages in Israel's history'.

Those dark ages include Israel's sin of idolatry, which was followed by God's judgement upon the nation in the form of foreign oppressors invading the country. Israel then cried out to the Lord in repentance and prayed for deliverance. God heard their prayer, and deliverance was brought about by God raising up judges to inspire Israel to drive out the oppressors. The cycle repeats itself many times in the period covered by the book of Judges.

However, Israel did not start off with defeat or idolatry, for with the death of Joshua, they turned to the Lord in prayer, 1. 1. They sought advice from God as to who would lead them into battle, as they now had no national leader upon whom they could depend.

The Lord answered their prayer in two ways. Firstly, they were told that Judah was to lead them into battle. Secondly, they were given assurance of ultimate victory over the people of the land, 1. 2. There then follows an account of Judah entering into battles and being victorious because 'the Lord was with Judah', 1. 19. Though God had given the promise of victory and it was only with His help and strength that it could be achieved, yet the battle had to be engaged, and the effort of campaign undertaken. Here are divine and human responsibilities working in harmony for the glory of God.

There is still need for firm decisive leadership in companies of God's people, and such leadership must be of God's provision, and rely upon God for His guidance and empowerment. Others should acknowledge this appointment by God, and offer their full and active support.

Judges 3. 9, 15

THE LORD RAISED UP A DELIVERER

The New Testament reminds us that 'whatsoever a man soweth, that shall he also reap', Gal. 6. 7. This principle was certainly true for the nation of Israel, for they committed evil against the Lord and paid a heavy price for it. Their evil consisted of forgetting the Lord and serving useless idols. It seems incredible that they should so quickly forget the mighty miracles and victories which God had brought about for them. However, we should not stand in judgement as we can easily forget what our Saviour has done for us, and that is why we need to affirm regularly our focus on Calvary through breaking bread and drinking wine.

The consequence of the nation's evil was that 'the anger of the Lord was hot against Israel' and he allowed the land to be invaded and oppressed for eight years under Cushan-rishathaim with his Mesopotamian forces. This was the Lord's hand of discipline upon His beloved and chosen people, which enabled them to learn the lesson of dependence upon God as they returned to the Lord in prayer, seeking His deliverance. The Lord heard their prayer and brought deliverance through a famous family in Judah. Caleb's younger brother, Othniel, with the Spirit of the Lord upon him, 3. 10, led Israel to victory over the invasion force.

Later God brought about another invasion to discipline His people. This time it was a confederacy of Moab, Ammon and Amalek under the leadership of Eglon, king of Moab. It was a partial invasion which centred upon the city of Jericho in the tribal area of Benjamin, and lasted for eighteen years. Again the people raised up their cries of prayer to the Lord for deliverance, and He raised up a deliverer in the form of a left-handed assassin known as Ehud.

Ehud was chosen by God, being enabled to kill king Eglon, and then he led the army of Israel to a great victory over the forces of Moab. His weapon was a two-edged sword, reminding us that our evangelistic thrust is with 'the word of God' which is 'sharper than any two-edged sword', Heb. 4. 12.

February 21st

Judges 6. 11-14

THE LORD IS WITH THEE

It was once again a desperately unhappy time in Israel's history, for in response to their wicked idolatry God allowed the hordes of Midian to conquer the land and have the upper hand over Israel for seven years, 6. 1. The Midianites were as 'grasshoppers for multitude', 6. 5, which is surely a reference to their vast numbers. However, it also indicates that like the plagues of locusts which could strip the land bare, so Midian stripped Israel of its agricultural wealth. They destroyed the crops, stole the domestic animals, 6. 3-4, and reduced Israel to starving poverty and pathetic attempts to hide in the more rugged upland terrain. Israel certainly paid a heavy price for their wickedness.

Eventually the Lord intervened in response to their prayers and visited a young man named Gideon. He was from the tribe of Manasseh and was desperately trying to winnow some corn in a winepress. Such work was usually done on high ground where the breezes were blowing, so we can imagine Gideon feeling hot and sticky and generally frustrated at his slow progress working below ground level. His aim was to hide from the Midianites and produce a little grain for his family's needs.

In this condition the Lord visited him, appearing as an angel, though His true identity is revealed in verses 14 and 16. God described Gideon as a 'mighty man of valour', without apparent justification at that time, for Gideon felt disillusioned with the present situation which contrasted greatly with God's miraculous dealings with the nation in the past. They had then been victorious; now they were defeated, demoralized and felt forsaken by the Lord, and memories of the past only compounded Gideon's deep distress.

Yet Gideon was chosen by the Lord to go and liberate Israel from Midianite bondage, and all he needed to do was to obey the divine commandment. Likewise, we are called to go and proclaim deliverance to those bound by sin who need the liberating message of the gospel. Are we obedient?

February 22nd
Judges 6. 15-16

I AM THE LEAST

Gideon's response to the Lord's call teaches us some important lessons about our relationship with God. Firstly, we notice that he was genuinely respectful. He said, 'Oh my Lord'. This reveals very clearly that he recognized that he was talking with someone greater than himself and gave him due reverence in the title with which he addressed God. To appreciate the greatness and majesty of God is vital for our development as Christians.

Secondly, he showed real humility. He was 'little in his own eyes' and was not an arrogant or conceited person. He responded by saying that the Lord's message of leading Israel to victory seemed impossible, for Gideon belonged to a poor family in one of the least prominent tribes of Israel, and was considered least in his father's household. He was so low on the scale of importance that he had even been engaged in the menial task of winnowing wheat. This is always the sort of person whom the Lord can use. Humility means that we do not focus upon ourselves and think we can achieve something in our own strength, but we look to God and seek His resources to enable us to be successful in the task we undertake.

The Lord responded with two reassuring promises to Gideon. Firstly, the Lord's presence would go with him, for Gideon was given (as have we) the wonderful promise, 'Surely I will be with thee', 6. 16. Nothing can be of greater encouragement to the servant of the Lord as he steps out into Christian service than the knowledge of the Saviour's presence. Those were the words of Jesus to His disciples as He gave them the great commission, 'Lo, I am with you alway', Matt. 28. 20.

The second promise to Gideon was the certainty of victory. The great army of Midian would be struck down as if they were merely an individual soldier. The Lord had decided that His people had been disciplined for long enough and now was the time for their deliverance. Thus the Lord's discipline had achieved its purpose in bringing Israel to repentance.

Judges 6. 17-24

JEHOVAH-SHALOM

Gideon was wonderfully favoured by the Lord, for God in His grace had met with him and bestowed upon him the promise of victory over the oppressive forces of Midian. Though the immediate circumstances for Israel were difficult and restricted, God gave a glimpse of future freedom and the overthrow of the invasion force. Gideon would be the man to lead Israel to victory.

We can well imagine the impact upon Gideon's mind as he heard those awesome words. He wanted to be absolutely sure that this was God's message. So he sought a sign and asked the angel of the Lord to stay while he went and made a pot of broth and a basket of unleavened bread. This he offered as a present to the Lord and placed it upon a rock. The rock thus functioned as an altar and the food became a sacrifice to the Lord. With a touch of his staff the angel caused fire to ascend out of the rock and consume the offering, and with that the angel departed.

The enormity of what had happened must have weighed heavily upon Gideon, for fear engulfed him and he cried out in terror to the Lord. It was a desperate cry for he had seen an angel of the Lord face to face. 'Angel of the Lord' is widely used in the Old Testament to denote a manifestation of God Himself to men. Thus Gideon had seen the Lord and in fear for his life cried out to God.

God's reassuring voice came to Gideon, and with it peace to replace fear. Fear always robs us of peace, but as we learn to trust the Lord and rely upon Him we can conquer fear and experience true peace. The apostle Paul made this clear when he assured the Philippians that the truly prayerful Christian will enjoy God's wonderful peace, Phil. 4. 6-7.

So Gideon was told that he would not die, but live to secure victory over the Midianites. He then built an altar to the Lord and called it 'Jehovah-shalom', which means 'The Lord is peace'. We can imagine that such a sentiment echoed the feelings of Gideon's heart, for he now knew calmness within—but it also focused upon the future peace and freedom from oppression which would be secured for Israel through Gideon. Today the Lord Jesus gives His people true peace of heart.

February 24th

Judges 10. 10-16

WE HAVE SINNED

The Ammonites had invaded the land of Israel by attacking across the Jordan into the tribal areas of Judah, Benjamin and Ephraim, and the whole of Israel was affected and felt the disruption of invasion. The nation's response was to cry out to the Lord in confession and two sins were mentioned.

Firstly, they had forsaken their God. Somehow they had turned their backs upon the Lord by failing to obey Him and neglecting to bring Him the true worship of their hearts. Secondly, they served false gods. These gods of Canaan were known as 'Baalim' or 'Baals', and such a title appears to have been a 'cover' word for all the many idols in Canaan. However, it eventually came to apply to the fertility god of the Canaanites. Such idols became the focus for Israelite worship in direct violation of God's commandments, and the result was the punishment of invasion by the Ammonites.

In response to Israel's confession, God sent a message, presumably delivered by a prophet. He reminded the people of the past when He had delivered them from the Egyptians, Exod. 1. 2–14, the Amorites, Num. 21, the Ammonites, Judg. 3. 13, the Philistines, Judg. 3. 31, the Sidonians, the Amalekites and the Midianites, Judg. 7. Despite such powerful victories Israel had still forsaken the Lord and turned to the worship of idols. So the Lord challenged Israel to pray to those idols for deliverance in their hour of need.

Such a challenge proved how futile it was to worship man-made gods, for such gods were utterly incapable of delivering Israel from their desperate plight. It galvanized the nation to change course and they forsook the idols and once again sought to serve the true and living God. Thus their confession of sin was effective for it led to the actions of repentance. We, as Christians, are instructed to confess our sins, 1 John 1. 9. Such confession is not simply a formula of words, but an action of forsaking and repenting of the sins which we commit, and this leads to God's forgiveness.

In the light of Israel's repentance the Lord's soul was moved by their sad situation. He could no longer bear to see His people so miserably treated and so He raised up Jephthah to lead them to victory, to freedom from the armies of Ammon.

A VOW UNTO THE LORD

Jephthah was God's chosen instrument to deliver Israel from the control which Ammon had exercised over the nation. Previously he had been rejected by Israel because of his mixed parentage, but in their hour of need they turned to him as a man of strength and leadership-capability. In addition 'the Spirit of the Lord came upon Jephthah', 11. 29. Thus he was empowered by God for the task of delivering Israel.

As he moved out with his forces to attack the army of Ammon he made a vow before the Lord. Many have felt that this was an unnecessary vow, for God would have delivered the enemy into his hand without such statements. Nevertheless, he vowed and solemnly promised that if God gave him victory, then on his return he would offer as a burnt offering whatsoever came out of his house to meet him on his return from battle.

Jephthah led his forces to complete victory over Ammon. The tide of invasion was turned and once again the nation was free. However, the effects of the vow caused Jephthah real sadness and heartache for his own daughter was the first to meet him as he returned home. She was his only daughter and she came to meet him with joy, excited dancing and the playing of musical instruments. The pleasure was short-lived, and victory turned sour for Jephthah as he recalled his vow. His daughter was given two months before he 'did with her according to his vow', 11. 39. The obvious inference is that she was actually sacrificed, though such human offerings were strictly forbidden in Israel. Yet Jephthah with half-Canaanite antecedents may have had less compunction about such things.

Some suggest that Jephthah's daughter was not actually sacrificed but that she may have been reprieved and instead 'sacrificed' herself to perpetual virginity, celibate and unmarried, which may have been worse for an Israelite maid than death. Whichever is right, it is a real lesson in taking care over the promises we make. God looks for faithful obedience and not the extravagance of outlandish vows.

However, Jephthah is given a place amongst the great saints of God, and his victories and faith are recorded for us very briefly in the New Testament, Heb. 11. 32.

February 26th

Judges 13. 8-21

THE PROMISED NAZARITE

Here we witness God answering prayer and giving the promise of a son to a childless couple from the tribe of Dan. Manoah's wife had been visited by an angel of the Lord and been told that she would have a son; she had also been given instructions concerning that child. When she informed her husband of the visitation he entered into prayer and entreated the Lord for a further visit so that they could be given advice on the upbringing of that son.

We notice that Manoah was a man of faith. He had total confidence in the word of his wife and never doubted that the child would be born. He knew that God had given her the message and that God's word would soon be fulfilled. He no doubt felt the enormous responsibility of impending parenthood and so wisely sought the help of God. It is always true that no parents can adequately discharge their responsibilities without the help of the Lord.

God answered his prayer and the angel visited the woman a second time. This time she called her husband and it was confirmed that the son would be a Nazarite and must conform to the regulations for Nazarites, Num. 6. This meant that Manoah's wife must not be defiled during pregnancy by indulging in wine or strong drink, and must not eat unclean food, 11. 4. Similarly, the son must abstain from these things, must never shave or cut his hair and should never be defiled by contact with dead bodies. The word 'Nazarite' means consecrated or dedicated. Thus the son was to be get apart for the service of God, and his lifestyle would clearly emphasize such a calling to the people of Israel.

We can imagine Manoah reeling from the impact of the angel's words, and yet at the same time he would be full of gratitude to God. That thankfulness was expressed by bringing a young goat, together with a cereal offering, to the angel. Manoah laid it upon the rock as a sacrifice, and as the flames rose from the offering the angel ascended up with them into the presence of God. The angel never again appeared to Manoah and his wife. He had kept his name a strict secret, for it was too wonderful to be truly understood by men, 13. 18, but they realized that they had been in contact with the Lord Himself.

Judges 16. 28-30

SAMSON'S FINAL PRAYER

In his life Samson won some great and notable victories over the Philistines, but he was eventually captured and humiliated by his enemies. Delilah had coaxed from him the secret of his great strength, and by cutting his hair had robbed him of his physical might. The Philistines had not only imprisoned him but had, in an act of intense cruelty, put out his eyes and blinded him. They had made him do the work of a slave girl, that of grinding in the mill, and then had him brought to the house of their god Dagon where they could mock and despise their captured enemy.

Samson's downfall had been his self-confidence. He had largely gone his own way regardless of his parents' advice and by ignoring the laws of God. He had become dependent upon his physical strength and failed to trust in the Lord. Maybe with sadness these thoughts went through his mind as he heard the mocking laughter of his Philistine captors.

At the centre of his jeering enemies, in a temple made for idol worship, Samson lifted up his voice for one final prayer. God heard that prayer and answered it in a wonderful way. The answer was to give Samson strength for one last great act and, though he died, so did many of the Philistines; his death was both a triumph and a tragedy.

It was a **triumph** because at least in part his honour was restored. Many of those mocking enemies of God were killed as Samson pushed aside the retaining pillars and the temple collapsed. In death he killed many more Philistines than he had in a lifetime of battling with them. As a result the Philistines were a broken force and it would take many years for such veteran soldiers to be replaced. Thus, Samson's actions in death prevented the Philistines from making effective incursions towards Israel for many years.

It was a **tragedy** because he need never have come to the point of imprisonment and weakness. His life, which had such potential, was undermined by personal weakness and failure to trust the Lord. Yet Samson is still remembered as a great leader in Israel and, despite his failure, his faith is highlighted in the New Testament 'hall of fame', Heb. 11. 32. God's grace focuses upon our faith and not our failures.

ISRAEL DIVIDED

This was one of the saddest incidents in the history of Israel. There was warfare between the tribes as Benjamin faced the judgemental wrath of the rest of the nation. This was the result of a particularly sickening incident which had occurred to the concubine of a Levite while making an overnight stay in a town under Benjaminite jurisdiction. The woman had been so badly abused that she had died, and the nation of Israel sought to punish the guilty, for such a gross moral lapse defiled the whole nation.

Benjamin refused to release the wicked men for trial and this led to the Israelite army being mustered for war. On two occasions that army was defeated by the much smaller Benjaminite forces. Altogether Israel lost forty thousand men in battle, and this was despite seeking the Lord's face and weeping before the Lord. It would seem that the whole nation was being taught a lesson, and so each of the tribes lost men in the battles.

The third battle led to the defeat and virtual annihilation of the tribe of Benjamin, with over twenty-five thousand of their soldiers being killed. This victory for Israel had been the result of 'all the children of Israel, and all the people' going to the house of the God where they wept and fasted, offered sacrifices and enquired of the Lord about their next course of action. This time 'the Lord smote Benjamin before Israel', 20. 35. Israel had been defeated twice, but this third battle was certainly the Lord's and the sinful tribe was punished most severely. Ultimately it took a great deal of thought and effort and considerable time for Benjamin to recover its strength from that defeat and to again take its rightful place amongst the tribes of Israel.

It is certainly true that sin amongst the people of God must be dealt with. However, it is never with anything but sorrow that individuals are confronted or disciplined. It must never be done without deep prayer and a true seeking of the mind of the Lord. There should be tears in our eyes and sorrow in our hearts whenever it is undertaken. The aim must be the conquest of sin and restoration of the errant believer into the household of faith and fellowship.

February 29th

Judges 21. 2-3

SEEKING RECONCILIATION

The effect of Benjamin's punishment had left the rest of Israel with a problem. The problem was the need for Benjamin to recover its strength after so devastating a defeat, and to take its place again in the councils of the nation. With commendable devotion the people went to the house of the Lord and lifted up their voices in prayer and wept tears for the needs of Benjamin.

Their approach to God was not just a matter of minutes or of hours. Most of the day seemed to be spent seeking the Lord, while on the next day they continued by rising early and building an altar to the Lord.

There is much need today for a single-minded approach to seek the will of the Lord through prayer. We need to be burdened in prayer for the decisions we make, the people in need and the work of the gospel. It is too easy to 'shrug off' prayer and put it on the sidelines as we use our minds in planning, organizing and engaging in the normal affairs of life. In the busy life which so many live these days the communion of prayer and intercession too quickly can be lost. Yet it has always been true that genuine prayer moves the hand of God. This was certainly seen in the early church, which engaged in committed prayer before it moved out into effective evangelistic work where thousands were converted.

It is also true that to rise early to commune with the Lord means that we are truly serious about our relationship with God. This was the practice of the Lord Jesus while here on earth, Mark 1. 35, and early rising has been a proven aid to Christian godliness. The psalmist wrote, 'In the morning will I direct my prayer unto thee, and will look up', Ps. 5. 3. To lift up our hearts to God in prayer before the day begins, honours God and starts our day aright.

It is interesting that the people of Israel wept in the presence of God. Such emotion is decried in our day but the Bible has a lot to say on the subject of weeping. To weep reveals a heart which is deeply concerned, and to weep over the condition of the lost shows a real compassion for them.

The Lord eventually answered Israel's prayer and enabled them to bring about the restoration of the tribe of Benjamin.

1 Sam. 1. 9-19

SUCCESSFUL SECRET SUPPLICATION

For Hannah—her name means grace—it was a day of external anarchy, Judg. 21. 25, and internal anguish, 1 Sam. 1. 10. Her distress was not only that she was childless, but that, as the text says literally, 'she had no children', and every Jewish woman longed to have a son. She had long borne the insults of Peninnah, Elkanah's other wife, who had children, but she did enjoy the love of her husband. In other situations women have been childless: one resorted to human machinations (Sarai, Gen. 16. 1); another had been praying but had stopped, Luke 1. 7, and of another we have no record of any prayer at all, Judg. 13. 2. Hannah's answer to her problem was continual prayer. Now, after many years of casting her care upon the Lord, her prayer was about to be answered.

Her husband Elkanah was fulfilling his obligation by appearing *before the Lord*, Deut. 16. 16, and he worshipped *before the Lord*, v. 19. Now Hannah prayed *before the Lord*, v. 12, and poured out her soul *before the Lord*, v. 15; hence her spiritual exercise was as valid as her husband's, even though she did not perform it audibly in public. Her fruitless physical condition was a picture of Israel's spiritual state at the time, and the answer was the same in both cases—the birth of Samuel. Her promise was that the child 'may appear *before the Lord*, and abide there for ever', v. 22. In fact Samuel eventually ministered *before the Lord*, 2. 18; grew *before the Lord*, 2. 21; poured water *before the Lord*, 7. 6, and laid the book *before the Lord*, 10. 25. All this was due to Hannah's spiritual exercise *before the Lord*.

Can prayer change God's mind? It certainly changes our minds! How long had Hannah only been praying for a son until eventually she was prepared also to vow a vow that the child would be given to the Lord as a Nazarite from birth, v. 11 (cf. Judg. 13. 5)? God was waiting for this prayer: it had the High Priest's blessing, and was answered.

The Lord Jesus Christ told His disciples that there were occasions when they should 'pray to thy Father which is in secret; and thy Father which seeth in secret shall reward thee openly', Matt. 6. 6. God was waiting for Hannah's silent prayer (cf. Gen. 24. 45; Neh. 2. 4), then He would bring in His answer to her sadness and the nation's weakness.

March 2nd
1 Sam. 2. 1-10

GLORYING IN GOD

There are in the scriptures a number of songs of thanksgiving to God from women, beginning with Miriam, Exod. 15. 20, but Hannah's is the first extended one from a single source, following that of dual origin from Deborah and Barak, Judg. 5. 1. Elisabeth's, Luke. 1. 42; and Mary's, Luke. 1. 46, are two later examples. Hannah left behind her a great example of spiritual prayer and praise to all believing womanhood. In it she rose to spiritual heights hitherto unknown for a woman, and she touched on issues we would have thought of little interest to a woman from an obscure place in Ephraim. Her spiritual perception is even more remarkable when we think of the spiritual darkness around her. What an influence she must have been on little Samuel!

There is a remarkable parallel between Hannah's praise and that of Mary, the occasion of both being the birth of a remarkable son. Both rejoiced in God and acknowledged His salvation, 1 Sam. 2. 1; Luke. 1. 47. This is paralleled for the believer today in that 'we ... joy [rejoice, boast] in God through our Lord Jesus Christ', Rom. 5. 11 (cf. Ps. 33. 1; Ps. 97. 12; Isa. 41. 16; 61. 10; Joel 2. 23; Hab. 3. 18; Zech. 10. 7). There is no higher boast than God Himself, so that we 'rejoice in Christ Jesus, and have no confidence in the flesh', Phil. 3. 3. Hannah had come to an end of herself and was totally dependent on God. She, like Mary, came to acknowledge His beneficial sovereignty and goodness to the humble, but not to the proud and self-sufficient.

Obviously, the one who had set herself up as her enemy was proud and arrogant Peninnah, v. 3, but God knew and would take account. However, Hannah is able to rise above her own situation and see the over-riding purposes and ways of the God who 'maketh poor, and maketh rich: he bringeth low, and lifteth up', v. 7. He is able, according to His will, to so control circumstances that He can cause even the beggar to rise from his dunghill and to sit among princes on their thrones of glory, v. 8; cf. Jude 24.

Last, we see that Hannah had an expectation of a coming king. There was at that time no king in Israel, but she looked forward to God's anointed king, v. 10. We should do the same in our day!

March 3rd

1 Sam. 3. 1-10

THE FAITHFUL SERVANT'S PRAYER

The scriptures carefully chart Samuel's physical and spiritual progress, beginning with his brief home life under the strong influence of a godly mother, to being brought as a young child 'unto the house of the Lord in Shiloh', 1. 24. There he was able to 'minister unto the Lord', 2. 11, and he 'grew before the Lord', v. 21, and 'grew on, and was in favour both with the Lord, and also with men', v. 26. Today, it is a good thing to bring one's children to assembly meetings as soon as it is judged that they are old enough.

God and the people were pleased with the innocence of young Samuel. To both, he was a breath of fresh air at the spiritually polluted sanctuary where the sons of Eli were stealing the best parts of the sacrifice from the people, 2. 12-16. 'The sin of the young men was very great before the Lord: for men abhorred the offering of the Lord. But Samuel ministered before the Lord', 2. 17, 18.

An open vision was a rare thing in those days; God did not often speak directly, but now that He had found a clean heart, Ps. 73. 1, He was going to speak again. For whatever reason, the lamp was about to go out before the ark in the tabernacle, 1 Sam. 3. 3 (but see Exod. 27. 20; 30. 7), and all were asleep. This was a picture of Israel's spiritual state of neglect and apathy.

Samuel's inexperience meant that it was not until God's third, and this time double, call that he answered. However, he prayed, and no doubt meant, the words taught him by Eli—'Speak, for thy servant heareth', 3. 10 (although he apparently missed out the word 'Lord'). God answered Samuel's prayer, but the answer gave him difficulties, for God confirmed to Samuel His earlier words of judgement, cf. 2. 27-36 and 3. 11-14. Samuel had to learn the difficult task of passing on unpalatable divine messages, which he did, 'Samuel told him every whit', v. 18. This difficult act of obedience was blessed: 'Samuel grew ... the Lord was with him, and did let none of his words fall to the ground ... all Israel ... knew that Samuel was established ... a prophet of the Lord', vv. 19, 20. May we too be as faithful as Samuel in telling to others the divine message, whatever its content, and whatever the personal cost.

March 4th

1 Sam. 7. 8-13

INTERCESSOR'S PRAYER

When the spiritually weak Israelites went out against the Philistines without the counsel of Samuel, a national disaster threatened. Even taking the ark of the covenant did not help them, because their hearts were far from God, 1 Sam. 4. 1. The ark was captured, the priests killed and the people left in disarray. Of course this substantiated God's earlier warning through Samuel that Eli's renegade sons would be killed and the family line wiped out, 1 Sam. 3. 13.

Then Samuel spoke to all Israel and said, 'If ye do return unto the Lord with all your hearts, then put away the strange gods and Ashtaroth from among you, and prepare your hearts unto the Lord, and serve him only: and he will deliver you out of the hand of the Philistines', 7. 3. After they had carried out exactly Samuel's commands, he gathered them to Mizpeh, promising he would pray to the Lord for them, v. 5. It was a day of true national repentance, when the people admitted that they had 'sinned against the Lord', v. 6.

However, the Philistines heard of this national gathering and took the opportunity for a major attack. The fearful Israelites turned to Samuel, asking for his intercession; in fact they implored him not to be silent but to call out for God's help in deliverance [literal translation]. Making use of a burnt offering that reminded them of their relationship with God, Samuel 'cried unto the Lord for Israel; and the Lord heard [Heb. answered] him', v. 9. God showed His power to save without any human agency: He routed the Philistines in the sight of Israel, who only then attacked the fleeing army.

Praying effectively for others is a great privilege but a heavy responsibility. We ourselves have to be in a fit spiritual state, as was Samuel, and we have to be prepared to pray fervently; for 'the effectual fervent prayer of a righteous man availeth much', Jas, 5. 16. Samuel continued his intercessory ministry, 1 Sam. 12. 19, 23, and he was later followed by the apostle Paul, as noted in nearly all his epistles, e.g. Rom. 1. 9; Col. 1. 3; 2 Thess. 1. 11. Paul just as frequently asked for the intercessory prayers of others, as when he wrote to the Thessalonians, 'Brethren, pray for us', 1 Thess. 5. 25 (see also 2 Thess. 3. 1; Col. 4. 3; cf. Heb. 13. 18).

March 5th

1 Sam. 8. 1-6

CONCERNED PRAYER

When Samuel was old he made his sons judges, but they were unspiritual men who took bribes and perverted the course of justice. This eventually resulted in national dissatisfaction and all the elders of Israel met together and came to Samuel to tell him the truth. This must have upset him, but what grieved him more was their suggested solution, 'make us a king to judge us like all the nations', v. 5.

God's way of national administration was then through judges circulating around the country, and even if these judges were unsatisfactory, it did not mean the system was wrong. The people's human solution was merely to copy other nations and lose their distinctively divine rule. Of course, in His own time God would bring in His king, but for the moment he explained to Samuel in answer to his prayer that 'they have not rejected thee, but they have rejected me, that I should not reign over them', v. 7. They had, as a nation, since God had brought them out of Egypt, consistently rejected Him. This was yet another manifestation of the same attitude, but now with Samuel as the target. Just as they had turned to the gods of the nations, rejecting their own God, so too had they now turned from the divine form of government as represented by Samuel.

God then tells Samuel to explain to them the painful consequences of their request. It would cost them dearly, in heavy taxes in money and in kind, and they would eventually rue the day they ever asked, but then it would be too late, v. 18. However, in spite of this dire warning; they refused Samuel's words and still insisted on having a king, adding that not only would the king judge them but also 'go out before us, and fight our battles', v. 20. What an insult to the God of Ebenezer!

Once again Samuel 'took it to the Lord in prayer', and now God tells him to 'hearken unto their voice, and make them a king', v. 22. In the end God grants them their wish, leaving them to discover eventually the folly of their ways. Then in His own time He would bring in His own king. Sometimes God allows even Christians to bring in unscriptural forms of government among His people, according to their desire, but this provides no proper solution to present problems.

March 6th

1 Sam. 12. 6-7, 13-19

THE POWER OF ANSWERED PRAYER

Having seen Saul formally installed as king, Samuel commanded the people to 'stand still, that I may reason with you before the Lord of all the righteous acts of the Lord, which he did to you and to your fathers', 12. 7. He then reminded them of Israel's sad spiritual history, starting from Egypt and ending with 'the king whom ye have chosen, and whom ye have desired', v. 13. Then he told them, 'If ye will fear the Lord, and serve him, and obey his voice, and not rebel against the commandment of the Lord, then shall both ye and also the king that reigneth over you continue following the Lord your God: But if ye will not obey the voice of the Lord, but rebel against the commandment of the Lord, then shall the hand of the Lord be against you, as it was against your fathers'. In order to substantiate what he said about the Lord's power, he told them to 'stand and see this great thing, which the Lord will do before your eyes', v. 16. Human activity has to cease so that divine words, works and wonders can be seen to their full extent; see other commands to 'stand still' to see the Lord working mightily, Exod. 14. 13; Job 37. 14; 2 Chr. 20. 17.

Samuel then told the people, 'Is it not wheat harvest to day? I will call unto the Lord, and he shall send thunder and rain; that ye may perceive and see that your wickedness is great, which ye have done in the sight of the Lord, in asking you a king. So Samuel called unto the Lord; and the Lord sent thunder and rain that day: and all the people greatly feared the Lord and Samuel', 1 Sam. 12. 17, 18.

Samuel had, in faith, fully committed God beforehand by stating precisely what He would do, in an act that, beyond any shadow of a doubt, would be a matter of divine intervention. Such a seemingly impossible event would later produce the proverb 'as rain in harvest, so honour is not seemly for a fool', Prov. 26. 1. Then 'the Lord sent thunder and rain that day', 12. 18, just as in Moses' day 'the Lord sent thunder and hail ... and the Lord rained hail upon the land of Egypt', Exod. 9. 23. The God of yesterday is always proved to be the God of today by the answer to believing prayer!

March 7th

1 Sam. 12. 19-25

THE INTERCESSOR'S PROMISE

Seeing the miracle of the thunder and rain, the people of Israel realized the power of God and the great danger they were in because of their sin, especially now that they had asked for a king, 1 Sam. 12. 19. They implored Samuel to intercede because they feared for their lives. 'Samuel said unto the people, Fear not: ye have done all this wickedness: yet turn not aside from following the Lord, but serve the Lord with all your heart', v. 20: nothing short of true repentance was called for. Then Samuel explained to them that the reason why the Lord was prepared, so far, to bear with them and not forsake them was 'for his great name's sake: because it hath pleased the Lord to make you his people', v. 22.

Although Samuel considered it a sin against the Lord in ceasing to pray for them, he tells them that the onus thereafter was on them to fear and obey the Lord, otherwise they would perish as a nation in the land.

Promises of, and requests for, prayer abound in the Scriptures when people had sinned or where there was weakness, failure or need. In the Old Testament, among those praying, or being asked to pray, for others were Abraham who prayed for Abimelech, Gen. 20. 7; Moses for Israel, Num. 21. 7; Moses for Aaron, Deut. 9. 20; Samuel for the people, 1 Sam. 7. 5; a man of God for Jeroboam, 1 Kgs. 13. 6; Isaiah for the remnant, 2 Kgs. 19. 4; Isa. 37. 4; the remnant for Cyrus, Ezra 6. 10; Job for his friends, Job 42. 8, 10; Jeremiah for Israel, Jer. 42. 2, 20; and Hezekiah for Israel, 2 Chr. 30. 18 ('The good Lord pardon every one').

We too have a ministry of prayer for others, first for unbelievers who cannot, and usually will not, pray for themselves: we pray for their salvation, especially those whom the Lord places on our hearts. Then we should be 'praying always with all prayer ... with all perseverance and supplication for all saints', Eph. 6. 18, and especially those serving the Lord, see v. 19; 2 Cor. 1. 11; Col. 4. 3; 1 Thess. 5. 25; 2 Thess. 3. 1. We have a suitable example in the apostle Paul who was always praying for such, Rom. 1. 9; Phil. 1. 4; Col. 1. 3; 1 Thess. 1. 2; 2 Thess. 1. 11; Philem. 4.

1 Sam. 14. 35-37

UNANSWERED PRAYER

Given the right circumstances, the Lord answered the prayers of national leaders who enquired about particular military matters, e.g., Judg. 1. 1; 20. 18, 28; 1 Sam. 30. 8; 2 Sam. 5. 19, 23. However, when the circumstances were wrong, He would not answer, e.g., 1 Sam. 28. 6; Ezek. 20. 3, and this incident concerning Saul was one such occasion.

Because of the singular bravery of Jonathan, the Israelites found themselves pursuing the Philistines, but they were in great difficulty because Saul had forbidden them to eat that day. Unfortunately, Jonathan had not heard his father's command, and inadvertently ate some wild honey. Worse was to follow, for eventually the pursuing Israelites were so hungry that, after over-whelming the fleeing Philistines, they took the spoil—sheep, oxen and calves—and ate them quickly without first bleeding them, which was a sin against the law, Lev. 3. 17; 7. 26, 27; 17. 10-14; 19. 26.

When Saul thereafter asked aloud if they should pursue the Philistines in order to complete the victory, the priest with him (Ahiah?, 1 Sam. 14. 3) suggested that they should first pray about the matter, possibly hoping to transmit the answer to Saul via the Urim, Num. 27. 21. When Saul then got no answer to his prayer, and he realized that something was wrong, he determined to find out who was responsible for the problem, saying that once found, they should die. Eventually Jonathan was selected by lot, as indeed he was the first to eat that day. Saul then, in order to vindicate his decision, was going to kill his own son, who of course had actually been responsible for the initial victory, but who had innocently broken his father's arbitrary and needless command. However the people told Saul 'as the Lord liveth, there shall not one hair of his head fall to the ground; for he hath wrought with God this day. So the people rescued Jonathan, that he died not', v. 45.

Saul's apparent religious zeal in first forbidding the people to eat had now caused them to sin, and then later, in suggesting that his own son should die, he had compounded his folly. God would have nothing to do with his prayer which was only prayed as an afterthought at the prompting of another. Prayer must be spontaneous and sincere if we want an answer.

March 9th

1 Sam. 15. 10-26

CONTINUED PRAYER OF A GRIEVED HEART

Samuel was grieved (literally angry) with Saul, of whom the Lord had said, 'he is turned back from following me, and hath not performed my commandments', 1 Sam. 15. 11. Samuel had passed on the Lord's message that, because of the Amalekites' history, Exod. 17. 8, Saul and the Israelites were to 'go and smite Amalek, and utterly destroy all that they have, and spare them not', 1 Sam. 15. 3; cf. Deut. 25. 17-19. However, after a swift and successful battle, Saul and the people of Israel spared Agag the king of the Amalekites, and 'the best of the sheep, and of the oxen, and of the fatlings, and the lambs, and all that was good, and would not utterly destroy them: but every thing that was vile and refuse, that they destroyed utterly', v. 9.

When Samuel confronts Saul, he at first claims to have obeyed the Lord. However, his obvious lies were eventually exposed and Samuel tells him, 'Wherefore then didst thou not obey the voice of the Lord, but didst fly upon the spoil, and didst evil in the sight of the Lord?', v. 19. Saul then says that 'the people took of the spoil, sheep and oxen, the chief of the things which should have been utterly destroyed, to sacrifice unto the Lord thy God in Gilgal', v. 21. Samuel replies, 'Behold, to obey is better than sacrifice, and to hearken than the fat of rams ... Because thou hast rejected the word of the Lord, he hath also rejected thee from being king', vv. 22-23. At this, Saul fully admits his sin, and acknowledges that he had 'transgressed the commandment of the Lord ... because I feared the people, and obeyed their voice', v. 24. Samuel tells him the sad truth that the 'Lord hath rejected thee from being king over Israel', v. 26, and that He had now given the kingdom to someone else, who was better than him, and that the Lord would not change His mind.

Samuel had realized the consequences of the Lord's decision, and had struggled with it all night, crying to the Lord. Later the Lord Jesus 'continued all night in prayer to God', Luke 6. 12, no doubt also praying for others. A night's sleep is often the price one has to pay for showing a real interest in the spiritual state of others.

March 10th

1 Sam. 16. 1-12

QUESTIONS

Although Samuel had passed on the Lord's message that Saul was rejected and that He had already chosen a new king—a neighbour of Saul's but not a relative—Samuel still mourned for Saul, even though he would never see him alive again, 1 Sam. 15. 35. No doubt his thoughts were akin to those of Abraham who had said, 'O that Ishmael might live before thee', Gen. 17. 18. However, now was the time for the Lord's will to be put into action, and Samuel had to facilitate it. The Lord said to him, 'I will send thee to Jesse the Beth-lehemite: for I have provided me a king among his sons', v. 1. Although he mourned for Saul, Samuel knew him so well that he was afraid that he would kill him if he found out what he was about to do, and so immediately he asked the Lord, 'How can I go?'. The Lord provided Samuel with a way of visiting Jesse without arousing Saul's suspicion.

Previously Samuel had found Saul 'a choice young man, and a goodly … from his shoulders and upward he was higher than any of the people', 9. 2, and had said to the people, 'See ye him whom the Lord hath chosen, that there is none like him among all the people?', 10. 24. Now the Lord said about Eliab, candidate for kingship, 'Look not on his countenance, or on the height of his stature; because I have refused him: for the Lord seeth not as man seeth; for man looketh on the outward appearance, but the Lord looketh on the heart', 16. 7 (cf. 2 Sam. 14. 25; 1 Pet. 3. 4; John 7. 24; 2 Cor. 10. 7). In fact when he found David, 'he was ruddy, and withal of a beautiful countenance, and goodly to look to … the Lord said, Arise, anoint him: for this is he', 16. 12. So 'Samuel took the horn of oil, and anointed him in the midst of his brethren: and the Spirit of the Lord came upon David from that day forward, v. 13; contrast v. 14.

For Samuel, doing God's will was difficult because of his sentimental attachment to Saul; and dangerous because of Saul's fierce temper; but in spite of his initial questioning, with divine help, he eventually did His will.

1 Sam. 23. 1-12

CONTINUED PRAYER

As soon as David heard that the Philistine armies were raiding Keilah, he prayed about it, and the Lord immediately answered him (cf. Saul's similar, but half-hearted prayer, 1 Sam. 14. 37), telling him that he should go and save the town. Unfortunately, David's men—who only numbered about 600 at that time—then told him quite honestly that they were 'afraid here in Judah: how much more then if we come to Keilah against the armies of the Philistines?', 1 Sam. 23. 3. Faced with this new difficulty, David prayed yet again, and again the Lord told him to go to Keilah, but this time He added the promise—'I will deliver the Philistines into thine hand', v. 4. David's men believed the Lord, overcame their fear and 'went to Keilah, and fought with the Philistines, and brought away their cattle, and smote them with a great slaughter', v. 5.

Abiathar the priest heard that David was in Keilah and he joined him, bringing the ephod. However, Saul had also heard that David was there, and he began to plan a siege of the walled town. But while Saul was preparing for the campaign, David found out 'that Saul secretly practised mischief against him', v. 9.

The ephod that Abiathar had brought would have been that part of the ceremonial vesture of the high priest (Exod. 28 and 39), which, with its attached Urim and Thummim, could be used to ask the Lord questions, cf. Num. 27. 21, but see 1 Sam. 28. 6. Ephods were normally kept in the tabernacle, 1 Sam. 21. 9, but as Abiathar had brought one to Keilah, David gladly made use of it (cf. 1 Sam. 30. 7), asking the Lord if the people of Keilah would give him up to Saul. The Lord answered that they would, so David was able to escape.

Today, we Christians do not depend on such devices as ephods, or Urim and Thummim, but there are at least three things needed to guarantee our prayers being answered. First, faith—'whatsoever ye shall ask in prayer, believing, ye shall receive', Matt. 21. 22. Second, the name of the Lord Jesus—'whatsoever ye shall ask in my name, that will I do, that the Father may be glorified in the Son', John 14. 13. Third, obedience to Him—'whatsoever we ask, we receive of him, because we keep his commandments, and do those things that are pleasing in his sight', 1 John 3. 22. Because our needs are continuous, we must needs continue in prayer!

NO ANSWER

Soon after Samuel died, Saul had to face his next predicament—
a massive Philistine invasion. He lined his troops against them
at Gilboa, but 'when [he] ... saw the host of the Philistines, he
was afraid, and his heart greatly trembled', 1 Sam. 28. 4 (cf. Isaac,
Gen. 27. 37). He desperately prayed about the situation, but the
Lord did not answer, even when he used every device he could
think of—Urim, dreams and prophets, 1 Sam. 28. 6.

Saul had been afraid before, when the Philistine champion
Goliath had taunted Israel, 1 Sam. 17. 11, but then the Lord sent a
saviour in David. Now He had forsaken Saul and no saviour
would appear. Such was his desperation that trying to get in
touch with Samuel, he eventually stooped to the depth of consulting a spiritualist medium ('a woman that hath a familiar
spirit', 1 Sam. 28. 7), even though he had previously banned such
people from the land, v. 3. Much to the consternation of the medium, Samuel did appear, and immediately announced Saul's
doom. Tomorrow, said Samuel, both Saul and his three sons
would join him in death.

When Saul had originally prayed, his situation was precisely
that described later in the Book of Proverbs, 'ye have set at
nought all my counsel, and would none of my reproof: I also will
laugh at your calamity; I will mock when your fear cometh;
when your fear cometh as desolation, and your destruction
cometh as a whirlwind; when distress and anguish cometh upon
you. Then shall they call upon me, but I will not answer; they
shall seek me early [i.e. earnestly, *Young's literal translation*], but
they shall not find me', 1. 24–28.

The Lord will never forsake us today, Heb. 13, 5, but to have
our prayers answered, there are conditions that He expects us to
fulfil. Hence in prayer we should be characterized by: **persistence**, 1 Thess. 5. 17; **faith**, Jas. 5. 15; **knowledge**, 1 Cor. 14. 15;
acceptance, Matt. 6. 10; **holy living**, Jas. 5. 16, and **reverence**,
Matt. 6. 9. Then we must never forget what the Lord said, 'If my
people ... shall humble themselves, and pray, and seek my face,
and turn from their wicked ways; then will I hear from heaven
... mine eyes shall be open, and mine ears attent unto ... prayer',
2 Chron. 7. 14, 15; cf. Isa. 65. 12.

March 13th

1 Sam. 30. 1-8

A DETAILED ANSWER

Achish, the Philistine king of Gath, had given David the city of Ziklag for the one year and four months that he lived in exile, 1 Sam. 27. 5-7. He and his men were returning there one day after a long journey and found that the Amalekites had invaded the district, burned their city and taken the inhabitants captive, including their families. They were distraught and cried 'until they had no more power to weep', 1 Sam. 30. 4. David's great distress for his two wives who had been taken captive (Ahinoam the Jezreelitess, and Abigail the wife of Nabal the Carmelite) was compounded by the talk amongst his men that he was personally to blame and they would stone him.

When all things seemed against him, 'David strengthened himself in the Lord his God', v. 6 RV; see 2 Tim. 4. 17; Heb. 13. 6 and cf. Psa. 52. 7. This strengthening naturally resulted in prayer and, making use of the ephod, David asked the Lord if he and his men should pursue the enemy and if they could then overtake them. The answer was very positive and specific, 'Pursue: for thou shalt surely overtake them, and without fail recover all', v. 8.

David and his six hundred men left immediately, but soon two hundred 'were so faint that they could not go over the brook Besor', v. 10. As the rest went on they came across a sick young Egyptian who was a slave of one of the Amalekites. He had not eaten for three days, but they soon revived him with food and drink. From him they found the details of the invasion and he was able to lead them to the enemy. They found them off-guard, celebrating their great victories and spoil. David and his army fought them 'from the twilight even unto the evening of the next day: and there escaped not a man of them, save four hundred young men, which rode upon camels, and fled', v. 17. The Lord had said that without fail David would recover all, and indeed he did, for the story ends, 'there was nothing lacking to them, neither small nor great', vv. 18–20. The Lord had answered exactly as He had promised. God hears and answers prayer!

March 14th

2 Sam. 2. 1-4

PRAYER FOR DIRECTION

David had eventually heard about the tragic death of Saul and his sons. He deeply lamented Saul's passing and that of Jonathan, 2 Sam. 1. 11–16, but now the question arose as to what he should do next. One possibility was to go straight home to Judah, and claim the crown—but how would he be received after living among the Philistines? Was it safe to go? If not, would it now be safe to stay? If he went, which city should he go to? The only thing to do was to pray about these matters.

David's prayer is very definite and to the point—'Shall I go up into any of the cities of Judah? ... whither shall I go up?'. The Lord's answers were equally as precise—'Go up ... unto Hebron', 2 Sam. 2. 1. So David, his men and their families went to Hebron, one of his old haunts, and settled there. It was not long before the people of Judah came and anointed David king over the house of Judah, v. 4. His first act as king was to honour the men of Jabesh-gilead who had removed the dead bodies of Saul and his sons from public display on the walls of Bethshan and given them a proper burial. David is fulsome in his praise; 'Blessed be ye of the Lord, that ye have shewed this kindness unto your lord, even unto Saul, and have buried him. And now the Lord shew kindness and truth unto you: and I also will requite you this kindness, because ye have done this thing. Therefore now let your hands be strengthened, and be ye valiant: for your master Saul is dead, and also the house of Judah have anointed me king over them', vv. 5-7.

A true person of prayer cannot be vindictive. Saul had been the Lord's anointed, even though he had relentlessly persecuted David. David never gloated over his death, or even his humiliation in death, and was now happy that he had been given a decent burial. But now one of the dangers that David might have anticipated was opposition from the followers of Saul. In fact they made Saul's surviving son, the forty-year-old Ishbosheth, king of Israel, v. 9. For six and a half years David was king of only Judah, during which time there was constant warfare between them, but 'David waxed stronger and stronger, and the house of Saul waxed weaker and weaker', 3. 1.

David asked the Lord about every important decision in his life. Do we bring our decisions before the throne of grace?

March 15th
2 Sam. 5. 18-25

REQUEST FOR BATTLE PLANS

On many occasions when David asked God specific questions, he got an immediate answer, see 1 Sam. 23. 2; 1 Sam. 30. 8; 2 Sam. 2. 1; 1 Chr. 14. 10; and now 2 Sam. 5. 19. The circumstances this time were as follows. All the tribes of Israel had come together to acknowledge David's God-given right to the throne of the whole country; 'the Lord said to thee, Thou shalt feed my people Israel, and thou shalt be a captain over Israel', v. 2. They solemnly accepted him and anointed him as king over all Israel, v. 3. His first action was to capture the hitherto unconquered city of Jerusalem and make it the new capital city. God blessed him, and 'David went on, and grew great, and the Lord God of hosts was with him', v. 10, and 'David perceived that the Lord had established him king over Israel, and that he had exalted his kingdom for his people Israel's sake', v. 12.

David won the acclaim of some neighbouring countries (e.g. Hiram king of Tyre, 2 Sam. 5. 11) but he was perceived as a serious threat by others, e.g. the Philistines, his erstwhile protectors. They invaded the country and camped in the valley of Rephaim, v. 18. Naturally, David 'enquired of the Lord, saying, Shall I go up to the Philistines? wilt thou deliver them into mine hand?', v. 19. The answer was very positive, 'Go up: for I will doubtless deliver the Philistines into thine hand', v. 20. There was no doubt about God's promise—this reminds us that 'all the promises of God in him are yea, and in him Amen, unto the glory of God', 2 Cor. 1. 20.

At first, when David attacked the Philistines, he had a great victory. However, the Philistines regrouped in the valley of Rephaim, so David enquired of the Lord again, this time about specific military tactics. The Lord replied 'let it be, when thou hearest the sound of a going in the tops of the mulberry trees, that then thou shalt bestir thyself: for then shall the Lord go out before thee, to smite the host of the Philistines ... David did so, as the Lord had commanded him; and smote the Philistines from Geba ... to Gazer', vv. 24-25. David really could trust and obey!

March 16th

2 Sam. 7. 18-29

WHO AM I, O LORD GOD?

The background to these words is most interesting. David was resting in his kingship, content that God had given him rest from all surrounding enemies. However, he was disturbed that he dwelt in a cedar house while the ark of the Lord rested in a tent. Nathan told him to do all that was in his heart, vv. 1-3, but God had other plans. In verses 4-17 the prophet gave a wonderful message to the king. David would not build the house, but later his offspring would erect a house for God's name, and his throne would be established with the kingdom for ever. This vision was explained to the king; it was tremendous and inspiring.

David's response was immediate. 'Who am I, O Lord God, and what is my father's house that thou hast brought me hitherto?' His unworthiness was deeply felt. God had spoken of blessings to come, and an overwhelming sense of God's kindness brought him very low. How often does God make us feel this way? True prayer will always remind us that God owes us nothing. Every favour, every grace given is unmerited. 'Who am I?' We come empty handed into the presence of our God.

'Wherefore, thou art great, O Lord God, for there is none like thee', v. 22. The thoughts of David move from his nothingness to the magnificence of God. History and experience had revealed his ability and power to do great things. This God had made the nation His own people. Such sense of greatness overwhelmed David. Surely he is **nothing** and God is **all**. He is **empty** but there is **fulness** with God. Thus, each time we spend in quiet prayer, we do well to meditate on God's complete sufficiency. We are blessed with every spiritual blessing in the heavenlies in Christ, Eph. 1. 3. Out of His riches in glory, God can supply all our needs, Phil. 4. 19.

'Therefore, now let it please thee to bless', v. 29. Each day we need to seek fresh blessings from our bountiful God. We dare not try to live on yesterday's blessing. David felt that God had given far beyond his expectations. Yet His promises made him hungry for more: 'Do as thou hast said', v. 25. David was bold in his asking. Be sure today to claim God's promises! Faith can prove that what He has promised He is able to perform, Rom. 4. 19-21.

Thought:- It is only an empty vessel that can be filled!

March 17th

2 Sam. 12. 13-18

DAVID BESOUGHT THE LORD FOR THE CHILD

The aspect of prayer we look at today is set against the background of David's most tragic sin. David's confession reveals his contrition, 'I have sinned against the Lord'. Psalm 51 shows his deep sense of shame. The Lord assures him that the child will die. Such was the tragedy of sin in the life of a king. But the Lord through Nathan assures him of forgiveness, 'The Lord also hath put away thy sin; thou shalt not die'. But even when God forgives, we know that sin will often take its natural course. Yet God is merciful.

David does not give up fasting and praying. He is brought very low, but does not give up hope. Then the child died. The servants hesitated to tell him, for David's reactions seemed to contradict reason. He immediately takes control and ate and began to hold the reins again. It was a strange way to take reverses for he washes, anoints himself and goes in to worship his God.

There are some helpful thoughts for us today. Prayer must be hindered where there is no **repentance** for sin. Every Christian knows what failure means. Unconfessed sin will spoil communion with God. Yet confession of sin brings forgiveness and cleansing, 1 John 1. 9. In the seeming contradictions of David's behaviour we see that in prayer he clung to the hope of God's mercy, 'Who can tell if the Lord will be gracious to me?'. To the person who prays there must always be this hope, that God's mercy is greater than all our sin. **Refusal** proved the governmental dealings of God with His servant. He does not act in grace at the expense of His righteousness. This tells us how necessary it is for us to 'walk in the light, as he is in the light', 1 John 1. 7.

There is a happy sequel to the incident. David comforted Bathsheba after the baby's death. The Lord gave him another son in whom His promises were fulfilled. Solomon was born and the Lord loved him. What a lovely touch to the story. David knew **restoration** after his fall, and **joy** followed. God makes every provision that we do not sin. But 'if any man sin, we have an advocate with the Father, Jesus Christ the righteous', 1 John 2. 1-2.

Thought:- 'God who is rich in mercy'.

March 18th

2 Sam. 21. 1-14

AND DAVID ENQUIRED OF THE LORD

David was perplexed! For three years there had been barrenness in the land. To David there seemed to be no rational explanation. But he knew where to go in his perplexity. 'David enquired of the Lord.' Why had he waited so long? We would have thought that the Lord would have been his first resource. Even so, better he acted now than too late! It was not long before the cause of the trouble was revealed and the requirements necessary to remedy the situation were taken. The blight was removed and the harvest restored. The cause of the famine was the withdrawal of God's favour, resulting from Saul's wrong treatment of the Gibeonites, long before. David did not hesitate to put matters right.

There is a useful lesson in this for us today. When we are baffled about our circumstances, prayer is a vital means of seeking God's guidance. Do you ever find the word 'problem' in the Bible? Yet references to prayer are numerous. Wrongs had to be righted, but it was no good enquiring of the Lord if the king had not been willing to obey. Yet the word is precious, 'Cast thy burden upon the Lord, and he shall sustain thee', Psalm 55. 22. How many times have such words been our comfort!, cf. Ps. 37. 5. The pathway to be taken was severe, even brutal. Innocent lives had to go. This was costly obedience, yet the pathway of obedience is always costly, and never easy. But such a way is the only way to blessing.

We are confronted with the fact that David needed a wisdom greater than his own. Events were not of his ordering but he realized action was necessary. As the king saw the sorrow of Rizpah, he acted in righteousness to the memory of Saul and Jonathan by gathering their bones and burying them in home territory. God responded by opening heaven's blessing. Do we need wisdom today to act rightly? James 1. 5-7 is so relevant. God gives liberally with no withholding. We may pause to ask ourselves if our 'enquiring' of the Lord, our seeking for His help, comes first in our reckoning. Or is it our last resource? 'David enquired of the Lord'—a wise course. **The Lord was waiting to bless**. Stores of grace are there for our asking.

Thought:- Turn your **problems** into **prayers**; **burdens** can be turned into **blessings**.

March 19th

2 Sam. 22. 1, 29-37

THIS SONG IN THE DAY THAT THE LORD DELIVERED

Prayer and praise go together. They must be inseparable. David had known many troubles in his life. Saul was his bitter enemy as he hounded him from place to place with intent to kill him. The Philistines and other nations had constantly fought against Israel. From his own family he had faced many problems, especially during the Absalom rebellion. But now the Lord had delivered him from **all** his enemies; no wonder he could sing praises to the Lord. He was a man delivered. Yet, when we look at these verses for today, there must have been times when the subjects of his praises were matters for his prayers. He sings, 'thou art my lamp, O Lord: and the Lord will lighten my darkness', v. 29. It was out of dark circumstances that David often prayed for light—the darkness of sorrow, persecution and a sense of abandonment. His cry went up, but now his song ascends; the Lord was his lamp.

Often he had experienced weakness, unable to cope with the pressures of his enemies—at the end of his tether. His words tell of many such times when he cried for strength. 'God is my strength and power', he says. He proved that, so often, God's strength is made perfect in weakness, 2 Cor. 12. 9-10.

There were times when David lost his way. He was bewildered and baffled, asking the Lord to teach him the way to go. Only with the Lord could his feet tread surely and safely. So now he could sing, 'As for God, his way is perfect ... he maketh my way perfect'. Here is a song that celebrates God's guidance.

There were many times when David was under siege, surrounded by his enemies. He was like an animal caught in a trap, not knowing where to turn. He was often in hiding from Saul and his army, waiting for capture. But now he sings, 'Thou hast enlarged my steps ... so that my feet did not slip'. He felt a sense of freedom; he could expand into liberty; he was in a large place. He could sing the song of a soul set free. This can be our song indeed, as we stand fast in the liberty with which Christ has set us free, Gal. 5. 1; John 8. 36. Thus we return to give God thanks.

Thought:- **Praying lives** will always lead to **praising lips**.

March 20th

2 Sam. 24. 10-17

I HAVE DONE VERY FOOLISHLY

David had sinned again in human weakness. Yet how faithful is the record that Scripture gives of human experience so we can identify with the lives recorded and with their God.

David suffered from the sin of **pride**; 'that I may know the number of the people', v. 2. Greatness that gloats in its achievements is displeasing to God. Joab recognized this and for once gave useful advice to the king. He was a good counsellor, but his counsel went unheeded and the deed was done. The extent of the kingdom was far-reaching. Joab's words are interesting; 'Now the Lord thy God add unto the people, how many soever they be', v. 3. It was God's business. Pride was out of place.

'David's heart smote him.' Tender of conscience, he did not need Nathan to tell him it was wrong. When he lusted after Bathsheba and fell, he needed his eyes to be opened to his wrong. But now he readily recognizes his sin, and confesses it. 'I have done very foolishly', he says. The accusing voice of conscience spoke. Perhaps this was a sign of his spiritual maturity; he had become more sensitive to sin. In the life of prayer and communion with God, there has to be a growing sensitivity to sin.

David truly humbled himself. His request for the measure of retribution that cast him wholly upon God proved this. 'The prayer of the humble is his delight.' Humble confession of sin, the contrite heart of repentance, will never go unheeded. The whole nation paid the price for his sin; this could not be avoided. But repentance brought forgiveness. In building our life of prayer, we have to learn that God hates pride and self-assertion. This was the primitive sin of the devil. 'Humble yourselves therefore under the mighty hand of God, that he may exalt you in due time', 1 Pet. 5. 6.

Sacrifice was the only basis for restitution. David would not make his approach to God by an easy way. For him, the costly basis of the offering was the only way. In our life of prayer today, surely we need to be at the cross. It was there sins were atoned for, and pardon found. In that one sacrifice all has been paid. Forgiveness and peace are there.

Thought:- For our **foolishness**, the **cross** is God's **wisdom**.

March 21st

1 Kings 3. 5-14

GIVE TO THY SERVANT AN UNDERSTANDING HEART

The passage for today is full of beauty. Solomon's dream brought him into touch with God. 'Ask what I shall give thee.' The Lord threw open wide His treasures, and put them at the disposal of the young king. What abundance is there! In his inexperience he could have made so many extravagant requests.

The request that he made revealed the attitude of his heart, 'I am but a little child; I know not how to go out or come in,' v. 7. Here is true lowliness of heart and mind. He faced a huge task for he was among a truly great people. Solomon realized that human ability was just not enough. Israel came to the zenith of its power and glory as a nation at this time. All the surrounding countries came to see and hear the wisdom and works of this great monarch. Yet 'before honour is humility'.

As Solomon prayed, we can see he appreciated four things. He appreciated *the kindness and goodness of God*, v. 6. Prayer is poor indeed if it has not within it a context of gratitude and thanksgiving. Solomon appreciated that without such mercy no throne would be his. We should pray with this constantly in mind, for where would we be without such mercy?

He also appreciated *his complete inadequacy* to rule in his own strength. Thus when given amazing scope for asking blessing, he asked for the most important. He spoke out of a humble heart. What are our priorities when we come seeking God's face? Notice what James says about right asking, James 4. 1-3. So often God has to bring us to an end of ourselves before we pray aright.

Then Solomon appreciated *the vastness of the task* with which he was faced. Israel were a great people who could not be numbered. They were God's people and the task was stupendous. In his prayer he faced reality. Let us be aware today, that if our lives are committed to true prayer, we shall be 'in tune' with the God who said that nothing is too hard for Him.

Finally, he appreciated that *only God-given wisdom* would be enough. And God gave him wealth, power and glory as well.

Thought:- God so often gives **more than we ask**.

March 22nd

1 Kings 8. 22-30

HAVE THOU RESPECT UNTO THE PRAYER OF THY SERVANT

Solomon's prayer at the dedication of the temple is one of the most beautiful recorded for us in Scripture. As with his prayer for wisdom, there is an overall atmosphere of humility and submission. He stands before the *altar*, the place of *sacrifice*. As we pray today, we remember that our entrance into the presence of the Lord is on the ground of Christ's one sacrifice, Heb. 10. 12-14. *Where* Solomon stood was interesting.

We notice his *approach*. He begins by affirming his appreciation of God's majesty and greatness, vv. 23, 27. There was a sense of awe and godly fear. There was no casual familiarity in his approach, and yet he could come with confidence in God's mercy and faithfulness. Here was a covenant-keeping God, v. 3. Solomon laid hold of the steadfast love of this faithful God—his very position on the throne he owed to God's fulfilled promises.

Pause as you pray today. How great does God seem to you? All notable servants of God through the ages have known this awe-inspiring sense of God's majesty. Beware of irreverence! As he prayed, Solomon's *appreciation* of the issues at stake are clear. All his achievements he reckoned small, even the greatness and magnificence of the temple he had built. No earthly dwelling could contain the God of earth and heaven. Also he realized that the building would be but a hollow shell without the presence of God. Long years before, God had promised to dwell among His people. No magnificence of man's creation could replace the magnificence of this promise. Let us remember today that we approach our God having nothing of ourselves, and that the experience of God's presence is indispensable to blessing.

Think carefully on this **appeal** of Solomon, 'Have thou respect unto the prayer of thy servant, and to his supplication', v. 28. Here was a great earthly king, appealing to the King of the universe. He knew he had the right to claim God's promise, but in humility he would request. This is indeed the true spirit of prayer. Note his sense of unworthiness, 'When thou hearest, forgive,' vv. 28-30. 'I have heard', says God.

Thought:- Humble requests are never wasted.

March 23rd

1 Kings 9. 1-9

I HAVE HEARD THY PRAYER AND SUPPLICATION

We often are heard to say, 'Our God hears and answers prayer'. This is a comforting thought, and one we, no doubt, have proved true. Sometimes the heavens are as brass, and God seems a long way off. Our study today speaks of God's willingness to hear the king's prayer. This prayer, at the dedication of the temple, is well worth a detailed study. It reveals a king who was a true Israelite, and one who was committed to the worship of God. He reverenced the greatness of God, and remembered His mercies.

Solomon desired that the **presence** of the Lord should sanctify the house of the Lord. The work was finished and done well. Wondering that God in His greatness could indeed dwell with men, he asked that the Lord should look favourably on the house, 8. 27-28. Thus God, in answering his prayer, gave assurance that His presence should be there. Pausing to think of our lives today, how much we need God's presence with us. It is marvellous that He will answer this prayer. As He did to Moses, He says to us, 'My presence shall go with thee, and I will give thee rest', Exod. 33. 14.

Solomon was also claiming the **promises** of God in his prayer, 8. 20. The Lord had promised David that He would establish the kingdom of Israel. There would not lack a man for the throne for ever. In responding thus to Solomon's prayer, God was fulfilling His promises. Prayer lays hold of the promises of God. Whatever He promises He surely will fulfil, Heb. 10. 23.

Solomon also prayed for God's **pardon**, His forgiveness for the people's sins, 8. 30. 'When they shall pray towards this place: hear thou in heaven thy dwelling place: and when thou hearest, forgive.' Within the scope of God's answer, there was the possibility of His pardon for their sins. In every prayer-experience, there must be the blessing of forgiveness. Unconfessed sin is a hindrance, preventing answers to prayer. And if there were no forgiveness, then no prayer would be possible, 1 John 1. 7. Notice the conditions, 'If … then', vv. 4, 5. Only 'if' the conditions were fulfilled would the Lord then bless. Today we can prove that God answers prayer.

Thought:- God says, '**I will**, if **you will**'.

March 24th

1 Kings 13. 4-10

THE MAN OF GOD BESOUGHT THE LORD

We look today at a prayer that was uttered under very sad and perplexing circumstances. Jeroboam was a wicked king, whose sins were never forgotten. He was the one who caused Israel to sin. The altar erected at Bethel was a disgrace to the kingdom, and a dishonour to God. This unnamed prophet came out of Judah and prophesied against the altar. He foretold its destruction, with all the associated idolatry. This looked on to many years later, to the judgement of Josiah's time. The evils of sacrilege would be answered in judgement, and the altar at Bethel would be destroyed.

Jeroboam's outstretched hand was withered. The altar was destroyed and the ashes poured out. So this wicked king asked the prophet to beseech the Lord for him. The prayer ascended, and the answer brought healing to the king. A godly prophet and a gracious God worked together in this healing. Notice today several points of interest in this prayer.

Those who have no regard for God, and never pray, will often turn to one who does in a time of trouble. They will say, 'Intreat now the face of God, and **pray for me**'. It is good for us to be known as those in touch with God, as those who **pray**. This was a time of crisis in the nation's history. The kingdom, once united, was now divided. Instead of one place where God's name was set, two altars were set up in disobedience to God's word. Through His servant, God not only spoke with a voice of judgement, but provided a means of mercy. This is so with people who pray. They are a people apart, yet they stand before Him on behalf of those in need.

In our needy generation, we today must pray for those who are out in the cold and far from God. Compassion must move us to intercede for those who desperately need His love, 1 Tim. 2. 1-6.

The beauty of this incident lies in the fact that the man of God besought the Lord and the king's hand was restored. Humble and unnamed though he was, he had power with God and prevailed. As we today go about our business among those that do not know God, let us pray for all. Who knows what God will do?

Thought:- Those who **do not pray**, owe much to **those who do**.

1 Kings 19. 1-8

NOW, O LORD, TAKE AWAY MY LIFE

The best of men are only men at the best. From the Bible this can be illustrated many times. Here is the hero of Mount Carmel running away from the woman he had defied. On Carmel he stood alone for the God of Israel, and he triumphed. What could have gone wrong to cause such a complete change?

This prayer has to be looked at in the context of Elijah's depression. He is not standing before the people now but sitting under a juniper tree. Dark depression has taken the place of courageous confrontation of Jezebel's prophets. Yet before we criticize, let us look within our own lives, for circumstances can so easily spoil our prayers. Elijah had lost his way and it reminds us that we cannot always be on the mountain top.

Elijah asked that he might die. He begins to remind the Lord of his faithfulness. 'I, even I only, am left; and they seek my life, to take it away', v. 10. He felt his ministry was over and that to continue was pointless. What a sad picture, yet there are lessons we can learn from it. What kind of prayer was this?

It was a **self-centred** prayer. The heart of it was 'I'. The moment a servant of God looks only at himself, trouble begins. Even worse, Elijah took his eyes off God and forgot that Carmel was a God-centred experience. Prayer can never succeed if **self** is at its centre. God is greater, cf. 2 Cor. 1. 8-10.

But also it was a **misguided** prayer. It was not for Elijah to say when his life should end. He said that he was the only one left, but God reminded him that there were 7,000 who had not bowed the knee to Baal. Depression can play sad tricks with our minds. God will never abandon those who faithfully witness to His name, 2 Tim. 4. 16-17.

Finally, it was an **unanswered** prayer. Think of what would have happened if God had answered his prayer. The on-going prophetic ministry would have been damaged! Elisha would never have been appointed! And Elijah was not destined to die— he went up in a whirlwind, with an accompanying chariot of fire!

Thought:- **Depression distorts our vision.**

March 28th

2 Kings 4. 18-37

WENT IN ... SHUT THE DOOR, AND PRAYED

In reading this passage today, we recall that Elijah had been faced with the problem of a child that died, and he had been able to bring him back to life. The Shunamite's son dies and Elisha is confronted with the sadness. Very little is said between the woman and the prophet. Gehazi enquires at the prophet's command, 'Is it well with the child?'. Her answer is sure, 'It is well'. Her heart must have been breaking, but her confidence is sure. It seemed as if she trusted in the God whom Elisha represented. She had seen from the start that he was a man of God. It is good to catch the assurance that God is in control, and therefore that things must be well.

When Elisha comes into the house the child is on the bed. Death is there with its coldness and sorrow. The prophet shuts the door on both of them. Can this be a challenge to us as we pray? Just two of them in God's presence. Jesus said in Matt. 6. 6, 'But thou, when thou prayest, enter into thy closet, and when thou has **shut thy door**, pray to thy Father which is in secret'. The shut door, the quiet time and the quiet heart are essential as we come before God for blessing. To be alone with God each day is a 'must'.

Notice how Elisha treated the child. He lay upon the child, mouth to mouth, eyes to eyes, hands upon hands, v. 34. So it is in dealing with those for whom we pray, especially when we are involved with the needs of children. We need to draw very close, very near. Compassion and understanding will have this effect on us as we draw near to the Lord on their behalf.

So it was that warmth came to the child's flesh and eventually he opened his eyes. The mother received back her son and she worshipped God as the result. To identify with the needs of young people today is not easy. The generation is hard, blind and godless. Yet our aim must be to be involved with them in such a way that we see their eyes open to Christ and eternal life. Said Paul to Timothy, 'From a child thou hast known the holy scriptures, which are able to make thee wise unto salvation ...', 2 Tim. 3. 15. Pray again for that child!

Thought:- A child won for Christ, a whole life saved.

2 Kings 6. 13-23

LORD, I PRAY THEE, OPEN HIS EYES THAT HE MIGHT SEE

Our thoughts today focus on a very important aspect of prayer. It is that of **perspective**. We must see and understand the real issues at stake when we engage in prayer. This prayer was for opened eyes. It was a request that the man might see things that were already there. The Syrian army was vast, and as the servant of God saw them understandably he panicked. 'How shall we do?' So the prophet prayed that his eyes be opened. What a contrast the second viewing opened to him. He saw the armies of the Lord encamped around the Syrian army. 'Fear not,' it was said, 'they that are with us are more than they that are with them'. This God-given vision enabled him to see the true position. What a blessing it is to see things from God's standpoint.

This could provide valuable lessons for us in relation to our prayer life. Prayer is no easy business. In forming our estimate of spiritual involvement we can make two mistakes. We can **underestimate** the strength of those enemy forces that are against us: thus we become complacent. Yet the reverse can be true! We can **overestimate** the enemy's strength, the powers of evil and Satan. We then forget the greatness of our resources, of strength in God. The first sighting of the man was that of Syrian armies surrounding a much weaker Israel. But then, with eyes opened, he saw the greater armies of the Lord. What should our perspective really be? Surely that of Paul when he said, 'What shall we say then to these things? If God be for us, who can be against us?'. So many tokens of God's grace and blessing have been revealed that we can say, 'Nay, in all these things we are more than conquerors through him that loved us'. Such confidence can only encourage intelligent prayer.

We may, therefore, take courage. 'Greater is he that is in you than he that is in the world', 1 John 4. 4. It was not long in the experience of this servant before he saw the might of Israel triumph. 'The Lord of hosts is with us; the God of Jacob is our refuge', Ps. 46. 7. May God give us right perspectives.

Thought:- If the first look frightens, ask for the second.

March 30th

2 Kings 19. 14-20

LORD, BOW DOWN ... AND HEAR:
OPEN ... THINE EYES, AND SEE

Of all the prayers of the Old Testament, this prayer of Hezekiah is perhaps the most poignant. It is born out of desperation, the cry of one who has no hope but in God Himself. Rabshakeh, the servant of the king of Assyria, had openly challenged Hezekiah's trust in God. He mocked at his godly rule, and his destruction of idols and idol worship in Israel. Samaria had been destroyed and so would Jerusalem. In the face of Assyrian might, the God of Israel and Judah and all who served and trusted in Him would fall. Thus the letter was received by Hezekiah.

It is good to notice the way in which the king approaches the challenge. First of all he rends his clothes and goes humbly into the Lord's house. The word is sent to Isaiah the prophet, asking for prayer to his God. But then as word of encouragement comes from the prophet, he quietly takes the letter and spreads it out before the Lord. So he asks the Lord to draw near, to see and hear the plea of His servant.

It is not very often that we find ourselves in such a desperate situation as this. The very foundation of his trust was shaken and his God was blasphemed. Overwhelming defeat seemed to be staring him in the face. 'He spread the letter before the Lord.' What lessons can we learn from this event? 'Before the Lord' is the place where we can bring desperate need. The writer to the Hebrews could say, 'Let us come boldly to the throne of grace', Heb. 4. 16. Listening to Assyria brought fear—understandably so. But fears can be banished when problems are brought before the Lord. Jesus the Son of God, our Great High Priest, has passed through the heavens. We can obtain mercy and find grace to help in every time of need. 'Open, Lord, thine eyes.' The all-seeing eyes of the Lord can appraise the exact dimensions of each trouble. He doesn't miss a thing. 'Bow down thine ear, and hear.' Not a whisper of our need will fail to reach His ear. This is a vital lesson.

Thought:- O what peace we often forfeit, O what needless pain we bear. All because we do not carry everything to God in prayer.

March 31st

2 Kings 20. 1-11

HE TURNED HIS FACE TO THE WALL AND PRAYED

A prayer such as we look at today could raise many questions. We of course wonder whether Hezekiah was right to ask to live when God has said that he would die and not live. No doubt from the king's point of view this came as a terrible shock and was beyond his understanding. He wept and brought before the Lord all the values of his godly reign. These were true but the Lord knew them all very well. At that stage it seemed that Hezekiah's life span was over and the decree was that he should die.

We know that life is precious and the thought of death is hard to accept. God answered his prayer, but it appears from subsequent events that Hezekiah declined in his way of life from that point onwards. We recall that during the extended period of his life, Manasseh, one of the nation's wickedest kings, was born. Also the king received a severe rebuke from Isaiah concerning his pride when the ambassadors from Babylon visited him. The people paid for this in later years, 20. 12-19.

Although life is very dear, the will of God with its priorities must be the higher law that governs our prayers. Jesus taught His disciples to say, 'Thy will be done in earth, as it is in heaven', Matt. 6. 10. Remember too His words in the garden, 'Not my will, but thine, be done', Luke 22. 42. When we bring our desires to the Lord in prayer, we can know that His wisdom and ability are infinite. His knowledge of life's pathway is perfect all the way through. We can trust Him.

There were times in Israel's history when we read that God granted them their request, but he also sent leanness into their souls. Physically they got what they wanted; spiritually they lost out. Perhaps we can detect this progression in Hezekiah's case, for God's response to his impassioned plea should have resulted in greater godliness, not dismal decline! We should take instruction from this. God's will is always best for us. He cannot make a mistake. Though we cannot see where He is taking us, we say as we submit, 'thy will be done', and simply trust. One day all will be clear.

Thought:- 'Our **trust** should submit to God's **timing**.'

April 1st
1 Chronicles 4. 9-10

JABEZ CALLED UPON THE GOD OF ISRAEL

The verses we have before us are part of the extensive genealogy which forms the first section of 1 Chronicles. They are remarkable in that they present narrative of considerable detail within the genealogy.

The subject of the narrative is Jabez. He was head of a family of Judah associated with Bethlehem, v. 4. His name means 'he causes pain', but he is described as being 'more honourable than his brethren', v. 9. This would suggest conflict in his life between the things of God and natural tendencies of the flesh, which has been the experience of all God-fearing persons down through the ages. Priority is given in the scriptural record to his honourable character, which suggests that he knew some degree of victory in this conflict. How blessed are those who achieve this in the power of the Spirit, but how gracious is the Spirit in that He reveals to us how Jabez achieved the blessing.

'He called on the God of Israel', v. 10. This shows deep concern, even distress, and is a cry for help to the God who had intervened in the affairs of the nation (the 'God of Israel') but who is also cognizant of the deep needs of individuals. The heart of Jabez' prayer was 'that thine hand might be with me, and that thou wouldest keep me from evil, that it might not grieve me!'. He had known the grief and consequences of sin in his life and recognized its constant attack: he needed to be kept from it as well as saved out from it. He was incapable of this in his own strength: his only help and hope was that the hand of the Lord might be with him. Other blessings were peripheral to this. Only when the heart of the matter was right did he know associated blessings from the Lord.

Despite the passage of time and the increase of human knowledge and sophistication, humanity is not able to alter its true nature. The conflict between this nature and the things of God remains as real today as in Jabez' day. Paul's letter to the Romans outlines his similar concern, 'O wretched man that I am! who shall deliver me from the body of this death?', Rom. 7. 24. His experience was 'I thank God through Jesus Christ our Lord', v. 25. May we have similar exercise before the Lord in our day about our spiritual condition, and may it be said of us as is recorded of Jabez, 'God granted him that which he requested'.

April 2nd

1 Chronicles 5. 18-22

THEY CRIED TO GOD IN THE BATTLE

Attention is now focused upon the family of Reuben. He was the eldest son of Jacob and Leah. The Scriptures generally present him in a favourable manner, but he was never able to escape the consequences of his sinful association with Bilhah, Gen. 35.22. He lost his birthright through this and the leading position of the tribe was taken over by Judah. He behaved nobly over his brother Joseph and his father spoke favourably of him just before he (Jacob) died, but added 'unstable as water, thou shalt not excel', Gen. 49.4.

The tribes of Reuben, Gad and half of Manasseh were herdsmen and asked to be allowed to settle on the border of the land, in Gilead east of the Jordan, as it was a 'place for cattle', Num. 32.1. Moses feared this would discourage other tribes from fully entering the land; he remembered the spy representing Reuben had brought back an unfavourable report. They were allowed to stay as long as they assisted in the battle, vv. 6-33.

The passage before us must be viewed in this context. The tribes of Reuben, Gad and half of Manasseh had tremendous potential for God, with a skilled army of 44,760 soldiers when they fought against the Hagarites, 1 Cnron. 5. 18, 19. They won a great victory that day. This was not attributed to their skill but rather to their trust in the Lord; 'they cried to God in the battle, and he was intreated of them, because they put their trust in him', v. 20. What potential for God! How great could be their achievements for the Lord! It was, however, not to be so because constancy and faithfulness in the things of the Lord were lacking. Jacob's statement concerning Reuben is shown to be true of the tribe and its associates—'unstable as water'. It is significant that the last statement recorded of the tribes is 'they transgressed ... and went a whoring after the gods of the people of the land', v. 25. God caused the Assyrian king to carry them away, v. 26.

How important are the solemn lessons brought before us by these verses: tremendous potential, awareness of the power of prayer at a time of extreme need, but finally ending in disaster because of unfaithfulness. The scriptures assert, 'the effectual fervent prayer of a **righteous man** availeth much', Jas. 5. 16.

April 3rd

1 Chronicles 11. 15-19

FORBID IT ME, THAT I SHOULD DO THIS THING

It was honour indeed to be included amongst the chiefs of king David's mighty men. Three of his chief men braved the might of the encamped Philistine army and went to him in the cave of Adullam. The Philistine army encampment extended from Adullam to Bethlehem, the town of David's birth. Remembrance of the days when, as a shepherd boy, he drank from the well near the gate of Bethlehem, stood in sharp contrast to his present restriction, and caused him to utter a longing to drink again of that water. The three, driven by devotion to their leader, 'brake through the host of the Philistines', v. 18, and made the perilous journey to the well and, returning, presented him with what they knew to be his heart's desire.

All that mattered was that their liege lord understood and accepted what they had done. They had demonstrated their love for him, gladly associated with him in the day of his rejection and served him willingly and totally. He, the king, acknowledged this in his record, but the Holy Spirit incorporated it in the Scriptures for our example and their eternal recognition. Typically, this carefully recorded event would speak of the believer's association with the rejected Lord Jesus in the day in which we live. O that we might be sensitive to the desires of His heart and conduct ourselves in the light of this.

David would not drink the water but poured it out before Jehovah as a drink offering with the prayer, 'My God, forbid it me, that I should do this thing: shall I drink the blood of these men that have put their lives in jeopardy?', v. 19. So precious was the water to David that he could not accept it for himself; rather he identified himself with it, and with those who procured it, and presented it to Jehovah as appreciation of faithful commitment to Him and His cause. Paul knew similar emotions when writing to the Philippian believers, 'Yea, and if I be poured out upon the sacrifice and service of your faith, I joy and rejoice with you all', Phil. 2. 17, 18. The exhortation of Romans 12. 1 is, in many ways, a parallel of this: 'to offer your bodies a living sacrifice, holy and well pleasing unto God, which is your reasonable worship' (CONYBEARE). This is the divine model for service in the day of our Lord's rejection.

April 4th
1 Chronicles 16. 7-11, 34-36

ALL THE PEOPLE SAID, AMEN,
AND PRAISED THE LORD

David's desire when king was that the ark of the Lord be brought to Jerusalem and set in its place. It had earlier been captured by the Philistines with disastrous results for them, 1 Sam. 5. They transported it by cart and on such a vehicle it finally returned to Beth-shemesh and Israel, 1 Sam. 6. In contrast to this, the people of God had been given specific instructions that the ark should only be carried by the Levites, Num. 3, and thus it had been transported through the wilderness and Jordan into Canaan. How remarkable that David chose the Philistine way of carrying the ark on a cart, 1 Sam. 6. 6-8; 2 Sam. 6. 3, with similar, disastrous results, 2 Sam. 6. 6, 7.

Conduct based upon the ideas of men relative to the things of God may be convenient, and even popular, but can never lead to the blessing of the Lord and the honouring of His name. The ark is a precious type of Christ. Right thinking and behaviour associated with it, as with Christ Himself, must originate from a source higher and beyond the thinking of men. Even though David was angry about the death of Uzza and was fearful before the Lord, he would not be moved from his purpose. He asks the question, 'How shall I bring the ark of God home to me?', 1 Chron. 13. 14, and finally finds the answer only in obedience to the word of the Lord.

The verses before us are taken from the prayer/psalm of praise which David uttered and wrote after the return of the ark to Jerusalem. Israel's thanksgiving finds its source in appreciation of who their God was and is and what He had done. We read, 'Give thanks unto the Lord', v. 8, 'make known his deeds among the people', v. 8, 'the Lord ... is good; for his mercy endureth for ever', v. 34, 'O God of our salvation', v. 35.

With the ark in the midst, David leads the people in thanksgiving and praise to the Lord. How delightful a picture is this! The principle is eternal. Our God still leads His obedient people to deeper appreciation of who He is and what He has done. He gathers them to His name and, with His presence in their midst, on to the delights of corporate worship. Our response must be that of the people in David's day, 'Amen, and praise the Lord'.

April 5th

1 Chronicles 23. 24-32

TO STAND EVERY MORNING TO THANK ... THE LORD ... LIKEWISE AT EVEN

Members of the tribe of Levi were given specific and unique responsibilities relating to the things of God. Their distinctive position grew from their faithfulness to the Lord at the time of apostasy, when the people made and worshipped a golden calf, Exod. 32. 25-29. The general responsibility of the Levites during the wilderness journey was the taking down of the tabernacle, its transportation and its erection, Num. 1. 51. They were the guardians of the things of God.

The passage before us relates to the time when the wilderness journey had been completed and the ark had been brought to a place of rest in Jerusalem. The work of transporting the tabernacle was no longer required, so the duties of the Levites needed to be revised. There is much for us to learn from this.

Whilst circumstances might change, God never changes. His holy character and power are constant and unassailable and will not and cannot adjust to the conventional thinking of any generation. It was the same Holy One who dwelt between the cherubim when the ark was in the wilderness that dwelt between the cherubim when the ark was in Jerusalem. We will be encouraged in our service only if we grasp the truth that the One who has proved faithful in the past will remain unchanged in present changed and changing situations.

It was the Lord God (through His servant David, 1 Chron. 23. 25) who indicated the need for change; it was not the idea of the Levites. Change was not introduced to enhance the standing of the Levites in any way, indeed their role was more subservient as a result of the change. It was only the direction of their service changed; its character was not altered, nor was its importance in God's eyes diminished in any way.

The level of commitment required was increased; David told the Levites that they would 'dwell in Jerusalem for ever', v. 26. The service required now was a constant service of prayer and praise necessitating that they should 'stand every morning to thank and praise the Lord, and likewise at even', v. 30.

April 6th

1 Chronicles 29. 10-19

WE THANK THEE AND PRAISE THY GLORIOUS NAME

David's prayer recorded in these verses is an expression of appreciation to the Lord for His kindness towards him, his family and the people of God. Under David's leadership the kingdom had been extended and a period of peace introduced and sustained. His exercise and desire was to build God a house. This privilege was to be denied him but would be given to his son, Solomon, 1 Chron. 28. 3-6. The Lord would, however, reveal the pattern of the house to David and he, with the people, would contribute richly to its materials before his death. David accepted God's will in the matter and was satisfied.

The prayer expresses appreciation of the greatness of the Lord, v. 11. David had come to know and to rest in the One who is omniscient and whose ways are inscrutable. Our God does not merely know the end from the beginning. He established the beginning and maintains it to the end according to His character and eternal purposes. It is on this that His people are able to rest.

The prayer recognizes the Lord as the only source of blessing, materially and otherwise; 'for all things come of thee, and of thine own have we given thee', v. 14. This is always the humble position of the people of God throughout the ages; we are what we are by grace and not by personal status. The apostle Paul, inspired by the Holy Spirit, wrote, 'to every man that is among you, not to think of himself more highly than he ought to think', Rom. 12. 3, and 'what hast thou that thou didst not receive? now if thou didst receive it, why dost thou glory ?', 1 Cor. 4. 7. We are only able to offer to our God that which we have received, be it material things, personal commitment in His service, or appreciation of Him in worship.

There is also recognition in the prayer of a particular joy which results from harmony amongst the people of God; 'I have willingly offered all these things; and now I have seen with joy thy people ... offer willingly unto thee', v. 18.

It is only when we are brought to this position and condition that we can truly say, 'Now therefore, our God, we thank thee, and praise thy glorious name', v. 13.

April 7th

2 Chronicles 14. 9-15

WE REST ON THEE, AND IN THY NAME WE GO

Asa, the third king of Judah, was 10 years old when his father Abijah died. During his minority he would have been tutored by the priests, and this had consequences when he came to the throne. During his reign he removed idols and shrines and did not allow family relationships to stand in his way: his grandmother, who had taken on the role of 'queen mother', during his minority, suffered under these reforms, 1 Kgs. 15. 13. Asa also fortified frontier cities and raised an army of some 580,000 men. His reign was, generally, peaceful and Scripture records that he 'did that which was good and right in the eyes of the Lord his God', 2 Chron. 14. 2. How important were those early years of tutelage!

At one stage, Asa's reign was threatened by a massive Ethiopian army of about a million led by Zerah, 2 Chron. 14. 9. The armies confronted each other in the valley of Zephathah (a strategic point in the defences of Judah) where the strength and size of the Ethiopian army could be clearly seen. Humanly speaking the position was hopeless and victory an impossibility. Asa and the people of Judah did not shirk the battle but prayed, out of their extremity, for God's help in the battle, 'Help us, O Lord our God; for we rest on thee, and in thy name we go against the multitude', v. 11. The Lord heard their cry and brought about a notable victory. It is only when we come to an end of ourselves and are cast entirely on the Lord that He is able to do His greatest work. We, in our day, need to learn this important, lesson as also did Abraham and Gideon, as well as Asa, in their day.

When the blessing came, Asa recognized it as coming from the Lord, 'the Lord smote the Ethiopians before Asa, and before Judah; and the Ethiopians fled', v. 12. Asa and the people were immediate beneficiaries, but the victory was so great that it had consequences well beyond the reign of Asa.

We must not turn from the battle whatever it may be, but it is only when we cast ourselves completely upon the Lord that He is 'able to do exceeding abundantly above all that we ask or think', Eph. 3. 20.

April 8th

2 Chronicles 15. 8-15

THEY SOUGHT HIM WITH THEIR WHOLE DESIRE

The subject before us is that of the peace and rest provided for the people of God, and the conditions under which enjoyment of these blessings is obtained. Asa was a good king and mostly set a good example, but there was indifference on the part of the people. The Lord made this clear through the words of Oded the prophet: 'The Lord is with you, while ye be with him;' v. 2, and 'Now for a long season Israel hath been without the true God, and without a teaching priest, and without law', v. 3.

God outlined the ground for restoration—total allegiance to Him requiring faithfulness and industrious outworking in their personal lives, and in the social and religious life of the nation. Any lack of rest was the result of their disobedience and a sign of God's displeasure; 'for God did vex them with all adversity', v. 6.

Even though it is recorded that 'the heart of Asa was perfect all his days', 2 Chron. 15. 17, Scripture also records some discrepancy between his love for the things of God and his ability to work this out in his own life and in the life of the nation. For example, he made an alliance with the king of Syria and imprisoned the prophet (Hanani) who opposed him, and he sought the physicians rather than the Lord during his illness, 2 Chron. 16. 10, 12. But God looked upon Asa's heart, preserved the good testimony of his reign, and followed instances of failure with examples of faithfulness.

Following Oded's prophecy, Asa gathered the people to him and 'they saw that the Lord his God was with him', v. 9, and they made a covenant with Him. Their covenant was to 'seek the Lord God of their fathers will all their heart and with all their soul', v. 12. Only Judah 'rejoiced at the oath: for they had sworn with all their heart, and sought him with their whole desire; and he was found of them', v. 15. All knew about the covenant but it was only fulfilled in Asa and the people of Judah. The things of the Lord transcend human wisdom but are not beyond human understanding in the power of the Spirit; we will only be faithful to the things of the Lord when they are precious to us and touch and move our hearts. If this is the case, the result will be glorious, as it was to Asa and the people of Judah; 'the Lord gave them rest round about', v. 15.

April 9th

2 Chronicles 20.1-13

HE FEARED AND SET HIMSELF TO SEEK THE LORD

Jehoshaphat was the son of Asa and succeeded him as king of Judah. He came to the throne at the age of thirty-five years and reigned for twenty-five years. We see in his reign many of the things which characterized his father, 2 Chron. 17. 4. He strengthened himself against Israel but then made an alliance with Ahab its king, 2 Chron. 18. 1, which resulted in his eldest son marrying the daughter of Ahab and Jezebel. He showed zeal for the things of Jehovah and encouraged the priests to go throughout the kingdom taking the scrolls of the law with them and teaching the things of the Lord, 2 Chron. 17. 8, 9. He was made rich by tribute received from the surrounding nations and 'waxed great exceedingly', 2 Chron. 17. 10-12.

The verses under consideration record the threat brought upon Judah from the people of Ammon, Moab and Seir, 2 Chron. 20. 1. Jehoshaphat saw deliverance only by the hand of the Lord. None was able to help and, on this occasion, there was no benefit in any alliance. We read that 'Jehoshaphat feared, and set his face to seek Jehovah and proclaimed a fast throughout all Judah', v. 3 (NEWBERRY margin). The lesson is that which is constantly brought before us in the Scriptures, but how slow we are to learn it: God's greatest work can only be done when we recognize our total inadequacy and total dependence upon Him. It is sad when fear drives His people to this position but, in grace and mercy, Jehoshaphat's cry was heard and accepted. It is when we acknowledge our own inadequacy that we become aware of the greatness of our God, and only then is fear removed.

Jehoshaphat's prayer rehearses before the Lord that which was remembered of His greatness and presents his petition. The response, in its promise and realization, transcended his highest expectation. Any attempt to contribute to it could only detract from it; 'the battle is not yours, but God's ... Ye shall not need to fight in this battle: set yourselves, stand ye still, and see the salvation of the Lord with you', vv. 15, 17.

They went forth confidently and their returning indicated that their fear had been replaced by joy, vv. 20, 27.

When we are fearful we need only to 'seek the Lord'.

April 10th
2 Chronicles 26. 1-5

AS LONG AS HE SOUGHT THE LORD ...
GOD MADE HIM PROSPER

Uzziah's reign over Judah was a reign of sharp contrasts and strange contradictions. He came to the throne at the age of sixteen and reigned for fifty-two years. The greater part of his reign was remarkable for its achievements. His powerful armies defeated the Philistines and the Arabians and laid waste their cities; he strengthened the walls of Jerusalem, dug wells and his skilful engineers designed engines to shoot arrows and hurl rocks. At this time it is recorded of Uzziah that 'he did that which was right in the sight of the Lord', 2 Chron. 26. 4.

But Uzziah failed to appreciate the importance of right relationship and communion with his God. His many successes were due to God's power and intervention; he erroneously and fatally attributed his strong position to his own ability and strength. He thought his own plans could supersede God's word and after all his success he presumed to aspire to the office of priest. Uzziah was challenged in the sanctuary itself and 'while he was wroth with the priests, the leprosy rose up in his forehead', 2 Chron. 26. 19. He died in lonely isolation and his tragic death became a reference point in the writing of the nation's history, Isa. 6. 1.

As the people of God we must ever remember that we are only that which in grace our God has made us. Uzziah 'did that which was right in the sight of the Lord ... as long as he sought the Lord', and it was 'God made him to prosper', 2 Chron. 26. 5. The Corinthian believers were challenged by this, as are we in our day: 'what hast thou that thou didst not receive? now if thou didst receive it, why dost thou glory ... ?', 1 Cor. 4. 7.

God's word is eternal truth. We are blessed with the written record of this which must be accepted and trusted and must not be modified by men's ideas. The Lord Jesus said, 'blessed are they that hear the word of God and keep it', Luke 11. 28. Failing to understand this resulted in Uzziah's diminished love for his God and disastrous failure; 'his heart was lifted up to his destruction', 2 Chron. 26. 16. We must heed God's voice, speaking to us through His word, and seek His help that we may live our lives in accordance with His instruction.

2 Chronicles 30. 15-22

THE LORD HEARKENED TO HEZEKIAH

Hezekiah was king of Judah at a significant time in its history. His father Ahaz had been a wicked king and imitated the evils of the kings of Israel. Hezekiah was a good king and, from the commencement of his reign, was aware that to continue in his father's ways would only result in judgement. He, therefore, initiated a number of significant reforms. The subsequent fall and judgement of Samaria and the northern kingdom of Israel some years after he came to the throne, confirmed to him and the people the wisdom of these actions.

The portion before us outlines Hezekiah's appreciation of the need for preparation and sanctification if prayer and worship are to be acceptable. He had to learn that the evil activities which characterized his father's day could not be shed like a cloak. Defilement required cleansing, and the hearts of the priests, the Levites and the people had to turn again to the things of the Lord Jehovah. Such was the attitude of the day towards the things of the Lord that when runners were sent throughout the kingdom inviting the people to keep the feasts of passover and unleavened bread at Jerusalem, 'they laughed them to scorn, and mocked them', 2 Chron. 30. 10. There were those, however, 'who humbled themselves, and came to Jerusalem', 2 Chron. 30. 11. The prerequisite of **true worship** is a cleansed, prepared and humbled heart.

It was not possible to proceed immediately but the people of Judah were not to be deflected from their purpose and 'the hand of God was to give them one heart to do the commandment of the king ... by the word of the Lord', 2 Chron. 30. 12. God was gracious and merciful to them, and the passover, unusually, was kept in the second month, 2 Chron. 30. 15. The prerequisite of **corporate worship** is unity of heart.

Conscious of the solemnity of the occasion and the failings of the people, Hezekiah supplicated the Lord on behalf of the people. The result was glorious: 'The Lord hearkened to Hezekiah, and healed the people', 2 Chron. 30. 20. Our Great High Priest intercedes for us, Heb. 4. 16, but how important it is that we supplicate His throne on behalf of one another. The prerequisite of **harmonious worship** is a heart sensitive to the needs of others.

April 12th
2 Chronicles 31. 20-21

TO SEEK HIS GOD,
HE DID IT WITH ALL HIS HEART

The Scriptures sometimes bring before us examples of a process of review. God has always made rich provision for His people whatever their circumstances. He guides, protects, feeds and encourages them despite their frequent unfaithfulness and disobedience. God's faithfulness is unfailing, but we need ever to remember that in return He requires His people to be faithful to Him, and to the things that are dear to Him (as revealed by the Spirit through His appointed servants and, later, through the pages of His written word).

Amos saw a vision of the Lord standing 'upon a wall made by a plumbline, with a plumbline in his hand', Amos 7. 7. The apostle Paul wrote to believers: 'every one of us shall give account of himself to God', Rom. 14. 12. New Testament believers build upon the sure foundation of the Person and work of Christ, and the materials with which they build (gold, silver, precious stones, wood, hay, or stubble) will be tried by fire: the 'fire shall try every man's work of what sort it is', 1 Cor. 3. 13. We do well, personally and corporately as the people of God, to note these scriptural precedents and engage in humble review before Him in anticipation of that great day.

The verses before us relate to Hezekiah and the manner in which God reviewed his faithfulness to the house of God, the law and the commandments. That which he undertook was declared to be 'good and right and truth', 2 Chron. 31. 20. How Hezekiah achieved this is also revealed. Firstly, he saw it all as the work of the Lord and approached it in a spirit of prayer, supplication and submission. His first step was 'to seek his God', v. 21. Then, we read, 'he did it with all his heart', v. 21, and, finally, we note that this was true of each element of his service from the start, 'in every work that he began', v. 21.

As the people of God we are responsible for the work of the Lord as His stewards. The responsibility of a steward is summarized by Paul, 'it is required in stewards, that a man be found faithful'. If this is true in our case, Hezekiah's blessing will be our blessing. We read of him simply, 'and (Hezekiah) prospered'.

April 13th

2 Chronicles 33. 1-13

IN AFFLICTION HE SOUGHT THE LORD HIS GOD

Manasseh came to the throne at the age of twelve and reigned for fifty-five years. The scriptural record of most aspects of his reign is scathing; 'he wrought much evil in the sight of the Lord, to provoke him to anger', 2 Chron. 33. 6, and he 'made Judah and the inhabitants of Jerusalem to err, and do worse than the heathen', v. 9. He compromised the 'religion' of Judah and imported and encouraged indulgence in the religions of the surrounding nations with their associated immorality, witchcraft and evil ritual; 'he caused his children to pass through the fire in the valley of the son of Hinnom', v. 6.

Manasseh was warned by God but continued in his evil ways. He was taken captive and unceremoniously transported to Babylon; 'the king of Assyria ... took Manasseh with hooks, and bound him with fetters, and carried him to Babylon', v. 11 (NEWBERRY margin). This was retribution for his evil conduct, but God's judgement is always tempered with mercy and is designed to bring repentance before the final judgement falls. So we read of Manasseh, 'in affliction, he besought the Lord his God, and humbled himself greatly', v. 12. Through his prayer of supplication, backed by humble, true repentance, the Lord 'was entreated of him, and heard his supplication, and brought him again to Jerusalem into his kingdom. Then Manasseh knew that the Lord he was God', v. 13.

Despite the depth of Manasseh's depravity and sin, God had mercy upon him; 'It is of the Lord's mercies that we are not consumed', Lam. 3. 22. Note, however, that the activities of Manasseh's reign had dire consequences which could not be eradicated from the pages of history. His repentance occurred late in his reign, and whilst God forgave him, the testimony of his reign remained—'but did that which was evil in the sight of the Lord', v. 2. It was not until the reforms during the reign of Josiah (Manasseh's grandson) that the people returned to the things of the Lord. We rejoice in forgiveness but how we need to learn that the testimony of our lives and of the people of God, be it good or less good, is that which is etched deeply and is not easily changed in the eyes of men.

April 14th

2 Chronicles 34. 1-3

WHILST HE WAS YET YOUNG, HE BEGAN TO SEEK AFTER ... GOD

Josiah inherited the shame of his father and his grandfather, former kings of Judah. They had debased the worship of the Lord and had placed Judah under threat of divine judgement. Amon his father had been assassinated after reigning for only two years, but in that time had demonstrated his waywardness. Add to this the tender age of eight years at which Josiah became king and all would seem to be hastening on to disaster. But God is sovereign and He specifically prepared His instrument for just this situation. Josiah was this instrument.

Josiah was faithful to the things of the Lord and the Scriptures carefully outline this for our learning and encouragement, 2 Kgs. 22-24; 2 Chron. 34-35. He journeyed throughout Judah and Israel personally supervising the removal of the artefacts of idolatry. A special commission was appointed to renovate the temple which resulted in the finding of the neglected scroll of the Law. This was received as the word of the Lord, was read to the people and became an encouragement to them in the work of the Lord. In the eighteenth year of his reign, Josiah with the priests and the people reinstituted the passover feast as the scroll indicated. We read, 'There was no passover like to that kept in Israel from the days of Samuel the prophet; neither did all the kings of Israel keep such a passover as Josiah kept', 2 Chron. 35. 18.

The record of Josiah's reign indicates the secret of its success: 'he did that was right in the sight of the Lord', 'when he was yet young he began to seek after ... God', vv. 2-3. To seek the Lord was Josiah's habit. Huldah the prophetess said of him, 'thine heart was tender and thou didst humble thyself before God', v. 27. There is no direct reference to a prayer of Josiah in our passage but it shows he communed with his God, actively sought His mind and was directed by Him. This is the attitude of prayer and is the foundation upon which his reforms and his successful reign were built.

The responsibilities which rest upon our shoulders are less than those of Josiah but the resources available to us are the same, as will be the blessings, if we are faithful.

April 15th

Ezra 3. 1-13

PRAISING AND GIVING THANKS UNTO THE LORD

In verse 11 of today's portion we read, 'And they sang together by course', or, as the RV renders it, 'sang one to another', which suggests some form of antiphonal singing. We may ask, *who* sang in this way? *what* caused them thus to sing? *why* was it so remarkable that mention should be made of their singing?

Who? Away in Persia there were Jewish captives who had been carried there in the days of Nebuchadnezzar, the Babylonian monarch. In the year 538 B.C., Babylon fell and the great Babylonian empire passed into the hands of Cyrus, king of Elam and Persia. The conqueror's first act was to issue a decree saying that the Lord God of heaven had charged him to build Him a house at Jerusalem which is in Judah, Ezra 1. 1, 2. Therefore he called for such Jewish captives who were willing, to go up to Jerusalem. He also brought forth the vessels of the house of the Lord, which were kept in the house of his gods, and counted them over that they might be carried back.

Those who returned numbered 42,360, besides their servants and maids who numbered a further 7,337, Ezra 2. 64, 65. Among these were elders, priests, Levites, singers, porters and Nethinim. It was these who gathered themselves together from the cities where they dwelt, as one man to Jerusalem, Ezra 3. 1. It was from these that the singers were drawn.

What? In the seventh month of the first year of their return they built the altar, setting it on its base, and offered burnt offerings thereon morning and evening. But it was when the builders laid the foundation of the house that the priests and the Levites were set to praise the Lord, with glad thanksgivings.

Why? Why was this so remarkable? Well, here was a people who for many years had been captives in a strange land. There they had had no desire to sing. Even when their captors encouraged them to sing they could not. We can read about it in Psalm 137. 1-4, and reflect that there can be no real praise and thanksgiving to God when the people of God are in bondage to the world. Can we truly sing praises to our God in the company of those who have never bowed the knee to Christ? Never!

Ezra 8. 21-23

SO WE FASTED AND BESOUGHT OUR GOD

In the course of history kings come and go. Here we read that Cyrus was succeeded by Darius, and he in turn by Artaxerxes. Now it was in the days of Artaxerxes, king of Persia, that Ezra went up from Babylon to Jerusalem by the king's decree, to appoint magistrates and judges; to teach the laws of the kingdom and to beautify the house of the Lord, Ezra 7. 25-28.

The Halt. On the way a census was made of those accompanying Ezra. The repatriates halted for three days by the river that ran to Ahava, and to his dismay Ezra found that there were no Levites in the company, 8. 15. Without wasting time, he despatched a message to a certain Iddo to send to him ministers for the house of God. In response, 'by the good hand of our God upon us', some thirty-eight Levites and two hundred and twenty Nethinim were brought. The halt, the census and the deficiency in the company had made Ezra realize that so great was the task committed to him that more time was called for to wait upon God, if it was to be done properly and worthily of God.

The Fast. Certainly humbled, and possibly somewhat ashamed, to think that they had started out inadequately prepared to carry through such a responsible undertaking, a fast was forthwith proclaimed. But yet another concern troubled the mind of Ezra. They were carrying with them considerable amounts of silver and gold 'which the king and his counsellors freely offered, and all the silver and gold that could be found in all the province of Babylon', 7. 15, 16. Also there were supplies of wheat and wine, oil and salt, and all without any protection from those who might waylay them. The king would have supplied soldiers and horsemen, but Ezra had assured him that there was no need, seeing 'The hand of our God is upon all them for good that seek him', 8. 22. To ask for help now would have been like saying that the earlier confidence in God was misplaced.

The Prayer. So they sought their God for this. He who was testing their faith would be intreated of them. One of life's great lessons is that implicit confidence in God at all times is never misplaced. Let us then pray on fervently, for God who never changes is always for us.

I FELL ON MY KNEES AND SPREAD OUT MY HANDS

Things had seemingly gone well so far. The king's instructions had been delivered to the governors acting for him 'on this side of the river', and they furthered the people (i.e. those who had returned almost sixty years before) and the house of God, 8. 36. But in truth all was far from well. For the people, 'the holy seed', had not kept themselves separate from those of the other nations in the land, and had even done according to their idolatrous practices. Indeed, the princes and rulers who should have known better, and set a right example in holiness, had been first in this trespass.

When this came to the ears of Ezra he felt so greatly humiliated that he sat down overwhelmed in heaviness by it for the remainder of the day. This had a profound effect on 'everyone that trembled at the words of the God of Israel', and they gathered themselves to him. By the time of the evening sacrifice, the hour of the day when God's oblation was being offered, Ezra rose up from his heaviness, even with his garment and mantle rent, and fell on his knees, and spread out his hands to the Lord his God.

Let us take time to ponder the state of this great man: disheveled, distraught and bowed down with the weight and gravity of the circumstances with which he fully identified himself.

There is given to us, from 9. 6-15, one of the most detailed prayers of confession in the whole of Scripture, one which in many ways is paralleled by Daniel's, see Dan. 9.3-19. Ezra goes to God as a true intercessor. He leaves no stone unturned in exposing the guilt of the people, summarizing his confession as one who was involved in it; because of '*our* trespasses ... *we* cannot stand before thee because of this'. Blushing to lift up his face he completely identified himself with a favoured remnant who had learned nothing apparently from the trespasses and judgement of their fathers.

What lessons there are for us all in this! Are we any better than our Christian forebears? Are we less likely to turn the grace of God into a licence to please ourselves and gratify our carnal desires? Who will intercede for us? See Hebrews 7. 25.

April 18th
Nehemiah 1. 1-11

I ... WEPT ... MOURNED ... FASTED ... PRAYED

Nehemiah tells the story of how a small remnant of Jews, return-ing from captivity in Babylon, were instrumental in rebuilding the walls of Jerusalem that had lain in dereliction since the city had been overthrown by Nebuchadnezzar. This they did in the face of tremendous difficulties, and the autobiographical style of writing that is largely adopted by Nehemiah in presenting his account of the proceedings allows us a rare insight into the thoughts and feelings of the man. His was a veritable roller-coaster of experience, and during the various crises that oc-curred throughout those desperate times, one obvious character-istic of Nehemiah's is discernable—his attachment to prayer.

Although himself situated in privileged circumstances, being cup-bearer to the Persian king, Nehemiah held total allegiance to Jehovah, God of Israel, and His people Israel. His heart was far re-moved from the lavish surroundings he enjoyed in that centre of royalty and earthly power; he recognized it for what it was—not of the true God, but of this world, 1 John 2. 16. His heart was set in a place far away, a place chosen by God to set His name there, v. 9. So, making contact with those of his countrymen that had visited Judah, he enquires of them as to the state of the people there, and of the city of Jerusalem. The depressing report they deliver makes him distraught, and he turns to God as the only possible source of help in the circumstances. The words he utters in prayer are re-corded for us—they are most moving to read and consider, and fall into four sections. (i) He glorifies God, v. 5. (ii) He confesses the sins of his people, vv. 6, 7. (iii) He claims God's promises to them, vv. 8, 9. (iv) He intercedes on their behalf, vv. 10, 11.

Some points of practical application arise from this account. Our first allegiance must ever be to God, and the things of God, and we must never allow the congeniality of the circumstances in which God has placed us to distract us from this. Our heart must be set 'on things above, not on things on the earth', Col. 3. 1-2. After the manner of Nehemiah, our prayerful approach to God on behalf of His people, as individuals and in companies, should be based on *personal inquiry*, vv. 1-3; *practical involvement*, v.4; *prayerful intervention*, vv. 5-10; *passionate interest*, v. 11.

April 19th

Nehemiah 2. 1-8

SO I PRAYED TO THE GOD OF HEAVEN

The manner in which God works out His purposes through men is made evident in this short sequence of events described in to-day's reading. In addition, we have here an example of how God responds to prayer coming from men, so that in the midst of a wide-ranging programme dictated by His sovereign will He allows their prayerful interventions to be influential in the way that programme is completed.

Nehemiah has prayed his prayer of the earlier chapter, having taken account of the adverse report brought to him by Hanani and the men of Judah, and as with others who pray he waited for God's response. In fact, four months elapsed before his prayer was answered, and then in a manner that was both unexpected and testing. Performing his duties as the king's cup-bearer, and therefore being in regular contact with Artaxerxes, the deep-seated sorrow that Nehemiah carried at this time of crisis became obvious to the monarch. An aura of sadness had descended upon him, and despite all attempts to hide the fact, its appearance brought comment, and question, from his royal master.

We may detect from Nehemiah's immense fear at this development that there were possibly dire consequences should the king take displeasure from this. However, his overwhelming concern for his land and his people overcame any desire for self-preservation, and so Nehemiah declared the situation to his master, v. 3. The king's reaction to this, 'For what dost thou make request?', must have brought instant relief to his troubled servant, and an awareness that God was now answering his original prayer! How easy it would have been for him then, in the euphoria of the moment and the consciousness that God was adopting him as His agent, to have blurted out all the pent up hopes and aspirations of many days. But this was not Nehemiah's way of procedure, for the man of prayer is ever the man of dependence upon God. Even in a situation where, apparently, prayer has been answered he yet prays that he might go on to fulfil God's established will in every possible way. His prayer was short—it had to be in the circumstances! It was silent, and possibly wordless. He took up no obvious posture for praying, and prayed with eyes opened! But the 'God of heaven', to whom he prayed, heard him and responded instantly.

April 20th
Nehemiah 4. 1-6

HEAR, O OUR GOD; FOR WE ARE DESPISED

Nehemiah and his small band of followers had run into all sorts of problems as they set about the task of rebuilding the shattered walls of Jerusalem. The physical problems they faced were immense, for Nehemiah's reconnaisance of the site prior to commencement of repairs had revealed that unprecedented damage had been done by the invaders years before; 'walls ... broken down', 'gates ... consumed with fire', Jerusalem lying 'waste', 2. 13, 17. Once the repair work had commenced, there had been diligent support rendered by most of the people, but even then not all had offered their services, v. 5, so undermining the general effort. Then there was the problem of ridicule coming from their adversaries in a calculated attempt to undermine the morale of the workers. To be 'mocked', to be insulted, and to have the product of their labours demeaned in the most scathing of terms must have been altogether demoralizing. Even Nehemiah must have been affected by the barrage of insults and jibes that came from this quarter, so that altogether there was a very real risk that the enterprise might falter at this early stage!

As on other occasions, Nehemiah's reaction was to resort to prayer. The God who had brought them thus far, opening up the way whereby 'this good work', 2. 18, might be pursued, would doubtless enable them to triumph in a campaign of psychological warfare. But His help must be sought, and His intervention for the discomfiture of their enemies must be enlisted. So, without delay, Nehemiah utters his prayer, stating in succinct terms what the problem was, and praying for a positive answer from God.

It is interesting to note that, as in his first recorded prayer, in his approach to God, Nehemiah identifies himself with the people, v. 4. Many of God's great servants have followed the same line of approach, and it is one that becomes us all in our method of intercessory prayer. We have a great responsibility towards others of the Lord's people to support them in their failures and problems by praying for them. So, we identify with their situations and accept their problems to be our problems. Here we have another example of answered prayer, for we read that the work continued with workers remaining in good heart, 'having a mind to work', v. 6.

April 21st

Nehemiah 4. 7-9

NEVERTHELESS, WE MADE OUR PRAYER UNTO OUR GOD

To cope with the mockery and the derision of others is one thing, but to stand firm in the face of verbal hostility and aggression is another. The Jews' enemies, realizing that their first initiative had failed to undermine the spirit of the enterprise by causing the work-force to lose heart, now demonstrate their anger and assume a threatening posture towards Nehemiah and his loyal band. There is now talk of outright conflict, and of physical presence to hinder the work going on at Jerusalem, v. 8. As before, Nehemiah would have to consider the effect such a development would have upon his people, for it was likely to generate fear, even panic, amongst them. We have commented upon the sovereign purpose of God being fulfilled through human agency, and the entire story of Nehemiah demonstrates this truth. God triumphed through the triumph of His people on this occasion, and His triumph was not only over human adversaries that adopted such threatening posture against the remnant band of Jews, but over the forces of evil and darkness that motivated and would use these human adversaries. Our adversary, the devil, uses many stratagems against the people of God in his attempts to thwart God's purposes, and cause the work of God to cease. We should not be ignorant of his devices—alas, so often this is the case and we fail in times of testing!

Since the beginning, the devil has used the fear of man to affect adversely the people of God. It is fear that creates panic in the mind, overwhelms the intentions and the best efforts of those not able to cope with it. The great and the worthy have succumbed to it, and Elijah provides a startling example of this, fleeing after Jezebel's threat, and Peter, so bold before the event, after Jesus' arrest and trial, 1 Kgs. 19. 1-4; Matt. 26. 69-75. The band of disciples hid behind closed doors for fear of the Jews, John 20. 19. In all of these examples, one disturbing element arising out of their fearful reactions is that *their work for God is halted*, and so the devil triumphs! What can be done to thwart the intentions of the evil one? What did Nehemiah do, with his fellow Jews? They made their prayer to their God, and set a watch against their enemies day and night, v. 9, cf. Prov. 29. 25; Matt. 26. 41; 1 Pet. 4. 7; Heb. 13. 6.

128

Nehemiah 5. 14-19

THINK UPON ME, MY GOD, FOR GOOD

Having survived with God's help the difficulties presented by external adversaries, and taken realistic precautions to safeguard the continuance of the work of re-building Jerusalem's wall, Nehemiah may well have anticipated some respite and release from stress. However it was not to be granted him, for yet another problem arose, unanticipated, for it came from an unexpected quarter.

That some should exploit the current situation to the extent that their fellow workers in this great enterprise were being placed heavily in their debt through usurial practices was despicable, and likely to spoil the whole venture. This became the latest problem to dominate Nehemiah's thinking, and one that he must deal with expeditiously. We read that he was 'very angry' when he listened to the complaints of the victims, and we may judge it was what lay behind this example of human avarice that so affected him. Those taking advantage of their fellow Jews in this manner were motivated by greed and selfishness, and the manifestation of these unpleasant, unholy vices gave a clear indication of the true moral condition of the people. They might have been God's people, doing God's work, but their selfish actions at this time represented a dangerous threat to the whole operation. This was an 'enemy within' the ranks of God's people—but how must it be dealt with?

Firstly, Nehemiah administers a justifiable rebuke to the offenders, reminding them of their oneness with their brethren, and the necessity of their safeguarding rather than eroding their brethren's possessions. Those censured accept his suggestions, making promises to do what he requires of them.

Secondly, because Nehemiah realised that more was required of him than just words, he sacrificed his own privileges in order to demonstrate before them all an example of *unselfishness*. In this he shows true signs of leadership—leadership by example!

All that he had done to divert a crisis was not easy, and left him still with the kind of misgivings that all spiritual leaders must feel from time-to-time when dealing with the failings of their brethren. So he prays his prayer, 'Think upon me, my God, for good, according to all that I have done for this people'.

April 23rd

Nehemiah 6. 1-14

O GOD, STRENGTHEN MY HANDS

Although the task of rebuilding the walls and setting up the gates of Jerusalem was virtually completed, the implacable opposers of the project mounted yet another attempt at subversion. This time, the method used was that of craft and deception—how often have God's servants fallen prey to such furtive, insidious means whereby that old serpent which is the devil and Satan seeks to achieve his ends. He deceives individuals, with apparent ease, as he demonstrated with Eve, the first woman, Gen. 3. 13; 2 Cor. 11. 3; 1 Tim. 2. 14. He can deceive 'nations', indeed 'the whole world', for 'from the beginning' he 'abode not in the truth, because there is no truth in him. When he speaketh a lie, he speaketh of his own: for he is a liar, and the father of it', John 8. 44.

The beleaguered Jews must have realized by now that there would be no let-up by the opposition in their attempts to stop the work. However, they must have been kept wondering in what guise the next attack would come, and so left in a state of unsettlement. How great a need, therefore, for firm resolute leadership at such a time; leadership that was truthful, honest and reliable; leadership that was perceptive to discern true from false; leadership that was incisive in judgement and quick to act so that evil be defeated and truth prosper. Here, as before, Nehemiah manifested all these characteristics of true leadership, acting without hesitation to resist this latest attempt at encroachment. What he reveals, with typical honesty, is the extent of his own feelings in this emergency, wherein the threats came with the impressive voices of officialdom and religion to recommend them as authentic. How naturally and easily we are impressed by what is directed towards us from political and religious quarters—the devil knows that, and so employs these tactics to dissipate our energies and create fear in our hearts. The people were made afraid at this time, and so was Nehemiah; see verse 9, 'for they made us all afraid'. It is no surprise to discover that his immediate recourse is prayer—prayer that his hands and the hands of others shall not be weakened so that the work ceases—prayer that perpetrators of these devilish activities be dealt with by God. These were not long prayers, but who can doubt their effectiveness!

April 24th

Nehemiah 9. 1-6

AND CRIED WITH A LOUD VOICE

The massive task of rebuilding Jerusalem's walls and setting up the gates was now completed. All attempts by opponents to sabotage the project had failed and the sustained, heartfelt prayers of Nehemiah had been wonderfully answered by 'the God of heaven' to whom they had been addressed.

This wonderful title holds within it suggestions of 'glory', 'sovereignty', and 'power'. Others of Nehemiah's references to God indicate a more local appreciation of God than this. He makes reference to 'our God', 4. 4, 20; 5. 9, etc., that is, the God of Israel, to whom the nation could look for His special interest and divine favour. Nehemiah's companions would have taken note, and heart, from his words. Most moving of all, however, was Nehemiah's use of the term 'my God', both for reference and as a form of address. What confirmation of his personal experience of God! He had learned that the great God of heaven, the God of Israel, was the God of individuals, even hearing and answering the single prayers they utter, 2. 8, 18; 5. 19; 6. 14; 7. 5, etc.

When one task is completed, others remain to be done. One of the great lessons we must learn in the field of Christian service is that large-scale spectacular effort in a crisis situation is commendable, and often it brings about whole hearted response and support by the Lord's people for a short period of time. Thereafter, maintenance of long-term, routine programmes of service must be undertaken, and it is at this point that support begins to wane. Tasks of this sort were now facing Nehemiah and the Jews. Only thus could the original work be consolidated; indeed, the entire effort hitherto had been but a means to an end. God must have His people in a fit moral and spiritual state to mark them out as altogether distinctive among the nations. They must heed His voice and obey His commandments. They must be subject to a process of godly order in whatever they do. So, at this time, practical arrangements are established by Nehemiah; the law is read and the people unitedly respond to its strictures, confess their sins, and pledge themselves to follow its precepts. Then, they cried out with a loud voice of thanksgiving to the Lord, their God, 'Blessed be thy glorious name'.

April 25th

Nehemiah 13. 10-14, 22-31

REMEMBER ME, O MY GOD, CONCERNING THIS

The reason that the story of Nehemiah is so encouraging for the Christian of today is that it tells of revival among God's people, and of triumph in the face of adversity. The events described might have occurred a long time ago, but the circumstances are not dissimilar to our circumstances now. So we can take heart from this account, but also to some degree take warning from its later sections. Therein is included God's unerring comment on the aftermath of triumph and a postscript to revival, and in the light of all that has gone before it makes for disturbing reading! Notably, the lapses that we read about in the final chapter took place in the absence of Nehemiah, for according to arrangement he had returned to Babylon to resume his duties before king Artaxerxes as his cup-bearer. However, in due time, after a period of twelve years, he is allowed to return to his beloved Jerusalem to see for himself the state of affairs, and how his people are faring. He finds a number of things wrong, that have been allowed by others who choose to disregard the divine commandments.

(i) One of his original enemies, Tobiah the Ammonite, had been granted lavish accommodation in the precincts of the temple itself—the result of an arrangement between Eliashab the priest and Tobiah. (ii) The Levites could not function as God required, because they were not adequately supported by the peoples' gifts through tithing. (iii) The Sabbath Day was being profaned, and God's clear instructions ignored. (iv) Intermarriage with surrounding nations had become accepted.

What lessons for God's people today may be read into these developments. In Nehemiah's time they would have been justified in terms of 'bridge-building', and 'moving ahead with the times'. Nehemiah saw them differently, and so should we. Notice the urgency with which he acts, and his resolution to uphold all that God has established for order amongst His people. Out go Tobiah and his belongings, and the chamber is cleansed. Sabbath Day requirements are re-established. Levites receive proper support through the people's gifts. Intermarriage is banned.

Significantly the book ends with prayer, reminding us that the man of resolute action was ever a man of prayer!

April 26th
Job 9. 25-35

THOU WILT NOT HOLD ME INNOCENT

Job is held up before us as an example of patience (endurance) in the face of extreme adversity, Jas. 5. 11. We might add that his endurance was the more remarkable because of the special circumstances that surrounded his testing, for he had no real inkling as to why he was allowed to suffer so. We are told that Job was a God-fearing man; God describes him as 'perfect' (blameless, NKJV), 'upright', and shunning evil, yet he was to be tested to the limit at the hand of Satan. Job's sufferings from this quarter were allowed by God as a means of demonstrating to Satan, and all else, that the integrity of this man was authentic, and would survive the sternest of tests. But Job did not know he was on trial, neither did his friends who came to comfort him in his adversity.

As they sat with him they attempted to define the reason for all that had befallen him, arguing that in some way he must have offended God and that this was justifiable retribution from God. Job's protestations were dismissed, for they argued that such sufferings as Job knew must indicate inherent latent sin, even though appearances seemed to contradict this conclusion. In the various discourses that occur in this book, attempts are made by the participants to describe the greatness of almighty God, and to define His characteristics and His relationship with frail mortal man. We see this in chapter 9, Job's answer to Bildad, commencing with the question, 'how should man be just with God?'. The prevailing thought upon Job's mind at this time is the immensity of distance that must exist between a remote God of awesome greatness, and poor weak man. Any attempts by man to present his own case for blamelessness and acceptance before God must be rendered impossible by the obvious problems of communication involved in such a process. What is required is a 'daysman' (an 'umpire', a 'go-between'), someone capable of presenting with full understanding man's case to God, and of speaking for God to man with full knowledge of God's requirements. Such a 'daysman' would have to be God and yet man in one person! We know this was God's provision in the person of His own dear Son—'God was manifest in the flesh', 1 Tim. 3. 16.

April 27th
Job 10. 1-13

THOU HAST GRANTED ME LIFE AND FAVOUR

Job gave vent to his feelings of bitterness as he prayed this prayer to God, v. 1. His attitude is one of contention, and he speaks out against the injustice of his afflictions, considering them to have come upon him from the hand of God. Acceptance of circumstances that befall us in life as part of God's dealings with us for good becomes us as Christians. It should be a characteristic of ours, and certainly will be noted by our fellows who look to see how we react in situations of difficulty and trial. Should we express seething resentment at our lot it is tantamount to criticizing God's chosen method with us, and questions the wisdom of His judgement in our case. It is, of course, the antithesis of our Lord's reactions during His life of trial and suffering—these He accepted with patient submission and humility of spirit, acknowledging not only God's right to impose upon Him any form of testing, but also rejoicing that God's will would be done thereby. That 'patient' Job should speak in such a way indicates the immense gulf that separates an exemplary man of earth from the One who came out of heaven to tabernacle on earth.

Job begins his prayer impressively, with admission of his own frailty and brevity of life, and acknowledgment that he owes his existence to God. God is his Creator and it is God who sustains him in life. He ends dismally, with gloomy anticipation of death in a land of darkness, but before this he presumes to express his feelings to God, and asks his question. It is one that many a stricken saint of God has asked when brought to a point of despair by overwhelming stress and sorrow; 'Why?'. If we construe this to be a question of annoyance at the injustice of God's treatment of Job, let us compare it with the sentiments he expresses in his much shorter prayer at the end of his experience. The first represents an outburst of misunderstanding, at why God could allow such unjustified suffering—the last represents acceptance of God's will, in whatever way He chooses to work it out in human lives. Job's experience brought about within him such massive change of heart, and he must by then have realized with certainty that herein was one of the reasons *why* God had allowed him to suffer so much!

'God moves in a mysterious way His wonders to perform.'

APPOINT ME A SET TIME AND REMEMBER ME

In the course of his response to Zophar's discourse, Job asks searching questions as to man's fate. We must recognize that Job's questions are prompted by his imperfect knowledge at this stage for, unlike us, he did not have the benefit of the Scriptures to enlighten his understanding. So in verse 10 he asks 'man giveth up the ghost, and where is he?'. Again, in verse 14, he asks, 'if a man die, shall he live again?'.

Looking to the future with such uncertainty of mind, in the midst of his solemn and depressing reflections on the brevity of man's existence and the certainty of his mortality, he breaks off to address God directly and express to Him his deep concerns. A superficial assessment of his appeal might result in our judging it to be merely a request for enlightenment—a desire that natural curiosity might be satisfied concerning the unknown future that lies beyond death. But surely we can read beyond this assessment in Job's case, for here, as in other statements that he makes throughout his book, we can detect signs of a hope to which he clings for life to be extended beyond the grave. If such a possibility exists then it is only because of God's almighty power to create it. So Job expresses a hope that he might be hidden in the grave (Heb. *Sheol*, here used in the sense of a last resting-place) until, at a set time of God's appointment, he is remembered by God.

We do not share the uncertainties that clouded Job's mind, for we have an assurance of 'eternal life through Jesus Christ our Lord', Rom. 6. 23. It is by Him that 'life and immortality' have been brought to light through the gospel, 2 Tim. 1. 10, so that ours is a sure and certain hope as we rest in Him! It is both touching and alarming that the vast majority of people cling blindly to a hope of life beyond the grave. Others, in total disbelief, reject the entire concept and claim that death is annihilation. Our prayers should extend to both groups, for we know that to die without Christ is to die without hope. Let us pray, and continue to pray, for the unsaved of our acquaintance, those we know and love who face a lost eternity.

Job 19. 23-27

OH THAT MY WORDS WERE NOW WRITTEN

Some of Job's most moving complaints are uttered in this chapter. It forms Job's reply to the discourse of Bildad, one of three friends who came to 'comfort' him in his affliction. It would seem these friends had precious little to offer him by way of 'comfort', and that in fact their messages to him were likely to depress him still further. How concerned we should be in the manner of our approach to others of our acquaintance who pass through troubled waters. With what care should we choose our words in seeking to minister comfort to them. Job's comforters relied heavily upon human wisdom in their analysis of why his circumstances had lapsed into tragic decline. As we read the book of Job we are made aware of how misguided their comments were, and of how, in a sense, they added to Job's agony of mind. This is Job's first complaint, and to it he adds others. God, who has dealt with him so summarily, is deaf to his entreaty; friends and family have forsaken him; servants ignore his requests, as does his wife; children react to his condition with abhorrence. In complete and utter dismay he appeals to his friends, asking for their pity, and begging them not to persecute him any more. That the saga continues would indicate that his cry went unheeded, and that he must still endure misery coming from that particular quarter.

Then he makes another appeal; this time it is to God, who both hears and responds to his request. He asks that his words might be written and printed in a book, and that they might last for ever, vv. 23, 24. Today, we have the words of Job eternally enshrined in the canon of Holy Scripture—God in His love granted Job's wish, thereby fulfilling His own sovereign will and purpose, and benefiting His suffering saints of future generations. They may turn to that blessed book, and take comfort from Job's experiences and ultimate blessing at the hand of God.

In expressing the yearnings of his heart, Job had hope that God might grant him this request. Also, he embraced other hopes for which he looked to God; hope of bodily resurrection in a future day, and hope of then meeting his Maker, vv. 25-27.

These were certain hopes, for he presents them as statements of fact!

April 30th

Job 40. 1-5

BEHOLD, I AM VILE: WHAT SHALL I ANSWER THEE?

After the long and profound discourses of Job and his companions that are recorded earlier in this book, we come to the section where God speaks directly to Job and allows Job to directly respond, 38. 1. Job heard God's voice coming 'out of the whirlwind', and we might reflect on how appropriate this was in the light of what had gone before. Job's settled existence of former days, with its blessings of family-life and material prosperity, had been caught up and smashed to smithereens by the ferocity of the whirlwind created by Satan, and allowed by God.

Early chapters of the book inform the reader of what had gone on behind the scenes, but the central figure, Job, was kept in ignorance, and left in a state of bewilderment by the turn of events. In the circumstances his stoicism was remarkable, as was his resilience in seeking to refute the accusations of his friends when they looked for a reason to explain his discomfiture at the hand of God. So much had been said by men; insinuations, accusations, protestations, justifications, explanations, without reaching a point of finality in the argument. But now God would speak, and men must listen, for the majestic voice rising above the roar of the mighty wind was undeniable. It is a point at which all human reasoning becomes irrelevant, and all human argument must cease.

God's statements come upon Job like blinding flashes of light, and the questions He asks register upon the ears like claps of thunder. Job's answer is predictable, and noteworthy in the light of his dogged defiance in the face of men's words. Now, challenged by his Maker, he capitulates entirely, and acknowledges that before a righteous and holy God he appears in all the vileness of a spiritual and moral leper. Such an awareness inhibits all further speech on his part—the debate has concluded and all the argument is settled. Take note of this development and remember: – (i) God has once spoken in His Son, Heb. 1. 1-2, yet men have not heeded. These Christ-rejecters will stand dumbstruck before His face, and at His word, in a coming day of judgement, Acts. 17. 30-32; Rev. 20. 11. (ii) I must confess that 'in me (that is in my flesh) dwelleth no good thing'. All my glorying must be 'in the Lord', Rom. 7. 18; 1 Cor. 1. 31.

May 1st

Job. 42. 1-6

I KNOW THAT THOU CANST DO EVERYTHING

This short section contains the prayer Job made at the end of his dialogue with God. Job had uttered a multitude of words in his exchanges with his equally wordy friends who came to 'comfort' and counsel him, but such a response to God would have been unthinkable. God who knows the very thoughts and intents of our hearts does not require from us a torrent of words in order to be convinced of the yearnings of our hearts. Our Lord emphasized this truth when stating that we are not heard for our much speaking in our prayers, using vain repetitions, Matt. 6. 7-8.

Consider how much is contained in this brief prayer! (i) *Recognition* of God's greatness, and sovereignty, v. 2. (ii) *Admission* of Job's inadequacies, v. 3. (iii) *Petition* that he be heard by God, v. 4. (iv) *Vision* of God whose voice he had been hearing, v. 5. (v) *Submission*. 'Wherefore I abhor ('loathe') myself', v. 6. (vi) *Contrition*. 'And repent in dust and ashes',v. 6.

The first statement Job makes is magnificent. He recognizes God can do 'all things', and that none of His purposes can be restrained. What a way to begin our prayers, with a declaration, born out of conviction, that the God we address has the power to do *anything*! In his last statement, Job repents 'in dust and ashes', v. 6. He had once been compelled to accept such a position of abject humiliation by the weight of affliction imposed upon him from an outside agency, 2. 8. Now, after his experience of God, he adopts it voluntarily as being the only fitting place before God for a poor vile sinner, v. 6. Acknowledgement of our own unworthiness is never out of place in our prayers, and God takes note of our humility of spirit as we approach Him in this appointed way.

At first sight it is hard to read this confession of Job's as a triumphant climax to all that had gone before! But so it is, and we can perceive the entire account to be a vivid illustration of how God can work out His purposes of grace for us through unlikely circumstances of life. Whatever Job had been in chapter 1, revered by men and esteemed by God, he was now a changed man, and we can regard this as God's intention from the beginning. The 'end (purpose, RSV) of the Lord', 'full of pity, and merciful', had been accomplished in his life, Jas. 5. 11.

MY SERVANT JOB SHALL PRAY FOR YOU

The final verses of this remarkable book provide a fitting epilogue to all that has gone before, and we find here the 'happy ending' we would hope to reach at the end of any such harrowing account of human suffering. We are told that all that Job had lost initially, in such tragic circumstances, was restored to him eventually in abundance. One lesson we can appreciate from this is that should God at any time allow radical change to occur in the pattern of our lives, causing suffering and loss, it will be seen in the end as leading to ultimate benefit. It certainly was with Job, for God blessed him latterly with double blessing—all his material possessions of former days were restored to him on a basis of two-for-one! Even in terms of his family this formula held, for Job's unshakeable belief in a future day of resurrection offered him the prospect of reunion with departed loved-ones, and, with eternity in mind, the knowledge that his sons and daughters had doubled in number.

God delights in giving, for He gives out of love, and His love is limitless. We have need to recognize that material blessings from God are but a small part of His generosity. We should appreciate the magnitude of His giving in that, here and now, He makes available to us those limitless spiritual blessings that are ours 'in Christ', Eph. 1. 3. Bear in mind, too, that He promises us rich rewards in a coming day for our faithful service for Him now.

At the conclusion of the story, when God would endorse the claims of His servant Job, He expresses also His displeasure at the conduct of Job's three friends, for they had offended Him with the folly of their reasoning. So He commands that they offer burnt offering for His appeasement, with requirement that Job shall pray for them. Job's prayer would have been one of intercession on behalf of those who had served him ill. Such prayer becomes the believer, for it is after the manner of our Lord. God makes clear that Job's integrity, and record over past days, would recommend his prayer for them. In such a way did this enduring servant of God emerge from black days of deep testing, to enjoy a bright future of blessing from God.

Psalm 3

LORD, HOW ARE THEY INCREASED THAT TROUBLE ME

The divinely-inspired title indicates that this psalm relates to the time when David fled from his son Absalom who was leading a rebellion against him. Psalm 2 speaks of *external* opposition; whereas Psalm 3 presents *internal* opposition. It is one of the many psalms where David is in danger and distress. In such depressing circumstances he found solace and encouragement when praying for the Lord's deliverance; the graphic historical background is in 2 Samuel 15-18.

This psalm is closely connected to Psalm 4 with which it has many similarities. Psalm 3 is a morning hymn after spending a safe night in the midst of danger, whereas Psalm 4 is an evening hymn when the danger is still present. David had many desperate situations to face but none more than the heart-rending rebellion through his son, Absalom. David looks for *the* salvation of the Lord, v. 8. He was a man after God's heart, and, although he failed, he loved God and desired the best for God's people, v. 8.

Psalm 3 relates to one of David's darkest periods due to the Lord's judgement on him because of his sins with Bathsheba. The Lord said through the prophet Nathan, 'the sword shall never depart from thine house', 2 Sam. 12. 10. Nevertheless, he confidently casts himself upon the Lord for deliverance. Even in his desperate situation through Absalom's disloyalty, he knows that one man/woman with God is a majority! **rebellion** in man is matched by **resource** in God!

David is convinced that all human schemes are incapable of frustrating the Lord's purposes and expresses a noble attitude towards God's people. It is encouraging that in dire circumstances the Lord provided associates who highly regarded the king and would gladly lay down their lives for him, 2 Sam. 15. 15, 21. We, too, may feel the presence of misguided opposition and the intensity of betrayal by those near to us, even close relatives. David illustrates that we should rely solely on the Lord who is an ever-present comfort and able to answer the prayers of His servants. As Psalm 3 puts it, **trial** (vv. 1-2), leads to **trust** (vv. 3-7), and concludes in **triumph** (v. 8).

May 4th

Psalm 4

I WILL ... LAY ME DOWN ... AND SLEEP: FOR THOU ... MAKEST ME DWELL IN SAFETY

This psalm has similarities with Psalm 3 and may very well be connected with the rebellion under Absalom, as indicated in the title of Psalm 3. Psalm 4 contrasts the outlook of others with the attitude of David. Even in very difficult circumstances, he was rejoicing in the Lord, v. 7. There is much in the psalm which brings Absalom to mind. Amongst other things, we recall that Absalom was a man of considerable beauty, albeit with great vanity. However, David was far more interested in the countenance of the Lord and the blessing that would bring, v. 6; Num. 6. 24-26. Absalom instigated rebellion and revolt, not peace. In contrast David delighted in genuine peace, v. 8.

Despite the extreme danger he faced, he was able to lie down and sleep in peace and safety. He had proved his God many times before and would do so again. Quite evidently the Lord meant more to David than anything else in life. We see hints of wonderful New Testament truths in the psalm: v. 1, *Justification* (Rom. 3. 24); v. 3, *Sanctification* (Heb. 10. 14); v. 3, *Acceptance* (Rom. 5. 2); v. 8, *Assurance* (Rom. 8. 37-39). Absalom was taken up with **callous rebellion** whereas David knew **complete repose**, v. 8. The Lord set David apart, v. 3, and David set the Lord apart, v. 8. Bearing in mind the critical situation which David faced in connection with Absalom's rebellion, it is quite breathtaking to read the words of v. 8. He is not only going to sleep but quite deliberately he says, 'I ... lay me down'. What confidence and assurance! Here is the supreme joy of perfect trust. The Lord is for him, with him, and surrounds him with His love and mercy. The Absaloms of this world come and go but the Lord Himself remains, and is determined to fulfil His purposes through faithful servants like David.

Neither Absalom, nor the dire circumstances he brought about could alarm David. His confidence, assurance and security were in the Lord who knew fully the justness of his servant's cause. Consequently, David could rest in complete repose because the Lord would ensure his safety. May we be encouraged to place our confidence always, unreservedly in the Lord, Prov. 3. 5-6.

May 5th

Psalm 5

MY VOICE SHALT THOU HEAR IN THE MORNING

Psalm 5 could well be associated with the same period as Psalms 3 and 4. It is a morning prayer uttered by David when he is exposed to danger from implacable and deceitful enemies. The Jewish day had three times reserved for prayer; evening, morning and noonday. The evening and morning prayers coincided with the evening and morning sacrifices. David adhered to this practice, as did the godly Daniel. In a number of psalms, David emphasizes the need of rising early to pray, Pss. 57. 8; 63. 1; 108. 2. The supreme example for us is the Lord Jesus. We recall some Scriptures indicating times for prayer:-

Morning—Psalm 5. 3; Mark 1. 35. The Lord Himself shows the importance of early prayer before the other activities of the day.

Noon—Psalm 55. 17; Dan. 6. 10; Acts 10. 9. In the middle of the day, with various pressing matters, and even problems to face.

Evening—Psalm 141. 2; Acts 3. 1; 10. 3, 30. The time of the evening sacrifice. Turning to the Lord towards evening.

Midnight—Acts 16. 25. Paul and Silas were in prison where they prayed and praised, Ps. 119. 62. Things can happen when we pray—they did at Philippi! Do I pray in unusual circumstances?

All times—1 Thess. 5. 17. 'Pray without ceasing'. It should be the habitual practice of the Christian, Luke 18. 1. *If I find I am too busy to pray, I am too busy!*

David starts his day with God, Pss. 55. 17; 59. 16; 88, 13; 92. 2. Prayer was his first thought of the day. In verse 3 of our psalm we note 'the morning' is repeated for emphasis. A world at enmity with God awaits us, vv. 8-9, and like David we need to commence our day requesting the Lord's guidance, v. 8, and rejoicing in divine protection, vv. 11-12. David's morning prayer was directed (ordered) or arranged as by a sacrificing priest, Lev. 1. 7-8; 6. 12, and is essentially personal. Note the repeated 'my' in the psalm. King David served a greater King, v. 2, and so he could look up, v. 3, i.e. 'wait expectantly'. He had an appreciation of the balanced character of his God who is both righteous, vv. 4-6, and loving, v. 7. Therefore, all could be left in the hands of Him who hears and answers prayer.

May 6th

Psalm 7. 1–10

O LORD MY GOD, IN THEE DO I PUT MY TRUST

The title of this psalm is 'Shiggaion (an elegy or an ode of wandering, see Hab. 3. 1) of David, which he sang unto the Lord, concerning the words of Cush the Benjamite'. The content of the psalm is in keeping with the anguish of the wanderer expressed in the title. Cush is not mentioned elsewhere in Scripture but it is evident he was a supporter of his fellow-tribesman, Saul, in the persecution of David, 1 Sam. 22. 8.

The historical background is found in 1 Samuel 21-26, when David was being hunted as a fugitive by Saul. There are many similarities of expression in those chapters with Psalm 7, which reflects not only opposition but deep seated hatred towards David by Saul and his sympathizers. David is attacked by ruthless enemies who are determined to kill him, v. 2, charging him with dreadful crimes, vv. 3–5. He claims his innocence and appeals to God to vindicate him completely, vv. 6–10; 1 Sam. 24. 9–15; 26. 18-24.

The psalm outlines very closely the circumstances of David at this period in his life. Imminent danger, the deep sense of injustice and strong faith in the righteousness of his God are its main themes. Ancient Jewish tradition prescribes its use during the feast of Purim, recalling the book of Esther and the victory of the Jews over the hateful Haman.

Our heading for today is the commencement of the psalm. David's cry for help is based on his relationship with the Lord. He expresses his complete trust in his God; 'in thee have I taken refuge', v. 1 lit. This is a recurring theme in the psalms, 11. 1; 16. 1; 31. 1; 57. 1; 71. 1; 141. 8. David has put himself under the Lord's protection and appeals to Him on the ground of this relationship. It could be rendered, 'seek shelter'. Ruth found refuge and shelter in the Lord, Ruth 2. 12, although she was an alien in Israel. Nahum's encouraging word is, 'The Lord is good, a strong hold in the day of trouble; and he knoweth them that put their trust (find refuge and shelter) in him', Nahum 1. 7. Similarly, the remnant of Israel will find refuge and shelter in the name of the Lord, Zeph. 3. 12. David himself proved, 'Blessed is the man that trusteth (finds refuge and shelter) in the Lord', Ps. 34. 8.

Psalm 8. 1–9

WHAT IS MAN, THAT THOU ART MINDFUL OF HIM?

This is one of the messianic psalms quoted a number of times in the New Testament and always applied to the Lord Jesus. It begins and concludes with a beautiful doxology in the same words. Today's title commences the section in the psalm which deals with the dominion of man, vv. 4–8. Reflecting upon the question, 'What is man?', we offer three answers. Man is:-

1. **Small.** We *look up* to view the grandeur of the moonlit and starry sky. The work of God's fingers, 'His embroidery!'. The Lord made the stars, Gen. 1. 16. He knows their number and names, Ps. 147. 4; Isa. 40. 26. In contrast, man is small and insignificant. Why should the Lord concern Himself with mere earth-dwellers in view of His creation of the vast universe? (And **to visit us**, Ps. 144. 3-4.) Small wonder David is moved to offer praise at the commencement and conclusion of our psalm. Similarly, at the birth of the Saviour, the wise men were moved to worship, not the guiding star, but the One through whom all the stars were made, Matt. 2. 1–12.

2. **Sinful.** We *look back*, Gen. 2–3, and note that man was created by God but subsequently sinned against Him. Our psalm presents 'feeble and frail mortal man' whom God intended to have dominion in the earth. However, through his sin the first Adam lost this position and brought downfall and misery to himself and to God's fair creation. Nevertheless, the Lord is mindful of failing man, considering us to such a degree as to visit us uniquely in the incarnation of Christ.

3. **Special.** We *look forward*, Heb. 2. 6-12. The awful consequences of Adam's sin made all his descendants sinners, Rom. 5. 12. However, believers in Christ are brought into the good of His restoring grace through their union with Him. Christ as the last Adam, the second Man, 1 Cor. 15. 45–47, is crowned with glory and honour in contrast to the first Adam who had lost his crown and glory through sin. Only in Christ, the true Son of Man, is man's dominion and sovereignty restored over a redeemed creation. Truly, Christ has restored that which He took not away, Ps. 69. 4. In Him we are remembered (*consideration*), visited (*incarnation*) and exalted (*exaltation*).

May 8th

Psalm 17. 1–8

HIDE ME UNDER THE SHADOW OF THY WINGS

The psalm presents a situation of difficulty and danger for David. Quite possibly it relates to his outlaw life in the time of Saul. David pleads his just cause and looks to the Lord to save and vindicate him. There are many challenges for us in the psalm, vv. 3–5, but also a beautiful appreciation by David of his God, 'Thy marvellous lovingkindness', v. 7. In addition, there is the care of the Lord for His own, as indicated in today's title.

'The shadow of thy wings' is a favourite figure in the psalms, taken from the care of the mother-bird for her young, 36. 7; 57. 1; 61. 4; 63. 7; 91. 4 (See Matt. 23. 37). It is a striking picture of the Lord providing refuge and rejoicing for His own people. David says, 'Thou art my hiding place; thou shalt preserve me from trouble', Ps. 32. 7. Others, like Zephaniah, encouraged the people to find hiding and refuge in the Lord, Zeph. 2. 3. For the Christian, his life is hid with Christ in God, Col. 3. 3.

David requests of the Lord, 'keep me' and 'hide me'. We are precious to the Lord and need to be guarded with the utmost care, 'as the apple of the eye'. In addition, we need to be *under* special protection when danger threatens—'under the shadow of thy wings'.

David prays for **protection** from those who bitterly oppose him. He looks outside of himself to the Lord for His special care in dangerous circumstances. With lions about, v. 12, he particularly needs the refuge provided by the Lord, Ps. 91. 1-4.

It is a most **personal** matter—'me'. There is a time for corporate concerns in prayer, but in trying times we will be found with a personal request on our lips, Luke 5. 12; 18. 13, 38-39; 23. 42. The Lord is concerned for us as individuals and David recognizes His vital interest concerning his personal welfare.

The **provision** of the Lord is seen, 'under the shadow of thy wings'. Not *above* where danger still lurks but *under*. And not only 'under thy wings' but 'under *the shadow* of thy wings', indicating great care in the protection being provided. Finally, the *full* provision is available—not wing but 'wings.' It reminds us of the 'so great salvation' found in our Lord Jesus Christ, Heb. 2. 3. He not only *saves* but *keeps* us safe and secure from all alarms.

May 9th

Psalm 18. 1–6, 46–50

I CALLED UPON THE LORD: HE HEARD MY VOICE

The inspired title of the psalm explains when David composed this song to the Lord. At last the warrior-king is at peace. His amazing escapes from Saul and many more difficulties are over. He had been saved through every danger and is now the accepted king of a united people, his supremacy acknowledged by the surrounding nations. In addition, he rejoices in the prospect of a splendid future for his posterity. How appropriate that he should compose this magnificent hymn of thanksgiving to the Lord. He surveys the Lord's dealings with him and delights in what the Lord has made him.

The psalm is also found in its historical setting in 2 Samuel 22. Its personal message is seen in the opening verses; *my* strength, *my* rock, *my* fortress, *my* deliverer, *my* God, *my* strength, *my* buckler (shield), *my* salvation, *my* high tower. David's heart is lifted in a song of thanksgiving to the Lord for His deliverance and all His blessings towards him. It is evident that the Lord heard his frequent and repeated prayers. 'I called' and 'He heard'. And the Lord was pleased to answer His servant's prayers. David exults in the Lord Himself and in what He has accomplished for and through him, vv. 46–50. The Lord is the living God in contrast to the dead idols of the heathen. David had proved Him to be so in all the vicissitudes of his career.

Security and salvation are found solely in Him who had vindicated David and avenged him because of the cruel injustice of Saul, 1 Sam. 24. 12, the dreadful insults of Nabal, 25. 39, and the opposition of those who refused to own him as king in spite of divine appointment, 2 Sam. 4. 8. He gives thanks to the Lord for accomplishing, both within and outside of his kingdom, that which was beyond his power to establish.

The celebration of the Lord's faithfulness to His servant is not confined within the narrow limits of Israel. His praise is to be proclaimed among the nations; quoted by Paul in Romans 15. 9. The final verse in the psalm tells of the deliverances which the Lord wrought for His chosen king, and His lovingkindness towards His anointed and his seed for evermore. 'Great deliverance giveth he to his king' is literally, 'Magnifying the salvations of his king', cf. 20. 6. His way is perfect and He makes my way perfect, vv. 30–32.

May 10th

Psalm 23. 1–6

THROUGH THE VALLEY OF THE SHADOW ...
THOU ART WITH ME

This wonderful psalm commences with a wonderful *conclusion*! Instead of moving towards this as a grand finale, David gives his final analysis at the beginning—'The Lord is my shepherd; I shall not want'. David had well proved this great truth before writing this beautiful psalm. Many see much of David's life and experience here but he starts his psalm by testifying to the **Person** of the Shepherd and then to the **Provision** of the Shepherd. He knows Him and therefore knows He will provide. He proceeds to express the Shepherd's **direction**, v. 3, and His **defence**, v. 4, as he 'walks through' and 'fears not'. Because of his Shepherd, he knows neither want, v. 1, nor fear, v. 4; Deut. 2. 7; 8. 9. The title for today reminds us of the valley of Elah, which could have been a valley of death for David. However, by the Lord's presence and enabling he overcame the giant Goliath. He is not walking or even running **in** the valley but rather walking **through** it. He knows the Lord's presence with him and anticipates being brought out of the valley of the shadow of death. It is noticeable that David moves from speaking **about** the Shepherd, vv. 1–3, to speaking **to** the Shepherd, v, 4. How encouraging to know that He is **with** us, and He is **for** us to provide help, however difficult the circumstances may be! We should be seeking and knowing His presence constantly, Heb. 13. 5.

'**Thou art with me**':-

'**Thou**'—**Privilege** indeed! Not a theory, philosophy or even a religion, but the Lord Himself.

'**Art**'— **Present**. He is constantly with me in the present trial and difficulty. He is more concerned about me than He is about my troubles, 1 Pet. 5. 7.

'**With**'— **Presence**. 'Notwithstanding the Lord stood with me, and strengthened me', 2 Tim. 4. 17.

'**Me**'— **Personal**. David's prayer is addressed to One he knows intimately. He is my Shepherd and I can rely on Him to care for and to protect me. In addition, He makes full **Provision** for me, vv. 5–6.

May 11th

Psalm 25. 1–10

SHEW ME THY WAYS, O LORD;
TEACH ME THY PATHS

Here we have one of the acrostic psalms based on the letters of the Hebrew alphabet. It is a psalm of prayer—beginning, continuing, v. 11, and ending with prayer. Despite troubles and trials, and even his own sin, David is seeking the Lord's guidance. He requests the Lord to 'shew (make known) thy ways ... teach me thy paths'. He has the prerequisites for knowing the Lord's will—a teachable spirit, and a preparedness to do God's revealed will, cf. Isa. 6. 8; Acts 22. 10.

David continues, 'The meek will he guide in judgment: and the meek will he teach his way', v. 9; 'What man is he that feareth the Lord? him shall he teach in the way that he shall choose', v. 12. David knows that the Lord will teach the teachable! Many of his psalms give testimony to this, 27. 11; 32. 8; 143. 8–10; cf. Isa. 48. 17; 58. 11. Asaph also shows a similar spirit, Ps. 73. 24. In Psalm 86, David prays, 'Teach me thy way, O Lord; I will walk in thy truth: unite my heart to fear thy name (give me an undivided heart to fear thy name)', v. 11. In our psalm, he requests, 'Shew me ... teach me ... lead (guide) me', vv. 4–5. As the old Welsh hymn says, 'Guide me, O Thou Great Jehovah'.

In the matter of seeking the Lord's guidance, it is essential to have a high regard for His ways, paths and truth. It is not worth looking for His endorsement of my ways if I have no intention of carrying out His truth. Mary's timely advice to the servants at Cana is still apposite; 'Whatsoever he saith unto you, do it', John 2. 5. The Lord Jesus Himself is the supreme example in seeking God's will; 'Not my will, but thine, be done', Luke 22. 42. To know the Lord's guidance we need to be acquainted with His word so that He may 'shew, teach and lead us' in His way.

David, in our psalm, is encouraging us to seek out and to carry out the Lord's will in our lives. **The guidance** comes from Him; **the obedience** comes from us! It is evident that David has the correct attitude concerning his desire for guidance from the Lord. The Lord Jesus emphasizes how essential it is to have this attitude, John 7. 17. Am I prepared to do His will? If so, then I can with confidence request His guidance, for His way is perfect, Ps. 18. 30.

May 12th

Psalm 19. 1–14

KEEP BACK THY SERVANT FROM PRESUMPTUOUS SINS

This psalm consists of three distinct parts. The first speaks of the revelation of the power and majesty of God in creation—its unceasing and universal testimony to the Creator, vv. 1-6; cf. Rom. 1. The second part speaks of the beauty of the word of the Lord, vv. 7-11. The third section sees the psalmist examining himself in the light of this law of the Lord and desiring pardon, preservation and acceptance, vv. 12–14.

David sees the **glory** of God in the heavens and the **will** of the Lord in the law, which leads him to plead for justification and sanctification. An outline of the psalm could read:–

1. The **Universal Report** of God in creation, vv. 1-6.
2. The **Unerring Revelation** of the Lord in His word, vv. 7-11.
3. The **Unfailing Result** of contemplating His word, vv. 12-14.

As LES RAINEY has said, 'In this chapter we are told to look to the **skies**, the **scriptures** and the **soul**. The stars tell much, the Bible tells more, but it is in personal dealings with God in the soul that we learn most!', cf. Matt. 2. 1–12. Like the Lord's work, way and will, Deut. 32. 4; Ps. 18. 30; Rom. 12. 2, His law is perfect, Ps. 19. 7. His word is complete, flawless, without defect or error; a guide which cannot mislead or fail. It is perfect, sure, right, pure, clean, enduring, true, altogether righteous, desirable and useful! Its effects are restoring the soul, making wise, rejoicing the heart, enlightening the eyes, convicting in its power and very much more! Many live beneath the rays of the light-giving sun yet remain in spiritual darkness because they know not the Son of God through the Scriptures, 2 Tim. 3. 15.

God's word is perfect, v. 7, precious and pleasant, v. 10. The effect of His word on the exercised heart is stressed as we approach the end of the psalm. David desires to be kept from wanton and blatant sin (the opposite of sinning through weakness). Some Scriptures for consideration in connection with presumptuous sins (or sins of proud defiance; high handed rejection of God) are Gen. 20. 6; Exod. 21. 14; Num. 15. 30-31; 1 Sam. 25. 33–34, 39. Presumptuous sins can become dominating sins. Hence the plea that such sins should find no place with the psalmist, Ps. 119. 133; John 8. 34; Rom. 6. 12-14.

May 13th

Psalm 30. 1–12

I WILL EXTOL THEE, O LORD; FOR THOU HAST LIFTED ME UP

This psalm is a thanksgiving for recovery from a severe illness and a reflection on the lessons which this would teach, cf. Ps. 119. 67. In answer to David's prayer the Lord preserved his life and he praises Him for this, vv. 1–3. He encourages the godly to join in his thanksgiving, vv. 4–5, and continues by relating his own appreciation of the Lord's mercy towards him, vv. 6–10. His prayer was heard and answered, his life was spared that he might praise the Lord and continue in thanksgiving for ever, vv. 11-12.

Today's title is the commencement of our psalm. David says he will extol the Lord. 'Extol' could be rendered 'exalt', a well-used word in various Old Testament passages, cf. Ps. 34. 3; Isa. 25. 1. Ideas associated with the word are 'to be high' or 'lifted up'. David continues, 'for thou hast lifted me up'. He lifts up the Lord because He has lifted up His servant. This relates to physical and spiritual deliverance. David not only recovered his health but he was also delivered from his enemies. He was lifted, or raised up. The idea is 'drawn me up' from the depths of trouble and despair, as out of a well. The Christian has been lifted up with Christ and made to sit with Him in heavenly places, Eph. 2. 6.

After his deliverance, David ascribes praise and thanksgiving to the Lord. We are reminded that the Father sent the Son to be the Saviour of the world, 1 John 4. 14. The Father also seeks true worshippers, John 4. 23–24. May we gladly offer our praise and worship to Him for all He has accomplished for us in Christ, Eph. 1. 3.

At the beginning, v. 2, and the conclusion, v. 12, of this psalm, David prays, 'O Lord my God'. Thomas addressed the Saviour as 'My Lord and my God', John 20. 28. The Lord Jesus is nothing less than very God. In effect, Thomas asked, 'How can He be alive after the horrors of crucifixion?'. The answer is, 'My Lord and my God'. We, ourselves, are encouraged with the Lord's further word to Thomas, John 20. 29; ct. Mark 15. 32. As David understands in our psalm, seeing does not automatically lead to believing, but to believe must result in our seeing. 'O Lord my God, I will give thanks unto thee for ever', v. 12.

May 14th
Psalm 32. 1–7

I ACKNOWLEDGED MY SIN ... MINE INIQUITY HAVE I NOT HID

This penitential psalm is generally thought to have been written by David about a year after his awful sin with Bathsheba and the murder of Uriah. He stubbornly refused to acknowledge his sin, until God sent the prophet, Nathan, to accuse and condemn the king, with the promise of forgiveness, cf. Ps. 51. The opening verses of the psalm give us four words for wrong-doing from the many expressions used in the Old Testament:–

1. **Transgression**. Rebellion, revolt or moving from right to wrong—as the young child might say, 'I want to do what I want to do!', Ps. 51. 1-3.
2. **Sin**. Missing the moral mark, falling short, Rom. 3. 23.
3. **Iniquity**. Depravity as a result of distorted moral values; perverseness expressed by careless indifference, Exod. 34. 7.
4. **Guile**. Duplicity, insincerity, 1 John 1. 8; cf. Prov. 28. 13.

David's terrible sin shows his rebellion against divine authority. He had fallen short of God's standards. He had been perverse and deceitful in committing and concealing his sin. All of this he confesses in the opening words of our psalm. Small wonder he is joyful because of the Lord's forgiveness towards him. How precious to know transgression forgiven, the covering of sin, and not to be reckoned as unrighteous or insincere. The Lord had taken his sin away, covered and cancelled it. Paul quotes the earlier verses of the psalm in Romans 4. 6–8, when explaining justification through faith in Christ. We are reminded of Jeremiah's words, Jer. 17. 9, as well as Paul's reference to the exceeding sinfulness of sin, Rom. 7. 13. How glad we are to be in the good of Christ's once-for-all sacrifice for sins, Heb. 10. 12. He has taken away our burden, John 1. 29, brought us complete covering and cleansing, 1 John 1. 7, and cancelled our debt. This forgiveness is **free**, **full** and **final**.

Here we are told of David's conscious guilt, vv. 1–4; his conviction of sin; his confession **directly** to the Lord; and his confidence of forgiveness, v. 5; cf. Luke 15. 21–24; 1 John 1. 7–9. May we, like David, prove the Lord to be completely sufficient to forgive all our sins and to enable us to live for His praise and glory, v. 11.

THIS POOR MAN CRIED,
AND THE LORD HEARD HIM

Here we have another song of praise, cf. Ps. 33. In the first half of the psalm, David exalts the Lord and invites others to join him in rejoicing in the Lord's care for those who fear Him. He greatly appreciates the Lord's concern for him and for many other God-fearing yet troubled saints, vv. 1–10.

The psalm, like Psalm 25, is alphabetical. The title assigns it to David, 'when he changed his behaviour (feigned madness) before Abimelech; who drove him away, and he departed'. The historical background is found in 1 Samuel 21, where we find David fleeing in desperation to the Philistines. He was discovered and only escaped by feigning madness, cf. the title of Psalm 56. What lessons David learned from this particular episode in his life! With the threat of Saul and his associates ever before him, David goes outside of Israel into the land of the Philistines. He was at the mercy of Achish, king of Gath, and was only able to extricate himself from the dangerous situation by acting as if mad. David's faith had been far greater before this occasion, and after being cast out by Achish he wrote this psalm. Now he says, 'I will bless the Lord **at all times**: his praise shall **continually** be in my mouth', v. 1.

'In the Lord', v. 2, is in the emphatic position at the beginning of the verse. In Him alone and in nothing and no one else! Truly, the Lord had delivered him from all his fears and all his troubles, vv. 4–6, 17. He had proved that the Lord **protects**, 'The angel of the Lord encampeth round about them that fear him', v. 7. And also that the Lord **provides**, vv. 8–10.

In the second half of the psalm, David takes on the role of the teacher. He emphasizes the essential characteristics of the fear of the Lord and the many blessings which attend those who fear Him, vv. 11–22. A literal rendering of our heading for today would be, 'This afflicted man called, and the Lord heard, and saved him out of all his distresses', v. 6; cf. v. 17; Ps. 31. 7. How David proved the truth of verse 6 in his career, and especially so in his excursion into Philistine territory!

May 16th

Psalm 36. 1-12

HOW EXCELLENT IS THY LOVING KINDNESS, O GOD!

This psalm presents two great contrasts. The first picture relates to godlessness, vv. 1–2, and its awful results, vv. 3–4. The second presents the glorious attributes of God, vv. 5–6, and His lovingkindness to man, vv. 7–9. Then David prays for blessing, v. 10, protection, v. 11, and is confident of the overthrow of the wicked, v. 12. The wicked have no eye for God's providential dealings and defy Him, but David sees ultimately His attributes and dealings as supreme, and His purposes must be fulfilled.

The two main parts of the psalm are similar to a proverb presenting opposition of ideas, Prov. 14. 22. David compares God's attributes to His creation, 'Thy mercy (lovingkindness), O Lord, is in the heavens; and thy faithfulness reacheth unto the clouds (skies). Thy righteousness is like the great mountains (mountains of God); Thy judgments are a great deep: O Lord, thou preservest man and beast', vv. 5–6. In contemplating such a glorious One, David expresses, 'How excellent is thy loving-kindness, O God!', v. 7. In contrast to the godless, he finds God's lovingkindness excellent ('how precious'). It is his treasure, Ps. 139. 17. The substitution of 'God' for 'Lord' is significant. David is speaking of a love which embraces all mankind, cf. John 3. 16. 'The children of men put their trust (take refuge) under the shadow of thy wings', v. 7. But He is much more than a protector. He makes rich provision for men, as was His original intention (pleasures, v. 8, is a cognate of 'Eden', Gen. 2. 8). God is the source of life and light, v. 9. Gems like this verse anticipate the gospel of Christ, John 1. 4.

David prays for the continuance of God's lovingkindness and for protection from the wicked, assured of the final overthrow of evil-doers, vv. 10–12. The lovingkindness of God is **preferable** to the ways of the wicked, vv. 1–4, **precious** to the believer, giving great **protection**, **provision** and **pleasure**, vv. 7–8. David continues, 'in thy light shall we see light', v. 9. Only as God reveals Himself can we know anything of Him. He has fully revealed Himself and His lovingkindness in the matchless Person of the Lord Jesus Christ, John 1. 18. How excellent! How precious!

May 17th

Psalm 39. 1–13

HOLD NOT THY PEACE AT MY TEARS

Psalm 39 continues the theme of the preceding psalm. David has been seriously ill, almost to the point of death. However, he has been spared and the opposition of his enemies has temporarily ceased. He finds it difficult to understand his own suffering when set against the seeming prosperity of the wicked. He is tempted to complain but resolves to stay silent. Notwithstanding, the fire of emotion within him is still very strong, vv. 1-3. He seeks relief in prayer so that he may understand the transience of human life and the vanity of worldly aims, vv. 4–6. His only hope is in the Lord, to whom he turns in silent resignation, vv. 7–9; cf. Ps. 38. 15; 40. 1. Finally, he pleads on account of the frailty and shortness of human life and prays for relief and respite, vv. 10–13.

The psalm has similarities with Psalm 62 and there are parallels with the book of Job, v. 13. David's prayer, cry and tears come before the Lord, and he sees himself as 'a stranger with thee, and a sojourner, as all my fathers were', v. 12. 'Strangers' and 'sojourners' were aliens residing in a country to which they did not belong, having no rights of citizenship, Gen. 23. 4; Lev. 25. 23. Peter applies this to the Christian with some force, 1 Pet. 2. 11; cf. Heb. 11. 13. In addition, as the strangers and sojourners amongst them were especially commended to the care of Israel, Exod. 22. 21, so David pleads to be treated by the Lord in a similar way.

When we are reduced to tears in the Lord's presence, we will discover 'there is no door through which tears do not pass'. Tears have a message all their own! The literal rendering of our title reads, 'be not silent at my tears'. He is looking to the Lord to hear and restore him, both physically and spiritually. Like David, we have every encouragement to look to the Lord, 1 Pet. 5. 6–7. We marvel that the sinless One from heaven, in the days of His flesh, offered up prayers and supplications with strong crying and tears, Heb. 5. 7, in order to become a suitable High Priest to minister to us, 2. 17–18. He not only answers our prayers but He fully understands our situation. Whilst He does not share our sinful nature, He most certainly shares our human nature, 2. 14.

However desperate you may feel today … **bring it to Him**.

May 18th

Psalm 40. 1–5, 11-17

THY WONDERFUL WORKS ... AND THY THOUGHTS

This is one of the Messianic psalms. Verses 6–8 are quoted and expounded in Hebrews 10. 5–10, showing that the words of David find their complete fulfilment in the Person and work of our Lord Jesus Christ. A suggested outline of the psalm is:–

(1) **David's trial and triumph**, vv. 1–5. (2) **David's testimony to the Messiah**, vv. 6-10. (3) **David's prayer for deliverance and his delight in the Lord**, vv. 11-17.

We cannot be sure which period in David's life provides the historical background to our psalm. Whatever the exact circumstances, it is evident he was desperately depressed, yet in looking to the Lord he found deliverance from his great trial. Furthermore, he was established in his faith and greatly rejoiced in the Lord, v. 5. Numbers of times in the psalms, '**The blessed man**' is before us. A selection of quotations tell of one whose sin is covered, 32. 1; one who makes the Lord his trust, 40. 4; one who fears the Lord, 112. 1; one whom the Lord chastises, 94. 12; and, one whose strength is in the Lord, 84. 5. Today's psalm indicates the experience of such a man.

1. The **Vindication** of the **Patient** Man, v. 1.
2. The **Elevation** of the **Triumphant** Man, v. 2.
3. The **Jubilation** of the **Glorified** Man, v. 3.
4. The **Description** of the **Blessed** Man, v. 4.
5. The **Meditation** of the **Enthroned** Man, v. 5.
6. The **Devotion** of the **Obedient** Man, vv. 6-8.
7. The **Declaration** of the **Faithful** Man, vv. 9-10.
8. The **Identification** of the **Sacrificing** Man, vv. 11–12.
9. The **Supplication** of the **Humble** Man, vv. 13-17.

David testifies to the uniqueness of the Lord which is beyond human powers to fully comprehend, Pss. 71. 19; 89. 6; 92. 5; cf. John 21. 25. The central section of our psalm clearly refers to the incarnation and work of Christ for our eternal salvation. The third section of the psalm returns to David's prayer which involves conviction, confession, cry and consolation, vv. 11-17. Like David, vv. 14-17, may we make the Lord our strength, song, salvation and stay.

May 19th

Psalm 42. 1–11

THIRSTY? LONGING?

Evidently the writer was prevented from going up to the sanctuary at Jerusalem at the feast-times and he expresses his grief. He longed to appear before God in the sanctuary. How different to many today who would not take the trouble to cross the road to meet with God's people. Yet this was something he longed to do; 'When shall I appear before God?'. He longed for this intensely, and with an overwhelming sense of want, v. 1, like that of a deer panting for the water brooks. His desire was insatiable for a sense of the divine presence. It was not God's blessings he sought, but the Blesser Himself. 'My soul thirsteth for God', he cried, 'When shall I come before him?'. He who loves God loves the gatherings wherein God is adored. He was never so much at home as in the Lord's house. He was not content with private worship; he did not **forsake** the place where the saints assemble, but he **could not get there**, and he was depressed accordingly, v. 3.

Now, if there are streams for thirsty deer, there must be streams for thirsty men, Isa. 55. 1, 2. The psalmist's thirst was not for money, or fame, or pleasure, or power—it was a thirst for God, and he knew with the utmost confidence that there was a God to quench that thirst. The prerequisite condition is thirst. Satisfaction is promised, Matt. 5. 6. The soul longing for God finds complete satisfaction in Christ. He is the answer to the cry of the human heart for God. Without Christ, God is invisible and incomprehensible. His spiritual nature necessarily transcends our ability to understand Him. His greatness overawes us, and His power overwhelms us. But in Christ He graciously draws near to us that our eyes should behold Him, our ears should hear Him, and be thrilled by His love and compassion, and that it should be still possible for us to enjoy intimate fellowship with Him.

God was to the psalmist the supreme necessity of his being. So, too, we need His power, we need His love, we need His salvation. He is 'the living God', v. 2, 'the God of my life', v. 8, and 'God my exceeding joy', 43. 4. 'If any man thirst', the Lord Jesus said, 'let him come unto me and drink', John 7. 37.

THOU ART THE MAN

Even in its heroes, the Bible does not cover up nor excuse sins. David was one of its heroes. The background to this psalm is found in 2 Samuel, chapters 11 and 12. It was a time of war. David should have been at the front with his army. He fell through a 'look'. He was not the only one to do so, Gen. 3. 6; 13. 10, 19, 26, etc. Later, the sin he committed with Bathsheba could not be hidden. Bathsheba was pregnant and David was going to be found out. It led to Uriah's murder. The story would never be revealed. But David reckoned without one important factor, 2 Sam. 11.27 —all was known to God. What happened in the year following is told in Psalm 32 verses 3, 4. Then Nathan is sent to David with his story of one little ewe lamb. David's anger is aroused, but he does not see himself in the story. Oh the blinding effect of sin! We are strangely blind to our own faults and sins. We excuse sin in our own lives and are very critical of it in the lives of others. God seeks to tear down the veil and show David his sin as it really is. 'Thou art the man', Nathan tells him. God desires to show mercy to David, but he can only do so when David repents and confesses his sin. David's response is 'I have sinned against the Lord'. Nathan's reply is immediate; 'And the Lord hath made to pass the iniquity of thy sin'.

Such is the background to this psalm. David is made conscious of his sins. He calls them his 'transgressions' (rebellion, overstepping the line); his 'sins' (missing the mark, coming short of God's standard); his 'iniquity' (moral crookedness). He prays for the blotting-out (the rubbing out) of his transgressions. He prays, 'wash me thoroughly', for sin is a polluted garment, and defilement must be removed. He asks for cleansing, just as the leper was cleansed. He acknowledges that his sin is essentially against God, v. 4, and it springs from a fallen nature, v. 5. God has provided the cleansing for which he pleads—'purge me', v. 7, 'wash me', v. 7, 'blot out', v. 9. He gladly recognizes God's power to forgive and remake—'Create in me a clean heart, O God', v. 10. Happily he can say, 'Blessed is he whose transgression is forgiven, whose sin is covered ... unto whom the Lord imputeth not iniquity', Ps. 32. 1, 2.

May 21st

Psalm 52.1-9

THE MALICIOUS TONGUE

The background to this psalm is found in 1 Samuel 21. 1-9; 22. 2-23. Doeg's betrayal of Abimelech leads to the slaughter of the priests. The psalm expresses David's righteous anger at this, and it is also the denunciation of a practised liar. There are contrasts drawn in the psalm. There is the contrast between the man who boasts in the mischief he has done, and the man who boasts of the mercy and goodness of God—'Why boasteth thyself?', v. 1—'I trust in the mercy of God', v. 8. The 'mighty man' is like a tree rooted up, v. 5, but the psalmist is like an evergreen tree, ever flourishing, v. 8. The former will be snatched from his tent by God; the latter, as an olive tree, abides in the house of God.

Verses 1 to 5 describe the **Condemnation of the Malicious Tongue**. Doeg's story had been told with malicious intent and fatal results. 'O thou deceitful tongue', says the psalmist, boldly identifying the offender with the offending member. What anguish has been caused by the malicious tongue, Jas. 3. 1-12. How often in the Bible the sins of the tongue are denounced—falsehood, slander, false witness, Pss. 5. 9; 10. 7; 12. 2f; Mic. 6. 12; Jer. 9. 3.

As Doeg's speech had wrought the destruction of innocent lives, so likewise God would utterly destroy him, v. 5. One cannot but rejoice that God's justice is such that even here wickedness can meet its reward as well as hereafter. This is the righteous judgement of God.

The second half of the psalm, vv. 6-9, demonstrates the **Vindication of the Righteous**. The righteous shall contemplate God's judgement with solemn awe, but also with joy at the downfall of a tyrant; awe producing a deeper reverence for God, and joy at the proof of God's just government of the world. The psalmist, expects not only the destruction of the wicked, but his own salvation. The wicked has not made God his strength, v. 7, but the psalmist loves and prospers in God's house. He is God's guest, enjoying His protection and favour, v. 8. He fears no uprooting, but lives in the enjoyment of God's fellowship. O to be one of God's green olive trees, drawing upon supplies from roots struck deep into Him, and trusting always in His mercy! Let us praise Him, with sincerity, and with heartfelt gratitude!

May 22nd
Psalm 54. 1-7

HELPER AND UPHOLDER

Once again David experienced betrayal, this time by the Ziphites. For the background read 1 Samuel 23. 19ff. Reference to the background is made in verse 3. The 'strangers' were the Ziphites, belonging to the same tribe of Judah as David did. But they had pledged themselves to seize him and deliver him up to Saul. They were alien in spirit both to himself and to the Lord. They were men with no regard for God; they acted as though they did not remember or believe in God's existence. They would deliver David up. Ordinarily this might have been their duty as subjects. In this case, however, it was godlessness, v. 3. If they had feared God more than man, they would not have made themselves the instrument of Saul's blind fury. Already God had, plainly enough, acknowledged David, but they had no concern for His will.

From his enemies, David turns to his friends, vv. 4, 5. Over against those risen up against him, he sets God who is his helper. Over against the violent men who seek after his life, he sets the Lord who upholds his soul, vv. 3, 4. Taught by past experience he can say not only that God will help him, but that God is on his side. There can be no doubt about the issue. **God is his helper**, there and then, not at some time in the future. 'God is a very present help in time of trouble.' He is the upholder of David's soul; not one of many helpers, but the **only** true helper, **supremely** the helper and upholder.

David's response is, 'I will offer a freewill sacrifice'. The faith with which He prayed has become so sure of answer that already it begins to think of thanksgivings. It was with a glad and willing heart he would bring his sacrifice—not under the compulsion of a vow.

He knows that he is heard. The 'perfect' tenses in verse 7 do not denote that the deliverance is already accomplished, but indicate the confidence of faith that it will be. So, surrounded by enemies who are seeking his life, the psalmist quietly stretches forth the hand of faith, and lays hold of the morrow—then he will look back on scattered enemies and he will present glad sacrifices. Let us in faith present our petitions to God, and anticipate, with relief and joy, the answers to our prayers.

159

May 23rd
Psalm 56. 1-13

I AM AFRAID ... I WILL TRUST

David was in Gath and had feigned himself mad. His faith was not strong enough to keep him from an unworthy disguise, but still faith was there, and this psalm states that, vv. 3, 4, 11. The background to the psalm is found in 1 Samuel 21. 18ff, the same as for Psalm 34. It is a strange combination—feigning madness in terror, and compiling psalms in heroic trust. The existence of **fear** with **trust** is acknowledged by the psalmist, v. 3. There are two main sections to the psalm, each ending with the same refrain, vv. 4, 10, 11. In both he passes from fear to confidence and that because of trust in God.

He prays for mercy, v. 1, and that because of his enemies who surround him like voracious animals, vv. 1, 2. His fear is a reality, yet it is a blessed fear that drives us to trust, v. 3. Trust may vanquish fear, or may like Peter, as he was drowning, have strength only to cry, 'Lord save me, I perish'. Faith does not make us cease to be men with men's emotions, but in the very midst of fear there comes to us a still small voice which says, 'Fear not, for I am with thee'.

The psalmist is very emphatic about his trust. Note the first pronoun singular in verse 4. Note, too, the repetition of the words 'in God'. His faith is valid because of the faithfulness of the One in whom he trusts.

Then he returns to his present distress, v. 5, and to his enemies who misrepresent his words and seek his destruction. He spreads his case before the Lord and puts himself under divine protection. He encourages himself by describing the tenderness of his God. God knew all about the wanderings of his life and the insecurity. God kept an exact account of those wanderings. His tears, registered in heaven, were precious in God's sight. What a sweet thought is here suggested of God's remembrance of His people's afflictions. No tear of any child of God falls unnoticed, or is forgotten by Him.

Against all adversaries, God is for him, v. 9; cf. Rom. 8. 31. The end of the psalm shows that faith has banished fear and replaced it with exuberant confidence. Deliverance is so sure that he thinks of preparing his sacrifice of praise. How good it is to render thanks to God for good received.

May 24th

Psalm 57. 1-11

THE SHADOW OF HIS WINGS

The background to this psalm is found in 1 Samuel 22, 24. The cry of the psalmist is the same as in the previous psalm—'Be merciful unto me'—but the reason is not the same. There it was a cry born of the oppression of the enemy; here it is born of the vision of God and of trust in Him. By name and title God is referred to 20 times in these eleven verses. In Psalm 55. 6 the desire was expressed for the insufficient wings of a dove for flight. Here the song is of the sufficient wings of God for refuge until calamity is past. Calamities send the psalmist to God. He is a fugitive seeking shelter, and he knows that there is no refuge so strong as the sheltering wings of God. There he will hide until the storm has spent itself. Faith does not free us from trial, but it does enable us to triumph over it.

The psalmist speaks of two environments. In verse 1, his refuge is in God, under the shadow of His wings. The figure is used several times in the psalms—17. 8; 36. 7; 61. 4; 63. 7; 91. 4. It was also used by Boaz of Ruth, 2. 12. It is a beautiful metaphor relating to the care of the mother bird for her young. When danger threatens they run to her for safety. Moses used the figure, Deut. 32. 11, and the Lord Jesus did so, Matt. 23. 37. God's care is like an eagle's wing for strength, and like a hen's for gentleness. The **shadow** of God's wings is the **shelter** of His sweet and gentle love, and the **shade** of His wings is the **refreshing comfort** derived from this protection.

His other environment is found in verse 4. He is among 'the lions', his ferocious enemies. His position was, in itself, one of dire peril, and yet faith made him feel secure, so that he could lie down. He felt secure under God's protection. The wicked become the victims of their own evil designs, v. 6, as Haman did, Esther 7. 10.

Behind all there is a divine hand which makes the wrath of men to praise Him. But the psalmist's heart is now fixed, v. 7, firmly resolved and proof against all fear. He is steadfastly resolved, grounded and settled, and 'not moved away', Col. 1. 23. How then has he managed to win through? He has learned fixity of purpose under the shadow of God's wings.

161

May 25th

Psalm 59. 1-17

THE GOD WORTHY OF UNSHAKEN TRUST

This psalm shows the psalmist's unshaken trust in God in circumstances of difficulty and danger. Its background is found in 1 Samuel 19. 8ff. The first half of the psalm, vv. 1-9, is a prayer for deliverance from his enemies, and the second half, vv. 10-17, a prayer for their defeat. Notice the verbs in verses 1 and 2, 'deliver', 'defend', 'deliver', 'save'. Four times the persecuted man cries for help.

Consider the description of his enemies—workers of iniquity, men of blood, plot weavers, insolent in their might. He is in the midst of trouble, the victim of unprovoked hatred, v. 3. Like wild beasts they crouched, waiting to make the fatal spring. What could he do? He laid the matter before the Lord. While the enemies were waiting in the posture of a beast for attack, the psalmist went before God in the posture of prayer. 'I will wait upon thee', he says, v. 8.

What a God to wait upon! Jehovah, the unchanging; Elohim Sabaoth (God of hosts), indicating the resources at His command; Elohe Israel (the God of Israel) in His covenant relations. Each is a new plea which God cannot resist. The names suggest reasons why his prayer should be answered. The One to whom it was addressed was not only the eternal, self-existent God, the Sovereign of the universe, but the God of Israel, and therefore bound by covenant to save His people. Each of the divine names is an appeal to God's ability, power, will and promise. He is the Lord of hosts and therefore able; He is the God of Israel, and therefore willing. Each name suggests something in God which encourages hope that God will act on his behalf.

Perhaps there is no more beautiful description of what God is to His people than that found in verse 9—'my defence' (my high tower). It suggests at once peace and strength, a **tower** against which all the might of the foe hurls itself in vain. But it is a **high** tower, lifting us far above the turmoil and strife, providing a vantage ground of perfect safety. How beautiful, too, the title, 'God of my mercy', v. 10. How often we are met with 'preventing' mercy for He has gone before us, providing supply before need, and refuge before danger.

May 26th

Psalm 60. 1-12

VICTORY AFTER DEFEAT

In verses 1 and 2 a crushing defeat is indicated. The background is found in 2 Samuel 8. 13ff and 1 Chronicles 19. 6-9. The words 'cast off' indicate at least a severe check, if not a defeat, of David's main army.

David expostulates with God for having abandoned His people to disaster and defeat, vv. 1-4. He sees the Lord's hand in their defeat and pleads with the Lord concerning it. He bases his appeal on the greatness of Israel's need and upon Israel's relation to God. They were His people, His 'beloved', v. 5; cf. Deut. 33. 12; Jer. 11. 15. Had He not given to them the banner of victory?, v. 5. Surely God would save those who marched beneath his banner? They believed themselves to be the people of the Lord, but the banner which He had given them in this instance had simply led the way to flight, Exod. 17. 15 margin. (See RV margin v. 4.) Victorious over Amalek, but here defeated by Edom, David's appeal for help is based on the recognition of the true vocation of his people. They bore a banner for the display of the truth. Israel was to be a witness for God to the nations. David looked upon the warfare with Edom as a rising-up for the truth in accordance with his nation's calling. So he pleads for help, v. 5, the king of Israel representing his people in prayer.

Just so, the Lord has given us the standard of the gospel to uphold and defend. The faith has been once committed to the saints. The standard must be lifted high and never surrendered.

God's answer promised victory, vv. 6-8, and confirmed for David the unshaken possession of the whole of Israel's territory, vv. 6, 7, and dominion over the neighbouring kingdoms which were then rebelling, v. 8.

Faith is never happier than when it can fall back on the promise of God. These territories had originally been in the covenant with Abraham. Moreover, God spoke in His holiness these things, v. 6. This elevates God far above all His creatures and therein also is the pledge of the fulfilment of His word. God had promised Israel victory and David the kingdom. The grant made to Abraham long before was a sufficiently firm guarantee for the belief that Israel would be victorious in battle.

163

May 27th

Psalm 63. 1-11

O GOD, THOU ART MY GOD

The psalmist no longer has access to the sanctuary which he loves, so in the wilderness he feeds upon the remembrance of Him on whom he had gazed, v. 2. Our vision on the mountain should be our comfort in the valley. In days of rapture we should store up delights for days of depression. At a distance, then, from the sanctuary, and in peril of his life, the psalmist throws himself upon God. What he longs for above all things is the sense of God's presence as he had realized it in the worship of the sanctuary.

Here is the cry of a believer, one who can say, 'O God, thou art my God'. The Almighty and the Eternal gives Himself in the fullness of His being to the soul who seeks after Him. The first name, Elohim, implies strength and power, and the second, El, awe and permanency. So he addresses God in verse 1 as the mighty One to whom he can appeal with confidence in his need, One in whom in all his weakness he retains unbroken trust. Truly, God 'is a very present help in time of trouble'. He encourages us to come to Him, cf. Ps. 50. 15. David had personal dealings with a personal God—'Thou art my God'. This sums up the privilege of the child of God and holds for him all the blessings for time and for eternity.

'Early will I seek thee', he continues. That should be the cry of each one of us in the dawn of life, and each day. Why does he seek God? Because he has a want in his soul. He is athirst. Thirst is an irresistible longing for that which is an essential support of life. It cannot be denied, nor forgotten, nor ignored. It will be heard. So it is with the divine desire that the grace of God creates in our souls. Only God Himself can satisfy such a craving. 'Soul' and 'flesh' have this desire of longing, that is to say, the psalmist's whole being, cf. Psa. 84. 2. Only God can slake our spiritual thirst. The psalmist's passion of yearning after God rebukes and puts to shame our faint desires. This man's soul was stretched to grasp and to hold God. This was in 'a dry and thirsty land where no water is', cf. Isa. 32. 2. How weary and sad is life without God, John 4. 13, 14. If there is nothing here below and nothing within us to cheer, the Christian can look up and find all he needs in his God. 'Because thy lovingkindness is better than life, my lips shall praise thee', v. 1.

May 28th

Psalm 65. 1-13

THE COURTS OF THE LORD

This psalm was composed for use at one of the great festivals, the feasts of the Lord, vv. 2, 4; Lev. 23. There are three stanzas, vv. 1-4, 5-8, 9-13. Each presents a different scene: first the courts of the Lord's house, then the shore of the sea, and finally the cornfields and pasturelands. The first section takes us into the courts of the house of the Lord, with the idea of a grateful people assembled to render thanks to God. It is the duty of a thankful people to render thanks to God who is the hearer of prayer, v. 2. It is God's inalienable attribute, His nature and His province, to answer prayer. Taught this by his own answered prayers, the psalmist's eye travels beyond Israel and sees 'all flesh' coming before God. By the word 'flesh' he calls attention to our weakness and need as men, each deficiency on our part pointing us to God. The more needy we are the greater cause there is for going to God. By 'all flesh' he is descriptive of a multitude of all ages and conditions and races that crowd God's courts and pray, and that have an answer.

There is a problem for all who would come into those courts, v. 3; the question of iniquities and transgressions has to be dealt with. Here is the barrier, and the barrier is sin. In the very act of preparing himself to pray the psalmist is conscious of his own sinfulness. But with God there is forgiveness. 'Thou'—and the word is emphatic—'shalt purge them away', that is, make atonement for them. The consciousness of sin would deter from approaching a holy God were it not that He himself is graciously ready to purge guilt away. He alone can do that. None but God can deal with the evil things that are too strong for man. A man forgiven may then dwell with God, v. 4, be admitted into His presence and into communion with Him. Then, and there, we shall be so filled that nothing can be said to be lacking. What can be wanting in the house of Him who made everything, who is master of everything, in whom there is an inexhaustible treasure of good? Who would not be satisfied with 'the goodness of thy house'? Does He not 'satisfy our mouth with good things', and 'crown us with lovingkindness and with tender mercies'? Ps. 103. 4, 5. And finally, after a life spent in His courts, we shall be satisfied to awake with His likeness.

May 29th

Psalm 70. 1-5

MAKE HASTE, O LORD

This psalm was written under great pressure. The urgency and earnestness of prayer has become impatient. The petition of haste is repeated three times. There are nine petitions in the psalm's five verses. There is such urgency that there is only time to cry out. The prophets of Baal cried all day long and received no answer because there was 'none to answer', 1 Kgs. 18. 26. The cry of Elijah, however, brought an immediate response, v. 38. 'Before they call I will answer'; this is the anticipating grace of God. He sees the inclination of our hearts, and before the mind can think the petitions, or our lips frame the words, the answer is on the way. Men do not turn a deaf ear to a cry for help. Will God do any less? cf. Heb. 4. 14-16. Furthermore, verse 1 makes it clear that it is not forbidden to us, in the hour of distress, to ask for instant help on God's part in coming to rescue us. The psalmist was in distress for there were those who sought after his life, and others who rejoiced at his extremity and also treated him with ridicule, v. 3. 'Aha, aha' is a term of malicious pleasure at another's misfortune.

The psalmist has no doubt as to God's ability to help him. The only question is whether help will arrive in time. But seekers after God will always find Him. They who long for His salvation will receive it, and that reception will fill their hearts so full of blessedness that their lips will not be able to refrain from ever-new outbursts of 'The Lord be magnified'. The godly man boasts in God and is only eager that His name should be exalted, Phil. 1. 20.

What a description of a believer's life this is, always **glad in God**, v. 4, and continually **seeking the glory of God**! Note how God's friends are described—'those who seek thee', and 'those who love thy salvation'. Is not that also a description of what a Christian is? One who seeks God by earnest desire and prayer, and loves God's salvation for what it is—for Him who sent it and for Him who brought it? What follows this glad intercession for the saints is a plea of personal need, v. 5. God will not be slack to vindicate His servant's confidence and magnify His own name. This appeal goes straight to the heart of God—it is an appeal we must make urgently, and constantly.

May 30th

Psalm 71. 1-12

THE GOLDEN YEARS

Old age robs us of personal beauty and deprives us of strength for active service, but it does not encroach upon the love and favour of God. This psalm is the utterance of a faith which has proved the goodness of God throughout life; it is the prayer of an old man, v. 9. Evidently, God has watched over him since birth, and even before that, vv. 5, 6. His experience of God from birth justifies his confidence that he will be heard now. God will not let him down at the end. The petition of old age is for the continuance of the mercy of past years.

In this passage of the psalm such confidence is based on the psalmist's knowledge of God, upon what He does and will not do. **And what is God** to this psalmist? He is his 'strong habitation', v. 3, his 'rock of habitation', a high rock which cannot be stormed, and which provides a secure abode. He is his 'rock' upon whom he has built throughout a long life. He is his 'fortress', and within that fortress his heart has been garrisoned in peace. He is his 'hope', v. 5. Not only is our hope in Him, but He himself is our hope, 1 Tim. 1. 1; Col. 1. 27. They are highly favoured who can say like the psalmist, 'Thou art my trust from my youth', v. 5. Happy is the person who can say that God has been his hope and trust from childhood. God is his 'strong refuge', v. 7; having fled to Him for refuge, v. 1, he looks confidently to God, as in the past, so in the future, for preservation. He is a strong refuge, and if we are strong, it is only in God. If we are safe, it is because our refuge shelters us. He is our God, v. 12. Then **what does his God do**? He delivers, vv. 2-4. He pleads the righteousness of God in this, v. 2. Because of that unchanging rectitude which is an unfailing attribute of deity, God cannot desert His servant; He must be true to His promise, 2 Tim. 2. 13. The psalmist then quotes his history from infancy, vv. 5, 6. His God listens to his prayers; He inclines His ear. He will 'uphold', v. 6 (the divine response to 'trust', v. 5), a lifelong support. 'I have been holden up' is a wonderful description of what God is to those who trust Him. He is like a father who bears them as children in His arms, holds them to His bosom. What He will never do is cast us off, nor forsake us, v. 9; cf. Heb. 13. 5, 6.

May 31st
Psalm 86. 1-11, 16, 17

GOOD, GREAT, UNIQUE AND COMPASSIONATE

The whole psalm is called a prayer because it is made up entirely of direct petitions, and of arguments intended to enforce them. The petitions are accompanied by reasons why they should be granted. The prayer consists of many quotations from other psalms, in total about twenty, and also thoughts from other books such as Exodus and Deuteronomy. The psalmist is not less burdened because he expresses his petitions in well-known words. God does not require originality of expression as a condition of acceptable prayer. The virtue and value of prayers do not consist necessarily in their originality, provided that they are the genuine expression of hearts opened to God. A prayer full of quotations may be heartfelt, and it will be heard and answered. Others may have made the same petitions before him but that does not preclude the psalmist from making them now. His experience in uttering such petitions is still his own.

This prayer is full of the Lord. Note the divine titles. The psalmist uses the word **Adonai** seven times, vv. 8, 9, 12, 15. It indicates 'absolute lordship'. By the use of it the psalmist shows his sense of submission and loyalty. It expresses the consciousness of specially belonging to Adonai, and standing under His immediate guidance and protection. He is the Master, the Owner, the Sovereign. The word **Elohim** is used five times, vv. 2, 10, 12, 14, 15, the 'mighty One', the 'great and powerful One'. In the hour of this man's great need he turned to God who is omnipotent. The name **Jehovah** is used four times, vv. 1, 6, 11, 17, the 'covenant-keeping God', the 'God who is utterly dependable', the 'God who never breaks His word'. If He had broken one word of any of His promises we would have to accept His word with reservation. But He is a covenant-keeping God whose word cannot be broken.

There are four great statements the psalmist makes of his God. His God is good, v. 5. He is not only the Sovereign of His people, but good and benevolent in His own nature, plenteous in mercy. He is great, v. 10. Greatness and goodness are in Him united. He is God alone, v. 10, unrivalled, incomparable, unique. His God is full of compassion, v. 15, the God of infinite pity and lovingkindness. And such a God is our God. We can with confidence appeal to Him in prayer!

June 1st

Psalm 90. 12

TEACH US TO NUMBER OUR DAYS

We only really number the items in our lives that we **value** the most. Therefore to count something is to take **quality** as well as **quantity** into account. When we have an abundance then we don't care to know how much of it we have and it can lead to a spirit of carelessness or neglect.

What do you value most and account as very precious in your life today? The Lord taught that our most valuable possession is our 'soul', Matt. 16. 24-26. This He clearly links with the way in which we spend our lives.

This psalm contrasts aspects of the nature of God with those of men, and in particular His eternity against the brevity of our lives, vv. 2, 10. Moses, the author, considers the generation that fell in the wilderness, 1 Cor. 10. 5. He had, under God's hand, brought them out of Egypt with potential to inherit their Promised Land. The actuality had proved to be so different. The years had been characterized by rebellion and unbelief resulting in discipline and trouble, vv. 7-9. The judgement of God made it a generation that would not enter into His rest, Heb. 3. 17-19.

What a waste of human lives and their treasures lay strewn behind them on the floor of the desert. Forty years that were unfruitful and unfulfilling for them and for their God. This psalm is Moses' lament over wanderings that should never have happened.

Saint of God, are you brave enough to take a look today over the years that lie behind you?, see 2 Tim. 4. 7. Just how much of your life in Christ will outlast time and stand the test of the divine fire at 'that day'?, see 1 Cor. 3. 13-15; 2 Cor 5. 10.

The final part of the psalm gives us a glimpse of what should be a profitable outcome of our day-by-day experience with God. In response to the heartfelt plea to, 'Return O Lord', v. 13, we shall then see His work appear, His glory unto our children and His beauty upon us, vv. 16-17. What more could we ask for? These alone are what real day-by-day 'quality' living is about. These are the lives that count.

Take up 'today' as a precious gift, yield it to the Giver, apply your heart to wisdom and make it a profitable day today.

June 2nd

Psalm 92. 1

IT IS A GOOD THING TO GIVE THANKS UNTO THE LORD

Thankfulness is a major key to spiritual well-being. The thankful believer will be a fruitful believer. The psalmist provides us to-day not only with an exhortation but a reason and a demonstration of how and why we should 'give thanks'. New Testament teaching is just as demanding in relation to this exercise, Col. 1. 12; 3. 17; 4. 2. We ignore such exhortation at our peril.

His Person, 'O Most High', v. 1, and His works, vv. 4, 5, are unchangeable reasons for us to offer continual thanksgiving to our God.

We need to start the day with praise, v. 2. The morning brings forth the **light** and we are filled with a renewed appreciation of **His lovingkindness**. The night imposes the darkness and we anticipate **His faithfulness**.

This is not the mere pattern of outward acknowledgement required of us but a full-blooded, total celebration, employing our whole capacity to praise Him. It is to be 'an instrument of **ten** strings', v. 3. We are glad, and triumph on account of what He has been to us in the day, v. 4.

We cannot underestimate the preciousness of this continual stream of God-centred rejoicing to the heart of our God. From the larger proportion of men He has no such anthem. They are as the animals, unreceptive and unresponsive, v. 6. They flourish only to perish and be scattered. Ultimately they will be the objects of His just wrath, vv. 7-9.

How different are His purposes and His portion in us, His people—in you as His child. He has given us to bring forth **fruit** even to our last day on earth. We are now linked with a God who has made it possible for us to enjoy victory, stability, sanctity and full fruitfulness throughout the whole of our lives.

Saint of God, have you **lost** the sense of joy and purpose that produces thanksgiving in your life? Then seek an anointing with 'fresh oil' (increase of strength),v. 10, and the exalting of your horn. You are here in order to show that the Lord is upright. He is your Rock and there is no unrighteousness in Him, v. 15.

June 3rd
Psalm 102. 1-13

A PRAYER OF THE AFFLICTED WHEN HE IS OVERWHELMED

This is a soul searching psalm. There will be few who can honestly say they have never been in this place. It is the place of **affliction**. If this has not been so with you then probably you have never had meaningful dealings with God. It is an essential learning ground for all His true sons, Heb. 12. 5-10.

Thank God for the relief that the opportunity of speaking with Him procures for the weary, forlorn saint. A **prayer**, becomes a **cry** and a **calling** to God. There is a growing desperation to have the His **ear** to hear, His **face** to see and an assurance that **He** will bend down to listen, vv. 1-2. This is **real**, tangible converse with God. Commence today with a renewed determination to make your prayer life the very centre of your spiritual experience, see 1 Thess. 3. 7-10.

These deep soul afflictions are learning phases through which we pass as the Lord deals with us. The areas of pressure and the associated effects and feelings are well described in verses 3-11. Another has aptly sectioned it as: 'Distressed in body', vv. 3-5; 'Desolate in soul', vv. 6-7; 'Derided by men', v. 8; and 'Disciplined by God', vv. 9-11 [A G CLARKE].

There can be dramatic physical manifestations during such deep exercises. This is not the pharisaical hypocrisy of those who seek the attentions of men, but a very real manifestation in one's physical being. Bones that burn, lack of appetite and drawn features declare the inner heart-searchings of soul, vv. 3-5. There can be a sense of isolation, and of rejection by others on account of the affliction.

Others can cause immense distress at times like this, some on account of their inability to truly sympathize, others out of a vindictive spirit to emphasize your calamity to satisfy their own ends, v. 8.

But, may you know this, child of God; His hand will only be upon you as long as He wills it to be. Let Him have His way, and believe. He hasn't changed, v. 12. He will not forsake you now and the time of His **favour**, that set time, may well dawn **today,** v. 13. Trust Him, 'for he careth for you', 1 Pet. 5. 7.

171

BUT THERE IS FORGIVENESS WITH THEE

Another prayer psalm which comes from heart-rending exercise before God. What **depths** are there now for the psalmist? They are experiences with which we are familiar. There is a sense of overwhelming woe and a fresh realization of impending disaster on account of '**iniquities**', v. 3. We are dealing with 'sins'. This matter cannot be sidestepped. It is basic to our spiritual health and to face the issue is of the deepest importance. It calls for acute agonizing before God.

Rejoice! Our God is all He claims to be. He takes full account of iniquities and yet with Him is found the **forgiveness** that we need, vv. 3, 4.

This forgiveness, which is His alone, enables the guilty to be justly cleared of all charges. It enables those who have sinned to possess and maintain a righteous acceptance with Him, Rom. 3. 21-26.

Who should stand were it not so?, v. 3. Thank God for Jesus Christ the righteous, 1 John 2. 1, 2. For this we will **fear** Him. Sin is never an idle or passing matter. We need to cultivate a holy hatred of it and a godly fear of Him with whom there is forgiveness, v. 4.

Thus we now have **hope** through **faith**. We **wait** for the Lord and **hope** for His word, vv. 5, 6. This **alone** is our rest in regard to these depths out of which we cry. It is the answer of our God, that which He has promised to all who believe.

Who are 'the morning watchers'?, v. 6. Perhaps those helplessly hanging to the storm-wrecked ship and longing for the morning light which may herald their deliverance. In their longing these could not long more intensely than we for the Lord. The reason? Well, His morning will be one 'without clouds … clear shining after rain', 2 Sam. 23. 4. His is a dawning this world has never yet seen, but when it comes it will manifest His mercy and plenteous redemption, v. 7. There is a restored Israel, v. 8, and a purged earth and a universe without sin. (No more depths to cry out of!) Saint of God, keep short accounts regarding sin and hope for the **morning of His Coming**.

June 5th
Psalm 142. 3

WHEN MY SPIRIT WAS OVERWHELMED ... THEN THOU KNEWEST MY PATH

The preface to this psalm makes us aware that it has our education at heart—'*maschil*' is teaching, instruction. It relates to one of David's cave experiences and reflects his years on the run from Saul. He identifies with those who are called upon to suffer unjustly for faithfulness to the will of God. It is part of the afflictions given to those who have purchased the 'true gold' and 'the eyesalve' that enables you to see, Rev. 3. 18. Surrounded and hounded by those who will not walk with you and prefer not to know you, it's then you find your **true refuge** and **portion** in the 'land of the living', vv. 4, 5.

The outworking of this situation causes us to seek our God. We will 'cry', we will 'make supplication', 'pour out our complaint' and show Him our trouble, vv. 1-2. It's not that He is unaware of the details. This necessary agony relieves our souls and enables us to 'walk through it' with Him. It will reveal much to us of the situation we don't understand and will confirm our certainty of the fact that the Lord is in control. Note the 'when' and 'then' of verse 3.

'No man would know me.' We engage in this reliance upon men until we are convinced about their inability to meet our need. No one would stand on the psalmist's right hand as an advocate. 'Refuge failed me'—men are not sufficient to cover us. 'No man cared for my soul'— men can be totally callous, v. 4.

Only when we have come to the end of appealing to men do we discover that our true **refuge** and **portion** is the Lord. He may have to bring us very low in order to convince us of this.

Then we can seek deliverance from the oppressor and liberty from the prison of these circumstances, vv. 6, 7. Only a 'Christ-centred' believer is a truly 'liberated' believer. Don't allow yourself to be in bondage to men. Seek the liberty of those who only seek the will of God and His sufficiency to fulfil it.

You will find there are others who have done the same and they will show you fellowship, sharing with you the matchless bounty of God's provision for 'the righteous', v. 7.

I WILL BLESS THY NAME

This psalm fittingly concludes the Psalter. The rest of the psalms are a supplement to the book. It is fitting because its author is David, 'the sweet psalmist of Israel', 2 Sam. 23. 1, and because it is 'a Witness in Praise'. Thus it represents a fitting consummation to all David's utterances.

'Prayer' centres on our needs, 'thanksgiving' on our blessings, 'worship' on our God (His Person and attributes), but **praise** is to 'speak well of', to tell out the excellent qualities of our God. The Blesser is greater than the blessings He bestows. He is more precious than His gifts, and thanksgiving is the overflowing of our love to Him.

Seven times David declares his intention to praise God. By the end of this reverberating anthem of exaltation he is saying, 'let **all** flesh bless his holy name'. He anticipates a day when there will be, willingly or unwillingly, universal acknowledgement of God's worthiness to be praised. What a privilege to commence and be part of that anthem now.

How do we do that? The psalm provides the answer. We 'extol'—(lift up, exalt) Him, 'bless' Him (pour out our joyous thanks). We 'speak' of His honour, majesty, wondrous works, might and terrible acts, v. 5. We 'declare', 'utter' and 'sing' of His greatness, goodness and righteousness, v. 6. We 'speak' and 'talk' and 'make known' His glory, power and mighty kingdom, vv. 11-13. How can we ever be silent before Him?

No wonder David says so often in this psalm what 'the Lord is ...' He is 'greatly to be praised', v. 3, 'gracious, and full of compassion', v. 8, 'good to all', v. 9. He 'upholdeth all who fall', v. 14. He is 'righteous in all His ways', v. 17, 'nigh unto all them that call upon him', v. 18. He 'preserveth all them that love him', v. 20. He will always act according to His unchangeable character. May we each get to know Him better today.

Praise will dominate a future eternity, the 'for ever and ever', but from now onwards, in tune, let 'my mouth ... speak the praise of the Lord', v. 21.

June 7th
Proverbs 3. 1-12

TRUST IN THE LORD ... ACKNOWLEDGE HIM

Today we can take the opportunity for the truth of these verses to grasp hold of our lives and begin to make them effective for God. They form the word from a father to his son and were intended to direct him into the very best that life could offer him, vv. 2, 4. Perhaps Solomon did not wish his son to make his mistakes.

Our Father fully intends for us to live satisfied and fulfilled lives. Here He relates for us the simple principles that produce it and asks us to 'forget not my law', v. 1.

Setting aside the material blessings that are mentioned, let us apply the outcomes to our own spiritual life. Do we desire to be knowingly in the will of God and in the good of understanding the path He sets for our feet?, v. 6. Do we want to be spiritually fit and robust?, v. 8. John says of the young men, 'Ye are strong, and the word of God abideth in you, and ye have overcome the wicked one', 1 John 2. 14. Would we be pleased to see our dry, parched, fruitlessness 'harvest' pressed down and overflowing?, v. 10. Would we be in the constant enjoyment of our Father's love and sense the pleasure and joy He receives from us day by day?, v. 12. If so, then here are the requirements.

Firstly, tell the Lord you want to fully **trust** Him and totally acknowledge Him in every aspect of your life. Tell Him you are casting aside your own understandings and the self-will that insists on having your own way. He must guide from now on, vv. 5-7. DO IT NOW.

Secondly, confess known sin and persistent ways of wickedness you have pursued in your life. Ask Him for help to develop a godly fear of evil out of awe of Him, v. 7. DO IT NOW.

Thirdly, give Him all you are and have. Let it all go. Yield it to Him for His use and service. You are **not** losing anything; just giving back that which is His already, v. 9. DO IT NOW.

Fourthly, yield to His discipline. Do not 'kick against the goads'—He knows what He's doing. The end will be well worth the journey, v. 11. Thank Him now for this crossroads in your life and ask for His grace to keep you on the right road.

June 8th

Proverbs 15. 1-9

TO PRAY IS TO PLEASE GOD

The Book of Proverbs seems to say so many things in a short compass. This is because it's written in unit proverbs. These are two line sayings, making distinct and complete sense on their own. However, the proverbs are in clusters which have a common theme. So what is the theme here?

Largely, it is to do with the commonest of human activities —**talking**. The author links what we **say** with what we **do** and shows how closely these are related to what we **are**. How revealing.

There are two distinct categories of people that the proverbs mention. 'The righteous'—those in a right relationship with God and actively in touch with Him. Contrasted with them are 'the wicked'—those who have no relationship with God and who proceed in life at the dictates only of their blind and evil hearts. The righteous are 'the wise', 'prudent' and 'upright', whereas the wicked are 'fools' and 'foolish'.

The divine eye monitors all the activities of each, v. 3, and responds to men according to their ways, v. 9. What does His eye see as He views you today? What is His response to your words and ways at this moment? Sadly, we can have a place amongst 'the righteous' but in our words and ways manifest the characteristics of 'the wicked'.

Let's seek to please Him today and start by cultivating the 'tongue of the righteous': a soft answer, instead of a bitter one, v. 1, using knowledge instead of making empty remarks, v. 2, providing words that 'heal', 'bind up' and 'refresh' rather than 'sting' and 'cut', v. 4. Try using your lips to 'encourage'. 'strengthen', 'aid' and 'edify', instead of holding back and saying nothing. Why not lift the telephone or take up pen and encourage someone today with 'good' words, v. 7.

Life can be so rewarding if lived as the righteous. Listen to His word, v. 5, even if it hurts. Follow the right way even if it's costly, v. 9. Accumulate in your home a treasure trove for God, v. 6. Talk to the Lord TODAY—give yourself to conversation with Him. **Your prayer**, however unworthy it might seem to you, is **His delight**, v. 8. What encouragement to 'give ourselves' to prayer!

June 9th

Proverbs 15. 23-33

HE HEARETH THE PRAYER OF THE RIGHTEOUS

We have another cluster of proverbs here that develops for us the theme of 'Words and Ways'. There is no getting away from it that these two are firmly linked together and it is a striking thought that even before God would say of His Son, 'Hear ye Him', He said, 'in whom I am well pleased'. Ways come before words. Whatever we say must draw its authority from what we are doing day by day.

We can all find things to complain about. There is no end to matters that upset us or cause us anger and to become despondent. How sad it must be if we allow our words to be constantly taken up with these things when there is so much of a positive and encouraging nature to be talking about as well.

In these verses the Lord will challenge us to change our topics of conversation so that we can reverse our own melancholy and raise the spirits of others.

Try the 'apt' or 'touchingly sensitive' answer and the 'word spoken at the right moment' as you respond to either saints or sinners today, v. 23. It will be a source of inner joy to you and a welcome comfort to those who hear it. A home or an assembly that has those within it who give themselves to provide 'a good report' rather than a negative one will provide those around with a spirit of well-being, v. 30.

The earnest soul will already be asking, 'Yes, but how do I do it?'. The answers are provided. It is the words of the **pure** that are pleasant words, v. 26, a clean heart and mind, emanating from a soul that lives in the sanctuary. Also, you will need to learn that cheap and quickly spoken words are rarely valuable. So, therefore, cultivate the heart that 'studieth'—this is to measure and weigh words, before offering them for public consumption, v. 28.

There is the need to be a good listener before you can have this ministry of 'healthful' words. Listening takes in those things that lead to life and understanding, vv. 31, 32. To have learnt to **fear** the Lord and to get down before you get up, v. 33, are the keys to this high service. Make it a matter of prayer **today**. Remember He's listening out for you, v. 29.

June 10th

Proverbs 28. 1-9

OBEDIENCE HAS ALWAYS BEEN THE KEY TO BLESSING

The proverbs before us today emphasize the need for behaviour to be directed by well defined laws that will govern the way we live as individuals and as a society.

The writer has in mind the laws made by rulers, and the responses of those that are ruled. It is no vain thing to respond to the many New Testament exhortations to pray for rulers and to be 'model' citizens in our society. These things please God and advance our witness, 1 Tim. 2. 1-3; 1 Pet. 2. 13-17.

There are no end to the problems that arise when wicked or wrongly motivated men come to rule. The proverbs here provide thought-provoking testimony to what is good and acceptable in this sphere, and what follows when there is unjust oppression or the rule of law cast aside. Pray for rulers and the ruled today. Make it a sacred trust to do so constantly.

There are two things identified here that men often aspire to—'power' and 'riches'. We need to be on our guard that whether we have them or not, we respond with uprightness of heart to both. A great deal can issue from the abuse of power or riches, vv. 2-6.

The pathway into which these proverbs direct us is one of a right relationship with God and a responsible life lived in the light of the laws that govern our society. This will lead to a lion-like boldness and a willingness to contend for what is right, vv. 1, 4. Also, it leads to 'understanding', v. 5, and a display of wisdom, v. 7, that will mark us out as those that 'believe in God', Titus 3. 1-2, 8.

Scripture leads us to expect a decline in law abiding and in moral behaviour as we move towards the last days and the coming of Christ, 2 Tim. 3. 1-9.

On account of this we must be on guard not to allow our lives to deteriorate in these areas. Any form of practice that is unlawful cannot be pursued by the Christian—it is a betrayal of his Christianity and is bound to affect his prayer life. You cannot approach the holiest of thrones if you are prepared to be unholy in your lifestyle, v. 9. Think about it today.

TO COVER UP OR CONFESS? THAT IS THE QUESTION

God would have us to understand more fully just what it is that causes us to prefer a 'cover up' to a 'clean up'. There are paths in the verses that we need to be warned about.

Beware of leading others down the way we are going in order to ease our own doubts or concerns about our progress. A crowd contributes to the blurred appropriateness of a thing and company halves the guilt, v. 10, see John 21. 2-3.

Again, we can be overconfident in our own knowledge or understanding so as to dismiss with scorn any challenge to the rightness of what we are doing. We don't like to feel that we could be wrong and so we allow conceit to cover up for us, v. 11.

Also, we can conceal and hide so as to avoid the discovery of some personal sin, our secret transgression. We can accommodate these things if we are determined to do so, v. 13.

We might possess a hardened heart—one that has been dulled and made insensitive by a continued process of refusing to face up to things. We may adopt a deliberate policy of ignoring that which we would cover. Remember, it doesn't ever go away, and can only cause continued damage wherever it is. It can even dig a 'pit' of mischief for us, v. 14.

So what are we to do? Clearly we need to have dealings in the open with God about these matters. Life will really begin to develop when we break the shackles and find the mercy our God longs to bring to us, v. 13.

The word is for us to **confess** and **forsake** these 'hidden things of darkness'. Bring them under the divine searchlight to be revealed for what they are, and then put them utterly out of our lives.

John's first epistle makes plain the process, 1 John 1. 9. **Confess** is to declare openly the facts as they are; to admit to the offence as God declares it to be an offence. This results in a deep inner conviction of sin. It is then that we find the **blood** that cleanses, an **Advocate** who will stand for us and the **mercy** that will heal and restore. Take advantage of it now if you need to.

CAUTIONARY COMMENTS REGARDING PRAYER
IN THE HOUSE OF GOD

In the fulfilment of his duties, the 'preacher' or 'caller of assemblies' requires that we listen attentively to his words and their wisdom. However, it must be understood that he always speaks as a man who is viewing things from 'under the sun'. That is from the viewpoint of a worldly wise man. He sets about his self-imposed task 'to seek and search out by wisdom concerning all things that are done under heaven', 1. 13, in a variety of ways. Our verses today are part of his response to what he saw in his many, varied, fact-collecting expeditions, 4. 1.

His observations cover many aspects of human life and condition. Here he ventures into the realms of piety and human aspirations after God. His exhortations are very wise and will be confirmed by our own experiences of God's sanctuary. If you are not given to moving in the presence of God then pay heed to 'the preacher'. His warnings are not vain.

He exhorts to a right preparation. **Concentrate**, give your mind to what you are doing. See Jacob's exercise in Genesis 35. 1-4 if you want to know what concern it caused him. **Be ready to hear**—it is sometimes more important to listen to the Lord than to speak to Him. It is preferable to be silent than to blurt out that which is unmeaningful, an offending offering, that which dishonours God, v. 1.

When it comes to saying anything, **don't be 'rash',** (that is 'pushed by the tongue') v. 2, nor 'hasty' (that is just 'led by your heart'). Make a wise choice of your words sparingly and avoid the voice of the fool who speaks much and says nothing, v. 3.

The rest has to do with **vows**, vv. 4-7. These are solemn and binding declarations of intent. Remember how Jephthah vowed, the consequences of which perhaps he did not consider at the time, Judg. 11. 30-31. Jonah ran away from his vows only to be divinely disciplined to recognize his commitment to them, Jonah 2. 9. Today's reading would aid us to measure and weigh our words so that when we do speak we fully understand the implications, v. 7.

June 13th

Isaiah 1. 1-20

ARE WE HIDING?

This is a very dramatic opening to the prophecy. God has called in witnesses. The moment He has postponed for centuries, but can delay no longer, has come. The nation must be exposed to the 'heavens' and the 'earth', that these may testify to His words of condemnation, vv. 1, 2. The details that follow are a painful revelation of privilege despised and potential unfulfilled. Be it in sonship or servanthood, they had acted as rebels and strangers, turning away from Him at every point, vv. 3-4.

Unresponsive to His disciplines, they were now like a body ravaged by disease, a building burned and desolate, vv. 5, 6. Their continued existence was only on account of divine sovereignty and nothing else, vv. 7-9.

To the leaders of the people He identifies the religious charade of superficial service to Him with which they had tried to cover up their departure. Every act of theirs rose up as a vile stench. The lifting up of their hands and many prayers were of no efficacy with God, 'I will not hear: your hands are full of blood', v. 15.

How do such statements find you and me today? Have not the years reduced our witness to a shell, a facade for the real thing? Are we not also guilty of denial and departure? Have we not also set our ways so that a vain tradition has substituted a spiritual reality? Are we yet prepared to brazen our way out of the present lack of sincerity and power with a continuing sham performance that will only end in the removal of the lampstand? Nothing is hid from Him.

What then are we to do? The answers come thick and fast. Deal with sin by open confession. Turn from the evil. Change our ways, vv. 16-17. Respond to need with compassion and seek the divine wisdom to act justly in dealing with wrongs. Support the weak and vulnerable, v. 17. It is in the environment of prayer that we can talk the matter through with God. He is not remote from our true pleadings and with Him alone lie the ultimate remedies, v. 18. Let's make up our minds to do the right thing. Let's face the issues and choose His way, rejecting all that is spurious, however attractively it might be presented. Our God is real, and our faith in Him must be real, as in real prayer we seek from Him real blessing.

June 14th

Isaiah 6. 1-10

A FRESH VISION OF THE LORD

Prayerful communion with God brings fresh vision of the Lord. Each vision will give us the aspects of the divine that most fit our circumstance and need. So it is when Isaiah 'sees the Lord', v. 1.

The vision conveys certain attributes of God that His servant will need to be in the good of to fulfil his ministry. There's His absolute **sovereignty**—He is the *'Adonai'* seated upon the exalted throne—in Him alone is vested all power. He is **purity** and **perfection**—His train which is light, Ps. 104, fills the sanctuary in harmony with the glory of His presence, v. 1. He is unapproachable **holiness**, for seraphim with fiery vigilance guard His Person, v. 2.

The seraphim declare one to another recognition of His holiness and give testimony to His glory throughout the earth. There will be a day when men will know the Lord and His glory will fill the earth to universal recognition, Hab. 2. 14.

There are immediate results from this vision. The first is 'monumental'; foundations are shaken, established orders are disturbed and men can do nothing but tremble, v. 4. The second is 'environmental', the sanctuary is filled with smoke as the sweet smelling offering of appreciation issues from the altar of incense. The third is 'personal', the prophet agonizes at the exposure of his condition and that of the people, v. 5.

The fact is that he has been a spectator of something that will affect the rest of his life. He will be turned upside down, remotivated and redirected. He has '**seen** the King, the Lord of hosts', v. 5. When did **we** last see Him? We need a fresh vision every day.

The prophet's responses follow swiftly and we see the Lord dealing with him in order to fit him for service to the nation. He is convicted and this leads to confession, v. 5. Application of the effect of the sacrifice removes and expiates his defilement.

Then he is open to hear what the Lord is saying. He will respond submissively and unhindered to fulfil the divine will. Can we today use Isaiah's response as our response to God?

June 15th

Isaiah 7. 1-16

DO WE TRUST HIM ENOUGH?

We all react differently under pressure. Often, in trying in many ways to prevent ourselves going under, we resort to those who dishonour the Lord and fail to recognize His place in the scheme of things. Beware of such a course of action!

Pekah, king of Israel, aligns himself with Rezin, king of Syria, and united they represent a fearful threat to Judah. Understandably, the smaller and weaker nation is moved to fear the worst, vv. 1, 2.

Immediately the Lord moves to comfort His people. Firstly, Isaiah is to take his son with him. The **presence** of Shear-jashub is a token that reminds Ahaz, king of Judah, that there is a divine **purpose** for them that cannot be changed. His name means 'a remnant shall return', v. 3.

There follows a clear **explanation** of the whole situation in considerable detail. Understanding the elements of any problem is always part of the Lord's way of enabling us to tackle it, vv. 4-6.

He will then **promise** that this alliance and its plans will not succeed, v. 7. Divine promises are there to stimulate **faith**. Our God is not obliged to make them. They are part of His way of dealing with us.

Isaiah calls upon Ahaz to believe, and makes it the requirement for his future security. 'If ye will not believe ...', v. 9. The rejection of mere reasoning allows the Lord to turn obstacles into manifestations of His glory.

Ahaz is then invited to ask a sign, v. 10. This is exceedingly gracious on God's part. It encourages us to appreciate **how much He values our faith**. For us this is asking for gracious confirmations from Him in response to our practical steps of faith and obedience, Phil. 2. 12, 13.

Ahaz refuses and so, under the pretext of piety, hides the rebellion of his self-will and unbelief, v. 12. Despite rejecting the offered blessing, it is provided by the unsolicited promise of mercy to the house of David, vv. 13-16. The lesson is that even our unbelief cannot deny God the fulfilment of His purposes of grace. Hallelujah!

June 16th

Isaiah 12. 1-6

THOU COMFORTEST ME

'In that day', v. 1, refers to the day of the millennial reign of Christ when Israel will once again be the cockpit of the nations through whom divine government will be administered. This prayer and call to praise will be uttered by those left of the nation, the faithful remnant who survive the Great Tribulation and who enter the millennial period.

Chapter 11 describes the conditions of that day with the regathering of God's ancient people and their enemies subdued. 'The earth shall be full of the knowledge of the Lord, as the waters cover the sea', v. 9.

vv. 1-3: Call to praise. In their prayer they praise the 'Lord' using the divine title 'Jehovah', v. 1; the title emphasizes His covenant faithfulness. In verse 2 the title used is 'Jah Jehovah', 'Jah' being a title linked with Israel's victory over her enemies, Exod. 15. 2; Ps. 118. 14. The One who had administered discipline is now the One who comforts, v. 1, delivers, removes fear, gives strength, gives a song, v. 2, and gives joy and spiritual refreshing, v. 3.

Those who have trusted Christ in this present day can experience the God who is ever faithful, One who will never let us down; though at times He has need to discipline His children, the issue will be joy and praise.

vv. 4-6: Call to publish His name. In the day of Christ's exaltation the call is to praise, calling upon His name, which involves conformity with His character and declaring His mighty deeds and exaltation, v. 4. The righteous administration of Christ will be acknowledged by all on the earth in that day, v. 5.

The name 'Zion', v. 6, emphasizes grace triumphing over judgement, e.g. 'Yet have I set my king upon my holy hill of Zion', Ps. 2. 6. In the context of the rejection of Christ and the intransigent opposition of the ungodly nations at the first advent, God's sovereign purpose will yet be fulfilled.

So it is with us—believers of the present day—that God in pure grace has overflowed to those who deserved nothing but judgement, and yet who have been brought into the fullness of God's salvation through His beloved Son.

June 17th
Isaiah 25. 1-12
THOU ART MY GOD; I WILL EXALT THEE

This is a prayer of godly Israelites who have experienced God's deliverance. The destruction of Babylon is in view in verse 2 with the consequent awe of other nations as they see the power of God in judgement, v. 3. In verses 1-5 there is a direct address to Jehovah, whereas in verses 6-8 things are said about Jehovah, and finally verses 9-12 speak of Jehovah's people and their attitude to Him.

vv. 1-5: Divine deliverance. They rejoice in the One who is ever faithful and true in His purposes, v. 1. Babylon was so magnificent that the city as a whole was viewed as a palace. The phrase 'it shall never be built' refers to a day yet future after her final destruction during the Great Tribulation, v. 2. Even in the time of her fierce persecution, described graphically as 'the noise of strangers', 'heat in a dry place', 'the blast of the terrible ones', and 'a storm', the Lord delivered the poor, v. 4-5. The 'branch' (lit. 'song') of their enemies is no longer one of victory but defeat, v. 5.

vv. 6-8: Divine protection. 'This mountain' refers again to Zion, and probably refers to a great inaugural feast at the beginning of the Millennium. There will be the enjoyment of well-flavoured wine, spiritually that which brings joy to God and man, Ps. 104. 15; Matt. 26. 29, and fat which speaks of full satisfaction. The veil of verse 7 probably refers to the blindness both of the nation of Israel and the nations right up to the point of Christ's return in glory, 2 Cor. 3. 15. Death is going to be 'swallowed up' (lit. 'devoured') at the first resurrection, referring to the Old Testament and Tribulation saints. (The saints of the present church age will be raptured prior to the first resurrection which will take place after the Great Tribulation, Rev. 20. 6.) Everything that resulted in sorrow will be removed, v. 8.

vv. 9-12: Divine judgement. Here we have a confession of the saved of the nation concerning Jehovah, the One for whom they have waited for centuries up to and including the Great Tribulation period. 'Lo, this is our God', cf. John 20. 6. 'He hath saved us' is the correct reading here, v. 9. In blessing His hand rests on Zion. With the sweep of His hand, as it were, Jehovah will destroy all those characterized by pride.

June 18th

Isaiah 26. 1-18

THOU WILT KEEP HIM IN PERFECT PEACE

After the second advent of Christ in glory there will be rejoicing in Israel. Their confidence will be in Jehovah who will restore all things according to His righteous values. This song is sung in the land of Judah, v. 1. In chapter 25 Babylon is destroyed, but here the city of Zion is surrounded by divinely appointed 'walls', each individual experiencing perfect peace, v. 3.

vv. 1-6: Perfect peace. No one will be able to touch the nation of Israel in that day. There will be no need for physical walls!, v. 1. Only the righteous will be allowed to enter the city, a reminder of the heavenly Jerusalem, Rev. 21. 27. It is good to have the 'mind stayed' (lit. 'leaning upon') Jehovah. Nothing can shake this confidence! The title 'Jah Jehovah' is again used here, emphasizing His absolute supremacy and stability. Israel in that day will know complete victory over her enemies, vv. 5, 6. God will take those who were insignificant and give them victory, v. 6.

vv. 7-8: Pathway of the just. In patience His people wait for Jehovah to manifest His power and vindicate His character, v. 8. How they longed for that day when He would be manifested and rule in perfect righteousness, v. 9. So today we look forward to the time when Christ will be manifested in glory. What a privilege is ours in this present day to be associated with Him, and be occupied in His service in this time of His rejection.

vv. 9-18: Pre-eminence of Israel over the nations. There is yet a glorious future for Israel. 'And so all Israel shall be saved: as it is written, There shall come out of Sion the Deliverer', Rom. 11. 26. However, unbelieving Jews will have no part in the redemption of the nation, v. 10. At the end of it all they will acknowledge that all their works were of God and nothing of themselves. This is true of each believer today, Phil. 2. 13. The false gods in whom the nations trusted will all be destroyed, v. 14. The terrible anguish of the time of Jacob's trouble is referred to in verses 16-18. They could not deliver themselves, v. 18; however, God's answer to this prayer follows. There will be a national resurrection in that day of His glory and power. Even those not regathered to the land who are faithful and believing will be included. 'Then he said unto me, Son of man, these bones are *the whole house of Israel*', Ezek. 37. 11.

Isaiah 29. 13-16

THE PRAYERFUL ATTITUDE

Chapter 29, verses 1-14 is a woe pronounced upon the formalists in Israel. In verses 15-24 a further woe is pronounced against those who try to deceive God. The word 'woe' reminds us that judgement is God's strange work, for it is uttered by Him with deep compassion, similar to the woe pronounced with deep sadness upon Jerusalem by the Lord Jesus, 'O Jerusalem, Jerusalem, which killest the prophets, and stonest them that are sent unto thee; how often would I have gathered thy children together, as a hen doth gather her brood under her wings, and ye would not'!

Ariel (lit. 'lion') is the name used by God for Jerusalem. His desire is not to destroy but to remove the chaff, v. 5.

Verse 13 tells how the traditions of men were taking precedence over the fear of God. Israel spoke things which seemed to honour God but their actions did not back up what they said. God was able to look into the heart and, as always, could see their true spiritual condition. 'Neither is there any creature that is not manifest in his sight: but all things are naked and opened unto the eyes of him with whom we have to do', Heb. 4. 13. Sadly their hearts had become cold, and their prayers did not reach the ears of God, but were like those of the Pharisee who prayed 'to himself' and not to God, Luke 18. 11. The Lord condemned the Pharisees for their hypocrisy, Matt. 23. 27.

Verse 14 speaks of a marvellous work of God. Even though this should be wrought, they will not be wise enough to receive it, for God steps in judicially to blind them. This is exactly what happened when Christ came.

Verse 15 in its local setting probably refers to a counsel of the nobles of Israel seeking help from Egypt. It is never right to seek help from the world in furthering the cause of God's kingdom.

In verse 16 they acted as if the One who had made the heart was unable to read it! 'The heart is deceitful above all things, and desperately wicked: who can know it? I the Lord search the heart, I try the reins, even to give every man according to his ways, and according to the fruit of his doings', Jer. 17. 9, 10.

In prayer, may the words that we speak be the true sentiments of our hearts!

June 20th

Isaiah 33. 2-6

A PRAYER OF DEEP ANGUISH

Here is a request from the remnant of Israel, uttered initially when Sennacherib leader of the Assyrian armies stood outside the walls of Jerusalem, 2 Kings 18. Already God has promised retribution on the enemy, who had attacked without provocation and dealt treacherously, v. 1. Hezekiah had promised tribute but Sennacherib broke the covenant, v. 8. This is the local or primary setting of the prayer uttered in verses 2-6. However, these events foreshadow the time of the end when again the king of the north will break the covenant and come down to destroy the land, 'like a whirlwind, with chariots, and with horsemen, and with many ships; and he shall enter into the countries, and shall overflow and pass over. He shall enter also into the glorious land', Dan. 11. 40, 41.

v. 2: The pleading voice. At a time of extremity, the remnant of the nation cry out in deep anguish. The situation seemed impossible and yet the truth of Romans 8. 31 is appropriate, 'If God be for us, who can be against us?'. This is a timeless truth applicable to both their situation and that of believers today! The prophet identifies with the people and intercedes for them, 'be thou their arm'. The ministry of intercession is a high one and should be the constant occupation of every believer on behalf of those in need !

v. 3: The predominant voice. The noise of the tumult refers to the Lord Himself, i.e. 'at the lifting up of thyself'. Revelation 14. 2 and 19. 6 describe the voice of the Lord as the sound of thunder, or many waters, a sound not to be ignored.

v. 4: The prophetic voice. The prayer is to be answered as pronounced in verse 1. Israel will be used in the judgement and spoiling of Jehovah's enemies, 'Behold, it is come, and it is done, saith the Lord God; this is the day whereof I have spoken. And they that dwell in the cities of Israel shall go forth, and shall set on fire and burn the weapons, both the shields and the bucklers, the bows and the arrows, and the handstaves, and the spears, and they shall burn them with fire seven years', Ezek. 39. 8-9.

vv. 5-6: The prospective view. The Lord will reign in perfect righteousness. Israel restored will be marked by the fear of the Lord, described as 'their treasure' JND. Godly fear is the fear of grieving Him. This should mark us today and until He comes!

June 21st
Isaiah 45. 11-19

THE MYSTERY OF GOD'S WAYS

Cyrus, an idolatrous Gentile leader who did not know God, vv. 4, 5, is chosen to deliver Israel from the Babylonish yoke. He is promised victory over other nations and a bounty of treasures. This he achieves, and acknowledges that his victories had been gained only through the power of the God of Israel. He is consequently charged by God to issue the decree for Israel to rebuild the temple at Jerusalem, Ezra 1. 2. God is able to take up whoever He will, whether believer or unbeliever, in fulfilment of His sovereign purpose for His people. In verses 9-13, Jehovah justifies His deliverance through this means to His people Israel who had resentfully questioned His method! Who were they, indeed, to question the One who is the Sovereign Creator? Verse 14 looks on to the day when all the nations will have been subjected to Christ. Only then will everything be made clear to those who passed through the times of testing and trial.

Verse 15 tells of the God who hides. This prayer uttered by the prophet is one of praise at the way God is to deliver His people. His purposes and method of deliverance could not have been imagined by any man, for His ways are inscrutable. Romans 11. 33, 34 is a commentary on this passage, 'O the depth of the riches both of the wisdom and knowledge of God! how unsearchable are his judgments, and his ways past finding out! For who hath known the mind of the Lord? or who hath been his counsellor?'.

> God moves in a mysterious way
> His wonders to perform;
> He plants His footsteps on the sea,
> And rides upon the storm.

His ways are always best, though maybe for a season hidden from His saints. Many reminders of this are found in the gospel records where the disciples could not discern the Lord's mind. He was the One who would accomplish a far greater deliverance for His people than Cyrus, but it was by way of His sufferings at Calvary.

Many times we as believers face circumstances of difficulty that defy human explanation, but though His way is hidden, let our prayer be as the prophet's here, 'Verily thou art a God that hidest thyself, O God of Israel, the Saviour', v. 15.

189

June 22nd
Isaiah 50. 4-9

A PRAYER OF THE PERFECT SERVANT

In verses 1-3 it is Jehovah's indictment. He had never been unfaithful in His covenant relationship with Israel, either in
divorcing them because of their unfaithfulness or in selling them
to a creditor; on the contrary, their own sin was the reason for
their misery. Verses 4-9 contain the prayer of the perfect Servant,
the emphasis being on His complete submission to Jehovah
Adonai. The divine title Adonai means literally, 'My Lord and
Master'. In verses 10-11 there is the exhortation of the prophet.
Two classes of people are addressed, firstly the faithful remnant,
v. 10, and then the unbelieving part of the nation, v. 11.

Listening and Speaking. Here is one who began each day with
meditation on the word of God, v. 4. When Satan tempted Him in
the wilderness the Lord used three scriptures from Deuteronomy
6-8. He was forearmed with the word from God appropriate for
that day, as will be the experience of every follower of His, if the
day is begun in quiet meditation. His ear was ever attentive to
Jehovah's voice. Psalm 40. 6 echoes this, 'Sacrifice and offering
thou didst not desire; mine ears hast thou opened'. His tongue was
ever ready to reveal the divine counsels, His followers being given
a word of encouragement and His enemies silenced, 'And no man
was able to answer him a word, neither durst any man from that
day forth ask him any more questions', Matt. 22. 46.

Submission and Suffering. His service involved the giving of
Himself in every way, His back, cheeks and face all being involved
in the terrible mockery and suffering at His trial and on the cross,
v. 6. Men would do their worst but they could not cause Him to utter one word of anguish. However, when it came to the atoning
sufferings of the Lord, He utters the most profound cry of Scripture, 'My God, my God, why hast thou forsaken me?', Mark 15. 34.
The prophet later speaks of His face as being 'so marred more than
any man', Isa. 52. 14, and His form also, so that He becomes unrec-
ognizable as a man! What depths of love are here displayed.

Dedication and Triumph. In verses 7, 8, His prayer ends on a
note of absolute confidence. He was not delivered from death
but He was saved out of it, Heb. 5. 7. In mighty power He rose
from the dead, signalling absolute supremacy!

June 23rd

Isaiah 55. 6-9

A PRAYER FOR SALVATION

In verses 1-5 the promise to Israel is that the Davidic covenant will be everlastingly established, while in verses 6-13 salvation is offered to Israel and her millennial joy is foretold.

In verse 1 the thirsty are addressed. They are exhorted to come and partake of the provision of God without self effort, though there is in the use of the word 'buy' an indication that some cost on their part is involved. It would be necessary to remove everything from life that would prevent them from putting the Lord first. All this world offers is empty and cannot satisfy; only the salvation available by God's provision will fill the deep wellsprings of man's innermost being, v. 2.

Counsel for the Seeker, v. 6. The prophet's exhortation is to seek the Lord. If He is to be found then it will involve seeking with the whole heart, cf. Deut. 4. 29. If His voice is ignored then it may be that all opportunity to find Him will pass. In the days of Noah this was true, for 'the Lord said, My spirit shall not always strive with man, for that he also is flesh: yet his days shall be an hundred and twenty years', Gen. 6. 3.

Comfort for the Supplicant, v. 7. The wicked man is addressed, speaking of the restlessness of a man's fallen nature which issues forth in lawlessness. The unrighteous man has evil thoughts which govern him and spring from the base desires of his sinful nature. Evil thoughts will need to be left behind. 'Bringing into captivity every thought to the obedience of Christ', 2 Cor. 10. 5. This is essential for the enjoyment of the salvation of God and His fellowship, and only possible in the life of a believer by the power of the Spirit of God.

God will have mercy upon those who come in sincerity. Mercy is defined positively as 'the pitying compassion of the Lord', rather than negatively as 'withholding judgement'. His abundant pardon is available for the very worst of sinners.

Confirmation of Supremacy, vv. 8-9. God's plan of salvation could never have been conceived by man whose thoughts and ways are infinitely lower than those of the Godhead. When we cried to God for salvation, He responded!

June 24th
Isaiah 56. 1-12
MY HOUSE A HOUSE OF PRAYER

Verses 1-8 speak of the terms of acceptance of the stranger and the eunuch, whereas verses 9-12 speak of the unfaithful leaders of Israel. Verse 1 refers to the physical deliverance of those who live faithful lives, this deliverance being accomplished at the second advent of the Lord Jesus. The conduct of the man who lays hold of this truth is governed by the hope of this salvation to come, v. 2! Every aspect of his life is affected by his view of that great day! The strangers, v. 3, or eunuchs, v. 4, who had become Jewish proselytes and who were obedient to God's commands, may believe that they will be in an inferior position in that day. They are assured, however, that this will not be the case, for they are to be given a place and name better than sons or daughters, v. 5.

v. 6: Acceptance. The 'strangers' of the Old Testament could not enter into the assembly, Deut. 23. 3, but there will be no such exclusion in the millennial day. The Lord notes their service, motivation of love for His name and taking hold of His covenant. Acceptance before Him is based on simple faith and trust in His revealed word, which works itself out in practical living. The Lord sees the secret motivations of the heart, Heb. 4. 13.

v. 7: The house of prayer. At Christ's first advent, sadly, there was great departure and the Lord Jesus rebuked the traders who had corrupted the temple with a quotation from this verse, Matt. 21. 13. The location of the house of prayer says the Lord, is 'my holy mountain'. This will be established according to Isaiah 2. 2 in the last days; i.e. the millennial reign. At that time all peoples will have access and will be able to bring offerings and prayers. The burnt offering contrasts with the other offerings in that it emphasizes Jehovah's appreciation and portion; the delight of the Father in His beloved Son. How beautiful that we can appreciate this aspect too, and dwell upon that perfect path of purest grace, which ever brought delight to the Father, and Jesus' offering up of Himself in perfect obedience to the Father's command.

We as believers today do not have to wait for millennial privileges for we can enter now the house of prayer, the very sanctuary of heaven itself, in Christ! 'Let us therefore come boldly unto the throne of grace ...', Heb. 4. 16.

June 25th

Isaiah 58. 1-14

YET THEY SEEK ME DAILY

In this passage Jehovah rebukes his people generally for their outward formality but promises blessing for individuals who are faithful to Him. It appears to be the time of captivity in Babylon, for there is no mention of sacrifices.

vv. 1-5: Approach. The prophet is requested to cry aloud, with full throat, a message of rebuke. Notice, however, the note of grace for, in spite of their transgression, Jehovah still addresses them as 'my people'. Though they are characterized by the fleshly nature of 'Jacob' their father, God speaks to them through the faithful prophet.

They sought Jehovah daily and professed to delight in His ways but the Lord could see the motivation of their hearts, and that their behaviour was mere outward formality. Their complaint was that the Lord did not take account of their spiritual exercises; however, even though they afflicted themselves and fasted, the Lord could see this was done only as a pretence of piety, v. 5.

vv. 6-14: Practice. Fasting should in the first instance be departure from evil, v. 6, then abstinence from food with a view to assisting in prayer. It was never intended to be an end in itself. However, at the same time as they practised these things, they were guilty of laying heavy burdens upon the oppressed and casting out those in genuine need, v. 7.

Profession of piety must be accompanied by a turning from all that is sinful in our practice, and godly living; only then will our prayers be answered. 'Then shalt thou call, and the Lord shall answer; thou shalt cry, and he shall say, Here I am', v. 9.

There is great reward in terms of light, health, righteousness, security, guidance, satisfaction, refreshment and glory to those who are faithful in these things, vv. 8, 10-14.

Above all, we shall find ourselves taken up with the Lord and transported above the circumstances of our lives down here. 'For God, who commanded the light to shine out of darkness, hath shined in our hearts, to give the light of the knowledge of the glory of God in the face of Jesus Christ', 2 Cor. 4. 6. What the Lord has spoken He will surely fulfil, v. 14.

June 26th
Isaiah 59. 1-2, 16-21
NEITHER HIS EAR HEAVY

The nation is in a desperate strait, not because of lack of ability on the part of Jehovah, but because of their own departure. He has already said through the prophet, 'Is my hand shortened at all, that it cannot redeem?', 50. 2. In verses 1-8 the cause of separation between God and His people is explained. In verses 9-15 there is a confession made by the godly remnant of the nation and in verses 16-21 the coming of the Redeemer is promised.

vv. 1-2: The hearing of Jehovah. The Lord does not say 'I cannot hear', but rather 'I will not hear', v. 2. This was because they had unconfessed sin in their lives. The truth of Psalm 66. 18 is applicable still, 'If I regard iniquity in my heart the Lord will not hear me'. The fact is that it was not Jehovah's ear that was heavy but theirs. In wilfulness they had rejected the word of the Lord and so He steps in judicially to 'make their ears heavy', Isa. 6. 10.

vv. 3-8: Their condition. They were guilty of serious sins including murder, v. 3, and perverted justice, vv. 4-5; those who sought to stamp this out were themselves bitten, v. 5. Their feet ran in the ways of evil, v. 7. No wonder the indictment of the Lord is that they should not know peace, v. 8.

vv. 9-15: A prayer of confession by the remnant. In contrast the godly remnant confess that which had been foretold by Moses had become true of the nation, v. 10; 'and thou shalt grope at noonday, as the blind gropeth in darkness, and thou shalt not prosper in thy ways: and thou shalt be only oppressed and spoiled evermore, and no man shall save thee', Deut. 28. 29. A bear roars when it is hungry, v. 11, exhibiting complete lack of satisfaction. Full confession is the only answer.

vv. 16-21: The Redeemer promised. When the Redeemer comes all injustices will be put right, v. 18. The mention of Zion, v. 20, in this context is significant as it is often linked with grace triumphing over judgement; cf. Ps. 2. 6. This truth is reiterated in Romans 11. 26, 'And so all Israel shall be saved: as it is written, There shall come out of Sion the Deliverer'.

The prayers of the godly are answered therefore, not according to their timing, but the Lord's.

Isaiah 62. 1-12

KEEP NOT SILENCE, AND GIVE HIM NO REST

The Spirit of Christ now speaks through the prophet, vv. 1-5. He cannot hold his peace and his continual intercession is that God will do what He has promised for Israel. In verses 6-9 there is a charge to the watchmen of Zion. The chapter ends with a command to clear any obstacles that might hinder the return of Israel to their land and blessings in that day of national redemption.

vv. 1-5: Provision for prayer. (The intercessor on high.) These verses remind us of the intercessory ministry of the Lord Jesus in this present day. He is engaged in ceaseless activity for His people, 'seeing he ever liveth to make intercession for them', Heb. 7. 25.

vv. 6-9: Persistence in prayer. (Charge to the watchmen.) These were set by the Lord and probably refer to those who remained faithful to Him. They are described as 'watchmen', reminding us of the solemn responsibility of every believer, cf. 1 Thess. 5. 6. The injunction was that, though they knew that the Lord's promises would surely come to pass, they were to continue praying and 'give him no rest till he establish', v. 7. 'And this is the confidence that we have in him, that, if we ask any thing according to his will, he heareth us', 1 John 5. 14, Where that which is prayed for is clearly according to His mind and will, as revealed in Scripture, it is to be prayed for without ceasing, v 7.

vv. 10-12: Product of prayer. (Prayer answered.) The local setting of verse 10 is that the captives of Israel would one day go forth through the gates of Babylon; however, it looks on to that time when those of the nation of Israel will go through the gates of their cities towards Jerusalem. The command to Gentiles in that day is 'Prepare ye the way of the people', v. 10. The Lord Himself will return and bring with Him His reward for those who have been faithful in their ministry of watching and prayer, v. 11.

As always, God answers the prayers of His people, for they will be called 'the holy people', 'a city not forsaken', v. 12. The national cleansing is so complete that the nation shall even be called by the name of the Lord. Then 'shall Judah be saved, and Jerusalem shall dwell safely: and this is the name wherewith she shall be called, The Lord our righteousness', Jer. 33. 16.

June 28th
Isaiah 63. 7-19

LOOK DOWN FROM HEAVEN

The opening verses of Isaiah 63 describe the returning Conqueror who, after carrying out the vengeance of God, will usher in the acceptable year of the Lord, cf. 61. 2. In verses 7-14 we hear the voice of the remnant of Israel as they remember past mercies and rejoice in present blessings. In verses 15-19 their plea is for God to show compassion on the ground of Israel's relationship with Him: 'Doubtless thou art our father', v. 16.

vv. 7-14: A prayer of thankfulness. It is always a good thing to give thanks to the Lord for His many blessings. His loving kindnesses are more than can be numbered, v. 7. God's expectation of His people is described in verse 8, and His care for them in verse 9. In all the circumstances they passed through He perfectly sympathized with them, 'For thus saith the Lord of hosts; After the glory hath he sent me unto the nations which spoiled you: for he that toucheth you toucheth the apple of his eye', Zech. 2. 8. This means that His care is comparable to the care for a most precious component of the eye, the pupil! This is true of each believer today! Such care is evident in spite of their unfaithfulness, vv. 10-14.

vv. 15-19: A plea for compassion. Their cry is one of intense anguish of heart, for the conditions on earth are far from those in heaven, and they long that conditions within the nation might improve. 'Look down from heaven, and behold from the habitation of thy holiness and of thy glory: where is thy zeal and thy strength, the sounding of thy bowels and of thy mercies toward me? are they restrained?', v. 15. So they plead with God on the basis of His deep yearnings for His people and His relationship to them. His name and character are immutable and so therefore His dealings with His people, v. 16. In verse 17 things are ascribed to God which really are only within His permissive will. 'O Lord, why hast thou made us to err from thy ways ...?'. He permits them to go after the tendencies of their hearts which He hardens judicially because of their folly.

This cry of the remnant as they bring before the Lord the sad state of the apostate nation should be the language of the godly saint today concerning the true condition of the church of Christ.

Isaiah 64. 1-7

O THAT THOU WOULDEST REND THE HEAVENS

In chapter 63 verse 15 the plea is that Jehovah should *look down* from heaven *in compassion,* but here the prayer of the remnant is quite different, that is, that the Lord should *come down* from heaven *in judgement.* The whole of chapter 64 is taken up with a prayer for God's intervention on behalf of His people, and judgement upon their enemies.

vv. 1-3: Prayer for the vindication of God and His people. Often in Scripture fire is used as a figure of God's righteous judgement, e.g. at the time of the second advent referred to by the apostle Paul, the Lord Jesus returns in 'flaming fire taking vengeance on them that know not God, and that obey not the gospel of our Lord Jesus Christ', 2 Thess. 1. 8. Here, every obstacle shall be removed, even the mountains, v. 1. In verse 3, 'when thou didst terrible things', probably refers to the judgement of the Red Sea, cf. Ps. 106. 22. When the people of Israel were in deep misery in Egypt, God came down, even though they did not look for Him; so how much more now, when those of the remnant are pleading on the nation's behalf!, v. 3.

vv. 4-7: Prayer of confession. Verse 4 is quoted in 1 Corinthians 2. 9, where 'him that waiteth for him' is rendered 'them that love him'. So waiting upon the Lord is synonymous with devotion for Him. Verse 5 refers to those who experience joy in working righteousness, no longer a duty, but a joy of heart to serve God. He has regard for those of the remnant in such a condition and comes to meet them. From verse 5 there is confession on the part of those praying. They own their uncleanness and look upon themselves as 'lepers' whom God has had to put away. Even those of the remnant who could be said by other men to be righteous have to confess that everything done is defiled in the sight of God. So the nation is like a tree in decline and scattered with the wind, v. 6.

All of this serves to remind believers today that apart from God's grace there is no justification before Him. Furthermore, if we accomplish anything in our service for Him, we will need to acknowledge this truth that, 'Every virtue we possess ... and every thought of holiness are His alone'.

June 30th

Isaiah 65. 17-25

BEFORE THEY CALL, I WILL ANSWER

In verses 1-7 of this chapter the Lord warns of judgement to come upon the apostates of the nation. Sadly, though God had made Himself available to them, there was no response on their part, v. 2. Verses 8-16 speak of the different treatments by God of the godly remnant and the apostate part of the nation. The passage for our consideration, verses 17-25, witnesses to the fact that the millennial day is but an earnest of the eternal state, v. 17.

vv. 17-23: God activates peace and prosperity. The creation of the new earth and new heavens will be so glorious as to remove even the memory of the former creation. The conditions of the new creation are finally described in Revelation 21. 1-8. These include there being no more sea, the tabernacle of God being with men (that is, He permanently dwells with them) and no more tears, sorrow, death, crying, pain, but an abundance of the water of life. No sin or anything that defiles will be present in that day, for all the ungodly will have been consigned to the lake of fire.

vv. 24-25: God anticipates prayer, and provides. Some of the truth in verses 20 to 25 relates to the millennial rather than the eternal state. The prayer of His people will be so aligned with His will, that He will answer even before they have finished praying. The fact that the Lord wishes His people to continue praying, even though He knows what they will pray, and is ready to answer before they articulate the prayer, is a mystery of His sovereignty. The answer to this mystery may partly lie in the fact that prayer has a reflexive effect upon the one praying, in that they are enabled by it to enter into the mind of God, and be more conformed to the image of His Son.

The Lord has always been willing to hear the sincere prayers of His people and never more so than today, for He 'is able to do exceeding abundantly above all that we ask or think, according to the power that worketh in us', Eph. 3. 20. With this knowledge let us be earnest in our attendance at the throne characterized by grace. There 'we have a great high priest, that is passed into the heavens, Jesus the Son of God', One who is 'touched with the feeling of our infirmities', Heb. 4. 14-16.

July 1st

Jeremiah 1. 4-10

I CANNOT SPEAK

One of the consistent features of Israel's history is that, whatever the circumstances, God always has His man. The period from good King Josiah to the puppet sovereign Zedekiah witnessed a slide from outward revival to brazen departure. One man was called to live through this, maintaining an unswerving ministry of correction.

But Jeremiah was hardly enthusiastic about it. The divine **appointment** of verse 5, announcing that he was foreknown, formed, sanctified and ordained of God, only provoked a response of understandable **anxiety**, v. 6. Any call to service is daunting. And Jeremiah's ministry was not going to make him a national favourite for, although it included judgement upon the Gentiles, vv. 5, 10, it was primarily focused upon the sins of his own people, vv. 16-19. Local assemblies today are in no less need of correction. Teachers are to proclaim the whole counsel of God, not just popular excerpts, speaking all the truth without fear or favour, Acts 20. 27.

His sense of inadequacy drove Jeremiah to prayer. The heartfelt admission, 'I cannot speak', is literally 'I know not how to speak', for he was not defiant but diffident. Like Timothy, he needed encouragement to fulfil his task, 1 Tim. 4. 14; 2 Tim. 1.6. And how graciously God met his fears! His brief confession of youthful timidity was granted an outstanding **answer**, vv. 7-10. To quell his fears, God promised His own sheltering presence, 'I am with thee to deliver thee', v. 8. And to counter his inability, God gave an insight into the mystery of inspiration, 'I have put my words in thy mouth', v. 9.

We should be thankful to Jeremiah. As a result of his nervousness, we have one of the most memorable descriptions of what Scripture really is: God's words in men's mouths. And as a consequence of his unfitness we are assured that all divine service depends upon divine power. As F B MEYER puts it, 'The best speakers for God are frequently they who are least gifted with human eloquence'. When the task seems too great, *pray*.

July 2nd
Jeremiah 2. 26-29

ARISE AND SAVE US

The history of the nation of Israel is a powerful testimony to the folly of idolatry. An idol, after all, is something that does not work. As Israel was attracted to the false gods of its neighbours so believers today can be lured into worshipping the current deities of the age: materialism, intellectualism, ecumenism, populism. Just as Israel's apostasy was led from the top, 2. 8, 26, so, it has to be admitted, much evil has entered local churches because of the ignorance or indifference of those who should have been spiritual guides.

Jeremiah's stinging words expose the utter folly of such departure; fancy crediting stocks and stones with generative functions! Yet this is no more absurd than the fashionable evolutionary myth which traces all things back to nothing and replaces the living God with a cosmic explosion. Such wilful blindness is an offence to God, 2. 27. But false gods prove their failure in times of emergency; Israel belatedly remembered its heritage and values 'in the time of their trouble'.

Peril stimulates prayer, Pss. 107. 13; 120. 1, but prayer is hindered by sin, Isa. 59. 2. If our lines of communication with God are utilized only in times of special need they will be found wanting, for the living God will not be treated like an insurance policy. Created and redeemed by Him, elevated to privileges past human imagination, gifted with the indwelling Spirit, and entrusted with the infallible word, believers are to be in the daily enjoyment of communion with heaven. Our blessings are sufficient to warrant eternal thanksgiving. Therefore, if anything or anyone has replaced the Lord in our affections let us cast that obstacle aside and return with repentant hearts to Him. It is only to the God and Father of our Lord Jesus Christ that we can truly say 'Thou art my father', v. 27; Matt. 6.9. And, whether speaking of creation or regeneration, it is to Him alone that we gladly cry, 'Thou hast brought me forth', v. 27; Ps. 100. 3; John 1. 13. Prayer is not merely for times of distress but for always.

July 3rd
Jeremiah 7. 13-16; 11. 14; 14. 11

I WILL NOT HEAR THEE

Prayer may be unanswered because of disobedience, Jas. 4. 3; it may also be forbidden. Jeremiah's was a painful ministry. Called upon to announce unavoidable judgement on the land and city he loved, he was also expressly denied the spiritual release of prayer on their behalf. The Babylonian captivity was fixed.

Our verses teach us that prayer, for Jeremiah, was an **instinctive** exercise. Clearly, his natural recourse when in distress of soul was to turn to God. The repetition of the words, 'pray not for this people', show how much he longed to speak to God about the nation. Perhaps we should ask ourselves if prayer is as natural and necessary to us, for it is one of the great hall marks of regeneration. The genuineness of Saul's conversion is summed up in the phrase, 'behold, he prayeth', Acts 9. 11. As THOMAS WATSON puts it: 'A godly man is a praying man. "Every one that is godly shall pray unto thee"'. As soon as grace is poured in, prayer is poured out'.

Jeremiah's prayer life was also **intense**. The terms of God's command make plain with what earnestness the prophet yearned to speak with his Master about Israel, 'neither lift up cry nor prayer for them', 7. 16. There is nothing perfunctory, mechanical, or formal about this. Rather, it is the expression of a deep heart-longing to God. Although public prayer must be controlled and coherent, lest others fail to understand and say 'Amen', 1 Cor. 14. 16, private prayer may often be interspersed with 'strong crying and tears', Heb. 5. 7. We cannot imagine that Samuel's prayers for Saul, or Paul's for Israel, would have been dry-eyed, 1 Sam. 15. 11, 35; Rom. 10. 1. How often have we wept for the needs of others?

The kind of prayer specifically forbidden is **intercessory**. Jeremiah's desire was for the good of Judah as a whole, not for himself, 14. 11. Alas, it is all too possible for our prayers to be self-centred. Yet Scripture exhorts that 'supplications ... be made for all men', 1 Tim. 2. 1. Those called to teach the word must especially intercede on behalf of those they seek to instruct.

July 4th

Jeremiah 10. 23-25

O LORD, CORRECT ME

Prayer, even more than preaching, manifests a man's deepest convictions. Jeremiah's fundamental beliefs shine through the words he utters at the close of this chapter of his prophecy.

First, he has no illusions about **the total inability of man**, v. 23. Boast as he will about technological advancement and humanitarian enlightenment, twentieth-century man is in the same spiritual condition as Jeremiah's contemporaries—completely incapable of governing either himself or the world around him, because of sin. That is why prayer is never addressed to men, however high their office, for man's splendour at best is a faded flower, 1 Pet. 1. 24, and his strength but a broken reed, Isa. 36. 6.

Second, he implicitly acknowledges **the sovereignty of God**; Jehovah alone is 'the living God, and an everlasting king', 10. 10, 23-24. Prayer presented to such a Lord must be grounded upon an intelligent appreciation of His unalterable power and purposes as revealed in the word. Bible study and prayer go hand in hand.

Third, he recognizes **the necessity for personal correction**, v. 24. Even the chosen prophet was no superman. Indeed, no servant of God more movingly confesses his weakness and pain than Jeremiah, 'Woe is me for my hurt! my wound is grievous: but I said, Truly this is a grief, and I must bear it', v. 19. It is in prayer that we confess our sinfulness and call upon God to mould, shape, correct and use us for His own glory.

Finally, he has an intense desire for **the prosperity of God's people**. Despite all their failures, despite their current exposure to divine discipline through the Gentile nations, v. 25, this faithful man of God longs for their spiritual restoration. The nation that rejected Jeremiah's testimony and wilfully resisted God's message, v. 21, was still dear to his heart. May our prayers for the saints in the local assembly where God has placed us be equally faithful and genuine.

202

Jeremiah 11. 18-23

UNTO THEE HAVE I REVEALED MY CAUSE

In life, Jeremiah showed characteristics that, at a later stage, were to be manifested in fulness by the Lord Jesus. In a land darkened by departure from God he shone as a bright beacon of truth, attracting hostility from those whose sin he condemned. Righteousness is always resented in this world. Some of his enemies even came from his own neighbourhood. Anathoth was his home, 1. 1, yet the men of Anathoth sought his life, 11. 21. He thus speaks of himself as 'a lamb ... brought to the slaughter', 11. 19, faintly illustrating the nation's future rejection of the Holy One, the true Lamb of God, John 1. 11; Isa. 53. 7.

It is never easy to be unpopular. Even the assurance of a righteous cause cannot entirely sweeten the bitter pill of derision. The faithful believer who stands against the current of religious apostasy will find himself isolated, accused of being unloving, ungracious, unhelpful. Like Elijah he will be denounced as 'he that troubleth Israel', 1 Kgs. 18. 17. Like Paul, he will see friends desert, 2 Tim. 1. 15; 4. 10, 16. Like the psalmist he will be the target of wicked gossip, Ps. 41. 5-9. All these things hurt. Yet how much better to be an Elijah than an Ahab!

So Jeremiah turns to God. He acknowledges the Lord's power as the 'Lord of hosts', the eternal commander of an innumerable army of glorious angelic beings. When you think you are outnumbered by the forces of wickedness, never forget this title of our God—a title not to be diluted by specious paraphrase. But God's righteousness and omniscience also fill the prophet's thoughts. It is *His* verdict that counts—not men's. With the utmost reassurance the believer can rest in the fact that whatever man may think or say, God knows the truth about us.

However, Jeremiah's request to see judgement upon his enemies marks the difference between the Old Testament prophet and the Son of God. While the former asked God to avenge him, the latter only prayed for forgiveness on His enemies, Luke 23. 34. If the prophet teaches us to **pray**, a greater than Jeremiah teaches us to **pardon**.

July 6th

Jeremiah 12. 1-3

THOU, O LORD, KNOWEST ME

The apparent prosperity of the wicked has often been a problem for God's people. Why should the godly suffer wrongfully when the unsaved live at ease? This disturbing inequity plagued the minds of David and Asaph, Pss. 37; 73, and both found the answer in the presence of God. Since the fall of man this world has been spiritually sick. Living on a planet which is in a state of rebellion against its Creator, it should not surprise us that everything is out of kilter. The clearest proof of this is the reception men gave to the Son of God when He visited them, Matt. 8. 20; 16. 21. If the **Lord of glory** was unrecognized in His own world, why should **His servants** expect better treatment?

Jeremiah's recourse to God in time of trouble is an encouragement to all beleaguered souls when events seem to conspire against them. Until the Lord returns to establish His reign of righteousness, Isa. 32. 1, right will not be seen to be done on earth. Yet, as the prophet confesses, God *is* eternally righteous. The solution is to 'talk with thee', Jer. 12. 1. The old chorus, 'A little talk with Jesus makes it right, all right', may sound trite but truly expresses a glorious divine reality. To speak to God *is* to have the heart strengthened.

We may notice Jeremiah's confidence in the Lord's knowledge of his situation, v. 3. We pray to a God of knowledge, 1 Sam. 2. 3, the unfailing Discerner of the thoughts and intents of the heart. Far from undermining prayer this great truth stimulates it: even when words fail our God can see beneath the surface. What an encouragement to frankness before Him! We may deceive our brethren with feigned piety, but God is never duped. Although it is important to speak to Him intelligently, we must never fall into the trap of thinking that prayer is a kind of *Open Sesame*, a magic formula which, correctly recited, bends the sovereign God to our will. Precision of utterance is never of greater importance than genuineness of heart. God forbid that it should be said of us, as Jeremiah had to declare of his people, 'thou art near in their mouth, and far from their reins', v. 2.

July 7th

Jeremiah 14. 20-22

WE WILL WAIT UPON THEE

During the long forty-one years or so of Jeremiah's prophetic ministry, Jerusalem experienced many severe trials. Included among them was a period of drought, which left the wells dry, the fields bare, and the people in desperate need, 14. 1-6.

The circumstances of Israel's history were never accidental. As God's covenant people they held a relationship with Him involving both glad privilege and solemn responsibility. 'If ye shall despise my statutes ... that ye break my covenant: I also will do this unto you ... I will make your heaven as iron, and your earth as brass: and your strength shall be spent in vain: for your land shall not yield her increase', Lev. 26. 14-20; see also Deut. 11. 17; 28. 23, 24. Affliction was therefore the good hand of God remonstrating with His wayward people.

Jeremiah's response to this external trial was prayer, 14. 20-22. Identifying himself with the sinful nation, he confessed Israel's disobedience and called upon God's mercy. Like Moses before him, he recalled God's faithfulness and sovereign grace in His past dealings with His redeemed people. Was not Jerusalem 'the throne of thy glory'? Though the nation had failed, God could never contradict Himself or deny His unconditional calling of Israel. Though the tenure of the land depended upon her obedience to God, her national preservation rested solely on Jehovah's election, 33. 17-26. All true prayer combines confession of personal guilt with confidence in God's faithfulness. The first on its own could lead us to despair; the latter to presumption. But Jeremiah is, as always, both reverent and real in his dealings with God. No other help could avail: only the Lord could save His people.

When we are at our wits' end because of adversity at home or apathy in the local assembly, let us learn from Jeremiah to wait upon the Lord, 14. 22. As he reminded God of His covenant, so we today can rest on even surer ground in our prayers, the once-for-all finished work of Calvary.

July 8th
Jeremiah 15. 15-21

O LORD ... REMEMBER ME

Jeremiah is not the only man to wish he had never been born, 15. 10; 20. 14-18. Job went though a similar period of depression, Job 3. 1-3, 11, as a consequence of the personal disasters which befell him. But while Job's misery sprang from external circumstances, Jeremiah's was tied up with his very office as a prophet of God. Called to preach not forgiveness, or long-suffering, or peace, but inexorable divine judgement upon a rebellious people, he obeyed. Yet the strain was great. Like all men of God he was no unfeeling preaching-machine, untouched by the terms of his message or the character of his audience's response. Like the Saviour after him, Jeremiah, in preaching, wept over the hardness of Jerusalem. Seeing the city already under judgement, assured of a coming Babylonian invasion, and facing the hostility of his compatriots who saw him as a traitor, Jeremiah was a social outcast, 15. 17.

When all others fail, to whom do we turn? Jeremiah comes before God with customary honesty and bares his soul in all its pain. Perhaps we have been called to a sphere of service which receives no loud acclaim and sees no bright success. To speak the truth in love today will cause offence in a religious world where the authority of God's word has been abandoned. When local assemblies flout the divine instructions about gathering, when biblical standards of marriage are disregarded, when even the gospel itself is trivialized into a cosy appeal to man's self-esteem instead of a solemn indictment of his sin, then we need men like Jeremiah. Jeremiah speaks to God about the sustenance he finds in His word, 15. 16. **God's words**—the plural form suggests the value of the smallest detail—are his source of **edification** (for he ate them), his **enjoyment**, and his **encouragement**, confirming the deep assurance that he belonged to Jehovah.

When the ministry to which God calls us seems painful and apparently fruitless, let us turn to Him and find succour in His unfailing words of truth. As the word calls us to prayer, so prayer will drive us back to the word.

July 9th
Jeremiah 17. 12-18

THOU ART MY PRAISE

As well as being unpopular, Jeremiah's message of impending devastation at the hands of the Babylonians seemed, for a time at least, to be unfounded. It is as hard to speak about darkness when all is light as it is to announce safety in the midst of a raging storm. Yet Jeremiah faithfully did the one as Paul did the other, Acts 27. 20-22. When the people of Judah challenged him with the words, 'Where is the word of the Lord?', 17. 15, they were only displaying man's natural contempt for God. The scoffers of the last days will echo the same taunt, 2 Pet. 3. 4. But the word of the Lord remains the same. Just as Jerusalem fell to Babylon, so too will this planet be exposed to the long-predicted intervention of the Lord Jesus Christ in judgement.

In the midst of such unbelief, the prophet found contentment in his God, 'Thou art my praise', 17. 14, and 'Thou art my refuge', 17. 17 RV. God was **the object of his adoration in days of departure**. He sought not the approval of men, fickle at best, but the delight of God. In finding all his resources in the Lord, Jeremiah acknowledged Him as the source of his being, actions, and life. He had good reasons for praise. The 'glorious high throne', v. 12, speaks of absolute sovereignty, while the 'sanctuary' speaks of ineffable purity. The title 'hope of Israel' emphasizes divine reliability—for how can one place any hope in the untrustworthy?—and the beautiful metaphor, 'the fountain of living waters', v. 13, suggests His eternal vitality as the spring of life and blessing. Each of these divine excellencies is attributed to Christ. He, the Holy One of God, Mark 1. 24, is enthroned in heaven, Heb. 12. 2, as our hope, 1 Tim. 1. 1, and the source of everlasting life, John 4. 14.

But Jehovah was also **the source of his preservation in days of danger**. Jerusalem would fall, its inhabitants be scattered, yet God remained the eternal hiding place of His saints, Prov. 18. 10. He has not changed. When the world seems to tremble beneath our feet, let us remember that Christ is our city of refuge, Heb. 6. 18.

July 10th

Jeremiah 32. 16-25

THERE IS NOTHING TOO HARD FOR THEE

Sometimes the Lord's servants have to do contradictory things. For years Jeremiah had been predicting the downfall of Judah and Jerusalem because of its sin, Jer. 1. 13-16. Now, however, the Lord instructed him to make a property investment in the very land that was facing imminent judgement. The date is the tenth year of Zedekiah, 32. 1; that is, just one year before the final conquest of the city and its destruction in 586 B.C., 39. 2, 8. The Babylonian army was already at the gates, subjecting Jerusalem to a cruel siege, 32. 1, 2. So the instruction to purchase a relative's land in Anathoth, a few miles outside the doomed city, came as a bolt from the blue. Why invest in what is to be destroyed and seized by an enemy?

Whatever Jeremiah may have felt, he obeyed without question, 32. 6-10. Obedience often has to precede complete understanding. When the Lord speaks to our souls through His word, may we have the courage of Jeremiah to obey despite all the difficulties.

But having obeyed, the prophet prayed. He honestly articulates his incomprehension of the ways of God at that moment, 32. 25, while never slipping into irreverence. Rather, he clings on to all that he knows of God, using that as the ground of his approach. This is a great lesson. We must never let local difficulties and misunderstandings obscure what we *do* know of our God. Jeremiah's prayer is therefore a potted history of Israel, seeing in all the nation's experiences, good and bad, the hand of God. To remind God, as it were, of His doings is neither presumption nor redundancy, but simple faith.

Such simple faith receives an answer, 32. 26-44. That problematic investment, so ludicrous in men's eyes, was a parable of God's purposes for Israel. Yes, Judah would fall, v. 29, but the people would later be restored to the very same land, vv. 37-44. Jeremiah's purchase was a concrete pledge of Israel's future return and revival, one ultimately tied up with the return of the Son of God Himself, vv. 39, 40; Zech. 14. 4-9. 'Come, Lord Jesus'.

July 11th

Jeremiah 33. 1-3

CALL UNTO ME

This is not so much an example of prayer as an encouragement to pray. We might have thought it was hardly needed. After all, Jeremiah was 'yet shut up in the court of the prison', 33. 1, and it is the experience of all God's people that suffering stimulates prayer. 'In my distress I cried unto the Lord, and he heard me', Ps. 120. 1. As THOMAS WATSON writes, 'Affliction quickens the spirit of prayer; Jonah was asleep in the ship, but at prayer in the whale's belly … In times of trouble we pray feelingly, and we never pray so fervently as when we pray feelingly'.

But Jeremiah, it seems, required some spur to kindle his praying spirit. He might have been out of the reach of men in the prison, but he was certainly not shut out from the presence and power of God! The invitation to 'call unto me' is peculiarly gracious, because it informs us that God enjoys communion with His people. The late twentieth-century communications explosion means that people are more accessible than ever before and as a consequence often resent the constant intrusion upon their time. But God delights to hear His children. Baal, like all fraudulent deities, remains stubbornly out of contact despite the loud cries and self-mutilations of his followers, 1 Kgs. 18. 27, while Jehovah can be approached by the simplest, briefest words of petition.

And if God rejoices in the prayers of His people, so may we in the assurance of His response, 'Call unto me, and I will answer thee', v. 3. The answer here is not so much a supernatural intervention as a disclosure of Himself and His ways. Jeremiah was not suddenly vindicated like Joseph, or elevated from misery to a lavish life-style. Rather, he got to know his God better. Prosperity theology, which claims, blasphemously, to command material blessing from the Lord, is naively only seeking the riches that are vulnerable to moth, rust and thieves. But to be brought into an intelligent enjoyment of divine counsels is wealth beyond measure. If we would progress in grace, we must pray.

July 12th
Jeremiah 42. 1-4

PRAY FOR US

Jerusalem fell as Jeremiah had predicted. King Zedekiah was slain and many Jews led into captivity. A few remained in the land, governed initially by Gedaliah, under Babylonian authority, and then by Johanan. It is hardly surprising that these disheartened people should turn to Jeremiah for counsel. Against all the odds his predictions had come true, and he was therefore fully accredited as a faithful prophet of God, Deut. 18. 20-22.

It is good when others recognize that believers have a genuine contact with heaven and request our prayers, 1 Sam. 12. 19; Acts 8. 24. It is, however, sadly true that many solicit aid either as a temporary circumvention of difficulties, or as a means of rubber-stamping their own decisions. In this case the prayer requests were feigned. Despite pious words, never a reliable guide to the heart, these people had no real love for the God of Israel. They pledged themselves to obey, 42. 5, 6, but were exposed as shams, 'ye dissembled in your hearts', vv. 20-22. Alas, they recapitulated the nation's empty gestures at Sinai, 'All that the Lord hath spoken we will do', Exod. 19. 8.

Such events are recorded in the word as a lesson in the importance of heart-honesty before God. The Pharisaical practice of lip-service, however impressive or plausible, will never satisfy the God who knows the thoughts of our innermost beings, Jer. 17. 9, 10; Matt. 15. 8, 9. To approach Him disingenuously, to ask for guidance when the mind is already fixed on its course, to attempt to deceive the God of heaven, is to court disaster. To the humble alone will God make Himself known, Isa. 66. 1, 2. If we would learn His will, let us remember the great precondition is that our will must be unconditionally subordinated to His. As the Saviour said, 'If any man will do his will, he shall know of the doctrine', John 17. 7. Prayer is no formal, impersonal request for information, but the outpouring of the heart before God, unreservedly surrendering ourselves to the One who knows what is best for His people. May we pray with a heart willing to obey.

July 13th

Ezekiel 11. 13-16

THEN FELL I DOWN UPON MY FACE

While Jeremiah remained in the land of Judah testifying to its imminent overthrow, his fellow prophet Ezekiel had been carried into Babylon at the second invasion of 597 B.C. His message, however, though distant in its delivery was identical in its theology: Jehovah would bring a final devastation upon the city of the Jews.

In spirit, Ezekiel saw Jerusalem's state of soul as exemplified by its leaders, vv. 1-3. Confident the war was finished they believed it right to settle in safety in their beloved capital. Like meat in a cooking pot, they were safe from the burning. The partial captivity of 605 and 597 B.C. would soon be over—contrary to Jeremiah's prophecy of a seventy-year captivity, Jer. 25. 8-14—and the warnings of God's servants could thus be disregarded. It is a feature of man's sinfulness that he refuses to receive God's blessings when they are proffered, or believe in God's judgement when it is predicted.

The Lord's response was to reaffirm the certainty of judgement because of sin, vv. 11, 12. Ezekiel's reaction to this was to fall before the Lord on behalf of his people. In this he displayed the heart of Moses and Paul in their tender concern for Israel, Exod. 32. 7-14; Rom. 11. 4, 5. Judgement was fully deserved, but the prophet could not callously abandon his own nation. Truthfulness and tearfulness are the qualifications of the man of God. The solemn message must be discharged even though the messenger's heart is breaking. Preachers of the gospel today have to announce God's eternal punishment of men outside of Christ; yet such preachers will also intercede earnestly with God on behalf of sinners.

Ezekiel's zeal is seen in the suddenness, the posture, and the volume of his prayer, v. 13. Mass emotion is easily manipulated and wisely distrusted, but here is a solitary saint overcome by the need and prostrate before God. Perhaps we are shy of such fervour. But, as C H SPURGEON writes, 'He who prays without fervency does not pray at all. We cannot commune with God, who is a consuming fire, if there is no fire in our prayers'.

July 14th

Ezekiel 36. 33-38

I WILL YET FOR THIS BE INQUIRED OF

The believer in contact with God will always have a long-term vision. Like every Old Testament prophet, Ezekiel was enabled to see beyond immediate judgement to national and spiritual renewal. Even as Israel was undergoing God's discipline at the hands of the Babylonians, Ezekiel was reassured that a day would come when they would be regathered to their land and restored to their God, 36. 24-30.

One of the evidences of this coming revival would be a new desire to pray to Jehovah, 'I will yet for this be inquired of by the house of Israel, to do it for them', v. 37. The God who had already said of His gracious purposes of blessing upon Israel, 'I will do it', v. 36, now makes plain that His acting will also be in response to Israel's asking.

It is a mark of spiritual grace when the believer is constrained to pray for the very benefits which God has in store for him. This, of course, reminds us that prayer is not a matter of cajoling a reluctant Giver; rather, it is calling upon the One who has the best in view for His children. Our God loves to 'give good things to them that ask him', Matt. 7. 11. If earthly fathers wish their children's good, how much more does God!

In such supplication we lean upon the foundation facts of God's eternal goodness, wisdom and power. All genuine prayer is grounded upon unshakeable doctrinal truth rather than being merely the whim of the moment. Therefore it follows that to know what God would do for His people we must spend time regularly, diligently, earnestly with the word. There can be no doubt that the two go hand in hand. It was Daniel's intense study of Jeremiah's prophecy which led him to understand that the seventy years of Judah's captivity were coming to an end, and to pray that God would look in mercy upon His scattered people, Dan. 9. 1-4.

If we long for spiritual refreshing in our souls, for the increase of the local assembly, for the conversion of sinners, we shall express these desires in earnest prayer.

July 15th

Daniel 2. 14-23

MERCIES FROM TIIE GOD OF HEAVEN

The position of Daniel and his godly companions was grim. They were in the service of an oriental totalitarian monarch whose word and whim meant life or death. Now, the king was angry because his wise men were unable to identify or interpret his troublesome dream! What was the dream that so disturbed this mega-monarch in mind and heart? Finding himself frustrated by the inability of his shamans, he lashed out in fury and commanded the destruction of all the wise men of Babylon. Although not present on that fearful occasion, 2. 2-3, Daniel, Hananiah, Mishael and Azariah were nevertheless included in the king's fiat of death, and were arrested by the chief executioner. Knowing nothing of the incident, and thus innocent of the charge, they sought audience with the king and requested, and were granted, time to show the king the interpretation. Thus they came with their lives forfeit to desire mercies from the God of heaven, v. 17. *Prayer* was their resource in the hour of peril and desperate need, and in this they stand as examples for believers of every age. God uses this means to reveal His secrets, and prayer was signally answered in their case. This is an instance of united prayer recorded in Scripture, and suggests the four young Hebrews were familiar with this practice, and that it was the secret of their holy and separated lives.

Their prayer, vv. 20-22, harnessed the wisdom of God, mobilized the might of God, and utilized the eye of God to penetrate this unfathomable mystery. 'He revealeth the deep and secret things', exulted Daniel. There is no mystery so deep, or situation so dark, that He cannot shine His light upon it and make the way clear. *But it is 'revelation' made known to 'prayer'*.

Please observe that the godly four met all the conditions for prevailing prayer: they (a) were in the place of divine appointment, and so in the centre of God's will; (b) were innocent of wrong and thus had God-pleasing lives; and (c) were fervent believers in God's Person and beneficence, cf. Heb. 11. 6.

Dear child of God, baffled, frustrated, and fearful—there is a God in heaven who 'knoweth what is in the darkness' and can shed light upon your urgent dilemma. Only, get down upon your knees and **pray**—for still today Daniel's God is your God. Hallelujah!

July 16th

Daniel 6. 1-11

AS HE DID AFORETIME

Another crisis in Daniel's life: this time in old age. Neither high rank nor advanced years put the faithful believer beyond the reach of persecution or temptation. But as in youth, so in age—*prayer* is the secret of his courage and consistency. Here, Daniel prays publicly, kneeling upon his knees three times a day before an open window, watched by enemies who hate his faithful life and have no fear of his unseen God. As a youth he proved God in prayer, and now in old age the habit of a lifetime will sustain him through this new danger, v. 10. He is courageous and calm because he is pious and prayerful—'as he did aforetime' is what he will continue to do, though his position be threatened and his life endangered. The secret of his faultlessness to the king, v. 4, and his integrity to God lay in his habitual prayer life. Daniel was a man of prayer.

Thus, when he knew the rash edict had been signed with all the unalterable finality of the law of the Medes and Persians, vv. 7-8, he still prayed according to godly habit three times a day! Further, he prayed publicly! Not as the hypocrites in order to be seen, Matt. 6. 5, but to stand as God's champion in face of the temptation to save his life by an act of idolatry or God-dishonouring compromise. Threat of horrible death will not make him waver in devotion to his God. Duty to God must transcend obedience to man when bad laws and unrighteous legislation mean sinning against divine principle.

Daniel 'prayed and gave thanks', v. 10. What could he find in his harrowing circumstances to 'give thanks' for? But 'give thanks' he did! Believing, prayerful spirits can look beyond immediate circumstances up to the throne, and find in God their exceeding joy, Ps. 43. 4. They have learned through prayer the secret of rejoicing in Him always, Phil. 4. 1, 4. This is the principle that put gratitude into Daniel's heart, and puts thanksgiving into the heart of the aged saint today racked with pain, or the terminally ill victim awaiting the end, or the grieving heart devastated by tragic bereavement.

The supplications, v. 11, on earth were heard in heaven. An angel was despatched to shut the lions' mouths, and the evil intended for the prayerful saint came upon his persecutors instead, vv. 22, 24; Prov. 28. 10.

July 17th

Daniel 9. 1-6, 17-19

O LORD, HEAR; O LORD, FORGIVE

Daniel's heart-cry and agonized plea was the result of a mind and spirit stirred by the word of God, 'I Daniel understood by books', v. 2. Daniel was not only a man of prayer, he was also a man of the Bible. Prayer and the word of God are complementary.

Jerusalem had been wasted and desolate for seventy years, and as once again the time comes to 'build the house of the Lord ... in Jerusalem', Ezra 1. 5, Daniel is found diligently searching the Scriptures in the prophecy of Jeremiah. His study of 'the books' (or Scriptures) led to his great prayer, and was used by God's Spirit as the means of fulfilling His word as to the rebuilding of the temple and the restoration of Jerusalem, Jer. 29. 10-14. This is in harmony with the divine principle, 'I will yet be inquired of by the house of Israel, to do it for them', Ezek. 36. 37.

So we see Daniel once again on his knees in prevailing prayer. As he considers the past seventy years of Israel's exile, Daniel recognizes God as, *'the great and dreadful God'*, v. 4. When he pleads for national pardon, he calls upon *a God of 'mercies and forgiveness'*, v. 9. Thus, he brings into focus both the goodness and severity of God, Rom. 11. 22. He recognizes God's holy nature and intolerance of sin, and His grace and compassion toward the repentant offenders.

Daniel's potent prayer was a blend of a *knowledge of God's will* from Jeremiah's prophecy, v. 2; a determined *perseverance*, v. 3; a *justification* of God's actions, vv. 4, 14; a *humility* in self-humbling confession, v. 5; an *identification* with the sinful nation that takes the sins of other upon himself, vv. 6-10; and a powerful pleading of God's *reputation* and name, v. 19.

The result of his supplication was an angelic messenger, v. 21, an assurance of heaven's approbation, v. 23. and the most complete prophecy regarding Israel's glorious destiny found anywhere in Scripture, vv. 24-27. It was the revelation of Israel's great seventy weeks. Dear devoted Daniel, the man 'greatly beloved', upon his knees in humble confession, exerted more real power than Darius did upon his throne, v. 1. Let Daniel's example of prayer inspire us today.

July 18th

Daniel 10. 1-12

THY WORDS WERE HEARD

As soon as a saint of God utters prayer from a burdened heart, that prayer is heard in heaven. 'From the first day ... thy words were heard', v. 12. A mighty angel was despatched to carry the reply, but for three weeks the powers of hell withstood the heavenly emissary, v. 13. Still, today, there is constant spiritual warfare in the cosmic realm, in which we have a share, Eph. 6. 12, and Satanic opposition is never more evident than in hindering the believer's prayers.

Now Daniel is seeking further instruction and understanding of the mind of God for Israel, v. 12. He is burdened about God's people there in Jerusalem, and beyond them desires divine light to understand what shall happen to Israel 'in the latter days', v. 14. Daniel is therefore deeply anxious to *find out the mind and will of God*. He has held high office now for over seventy years. He has shown himself a man of God, and had deep experiences of God. He is known in heaven as a man 'greatly beloved', and his life is saturated in prayer. Yet, as a very old man, he still feels the need, when seeking light and guidance from God, to give himself unreservedly and unremittingly to this great task.

The features that mark out Daniel's determination to know the will of God are (1) *A mighty burden to pray*. For three full weeks, day by day and throughout the day, week after week, he untiringly approached the throne of God with his prayers. If ever a man sought an answer from heaven, it was Daniel. (2) *A determination and urgency to catch the eye of God*. He mourned, he fasted, he gave no time even for his daily anointing, but devoted his whole energies to pleading with God. (3) *A perseverance in prayer until the answer comes*. His was no superficial, shallow asking which evaporated after a day. Daniel continued for three weeks to lay hold upon God until the answer came. The whole incident reveals the certainty of faith in the response of God. 'Ask, and it *shall* be given you', Matt. 7. 7. Dear fellow-saint, there is no alternative path today if we would certainly know God's will and receive answers to our prayers.

July 19th

Hosea 6. 1-3

COME AND LET US RETURN UNTO THE LORD

After a period of backsliding and departure there is such a thing as the prayer of repentance. This is the case with Israel here. In today's reading it is the humility and sorrow of heart, preceding the prayer of repentance, that we see in these poignant words.

This section properly belongs to the end of chapter 5, where God deals in severe judgement with Ephraim and Judah. The outcome of this discipline is the repentant cry, 'Come, and let us return unto the Lord'. In the immediate context this repentance was shallow, as the Lord's response in verse 4 indicates, 'Your goodness is as a morning cloud, and as the early dew it goeth away'. But viewed as a Messianic statement, and a figure of Israel's future national restoration, it has far-reaching significance.

Many see in the words of verse 2 a reference to Christ's death and burial as a consequence of bearing the divine judgement, and His resurrection on the third day ushering in life, the true knowledge of God, and the refreshing of the Spirit which followed. KELLY says, 'Can it be doubted that the passage does … refer to the resurrection of Christ?'. However, its immediate reference is to the Messianic people, Israel. See first of all the *rending* of Israel in disciplinary judgement, cf. 5. 14-15. This leads to their reviving in 'two days', v. 2 and the *resurrection* and *raising* of Israel on the third day, v. 2, in which they experience that renewal of knowledge that unveils the true identity of their Messiah. And finally the *refreshing* of a new dawn, and the abundant watering of the outpoured blessing of Jehovah.

How significant this prophecy is in light of 2 Peter 3. 8, where a thousand years are as one day to the timeless Godhead. After dark Calvary and the rejection of their Messiah, Israel have been 'torn' and under Jehovah's frown for 'two days'. The 'third' Millennial 'day' will be ushered in by the terrible 'rending' judgements of the Tribulation period, followed by the nation's repentance, 6. 1, and resurrection. They will 'know' their true Messiah, and follow Him into the glory and refreshing of that long anticipated Millennial glory, Ps. 72. 6-7; 2 Sam. 23. 34. Let us pray today for that glorious coming 'peace' of Jerusalem, Ps. 122. 6.

July 20th

Hosea 14. 1-4

TAKE WITH YOU WORDS

Under the powerful imagery of taking to himself 'a wife of whoredoms', chapter 1, Hosea has dramatized the wickedness of Israel in their departure from God. Hosea's marriage to Gomer was a covenant in which he had shown her loyal love, but she failed to show the same faithfulness in return. Thus had God betrothed Israel to Himself by covenant, and shown them love, but they had prostituted and rejected His love. God had pleaded with them in mercy, 'How shall I give thee up, Ephraim?', 11. 8. But with God's pleadings came His threatening; if sin is not repented of, then judgement must follow, 'For they have sown the wind, and they shall reap the whirlwind', 8. 7.

Our reading today brings us to the pinnacle revelation of God's love for His sinful people. In light of the fearful judgements of Jehovah, the prophet pleads, 'O Israel, return unto the Lord thy God; for thou hast fallen by thine iniquity'. Using Israel as an example, 1 Cor. 10. 6, we can discern abiding principles for every age of God's dealings with His people. Here is the way back from spiritual backsliding, and the assurance that God, in His pitying love toward us today, is the same as ever He was toward Israel in the days of Hosea.

'Take with you words'. (1) *A confession of sin*. The words to take are words of contrition as did David, 'a broken and a contrite heart, O God, thou wilt not despise', Ps. 51. 17. (2) *A desire for holiness*. 'Take away all iniquity'. The way back into the divine favour is to have all iniquity confessed and forsaken. (3) *A sincere consecration*. 'Receive us graciously' (lit, 'receive good'). The very 'good' received in God's pardoning grace is devoted now in willing service back to Him. A pardoning God is willing to receive the backslider into useful service once more. (4) *A renewed worship*. 'So will we render the calves of our lips'. As formerly the offerer came with sacrificial calves, our lips should now present the sacrifice of praise to God, Heb. 13. 15. 'Ransomed, healed, restored, forgiven, Who like thee His praise should sing?' Then the response of Jehovah falls like balm on the backslider's heart, 'I will heal their backsliding, I will love them freely: for mine anger is turned away', v. 4.

July 21st

Joel 1. 19-20

O LORD, TO THEE WILL I CRY

The terrible scourge of the eastern locusts has decimated the land, v. 4. The effect is as though fire has burned the earth, vv. 19-20. This was why the Romans called locusts, 'the burners of the land'. Joel views this locust invasion as a destruction from the Almighty, and a foretaste of a greater judgement to be expected in the future 'day of the Lord', v. 15. He calls for repentance and a day of fasting and prayer in the house of the Lord, v. 14.

As a prophecy, the nation, on their repentance, is promised blessing, 2. 12ff, restoration, 2. 25, a future outpouring of the Spirit, 2. 28-32, and judgement upon the Gentile nations, 3. 2, 12-15, after which there will be a reign of holiness and peace and the Lord will dwell in Zion, 3. 21. This will be fulfilled by the Tribulation judgements of the Day of Jehovah, and the coming of Israel's true Messiah, the Lord Jesus, to reign in Zion.

Our portion today, 'O Lord, to thee will I cry', v. 19, is a prayer, even a desperate cry, made to God when all hope has gone and total disaster stares them in the face. In verses 19-20 the people are at their wits' end, Ps. 107. 27. Like Israel, we sometimes feel that our hopes, ambitions, even our usefulness and testimony are burned up, and our pastures are devoured. The locusts of worldliness, materialism, self-centred ambition and refusal to submit to the will and ways of God in life and church testimony, have 'eaten' our years, 2. 25. Our green years for Christ, when we loved His word, gathered with His people, delighted in all things spiritual and heavenly, and witnessed to others of the great salvation we had found in Him, are seared and withered by these 'locusts'.

The remedy is found in the prayer of the prophet, 'O Lord, to thee will I cry'. Let us today turn to Him in the spirit of 2. 12-14, 'for he is gracious and merciful, slow to anger, and of great kindness, and repenteth him of the evil'. The **repentant cry** will always meet with the **restoring promise**, 'I will restore to you the years that the locust hath eaten', 2. 25.

July 22nd

Joel 2. 15-17

BLOW THE TRUMPET IN ZION

It is interesting to note the considerable space given to the subject of prayer in the Scriptures. From the beginning of the human story men began to call upon the name of the Lord, Gen. 4. 26. Jacob wrestled with the divine Stranger; Moses communed with God until his face shone; prophets and apostles prayed without ceasing. When God has made prayer so prominent in His word, it is in order that we should make it prominent in our lives.

There are times of peculiar need when we can do nothing but pray! It was thus with Israel at the Red Sea, Exod. 14. 10, and here, today, our reading is a trumpet blast calling the nation to prayer in the face of God's locust judgement against His people's sins in turning from Him. Today, we too, as a nation, have apostatized from God. Even as believers, we have turned away from the clear pathway of His word and followed our own devices, and mourn the consequent loss of power, joy, and increase in divine things.

Let us learn from Joel the requirements for God's pardon and blessing. (1) An inner desire for God Himself which touches our hearts and is evidenced by genuine sorrow, 2. 12. (2) A true heart-repentance and not mere superficial externalism, 2. 13. (3) A living hope in the known character of God, as a God of mercy and grace who can change judgement into blessing, 2. 14.

Then 'blow the trumpet in Zion'—summon the people to prayer and a solemn assembly. Let that assembly include whole families; let nothing, not even the nuptials of newlyweds, hinder this most solemn assembly in desperate prayer to the living Lord, vv. 15-17.

We live in similar circumstances, morally and spiritually, to Joel. We see massive departure from the Person and work of Christ, and culpable weakness among His assemblies. O for a trumpet blast in Zion today, calling for mercy because of our sins. If ever a solemn gathering of saints and their leaders, 2. 17, was needed, it is now! And let them say, 'Spare thy people, O Lord'. It may be the Lord will answer with His own blessing of fruitfulness and victory, 2. 19, and we shall see Him 'do great things', 2. 21.

July 23rd

Amos 5. 1-14

SEEK YE ME, AND YE SHALL LIVE

Amos was a herdsman and shepherd, a cultivator of sycamore fruit. He had never attended one of the 'schools of the prophets' as a prophet's son, 7. 14-15. A humble peasant, he had been commissioned by God as he followed his everyday task as a shepherd, 7. 15.

His message was grim, a declaration of judgement against a nation's ingratitude for God's love, their injustice and violence, and above all the adultery of heart which sought to combine their filthy calf-worship with the pure worship of Jehovah. Amos' authority lay in a strong conviction of his divine call, and the power of the message he delivered. He had deep dealings with God, and knew Him as few of his contemporaries did. So God took and used him as His prophet. God can do the same again today—speak through the lips of a humble dedicated 'nobody', one who is consecrated to Him entirely, Rom. 12. 1-2.

The great sorrow of Amos' time was that which should have been a living testimony for God had completely failed. His people had turned Bethel, the 'house of God', into Bethaven, the 'house of vanity', Hos. 4. 15. Gilgal (meaning 'rolling') where the reproach of Egypt had been rolled away and Israel became separated unto God, a holy nation, was likewise defiled by idolatry, 4. 4, and would be 'rolled away' into captivity. Similarly Beersheba, the well of the oath, and a glory in Israel's history, also had become a centre of abominable idolatry.

It is useless substituting past glories for present failure, and centering hopes on what was formerly blessed but is now corrupted. God calls His people to turn from their idolatry to Himself alone. The way of life is 'seek me and live', v. 4. This is the way of blessing today. To seek Him is to find Him, Matt. 7. 7, and to find Him is the only way to live spiritually. The source of so much of our barrenness today is that we put Bethel, Gilgal, and Beersheba—our past glories and blessings—in the place of God Himself. Let us seek Him in personal prayer; let us reach out to Him who is both Creator and Redeemer. Seek Him for Himself, and being filled afresh with His fullness, serve Him with renewed spiritual life.

221

July 24th

Amos 7. 1-6

O LORD GOD, FORGIVE ... O LORD GOD, CEASE

The intercessory prayers of God's servants have mightily prevailed down through the ages. Here is one of the mysteries of prayer. Prayer really does change things by moving the heart and hand of God. Prayer or 'asking', as petitionary prayer, is the justification and encouragement for the whole exercise of appealing to God in this way. We do not live in a rigid sphere of unalterable fatalism. This was demonstrated by Isaac who, when his wife proved barren, 'intreated the Lord for his wife ... and the Lord was intreated of him, and Rebekah his wife conceived', Gen. 25. 21. And Moses, by intercessory pleading with the Lord, averted the certain annihilation of the whole of Israel when they made their golden calf in rejection of the Lord. The prayer of intercession was all that stood between Israel and oblivion, and it was wholly effectual for, 'the Lord repented of the evil which he thought to do unto his people', Exod. 32. 7-14.

Thus it was with Amos here in chapter 7, with its three visions of the judgements God would bring upon Israel. First, the locusts (grasshoppers), devouring and destroying the nation of Jacob, vv. 1-3. Second, the fire which even destroyed the great deep—a more drastic judgement even than the locusts, vv. 4-6. Finally, the plumbline testing the wall, against which there could be no effective intercession, and judgement upon Israel and the house of Jereboam be made final, vv. 7-9.

The power of the prophet's intercessory prayer, 'O Lord God, forgive, I beseech thee', in the case of the locusts, turned God's wrath and produced His promise it should not happen, v. 3. The same with the devouring fire judgement: when Amos cried, 'O Lord God, cease, I beseech thee', God again repented and turned from judgement. It is instructive to see that Amos' intercession presented the argument of Israel's helplessness and littleness, v. 2, and thus the necessity of God's mercy or else His people were lost. How swiftly and graciously does God respond in both cases, 'It shall not be', when He is presented with such petitioning prayer. May the example of these great intercessors of old grip our souls today, and may we learn the lesson, 'The effectual fervent prayer of a righteous man availeth much', James 5. 16.

Jonah 1. 1-16

THE PRAYERLESS PROPHET

Nineveh was renowned for its power and wealth. Its fame as the capital of the foremost empire in the region made it *great*. That was man's assessment. But God saw its moral pollution, and judged it from heaven as fit for immediate destruction, clearly teaching that Gentile heathen powers have a moral responsibility to the one true God, and will be judged by Him according to the standards of his own holiness, Rom 1. 20.

Jonah's name means 'a dove'. As the dove gives a mournful call, so Jonah was commissioned to be God's mouthpiece against this Gentile sin-city. It was a message of judgement, 1. 2; 3. 4, but behind the cry of warning was the dove-like undertone of mourning love. Jonah knew God was more liable to be gracious and compassionate, 3. 1-2, than judgemental if Nineveh repented. So he fled to Tarshish by ship 'from the presence of the Lord', 1. 1-3. At this point of the history (for history it most certainly is, authenticated by the Lord Himself, Matt. 12. 40-41; Luke 11. 29-30), Jonah is a backslider outside the will of God. God had commanded him to go east, and he was stubbornly travelling west!

Jonah is an enigma in the ways of service for God. How can such a servant, totally out of sympathy with the heart and mind of God, be used at all? But sovereignty uses him, and his mission was wholly successful, 3 10, and his message blessed to the wicked Ninevites. Here is evidence of God's sovereignty in using whom He will, and that success in any particular endeavour for God is not necessarily a sign of divine approbation for the servant. It teaches us to give God alone the glory for sinners converted, and not to glorify the human channel used! Jonah in his experience is a type of Christ, but morally he is a failure.

The wind, v. 4, and the great fish, v. 17, render instant obedience to the Lord of creation, v. 9, and ungodly men honour Him, v. 14—only His stubborn servant refuses His command! Jonah cannot pray, vv. 5-6, because he is backslidden and disobedient. No backslider can effectively pray, for like Jonah he is asleep to reality, subject only to the contempt of the ungodly, and exposed to the storms of God's displeasure.

Jonah 1. 17—2. 10

I CRIED UNTO THE LORD

Prayer can be directed to the Lord from anywhere. If Jonah can be heard from the belly of the great fish, then there is nowhere his saints can cry unto Him unheard. From the deepest experiences and trials of life, from the lowest depression and the darkest pain: from the most impossible predicament, the prayer of desperation ascends surely and inevitably into His holy temple, v. 7. There is a divinely appointed law that invests prayer with its own heavenly homing capacity. It is never lost in the vast universe, or permitted to vanish into the spacious void of infinity. Every prayer directed to God flies, swifter than light, to the sympathetic ear of the universal King. When Jonah, inside the fish, a score of fathoms below the waves, even 'from the belly of hell', v. 2, cried out to God, he knew immediately, 'Thou heardest my voice'. If it was so with the backsliding prophet, much more shall it be true of you, beloved suffering saint, walking in the fear of God and invoking the fragrant name of God's Son, our Saviour, John 16. 23-24. Your prayer is heard, and your deliverance is certain, v. 9.

Jonah's disobedience and backsliding have brought him under the chastening of his divine Master. Prayerless in the bottom of the ship, 1. 6, he cannot remain prayerless in the belly of the fish, 2. 1. His rebellion gone, and his soul submissive, he mightily prayed unto the Lord. His experience, v. 2, is that of the psalmist, 'before I was afflicted I went astray; but now have I kept thy word', Ps. 119. 67. Jonah recognized God's hand in his discipline, and the billows and waves that swamped him were God's billows, v. 3, and so were sent righteously as well as lovingly. The spiritual deserter has now returned to his post and to his first allegiance. His vows are renewed, and his thanksgiving sincere, v. 9. He has learned that he too needs salvation as much as the despised Gentiles, and needs as much mercy as ever wicked Nineveh did, v. 9. Thus a long-suffering God brings His backslidden servant to repentance, and on the third day the Lord commanded the fish, and Jonah was vomited to safety, v. 10.

Jonah 3:1-10

CRY MIGHTILY UNTO GOD

Thus far in the history of Jonah we have seen *God's awesome power*. He prepares a *man*, 1. 1; He commands the *storm*, 1. 4; He prepares a *great fish*, 1. 17; and in chapter 4 He prepares a *gourd*, v. 4, a *worm*, v. 7, and an *east wind*, v. 18. As sovereign Creator He holds the reins of universal dominion, and all things own His mastery. In chapter 3 He prepares a *way of salvation*, vv. 2, 4, a message of judgement leading to pardon on the ground of repentance. Jonah is recommissioned as Jehovah's spokesman, and boldly prophesies the fall of the city, and with it the whole proud Assyrian empire. What courage Jonah now shows, and what dread power God has over the nations, Isa. 40. 17.

Beyond this we see *God's amazing pity* toward Gentiles. In sending Jonah to Nineveh we learn God's scrutiny of, interest in, and authority over, the Gentile nations, and that equally His word is for them as it is for Israel. This is seen today, during the present gospel age, in the universal commission of the gospel, Matt. 28. 19-20. How beautiful to see God's love and compassion for these distant Gentiles, even the worst of them. He sends a message of judgement to warn them in perfect consistency with His compassionate and merciful nature, 4. 2, so that they may come to repentance and be pardoned.

Again, we observe that unbelieving Gentiles can be influenced by the word of God, and won for Him! Even the most hardened and unlikeliest of men may be saved. Who would have thought that high and lofty Nineveh would sit in sackcloth and ashes, and repent and *'cry mightily unto God'*, vv. 5-9, but they did! O dear fellow believer, discouraged because of the immorality, violence, and unbelief of the Gentile society among which we live—it is but a reflection of Nineveh of old. In Nineveh we see that the hardest mission-field yields the most impressive response! Hallelujah!

What a marvellous illustration of God's pardoning mercy upon the most defiant of sinners when they humble themselves, tremble at His word, repent, and turn to Him. It is always true as David found, 'A broken and a contrite heart, O God, thou wilt not despise', Ps. 51. 17.

Jonah 4. 1-11

HE WAS VERY ANGRY. AND HE PRAYED

Jonah's bigoted anger at God's sparing the Ninevites found expression in complaining prayer, vv. 1-2. The presumptuous audacity of the prophet is matched only by *God's astonishing patience* toward His servant. We see in God's patience, with such an extreme case as Jonah, why he is long-suffering with His servants still today, whose tantrums are sometimes as fleshly as Jonah's. From Jonah's angry prayer, v. 2, we discover he fled to Tarshish not for fear of the fierce Ninevites, but for fear of the great grace and mercy of God which he suspected would forgive them. In Jonah we learn it is possible to serve God with seeming success, and yet be completely out of touch with His love and pity for the lost, and even resent His compassion for the distant sinner.

Jonah's story teaches us there is always a way out of spiritual responsibility when the task is distasteful. We all have our personal Nineveh, the place and people to whom God would send us, but how often we prefer a 'ship going to Tarshish'! Yet, as with Jonah, so with us; still God will use us and patiently remonstrate with our folly, vv. 9-11. God's pity is especially seen in the case of the children in Nineveh, v. 11. There were 120,000 children there not yet grown to years of accountability in the matter of guilt and judgement. They are innocent of *actual* sin although not of *original* sin, and this moves the pity of Jehovah's heart. Who can doubt such innocence will always be saved on the basis of divine pity, their inbred sin being covered by the sacrificial power of the blood of Christ.

The purpose of this book is (1) to manifest God's grace and love for Gentile sinners, even the worst; (2) to show His immense long-suffering toward His servants in their disobedience and pride; (3) to reveal His absolute sovereignty over creation to accomplish His purposes of grace; and (4) finally, to turn history into prophecy, for Jonah is a type of Him who was 'greater' than he. Thus in chapter 2 we have types of the sufferings, death, and burial of Christ, His resurrection, and His grace to the Gentiles in the message of life.

Ere we presume to approach God in prayer, let us despatch any angry thoughts that we might hold within us. Then let us freely acknowledge in His presence that it is only **'by grace'** that **'we are saved'**, and that **our salvation** is **'the gift of God'**, Eph. 2. 8.

July 29th

Micah 7. 5-9

MY GOD WILL HEAR ME

This particular portion of God's word has been a comfort to persecuted believers down the centuries. In our own generation, the Chinese preacher WONG MING—who when held for twenty-two years, almost all in solitary confinement, tortured and mocked for his faith in Christ—told this writer in Shanghai that the main Scripture portion that sustained his soul during all those years was Micah 7. 7-9!

For Micah, speaking as the representative of the spiritual remnant of Israel, it was an expression of faith in the ultimate triumph of God, and the vindication of His afflicted people. Good men had gone, and their influence, likened to precious and fragrant fruit, had perished. The land was morally and spiritually barren because the excellent, in whom was all God's delight, had been removed. The overwhelming influence was now degenerate and corrupt; to find a good man was like finding choice grapes when the vintage had been gleaned, v. 1. The whole of society was depraved, violent, evil, and corrupt, vv. 1-3.

It is amazing how, time and again, circumstances in Old Testament history reflect similar conditions in this modern age. Here is the value of such Scriptures; they encourage believers in parallel situations today to take hope. The godly of past generations lived under the same conditions, and came through victoriously for God.

Yet, verses 4-6 are also prophetic and quoted by Christ to show the kind of persecution His mainly Jewish disciples would suffer for following Him, with dark overtones looking on to the final apocalyptic endtime persecutions, the Tribulation, Matt. 10. 21-22, 35-36.

In the final section, vv. 7-9, Micah roots his faith and hope in the reality of God. If one cannot trust the nearest and dearest, or the old familiar friend, vv. 5-6, there is Another who is nearer and dearer still. It is the Friend 'that sticketh closer than a brother'. Micah *looks* to Him, *waits* for Him and *knows* that He will hear him. Let us also cry out in prayer when our hearts are overwhelmed by the darkness of the times. Our God will hear, and though we pass through dark days and appear to fall in the eyes of the enemy, v. 8, yet we shall arise and in the present darkness God shall be our light.

July 30th
Habakkuk 1. 1-4

HOW LONG SHALL I CRY AND THOU WILT NOT HEAR?

Habakkuk was perplexed by the problem of providence. Does God really rule? Does He really care? Is He interested in what happens in the world? Disasters, international, national or personal, thrust these questions on God's people still. The poet's words are so apt:- 'He hides Himself so wondrously, as if there were no God' (F W FABER).

In our verses, the heart of the prophet is wrung by **unanswered prayer**. Habakkuk had constantly been in God's presence, crying out because of conditions in Judah. He had prayed, not out of self-interest, but with the true interests of the nation and God's glory at heart. Yet, still, heaven was silent. Cruel, oppressive violence provoked his anguished prayers. Evil abounded. The wicked triumphed. Injustice prevailed. God's law was ignored. Human justice, such as it was, was perverted. Despite all this, God did not bare His holy arm. No latter-day flood burst on Judah, Gen. 6. 11. In the face of wickedness, God was inactive. In the face of prayer, God was indifferent. So it seemed to Habakkuk. So often his bafflement is ours.

From his heart cry we learn:

1. **Persistence in Prayer**. Habakkuk had persevered in his cries. His very persistence increased his distress. 'Still no answer, Lord, yet I've prayed so long'. Yet he didn't give up. He kept on praying. God may well delay His answers to produce in us the persistence in prayer He prizes. Keep on praying, Luke 18. 1-8; Eph. 6. 18.

2. **Concern in Prayer**. Habakkuk brought national needs and contemporary concerns to the Lord. There was a real depth and breadth in his prayers. He felt passionately the evil of his days. Do we mourn the violence and immorality of our society, the apostasy and ineffectiveness of the church, in prayer? Are we zealous for God's glory? Be earnest in prayer.

3. **Honesty in Prayer**. Habakkuk spilled out his emotions, and his frustrations to the Lord. Do we ever pray like that? God invites us to pour out our heart before Him, Ps. 62. 8. What a recourse! Be genuine in prayer.

July 31st

Habakkuk 1. 12-17.

O LORD MY GOD, MINE HOLY ONE

Habakkuk has wrestled with **unanswered prayer**. Now he must wrestle with an **unexpected answer to prayer**. God gave him a response, yet it deepened his perplexity. God will judge apostate Judah. He will raise up the Chaldeans to do it, Hab. 1. 6. What a judgement! An invincible, unstoppable military machine. 'Might is right' is their philosophy, Hab. 1. 7. 'Might is God' is their religion, Hab. 1. 11 (see e.g. JND, NIV).

Habakkuk is astounded. Judah is bad but Babylon is worse, Hab. 1. 13. How can God use them to judge His own people? How can He tolerate their cruelty? Will He endure their delight in aggression? Will the Lord allow their rampage to go on for ever?

Often, we too face mysteries in life. We need to take them to God as Habakkuk does. We should begin with what **we know of Him**. Habakkuk rehearses the attributes of God. We live in a man-centred age, and we can easily imbibe its spirit. We need to remind ourselves often of God's greatness and glory. Habakkuk grasps that God is everlasting. No one came before Him. None will come after Him. He recognizes Him as the Sovereign Lord, in grace and in judgement. The prophet bows before God's utter holiness, His radiant transcendence, perfect purity and absolute abhorrence of sin. He reminds himself that this God is the Rock (e.g. JND, NIV) ('mighty God' AV), totally reliable and wholly unshakeable. This is the God who invites us to draw near but whom we approach with awe.

Habakkuk rests on his personal relationship with God. Note 'my God' and 'my Holy One'. Like Paul, he knew whom he had believed and that He was able to keep him safe to the end, 2 Tim. 1. 12. God's people have a secure salvation because of who God is: so 'we shall not die', Hab. 1. 12. They are kept by His strong hold of them, not their weak hold of Him.

Habakkuk then leaves the enigma in the hands of the Lord. So should we. We cannot unravel all the tangled threads of life for this is beyond us. Instead we should be content like Habakkuk to rehearse what we know, rest on the Lord whom we know, and reserve what we do not know to His wisdom, goodness and power. Is that not to live by faith?, Hab. 2. 4.

August 1st
Habakkuk 3. 1-6

O LORD, REVIVE THY WORK

In Habakkuk chapter 2, the Lord answers the prophet's problem about His use of the Chaldeans. God tells Habakkuk that they will be judged, but at His appointed time. God's people will be delivered. Until then, the godly must wait, trusting God every day.

The prophet pens a triumphant psalm, responding in awe to this revelation. He pleads that God will bring His work to life again. He asks that God will do what He has promised in destruction and deliverance. He prays that the Lord will shorten the waiting time. Habakkuk yearns that the Lord will do in the future what He has done in the past. Verses 3-6 call to mind the glorious manifestations of God's presence. Habakkuk longs to experience that in his day.

We need to be aware of what God has done in Scripture and in church history. Our spiritual heritage should lead us to pray that the Lord will be with us as He was with our forefathers, 1 Kgs. 8. 57. Times of spiritual renewal are a return, at least in part, to the freshness of apostolic Christianity. The desperate spiritual and moral needs of our society should cause us to cry, 'Do it again, Lord!'.

Days of revival are days of divine visitation. God's presence is felt in a very real way. His word is preached in power, 1 Thess. 1. 5. Thus He is revealed in grace and glory. Earthly things become unreal. Eternity becomes the great reality to men and women. The transforming touch of the Holy Spirit is felt on individuals and communities. The imprint remains for generations.

Such days cannot be worked up. They can be prayed down. That is the challenge of our text. The great revival of 1858-59 began in a lunch-time prayer meeting in New York. When it was advertised first of all, the man who had arranged it was the only one present. Numbers grew. From that meeting revival fires blazed across North America. A few young men in County Antrim heard of the New York meetings and they too met to pray. From their humble gathering revival came to Ulster and from there to the rest of the British Isles. **Revivals are born in prayer**. 'Wilt thou not revive us again; that thy people may rejoice in thee?', Ps. 85. 6.

August 2nd

Habakkuk 3. 7-19.

THOU WENTEST FORTH FOR ... THY PEOPLE

Habakkuk continues his exultant psalm. In verses 7-15, he celebrates the victories of God. The Lord is dramatically portrayed as the divine warrior, Exod. 15. 3. The prophet weaves a glorious tapestry with the threads drawn from stirring events in Israel's past. The Exodus and the conquest of Canaan are depicted. God triumphs at the Red Sea. He opens up the Jordan. The sun and moon stand still at His command. All the forces of nature are under His control. The Lord subdues His foes in His all-conquering march. Throughout, He acts for the salvation of His people. But this history is also prophecy, for this mighty psalm looks to the destruction of Babylon as its immediate fulfilment and beyond that, to the final triumph of God in the end times. Victory is assured, for God will vindicate the cause of His people and above all of His anointed One, the Christ, v. 13.

Habbukuk celebrates God's faithfulness as well as His power. God did not intervene in nature because He had a conflict with rivers or seas. These miracles of natural upheaval took place because of the faithfulness of God to His sworn word, v. 9. God's promises cannot fail. He will not break His word nor can He be forced to break it.

No wonder Habakkuk rejoices in the Lord in the final stanza of his psalm, in vv. 16-19. In one of the most beautiful passages in Scripture, these moving verses express his confidence in God. The prophet trembles at the prospect of devastation facing his land. He foresees a situation which could not be any worse. Yet even if he loses everything, he still has his God and God is sufficient. Nothing can shake a personal relationship with the living God. This brings strength in weakness, joy in distress and deliverance in disaster. Even in the blackest hours of life we can share with Habakkuk a trembling, yet confident, faith in the God of our salvation.

August 3rd
Zechariah 8. 20-23

LET US GO SPEEDILY TO PRAY BEFORE THE LORD

Zechariah is supremely the prophet of Messiah's glory in His first and second advents. Our verses are the climax of a glowing prophecy of Israel's future restoration in Christ's coming kingdom. That glorious age will be an age of earnest prayer. True worship will then be universal. Israel, restored to God's favour, will be a messianic people—His representatives among the nations.

Zechariah foresees that God will replace Israel's fasts with feasts, solemn commemoration with joyful celebration. He will do this by miraculous intervention. God is the God of the impossible. These will be the days of the Lord's renewed presence in Jerusalem. Zion will know peace and security. Israel will be regathered and converted. God's holy jealousy will secure this happy future.

These coming days will be marked by deep desires to entreat the favour of the Lord and to seek His face. That will be the most urgent concern of life. City will spread to city the invitation to enjoy communion with God. Note the individual response in verse 21 to that earnest appeal, 'I will go also'. We should have the same commitment now to go on to seek the Lord's face and to encourage others to do so. Are these our most pressing concerns?

Longing for real communion with the true God will be universal. False religion will be no more. Jerusalem will be the centre of divine illumination for all the world. There the nations will stream to experience the Lord's presence. Let us take heart. God's cause will finally triumph. His truth will prevail.

God will give Israel a world-wide role. Their restoration will be a blessing to all the nations. The world will know that God is with them and will yearn to share His presence. Through the Jews the Gentiles will come to know God as verse 23 dramatically illustrates. May God give us, too, the privilege of leading others to share with us His blessing today.

August 4th

Zechariah 10. 1

ASK OF THE LORD RAIN IN THE TIME OF THE LATTER RAIN

This is 'one of the most beautiful Scriptures in the Old Testament in reference to prayer and God's manner of answering', DAVID BARON. God exhorts His people to ask Him for rain. The Old Testament, written in the Middle East, constantly stresses that the God of Israel and He alone is the giver of rain, Jer. 14. 22. The Creator and Sustainer of the universe is Sovereign of the weather. The latter rain is the spring rain. The autumn or former rains prepared the soil. The spring rains matured the crops for harvest. Both former and latter rains are promised by the Lord to His obedient people, Deut. 11. 13-15. Rain was indispensable for life in Palestine. Thus the rain includes all other temporal blessings and symbolizes all spiritual ones. Israel shall yet enjoy the full provision of her Shepherd King; God is the giver of every good and perfect gift, giving us richly all things to enjoy, Jas. 1. 17; 1 Tim. 6. 17.

God's promise is the incentive to pray. He exhorts us to seek His blessing and promises to grant it. The promises of God are the fuel on the altar of His people's prayers. It is in answer to believing prayer that He bestows His gifts. So often we forget this! James reminds us that 'we have not because we ask not'; God is well able to answer prayer. He delights to do so. The Lord Jesus promises that what we ask in faith we shall receive, Matt. 21. 22. Can we not take Him at His word?

God's liberality is the index of His response. He says that if asked for rain He will give 'pouring rain' (BARON). He is able to do exceeding abundantly above all that we ask, Eph. 3. 20. Thus He glorifies His grace and encourages us to trust Him and to value prayer. We can never ask too much.

God's fatherly concern secures the individualization of His promised blessings. To each is given 'grass in the field'. Not one is left out of the bountiful provision. The Lord knows all His people intimately. He is able to bless each of us personally with the very blessing that we most need. Seek that promised blessing as you seek His face today.

WHEREIN HAST THOU LOVED US?

Malachi begins with God declaring His love for His people. Yet Israel's response is a querulous 'Wherein hast thou loved us?'. They challenge God to prove His love. The assertion of divine love did not produce praise and devotion. Instead it revealed peevishness and doubt.

The Lord accepts the challenge. He enters a dialogue, explaining how He has loved His people. He reminds them of their ancestor Jacob and his twin, Esau. God's love is discriminating. God had displayed holy disfavour towards Esau and his descendants. Yet Jacob and his descendants were the objects of God's mercy. Likewise all that we are we owe to grace alone. All boasting is excluded. It is God who has made us to differ. We have nothing which we did not receive, 1 Cor. 4. 7. All our blessings have their source in God's eternal love, Eph. 1. 4.

That love is unconditional. It does not rest on human merit, Rom. 9. 10-13. It was Jacob, as Jacob, in all his twistedness who was chosen. He had no greater claim on God than Esau. Indeed Esau was the older twin. The vessels of honour are from the same lump as those of dishonour, Rom. 9. 21. God's love for Israel did not arise from anything in them, Deut. 7. 7-8; 8. 10-15. So too we can humbly and gratefully sing, 'Chosen not for good in me'.

God's love made a dramatic difference. He had restored Israel to their land. The Edomites had been dispossessed just as Judah had been. Edom lay a desolate waste, and so it would remain. God would dash Edom's plans to rebuild their cities; they would know no restoration.

Petra's ruins are a silent witness to the fulfilment of this prophecy. The destruction of Edom was due to God's judgement on her sins of selfish unconcern and proud hatred of Israel.

Solemnly God's name is magnified, both in wrath and in grace. What a debt of praise is owed by those who have known His mercy!

August 6th

Malachi 1. 6-8

WHEREIN HAVE WE DESPISED THY NAME?

Israel had failed to grasp God's gracious love for them. They doubted and disputed it. Not surprisingly, their devotion to God was minimal. God rebukes them with an illustration. Sons honour fathers and servants honour masters, yet Israel had no real respect for God, the supreme Father and absolute Master. The fear of the Lord was wholly absent; they knew no reverential awe. God challenges the priests directly. They above all should have honoured His name, but instead, they had despised it. Could anything better be expected of the people?

Their response is once again to demand proof from God. He demonstrates that Israel's devotion was defective. They dared to bring blemished animals for sacrifice, defying God's word. God demanded the best, yet Israel offered the worst. The altar was treated with contempt—blind, lame and sick beasts were presented as victims. With deep irony, God appeals once again to every-day life. 'Try offering them to your governor', v. 8 NIV. What mere man would refuse to accept was being offered to the Great King, v. 14. The Lord pronounces that all of this was evil, v. 8.

We cannot evade the challenge of this passage. Animal sacrifices are no longer required but God looks for the sacrifice of praise, Heb. 13. 15, monetary gifts, Heb. 13. 16, and, above all, ourselves, Rom. 12. 1. It is only too easy to forget the radical demands of consecration and settle down to a life of minimum Christianity. The Lord claims all that we are and have. Real Christian living involves cost and commitment, however unpalatable these ideas are today.

The Lord is more than worthy to receive **our best**. Dare we offer Him merely the 'left-overs' of our time, our talents and our treasure? May He preserve us from thus despising His name!

Malachi 2. 17.

YE HAVE WEARIED THE LORD WITH YOUR WORDS

Unlike us, God can never actually be weary, Isa. 40. 28. He is self-sufficient and all sufficient. No task is too much for Him. Nothing can tire Him, even the vastness of human need. Certainly He is never wearied by the authentic prayers of His people. He delights to hear and answer them. Yet, speaking after the manner of men, God can be wearied by our sins, Isa. 1. 14; 43. 24. This is a strong figure of speech, indicating that there is a limit to God's patience. Here the Lord expresses His weariness at the words of Israel. They challenge that assertion.

God replies to the challenge and justifies His distress—He was well aware of the people's words, but the attitude behind them was resentful and defiant. Israel had not enjoyed the material prosperity they expected, and this led them to question God's rule of the world. They said that God delighted in evil-doers—pagans were God's favourites. They challenged the justice of God in an arrogant question, 'Where is the God of judgement?'. These charges were monstrous and false. God does not esteem evil-doers as good, and He takes no delight in their deeds. Rather He delights in acts of righteousness, mercy and truth. In short, their words were 'nothing short of blasphemy' (W KAISER). God is a God of absolute justice.

God demonstrates this as He deigns to answer their question. The future will reveal that He is indeed the God of righteousness. They had asked for judgement, and judgement they would receive. The Lord would intervene. He promises a messenger to prepare His way. Then He Himself will come as the Messenger of the covenant, the Lord Jesus Christ. That coming will be a day of refining and a day of final judgement against all evil-doers. Thus, God will vindicate at last His own righteous character against all the calumnies of men. However, before that coming in judgement, the Lord has first come in grace. The day of grace, inaugurated at His first advent, is still running and the day of judgement is still delayed. What an opportunity of witness this affords us! May our witness be upheld by earnest prayer. We seek help from One who is never wearied at the words we address to Him in sincerity and in truth.

August 8th

Malachi 3. 7

WHEREIN SHALL WE RETURN?

In verse 6, the Lord declares His unchangeability, cf. Ps. 102. 26-27. God is perfect. Thus He cannot change for the better. Even less can He change for the worse. He is utterly dependable and wholly reliable. Apart from this, Israel could not have continued to exist. Characteristically, they were the sons of Jacob, marked and marred by sin as their father had been. They would have been consumed in judgement long since but for the constancy of their covenant-keeping God. Their security rested on God's purpose, and His purpose is anchored in His character. Our security too depends on the absolute faithfulness of our immutable Saviour.

The unchanging God calls on His people to change. Throughout their history they had continually failed to keep His commandments. Unlike the Lord, they had been fickle and unreliable. Now God calls them to return to Him, as he had done so often before. 'The message of all Israel's prophets could be put in this one word 'return', Zech. 1. 3-4' (W KAISER). It is repeated again here by the last writing prophet. The Lord graciously promises that, if they returned, He would return to His people in blessing. Instead of admitting their rebellion and changing course, the people once again reply, 'Wherein shall we return?'. They protest their innocence. In effect they are saying that they have no need to repent. They cannot see how they should return to the Lord. They seek to deflect the searing challenge of the living word of God. Do we not do the same?

Malachi's prophecy has already answered their question. It has told them clearly enough how they should return to God. **Reformation was the need of the hour**; in worship, spiritual leadership, family life and personal attitudes. God was seeking costly devotion instead of half-hearted formalism, 1. 6-14, exemplary teachers of His word instead of a corrupt hierarchy, 2. 1-9, fidelity in marriage not treachery in divorce, 2. 10-16, and humble faith, not arrogant unbelief, 2. 17-3. 5. Is not the message of Malachi a message for our own times?

237

August 9th
Malachi 3. 8-10

WHEREIN HAVE WE ROBBED THEE?

The Lord continues His debate with His people. Far from returning to Him, in truth they had robbed Him. They protest with yet another 'Wherein?' to this accusation. God spells out the charge of robbery. They had been parsimonious in their tithes and offerings, so that God was cheated of His due. Their failure to tithe deprived the Levites, the priests and the poor of resources, but it was actually the Lord Himself who was defrauded. As a result, the land languished under His discipline; poor yields and crop failure prevailed in field and vineyard.

The New Testament never imposes the tithe. No fixed percentage for giving is laid down. However, God is still concerned about how His people use their resources. Should not the response of the believer under grace be greater, not less, than in the Old Testament? Certainly we must give regularly to the Lord and in proportion to our resources, 1 Cor. 16. 1-2. We are to give gladly and with purpose—God loves the cheerful giver, 2 Cor. 9. 7. Ultimately, all we have comes from God and belongs to Him. The tithe was to remind Israel of that truth. God commands us too in these terms; 'bring the whole tithe in the treasure-house', v. 10 JND. This means first of all the **consecration of ourselves**, 2 Cor. 8. 4-5, and then the glad **committal of our every gift** (our money, abilities, efforts and energies). We hold all in trust for the Lord. Do we ever honestly assess our stewardship? Are we seeking to bring 'the whole tithe' or are we robbing God?

Here the Lord issues a challenge as well as a command. 'Put me to the test', He says. If the whole tithe is devoted to Him, cursing will give place to blessing. The desolate land will become delightful, v. 12. Indeed, God will open the floodgates of heaven and shower His people with superabundant blessing. He dares them to strain His resources and to drain them, if that were possible. What a promise! He who sows bountifully will reap bountifully, 2 Cor. 9. 6. Have we ever put God to the test? Have we obeyed His command, accepted His challenge and claimed His promise? Far from robbing God, let us freely offer to Him that which we have to give, so to prove by His response that our bountiful God is no man's debtor.

238

August 10th
Malachi 3. 13-18

WHAT HAVE WE SPOKEN SO MUCH AGAINST THEE?

As Malachi's prophecy draws to a close, the Lord again raises with the people the matter of their resentful murmuring against His providence. He tells them that their words were 'stout' AV, or 'harsh' NIV, against Him, v. 13. They were presumptuous and arrogant in their cavilling. This is only shown the more by their response in yet another impudent 'wherein?' RV ('what?' in AV). The Lord again proves His case. The murmurers and complainers had gone so far as to say that there was no point in serving God. They were getting no financial return from keeping His word. Indeed they proclaimed that the proud were happy. They declared that the wicked prospered and wholly escaped God's judgement, and that serving God made no difference in life. Actually one was better off wicked than pious, they affirmed. Effectively they were saying that they had put God to the test but He had failed them. Ironically they gave so little to the Lord yet expected so much materially in return. Their attitude was blasphemous. They had no fear of the Lord at all.

Yet not all of Malachi's contemporaries spoke like this. There was a godly remnant, and their hallmark was the fear of the Lord. They grasped His grandeur and glory. This sense of awe affected all of their life, and was the root of their whole life-style. Their minds were focused on the Lord. They loved fellowship with each other, sharing their thoughts of Him. God is still looking for people like this, and the question is raised, 'Are we among them?'. God was well aware of this company, and their names and actions were recorded in heaven. The Lord had been their special treasure, they would be His. He would wholly spare them from His future outpoured judgement.

That dreadful judgement will dramatically display that there is indeed a difference between godly and ungodly—those who serve God and those who do not. The day of the Lord is coming, and with it, absolute destruction of the wicked and complete deliverance of the righteous. Live in the light of eternity today. **Speak to Him** with a grateful heart, and with glowing lips **speak of Him**—we are assured that the Lord 'listens' and that he 'hears', see v. 16 NKJ.

August 11th

Luke 1. 5-17

ZACHARIAS

The Gospel of Luke is the gospel of prayer. Since the God who hears, also answers prayer, cares, loves, and has compassion, we hear the words 'Fear not' repeatedly in this Gospel; 1. 13, 30; 2. 10; 5. 10; 8. 50; 12. 7, 32.

Here the angel addresses Zacharias with these words, informing him that the time has come for his prayer to be answered in a wonderful, remarkable way, vv. 13-17. The message from the angel contains allusions and references to that with which Zacharias would have been very familiar, namely the Nazarite, in Numbers chapter 6 verses 2 and 3; Samson's birth, in Judges chapter 13 verses 3 and 5; the final message of the Old Testament, Malachi chapter 4 verses 5-6, with mention of Elijah. Yet Zacharias stumbles in unbelief at God`s answer, Luke 1. 20. How often we fail the Lord! If ever a man should have responded in faith it was Zacharias; note his pedigree, v. 5, his character, v. 6, the character of his wife, v. 6, and his activity and location when the answer is given, vv. 8-9.

We may contrast Mary's response to the angel's message to her: one of faith and submissiveness, yet she lacks the standing, background, experience and maturity of Zacharias. She is but a 'young sister'. Whilst Zacharias doubted whether **what** Gabriel said would happen, Mary was perplexed as to **the way** it would happen.

How vital faith is throughout life! The psalmist could say, 'I believed, therefore have I spoken', Ps. 116. 10; whereas Zacharias, not believing, could not speak. At the end of Luke we find the disciples 'in the temple, praising and blessing God', Luke 24. 53. Is not this what ought to be as we break bread; or are we dumb priests?

Here we have a long delayed answer to prayer, from our viewpoint; but God does not forget our prayers. How many answers to prayer have occurred subsequent to the death of the one who prayed? Our Lord's prayer for His own, John 17. 24, is still being answered today. We must leave the timing to Him, and watch and wait prayerfully as to the unfolding of His will and the outworking of His purposes, both generally and in our own lives.

SIMEON

Along with Zacharias, Elisabeth and Anna, Simeon follows in the line of those believers in the days of Malachi who, amidst apostasy and hypocrisy, 'spake often one to another', whom 'the Lord … heard', Mal. 3. 16. In those days there were men and women in fellowship with the Lord, and the Lord heard what they said. Here we have a man who hears what the Lord said, vv. 26, 29. Those who desire the fellowship of believers are those who desire fellowship with the Lord, and vice versa, 1 John 1. 3. This is seen in Mary's going to Elisabeth, subsequent to her hearing what the Lord said, Luke 1. 38-40.

Simeon, a 'just and devout' man, was 'waiting for' the coming of the Saviour. Here is something else that is linked in Scripture: a life of righteousness and an attitude of expectancy regarding the Lord's coming. Paul links a 'sober, righteous and godly' life with 'looking for the blessed hope and appearing of the glory of our great God and Saviour Jesus Christ'. The connection is more clear in the Greek, as the words for 'waiting for' and 'looking for' are the same, as is the case with the words 'just' and 'righteously', see Luke 2. 25; Titus 2. 12-13 RV. It is put succinctly by John in his first letter, 'every man that has this hope in him purifieth himself', 3. 3.

Simeon is in the right place at the right time, controlled by the Holy Spirit, and thus his words are fit words, words that honour God and exalt the Lord Jesus. His brief prayer exhibits a clear grasp of prophecy, v. 32; a definite understanding of the significance of what was happening before him, vv. 30-31; and a submissive spirit, v. 29. Simeon is now experiencing the promises of God being fulfilled in a specific and personal way, and his first and immediate response is to 'bless God', v. 28.

Those who are most in touch with heaven will most clearly convey what heaven communicates. If we would be effective preachers and witnesses to the world, we must be in close contact with the Focus of our preaching, and the Subject of our witness. The prayer life of the faithful witness and preacher is well known to the Lord.

August 13th

Luke 3. 21-22

THE LORD IN THE CRISES OF LIFE

It is well known that it is Luke of the gospel writers who draws attention to the prayer life of the Lord Jesus: there are eleven references, nine of which are peculiar to Luke, including the one here. Here indeed is the perfectly dependent man. In all the crises, significant moments and major decisions of His life, we find the Lord **prayed**: His baptism; the choosing of the twelve; the transfiguration; Gethsemane; the crucifixion. His praying here clearly demonstrates a spirit of submission and dependence on God right at the beginning of His public ministry. This needs to be emphasized today; it is not self-assertion, self-esteem and independence that God values in men and women, but a submissive spirit, an obedient heart, meekness and gentleness.

Here is the first 'official' view of its Messiah by Israel—a praying man, to whom 'the heaven was opened', v. 21.

He did not confess sins as did the others being baptized, Matt 3. 6, but He prayed as the others did. Here is Israel's Messiah being set forth publicly, and is the Lord's prayer a renewing of His commitment to the will and purposes of God? As the cross was ever before Him, especially during His years of ministry, were certain scriptures also ever before Him, in particular perhaps some of the psalms? Psalm 40. 7-8 may often have been on His mind, even at the time of His baptism, 'Lo, I come to do thy will, O my God'. His baptism was a major step on the road to Calvary and the declaration of John also clearly affirms this: 'Behold the Lamb of God, which taketh away the sin of the world', John 1. 29. In between the two would come the fulfilling of verses 9 and 10 of the psalm; the 'preaching of righteousness'; 'the declaring of God's faithfulness and his salvation', the 'not concealing of God's loving-kindness and truth from the great congregation'. All of these are very clearly exhibited in the gospel narratives.

The response from heaven, v. 22, shows that God heard the prayer of His Son. Whenever He prayed He was heard. In Hebrews we read that He was heard in 'that he feared', 5. 7. True, godly reverence characterized Him. In this, as in all things, He is our example.

August 14th

Mark 1. 32-39

THE LORD IN THE MORNING

The lives of servants in New Testament times must have been demanding, not least in the realm of time; there would be little spare time. We cannot read Mark`s Gospel without realizing how busy our Lord was, and how demanding His service, to such an extent that He and the twelve on two occasions had been so occupied that they had no leisure, so much as to eat, 3. 20; 6. 31. It comes as no surprise to find the first reference to our Lord`s praying in Mark is in the early morning, before work began, 1. 35, even though He had been extremely busy the evening before, vv. 32-34. There would be little opportunity to 'shut the door' later.

However, there are other reasons why the Lord prayed when He did. The service of the Lord was at the Father`s bidding. In Isaiah chapter 50 verses 4-6 we read of the Servant being wakened 'morning by morning', his 'ear' being 'opened' and 'wakened' to 'hear as the instructed', JND. The Lord waited upon God before the day commenced for the teaching He would give, the actions He would perform, the paths He would tread, John 5. 19, 30. As we peruse our chapter we hear 'the tongue of the learned' in verse 22; we see the weary sustained with a word in verses 30-31; and the Lord not being rebellious in verses 38-39. Later, He will fulfil Isaiah 50. 6, and not hide His 'face from shame and spitting', giving His 'back to the smiter'.

Did the Lord view prayer as supplementary to, or an integral aspect of, His work? Was prayer just as much work as preaching or cleaning His sandals? Was prayer the key aspect of His work; that which made the rest of it effective and God-honouring? Does prayer make fit for work and work necessitate prayer? We can cut, hammer, and nail so busily that the Architect has no opportunity to discuss His plans with us. We must view verse 35 in the context of verses 32-34 and 36-39. Similarly the apostles viewed their work, as 'prayer, and the ministry of the word', Acts 6. 4.

To rise early to pray was the Lord's practice; the Psalms furnish us with many examples, 5. 3; 59. 16; 63. 1; 88. 13. When God`s perfect Servant prayed is when assuredly His fallible servants ought to pray. Surely, He is our example.

THE LORD IN THE EVERYDAY

The Lord, as we have seen, prayed at the critical points of His earthly life; but, equally, He prayed in the ordinariness of life. So we find the Lord praying here. Communion and fellowship, between the Father and the Son was continuous, but at times the Lord was drawn to prayer by various factors. Was the chief factor here weariness in service? For the Lord had been giving and serving; we read that 'great multitudes came together to hear (Him), and to be healed by him of their infirmities', v. 15. Perhaps it was because the Lord had been cheered and encouraged by a simple believer, a leper, who had exhibited faith, and He wanted to share this with the Father? So out of' 'positive' and 'negative' factors we may be drawn to the Father in prayer—He is the One who ever listens.

There is potential temptation in many situations, such as we find in the Scriptures when the Lord prayed. How easy for us to become boastful, and puffed-up, feeling we are someone special if multitudes should follow us, if a fame went abroad about us, as happened here in verse 15. The remedy for this is also here— to draw aside, and to humble ourselves under the mighty hand of God. In His presence there can be neither boasting nor self-exaltation. The more we find ourselves in public prominence the more we need to put ourselves in the secret, private place before God, that we might be 'poor and of a contrite spirit', Isa. 66. 1-2. When Solomon had just been appointed king, in praying to the Lord, he refers to himself as a 'little child', who knew not 'how to go out or come in', and as God's 'servant', 1 Kings 3. 7-8. Happy would he have been, and his people, had he continued in that attitude.

The Lord withdraws into the wilderness, as no doubt was His practice, 'shutting the door', Matt. 6. 6. The busy hum of the world is not conducive to spiritual meditation. Sometimes He went to a solitary place, Mark 1. 35; sometimes to the hills and the mountains, Mark 6. 46; Luke 9. 28; and to a garden, Luke 22. 39. The example is clear; in any ordinary day we need a secret place, an inner chamber, to be alone with the Father—shut away from men, shut up to God.

August 16th

Luke 6. 12-13

THE LORD ON THE MOUNTAIN

Our Lord's practice was to pray in the morning, Mark 1. 35, but special prayer was engaged in at times. The choosing of the twelve requires care and wisdom. Is the Lord praying as to who to choose, or for those He has chosen? Since He knew all things, it was the latter; but the example is there for us, who do not. As He foresees their trials and temptations, as a result of being His followers, He prays for them. So later, foreseeing Satan's attack, He prays, Luke 22. 31-32.

This is the one occasion where we read of the Lord spending the whole night in prayer; as His public service continued so man's hatred and religious opposition intensified. We see this in the response of the scribes and Pharisees to the healing of the man with the withered hand, v. 11. When the world bares its fangs, in rage, hatred, animosity, we must seek the Lord, who is our refuge, consolation and strength. The Lord retired to pray when the crowds thronged Him and 'success' was His, 5. 15-16. Now He does this when opposition and 'set-back' are His portion. 'In all circumstances prayer was the resource of the perfect man', F B HOLE. Again an experience of the psalmist parallels that of the Lord, 'They have spoken against me with a lying tongue. They compassed me about also with words of hatred; and fought against me without a cause. (In return) for my love they are my adversaries: but I give myself unto prayer', Ps. 109. 2-4, see also Pss. 5. 7-9; 69. 9-13. Many psalms find their 'fulfilment' in the Lord's life.

The Lord prays on '**the**' mountain, JND, the article suggesting a familiar place, VINCENT. The mountain is a place from which everything can be seen in true perspective. Ten spies viewed Canaan's inhabitants as of a great stature and the sons of Anak as giants, but Caleb and Joshua saw them as defenceless. David viewed Goliath very differently from the rest of Israel. Elisha saw two armies from Dothan's walls, whilst his servant saw only one. In Exodus chapter 17 we have a clear relationship established between prayer on the mountain and conflict and victory in the valley. Let us view things from the perspective of the mountain of God, sustained by faith.

WHEN WE PRAY

The Lord's teaching on prayer focuses on (1) the place of prayer, (2) the purpose of prayer, and (3) the procedure of prayer. He clearly assumes we do pray—not 'if', but 'when' we pray, v. 5. Do we? This may seem a strange question. Nevertheless, we need to ask ourselves the question. For instance, how many of us, privately in our own homes, pray on the Lord's Day for the Gospel Meeting? If the extent of the blessing of God at these meetings was commensurate with the extent of our praying, how much blessing would there be?

The **place** of prayer is the unseen, unnoticed, private one. We are told to shut out the clamorous world, by the door that also shuts in the solitary worshipper and intercessor. Therefore we need a **time** when we shall not be disturbed. As we have seen, the Lord prayed in the early morning, Mark 1. 35. We need to be practical: sometimes the telephone and other distractions may prevent us regularly from putting into practice the Lord's teaching. Our lives need to be ordered if we are to do what our Lord requests. An ordered life, a closed door, an open ear, and an open heart are needed.

The **purpose** of prayer is to have dealings with our Father, to be 'seen' by Him; it is not for public acclaim, to impress others. Very simply, prayer is God-ward not man-ward. We need to remember this in assembly gatherings.

The **procedure** in prayer is to be simple, direct and brief. We are not to approach God our Father as if He does not know already what we need and are going to ask for, v. 8; as if He is reluctant and grudging in responding to us. The publican's prayer was readily answered, Luke 18. 13-14; and so was the dying thief's, Luke 23. 42-43. Many words are not necessary; He reads our hearts in any case. We do, however, need to **listen**, and there has to be time to listen. Habakkuk gives us a good example, 2. 1.

As our Father is wise, knowledgeable, and perfect, we can pray to Him in confidence and trust. The practice of prayer will open our lives to him, so that His will can be done in and through us; and so the happy Father/child relationship will deepen.

August 18th

Luke 11. 1-4

WHAT AND HOW WE SHOULD PRAY

How great is the power of unconscious influence! The disciples knew how often the Lord resorted to a solitary place to pray in the early morning, Mark 1. 35; had recently witnessed His face shining, and His being transfigured 'as he prayed', Luke 9. 29; and observed His looking up to heaven as He wrought some of His miracles, e.g. Luke 9. 16. They now wanted to pray like this, to enter into the secrets of prayer.

They must however have noticed that His praying was different: confession and contrition were absent. Thus it is a misnomer to call this prayer the Lord's prayer .

In its specific focus, this prayer is not for us at all. The disciples here are being seen as Jews, and it is in the Tribulation period that this prayer will find expression in its appropriate context, by all who do not bow down to 'the beast'. As Daniel, they will acknowledge the God of heaven, v. 2. They will honour His name, whilst the beast will blaspheme against God, 'to blaspheme his name', Rev. 13. 6; they will pray for His kingdom to come and His will to be done; and as they will not be able to buy or sell, they will pray literally for bread 'day by day'; and to be delivered from the 'evil one', Matt. 6. 13 RV.

Nevertheless, there are here **principles** of prayer. We must begin with God, His concerns, His praise. We must be reverent and respectful. The main things are God's name, honour and kingdom, whilst our requests are secondary. Yet the common things of life are not outside the scope of prayer, nor the concern of the Father; our needs are important, especially for forgiveness, moral guidance and succour. Forgiveness is very important. Do we sufficiently realize the importance of the need to confess our sins to God? John tells us to 'confess our sins', but do we?

God's will to be done: this is the grand objective of all true prayer, and nowhere is it more clearly demonstrated than in Gethsemane. The great overriding object of our Lord's life and prayer was not the laying down of His life at the cross, but the doing of the Father's will. That, and that alone, was all important, Luke 22. 42.

August 19th
Luke 11. 5-10

ASK, AND IT SHALL BE GIVEN YOU

The Lord here encourages His followers to pray persistently, earnestly and determinedly; to pray with their heart in it. Sometimes we are tempted in this matter of intercession and petition to give up, to ask for a while and then to forget the matter. The Lord enjoins us to keep on asking, seeking, knocking. God rewards those who are in earnest, for they are like Himself: He seeks the sheep until He finds it. The man in the parable is displeased at being asked for bread at midnight, whereas God is surely pleased when we supplicate His throne of grace. He is the only One who has the resources available. If we do not obtain from Him, we shall not obtain at all. All depends upon Him. So we can sow, but God alone can give the increase; we can labour, but He alone can build the house, 1 Cor. 3. 6; Ps. 127. 1. Are any of us sufficient? To meet the spiritual needs of others, as an elder, parent, Sunday School teacher, preacher etc., we must petition the throne of grace.

In the story, the man goes to a friend to obtain supplies for another friend. He asks, seeks, knocks until he obtains 'as many (loaves) as he needs'; which is what he asked for, v. 5. The man clearly did not have what was needed, nor do we. We have nothing to set before the people; but God has! The feeding of the five thousand also illustrates this truth. Additionally, we learn to come for others here, on their behalf.

Verses 9 and 10 are wonderful promises. 'The Lord doubleclasps His exhortations with assurances that '**every one** that asketh receiveth', etc. What a door is opened for us here, and what possibility of blessing is here unfolded! How rich may we all be, if we only will be, and what free leave we have to covet the best things!', F W GRANT.

Is there ever an inopportune moment with God? Here the man goes 'at midnight'. We ought **always** to pray and not to faint, Luke 18. 1. Examples in Scripture include the Syrophenician woman, Matt. 15. 21-28; the blind man in Jericho, Luke 18. 35-43; and Epaphras, Col. 4. 12.

'Praying always with all prayer, and supplication in the Spirit, and watching thereunto with all perseverance and supplication for all saints', Eph. 6. 18.

August 20th

Luke 11. 11-13

HOW MUCH MORE

Here the Lord moves on in His teaching on prayer, replying to the disciples' question, to emphasize the divine side. He has illustrated the human side, by speaking not only of an importunate petitioner but also of an unwilling provider; now He shows us that far from being an unwilling provider who needs to be awakened, as the great Provider, the Father, surpasses all men in goodness and willingness. He is ready and willing to give to us all good things, even the Holy Spirit. Even good men, fathers, who are evil in nature, give good gifts, suitable gifts, to their children. 'How much more shall your heavenly Father give'. These words, 'how much more', are logically irresistible and so they are heart-warming. Our God is the God of the 'much more', see Rom. 5. 10, 15, 17.

The character of God is a great incentive to prayer. He delights to give. 'Now the heart of God is declared as the ready and bounteous Giver, whose fulness cannot be exhausted, whose word to His people ever is, 'Open thy mouth wide, and I will fill it', Ps. 81. 10', F W GRANT. Thus Paul can affirm that 'He that spared not his own Son, but delivered him up for us all, how shall he not with him also freely give us all things?', Rom. 8. 32. Again the logic is irresistible: God has given us the best, the greatest, the highest, and therefore all other gifts, being lesser, inevitably follow. The words are also tremendously heart-warming. God is the great Giver. So here the Lord Jesus speaks of God as the perfect Father who gives the very best. He has given His Son; now He will give to us the Holy Spirit, v. 13. God gives Himself.

The Father will nourish us spiritually; so that we may be able to give to others. Bread, fish and eggs nourish and strengthen natural life; the Holy Spirit strengthens and nourishes spiritual life. The Father will not of course give us bad things, things not for our good; and this is one reason why He has to say 'no' to our requests on occasions. He is the perfect Father and we are to come to Him as His children in simple love, confidence and obedience.

August 21st

Luke 10. 21-22

JESUS REJOICED IN SPIRIT

In that hour Jesus rejoiced in spirit. 'In what hour?' we may ask. Seventy disciples had been appointed to go before Him to many towns and villages, Luke 10. 1. Now they are returning 'with joy', v. 17. They have experienced the power of the Lord's name, v. 17. The Lord rejoices with them; as He always rejoices at the outpouring of God`s grace, and true service in His name; as He also rejoices at the Father's ways of revealing things to 'babes' and not to the wise and prudent, v. 21; as He also rejoices at the salvation of souls. In the Lord's parables on the things lost this is delightfully conveyed: 'there is joy in the presence of the angels of God over one sinner that repenteth', Luke 15. 10.

The rejoicing and thanksgiving to God continue into verse 22 where the Lord speaks of the perfect understanding and mutual consciousness of Father and Son; and in their complementary work of revelation. The Father reveals to 'babes' the things concerning His Son, the purpose of His coming, and His saving work, v. 21, whilst the Son reveals the Father; see also John 1. 18.

As we have thought before, the Lord Jesus had the word of God ever before Him; He is the blessed man of Psalm 1, who 'meditates day and night' on the Scriptures. There are clear echoes of Psalm 8 here. He had sent the seventy out as 'lambs among wolves', v. 3, and speaks of them in prayer as 'babes'; this echoes verse 2 of the psalm. Likewise, Satan falls from heaven, as in the psalm the enemy and avenger is stilled, v. 2. The Lord addresses His Father as 'Lord of heaven and earth', so the psalmist speaks of the Lord's name being 'excellent in all the earth', v. 1. Finally He speaks of all things being delivered to him, and the psalm speaks of 'all things (being) put under His feet', v. 6.

Meditation on the word of God leads to praise and thanksgiving. GEORGE MULLER wrote, 'When I begin to meditate on the word of God to obtain food for my soul ... the result almost invariably ... [is that] my soul has been led to confession, or to thanksgiving, or to intercession'. Psalm 119 can be fulfilled in the life of the Christian, today.

August 22nd

Matthew 9. 35-38

PRAY

Yet again the assumption is obvious—we are a people who pray. **'When** you pray' says the Lord on another occasion. So the Lord says to Ananias concerning Saul, now converted, 'Behold, he prayeth', Acts 9. 11.

There are a number of motives and incentives to prayer. One is **human need**. How do we cast our eyes over people, whether individuals sprawled in a stupor on the steps of a night club, or raucous youths yelling on street corners, or groups of hopeful, yet hopeless, adults purchasing their lottery tickets? The Lord saw them with the eyes of compassion; for example, the rich young ruler, whom 'Jesus beholding, loved', Mark 10. 21; the woman taken in adultery, whom Jesus did not condemn, John 8. 11; or the crowds here, 'as sheep having no shepherd', v. 36. On another occasion He says to the disciples, 'I have compassion on the multitude', Mark 8. 2. This is an incentive to prayer; and we are to act in His Spirit, neither to judge nor condemn them, but to seek their salvation, John 12. 47. This is also shown on the occasion of the Lord being rejected by a Samaritan village. James and John react by wanting to invoke God's judgement on it, but the Lord told them that this attitude was not His attitude, 'ye know not of what spirit ye are', Luke 9. 55 JND. God has committed all judgement to the Son, and not to us.

The picture here is of a scattered flock of bleating sheep spread over a hillside. If we care we shall pray. 'All that love Christ and souls should show it by their earnest prayer to God, that He would send forth skilful, faithful, wise and industrious labourers into His harvest ... such as He will own in the conversion of sinners', M HENRY. Labourers are needed if the sheep are not to remain scattered and lost.

Then the picture changes to fields of waving corn, ripe for the harvest; but reapers are needed if the harvest is not to be lost. If we labour we must surely pray.

We must also be prepared to labour ourselves. So the disciples, having been told to pray for God to send out labourers, are themselves sent out, Matt. 10. 1. The Lord is Himself the perfect example, v. 35.

251

August 23rd

Luke 9. 10-17

LOOKING UP TO HEAVEN

The Lord Jesus is the Provider here. He provides teaching for the people, v. 11. In Mark's parallel account we read He taught them 'many things'. Then He provides food for the people, and they were all 'filled', v. 17. Both the spiritual and physical provision were substantial, abundant, sufficient, satisfying. Were the people as eager to listen as they were to eat? The teacher is to teach with substance, to lay a substantial meal before the people; and in our assemblies there ought to be adequate time set aside for this very purpose. Assemblies will not be built up on 'snacks'. Free samples are fine, provided the real thing in abundance is readily available.

The Lord also seeks to instruct and train His disciples. He uses simple, basic things; a boy's lunch. Do we put into His hands what we have, as Dorcas and her needle?, Acts 9. 39. Are our resources at His disposal, as His are at ours? He uses the disciples' hands; He fills their hands to enable them to give to the people. He shows them the need for order, v. 14. He unites them in a common purpose around Himself. He rewards them, v. 17; one basket per disciple.

The Lord looks up to heaven before He breaks the bread, v. 16. He receives from the Father to distribute to the disciples; they are to learn to receive from Him in order to distribute to the people. This truth He would express to them succinctly at a later date, 'as my Father hath sent me, even so send I you', John 20. 21. As He looked to His Father, so the disciples are to look to their Lord, see Ps. 123. 1-2.

Whenever we look to heaven what do we see? We see Jesus crowned with glory and honour sitting at the right hand of God; the One who was here is there, and is still the same, 'yesterday, and to day, and for ever', Heb. 2. 9; 8. 1; 10. 12; 13. 8.

Whenever we look at the common things of earth, such as food and flowers, do we thank God for them? 'Who giveth us richly all things to enjoy', 1 Tim. 6. 17. Ingratitude is a grievous sin, whether to God or man. 'Thank you' are simple words, but to the hearer they mean a great deal; our Lord set the example.

August 24th

Mark 6. 46-51

HE DEPARTED INTO A MOUNTAIN TO PRAY

The day has been very demanding; so much so, that the Lord along with the disciples, has not had any opportunity even to eat, Mark 6. 31. The crowds tracked Him down, and persisted in following Him, v. 33. He has then taught them, at some length, v. 34. He has healed all those who were lacking in health. Evening has come, and the Lord has provided a meal in the wilderness. Then the fragments have been gathered up, v. 43. Finally, He sends the disciples away by boat to Bethsaida. All this must have taken a considerable amount of time. His work was finished we might have thought, but it is not finished. He must now pray, v. 46.

The Lord's work is unfinished still. Yes, the work of Calvary is completed—the sacrifice has been made, never to be repeated, but our Lord is now working on our behalf in heaven, praying, interceding for us, Heb. 7. 25; Rom. 8. 34. His eye is upon us in the struggles of life (note: He saw them 'toiling in rowing', v. 48), in the darkness of this evil age, when we are alone. Here the disciples are three and a half miles from the shore, John 6. 17, 19, it is 3 a.m., Matt 14. 25. When will His work end? When His people are raptured? When Israel is rescued at the end of the Tribulation period with apparently all hope gone (of which this incident is a picture)? The Lord Jesus stated to the Jews on one occasion, 'My Father worketh hitherto (i.e. up to this point in time, continuously) and I work', John 5. 17. Is 1 Corinthians 15. 24-26 the answer? See also Rev. 20. 14-15, 22. 3-4.

And ourselves? When do we rest from our labours? Can we ever cease from the labour of prayer whilst on this earth? Can we not share in the great work of intercession with our Lord?

On this occasion for whom did the Lord pray? Was it the disciples in the boat, tossed about in the trials of life? Was it the multitude just fed that they might understand and apply His teaching which He had given to them before He had fed them? We need to pray regularly for individuals, assemblies, and the multitude.

August 25th

Mark 7. 31-37

THE PERFECT SERVANT

Few passages are peculiar to the Gospel of Mark, but this is one of them. So we might well expect to find a distinctive note here, a particular emphasis, which fits well with the writer's overall scheme, as guided by God's Spirit, and so it is. The perfect Servant is here shown performing a miracle using 'means' at His own disposal, costing nothing—His own saliva. He performs it in seven stages :-

> He takes the deaf man aside;
> He puts His fingers in his ears;
> He spits;
> He touches his tongue;
> He looks up to heaven;
> He sighs;
> He says, 'Be opened'.

The **sigh** expresses the sorrows and problems of earth which the Lord felt keenly, the burden of the world's sin which oppressed His spirit. The **look** expresses the resources and interest of heaven, for there is a heart in heaven that feels keenly, and the Lord Himself brings the two together. Similarly, when the Lord arrives at the sepulchre at Bethany, we read that 'he **groaned** in the spirit and was troubled'; and of another **look** and silent supplication: the Lord 'lifted up his eyes' and said, 'Father, I thank thee that thou hast heard me', John 11. 33, 38, 41. 'To God fine language is as sounding brass or a tinkling cymbal, but a **groan** has music in it', C H SPURGEON. As we find ourselves amidst such sorrows and problems we too must enlist the resources of heaven; and in the actual dealing with such things, a simple look shows where the answer is to be found. Similarly, as the Lord ministered to the multitude, just prior to breaking the loaves, He **looked** up to heaven, Mark 6. 41, exhibiting a dependent attitude God-ward. What worthy example for all of God's imperfect servants! So we read of Nehemiah's brief, simple **look** to the God of heaven, and his silent supplication, Neh. 2. 4, in a spirit of **mourning**, 1. 4, and sadness, 2. 2. God hears our sighing, and responds to our groans of supplication.

August 26th

Luke 9. 18-27

AS HE WAS ALONE PRAYING

The Lord's habitual life of prayer is brought before us again, v. 18. The Lord, though with the disciples, is nevertheless 'alone praying'. He does not invite them to pray with Him, for His relationship with God is not as theirs, as children to a Father, but is unique—as God's only begotten Son He addresses His Father. Moreover, His work of redemption is peculiar to Himself, and He has no need of forgiveness.

Again, we are not told **what** He prayed, but **that** He prayed; it is characteristic of Luke's record in the first half of his gospel. The main point is, He prayed—His life was a life of prayer. Prayer was as natural to Him as breathing. Let us pray 'without ceasing', 1 Thess. 5. 17. Pray always, pray everywhere. It is a blessed thing to tell God **everything** at any time, anywhere. 'Praying **always**', Eph. 6. 18, shows God would have us pray when off our knees ... All sorts of prayer, at all sorts of times, in all sorts of ways', W LINCOLN.

'Prayer is the Christian's vital breath,
   The Christian's native air', J MONTGOMERY.

Nevertheless, the context suggests that one aspect of the Lord's praying was what lay before Him, and what was drawing ever nearer; decreed in eternity, but now shortly to be actually brought to pass, His crucifixion and resurrection. Thus we note that He informs the disciples of these things, v. 22 (something He has not done previously); and 'His decease' will be the subject of the conversation on the mountain, v. 31. In addition, there was the declaration of Peter about to be uttered, v. 20, and bound up with it the disciples' false expectations, that they were now to reign and be acclaimed rather than to follow in His steps of rejection, suffering, self denial, vv. 23-26. Surely He was praying for them. And then, as the cross drew nearer, was there the daily renewing of His vows? 'Lo ... in the volume of the book it is written of me, I delight to do thy will', Ps. 40. 7-8. 'For thou ... hast heard my vows; thou hast given me the heritage of those that fear thy name (the eleven disciples here) ... so will I sing praise unto thy name for ever, that I may daily perform my vows', Ps. 61. 5-8.

255

August 27th

Luke 9. 28-36

TRANSFIGURED

Only Luke records the fact of the Lord's praying during this incident in His earthly life: a man praying to His God, v. 28, a Son speaking with His Father, v. 35. If we ask why was the Lord here, on this mountain, at this time, that is the answer—God directed His paths, the Father and the Son journeyed together. This former aspect is seen in the emphasis on Jerusalem as the destined place for the perfect Man, guided and led by God, Luke 9. 31, 51; 13. 33-34; 18. 31; 19. 41. The latter aspect reminds us of another father and an only son, Abraham and Isaac, who journeyed **together** to a mountain, seeing the place afar off, in Genesis 22; where this is doubly emphasized: 'they went **both** of them **together**', vv. 6, 8. We remember also that the Lord's first recorded words have as the main point 'my Father's business', and His last words, before He yielded up His spirit, begin 'Father ...', both recorded only by Luke, 2. 49; 23. 46.

True prayer is an expression of dependence, submission to the will of God, and concern for the glory of God. It was as He prayed that the Lord was changed and so will we be changed as we pray, 2 Cor. 3. 18. But we need to get apart from the world as the disciples here—for it is only thus that the Lord's glory is revealed to the soul.

Moses and Elijah represent Old Testament saints who put their faith in a sacrificial lamb, believing that God would provide the Lamb; who hoped for God's tender mercy through dark, troubled times, and for the Consolation of Israel, the Focus of prophecy. This last is what we find at the beginning of Luke, expressed through the lips of Zacharias and Simeon, members of the Jewish remnant, 1. 76-79; 2. 25, 30-32. Peter, James and John represent New Testament saints, who look back in faith to a crucified Saviour and upwards in hope to a risen Lord. All believers are represented here; their total well-being and future happiness absolutely dependent upon Him, on His 'accomplishing his decease' (lit. 'exodus'), v. 31. Is it any wonder that as the cross drew nearer He was found praying! We see this in Gethsemane, Luke 22. 39-46. All depends on Him, and, in His dependence on God, He prays!

August 28th

Matthew 18. 19-20

IF TWO OF YOU SHALL AGREE

Earlier in this very gospel the Lord had given instruction about private prayer in the closet. Now the same Lord speaks of public prayer in the church. The number may indeed be small—He mentions two—but the emphasis is more on the **unity** in the prayer of these two believers than upon the number who pray. They 'agree'. The Greek word is that from which we derive our English word 'symphony'. Here we have a beautiful picture of two believers harmonizing before the throne of grace. They bow their hearts together, they blend their voices together, and it all appears as a melody in heaven.

What significance this gives to united prayer! What importance this attaches to the prayer meeting of the believers! Such an occasion is here portrayed by the Lord Himself as a time of spiritual harmonization, and volume of sweet sound to God.

There is in the text a beautiful balance. We begin with 'two of you ... on earth'; and the text concludes with 'My Father which is in heaven'. How blessed it is to think of individuals on earth in prayerful contact with a Father in heaven. There is not only a precious harmony on an earthly plane between two agreeing believers; there is a precious communion between earth and heaven. Where such holy concord is enjoyed and demonstrated we have the assurance of the Saviour, 'it shall be done'. Such answers express the delight of our God in the holy harmony of His people.

This delightful symphony of spirit-touched hearts is not only sweet but sensitive. As in music a faulty instrument, a wrong note, a careless touch can easily turn concord into discord—so with believers. Let each of us so live that no word spoken, no act done, no attitude adopted will in any way mar the beauty of brethren dwelling together in unity.

Here we have the first mention in the New Testament of **assembly testimony**. In assembly life our collective prayers are an acknowledgment of conscious weakness and dependency. There is also a reference to disputes between brethren, and church discipline. Humble and harmonious prayer will see many disputes melt away, but should discipline be necessary, this verse indicates it must be administered in an atmosphere of prayer.

August 29th
John 11. 38-44

FATHER, I THANK THEE THAT THOU HAST HEARD ME

A climax has been reached. There have been many signs before this confirming Christ's identity, but the raising of a man who had been four days in the tomb was demonstration beyond doubt. This was not, however, the opinion of the chief priests and Pharisees, who would thereafter plot His death.

Before the performance of this wonder, the Saviour prays, and prays in public. He gives thanks for the resurrection of the dead man before it happened. Here we are witnessing the perfect communion between Father in heaven and Son upon earth. It is with a calm confidence the Saviour speaks these words.

It is not usual for the Saviour to speak to His Father in this audible way before performing a miracle. Are we to draw the conclusion that, if He did not pray publicly before a miracle, He did not pray at all. I think the opposite is the truth. His whole life was a prayer. When the Lord Jesus engaged in vocal prayer He was not moving from a state of non-prayer to prayer. This was the atmosphere of undisturbed communion in which He lived and which enabled Him to say here, 'I know that thou hearest me always'.

We are still asking why did He make His thanksgiving public on this occasion. He tells us it was 'because of the people which stand by'. It was certainly not a case of 'praying to the gallery', or praying to impress an earthly audience. There was a higher, nobler purpose. The Lord Jesus was publicly expressing His communion with, and His dependence upon, His Father in heaven. The Son would not act independently of the Father. There was a harmony of action between Father and Son. As the people would hear them speak together and see the proof of such concord in the mighty miracle, surely, as the Saviour says in verse 42, they would be convinced He had been sent by the Father.

The previous 'always' in this gospel is in chapter 8 verse 29, where the Saviour says concerning His Father, 'I do always those things that please him'. Here He says, 'thou hearest me always'. Let us seek to emulate this pattern, and our prayers will surely be heard by Him.

August 30th

Luke 18. 1-8

SHALL NOT GOD AVENGE HIS OWN ELECT WHICH CRY DAY AND NIGHT UNTO HIM

Perseverance is the word—keeping at it. This was the stamp of the widow in the Saviour's parable; she persevered. Even the unprincipled judge describes it as 'her continual coming'. Let this be a feature of our exercise at the throne of God. May we be continually coming with the assurance that He will never weary, but will respond to our persistence.

Her adversary was unjust and cruel; the judge was unscrupulous and unsympathetic; the widow's own position in ancient society, without the voice of her husband, was defenceless and vulnerable. These barriers were real, yet she overcame them all.

Importunity is a word often employed to describe her actions. An answer was important for this widow, and so despite repeated rebuffs she relentlessly pursued her goal. We are usually importunate about what is important to us. It is unlikely that we will keep praying about things unless we are convinced they really matter. It was more than personal vindication being sought. The widow was on the side of **principle**. Let us also pray for principles in a twisted world of injustice. Our faith may be tested by waiting, but the cause of righteousness will be vindicated in the end.

The parable presents a contrast. If a widow, by her persistence, was able to extract a positive response from a judge who was uncaring, how much more will God who knows and cares lend a ready ear to the constant cries of His own people.

This parable is an illustration for all times but especially for end times. The Saviour has in the previous verses been speaking of His second coming. That glorious event of deliverance will be preceded by dreadful days of tribulation and injustice. The faith of God's elect will be tried to the uttermost. Like the helpless widow a weak and persecuted remnant will cry to God. Their faith will be rewarded by the returning Christ, and their perseverance will be ultimately triumphant. Do we display the same patience and perseverance in this generation? It is not 'Will God answer?', but, 'Will we keep praying with faith and patience instead of fainting, though He long delay His response?'.

August 31st

Luke 18. 9-14

GOD BE MERCIFUL TO ME A SINNER

The setting of the Saviour's parable was a familiar sight in the first century. The scene is Herod's temple. The time is either the morning or the evening appointed time of prayer. The temple service is fully in operation. The priests are busy in their duty, and the sacrifice is burning on the altar. Presently, amid the normal business of the day with the general crowd moving to and fro, the Saviour focuses our attention upon two men.

The men are very different in **person**. One is a Pharisee the other a tax-collector. They are likewise different in their **position**. One confidently takes his place, and aloof from others he occupies as prominent a place as possible. The other man is ashamed and accordingly stands at a distance as one who, because of a sense of sinfulness, feels unfit for God's presence. They were also different in their **prayers**. The Pharisee's attempt to pray was more an extended soliloquy of self-congratulation than a supplication. He asked for nothing and received nothing. The other man was brief and broken in his plea. Their **profit** was also different. The only satisfaction the Pharisee obtained was the gratification of his **pride**. He made the parade of his piety and probably felt the better for it. The tax collector received the **pardon** of sin and was declared right before God.

His cry 'be merciful' is significant. It refers to the making of 'propitiation' for sins. It is a word that takes us to the altar where atonement is made. While he prays, the altar burns, and on the basis of the accepted sacrifice he pleads for mercy and receives forgiveness. It is also a word which takes us to the mercy-seat. This man, though standing at a distance in an outer court, has offered a humble, contrite plea such as reaches the innermost sanctuary of God.

The descendants of the Pharisee and the tax collector are with us still! Let us abandon all hope in self-righteousness, and let the cry of the tax collector be our cry. We find mercy flowing freely from the throne of God through a greater sacrifice. This is the ultimate sacrifice of all the ages, offered by the Lord Jesus on the cross.

September 1st

Matthew 19. 13-15

THERE WERE BROUGHT ... LITTLE CHILDREN
THAT HE SHOULD ... PRAY

A remarkable place in the ministry of the Lord Jesus is accorded to children. He, who passed His years of childhood in a simple Jewish home, displayed an unquestionable affection for children. Quite a number of His miracles were performed for the benefit of children and He often used them as positive illustrations in His parables and teachings. Such references confirm the depth of the interest in children of Jesus of Nazareth.

In the verses of the previous section the Lord Jesus had established the sanctity of marriage and the security of the family. It is fitting that children should be introduced in this section, for they are the ones who suffer most when family values are disregarded. The disciples regarded the request of the adults for these children as an unwelcome intrusion. Not so the Saviour! His priorities were different. His values were correct.

In these children the Saviour not only saw objects of prayer but He saw a picture of those who would enter and enjoy the kingdom of God. It is only available to those who are like children. Such are not **childish**, but they are **child-like** as displaying those qualities of humility and trustfulness, so essential for entry into God's kingdom.

We should follow the example of the Saviour here and pray for children. They are amongst the most vulnerable and exploited members of our society. Whether we consider the hungry and the homeless, the abused, the aborted, or the sick and suffering, we must admit that the plight of the children of our world is overwhelmingly pathetic, and utterly appalling. Present-day estimates suggest something like 100 million unwanted children roam the streets of our big cities. There are over five million children worldwide affected by AIDS.

Let us pray for children, not only because of their plight but because of their potential. **The child is father of the man**.

Perhaps in our private intercession today we could make special mention of **the children**—not just our own but **all the children of the world**.

261

September 2nd

Matthew 21. 18-22

ALL THINGS WHATSOEVER YE SHALL ASK IN PRAYER, BELIEVING, YE SHALL RECEIVE

In our materialistic society we are all too familiar with fantastic offers which, initially, appear so special until one reads the small print at the bottom. There are so many conditions attached that the fabulous can quickly become the futile.

The text before us today is not like that. Certainly it is a great offer, containing what seems to be an unlimited promise. It is like an open ticket or a blank cheque. All things possible to prayer! When, however, it comes to daily experience and the promise does not seem to work out, we ask, 'What is wrong?'. But we must ask ourselves again, 'Has one of the promises of Christ failed?'. Never! The problem is that we have not looked carefully enough at the condition which is very clearly articulated by the Lord Himself in the immediate context.

Prevailing prayer must be accompanied by **faith**. The operative word of the text is 'believing'. This is the faith, plus prayer, which can wither trees and uproot mountains. The Lord Jesus uses these natural objects as illustrations of what is humanly possible. Such situations can only be met by confident prayer. Many believers can testify to occasions when, confronted by human extremities, their confident cries God ward were matched by events nothing short of 'proofs' of God's omnipotence.

There is further amplification of this principle in the parallel passage in Mark 11. There the Lord Jesus adds, in verse 22, 'Have faith in God'. Here we learn that the faith in question is not blind, bare or baseless. It is the organ of the soul which rises from what is human to what is divine, from what is circumstantial to what is celestial, from what is earthly to what is eternal. Difficulties become designs, and obstacles become opportunities whenever faith brings God into the realities of life.

A further condition is introduced by the Lord in Mark 11 in the very same section. He says in verse 25, 'When ye stand praying, forgive'. Prevailing prayer must also be accompanied by a forgiving spirit. With faith Godward and forgiveness manward may our requests be increasingly fruitful to God's glory.

September 3rd

Mark 12. 38-40

FOR A PRETENCE MAKE LONG PRAYERS

It had been a busy day of argument. Differing parties had united to vent their opposition and malice upon the Saviour. The atmosphere is tense. Herodians, Pharisees and Sadducees all have had their turn. Their carefully crafted trick questions have been political, theological and hypothetical, but one by one the interrogators are silenced by the superior wisdom of the Son of God. Before he lets the crowd disperse, He puts them on their guard against the subtle, self-seeking scribes who were destroying the nation. Item by item he fills in the description of these scurrilous men, coming at last to their **covetousness**. They 'devour widows' houses, and for a pretence make long prayers'.

Just how it worked in practice is not altogether certain but whatever the nature of their fraudulent activities, it is clear that the Lord Jesus not only condemns their dishonest dealings but the pious dress beneath which they were concealed. While they 'prayed' with the widows, they 'preyed' upon them. Such duplicity, the Saviour declares, will earn for such men 'greater damnation'. Their profession of piety will bring a severer sentence upon their heads than will be visited upon dishonesty without the garb of godliness.

Hypocrisy is obnoxious to God, but never more so than when it touches the exercise of spiritual things. Prayers for a pretence! Imagine the most holy and elevated exercise of the human spirit being used as a cover-up. The prayers may have been long, but they were not able to provide in quantity what they lacked in quality. Let us cultivate integrity and sincerity in prayer. Let us examine our motives here. The supplication may be short but if it is sincere it will be pleasing to the Lord. How often public prayers have been used as a cover for correction, innuendo, or even point-scoring. We should call upon the Lord out of a pure heart. In the very next section in this gospel the Lord Jesus draws attention to a poor widow who gave her two mites. The **private sincerity** of this widow elicited Christ's commendation—the **parade of piety** in those scribes His condemnation. Let us aim at sincerity in all things, especially in prayer.

September 4th
John 12. 23-30

NOW IS MY SOUL TROUBLED ... FATHER, GLORIFY THY NAME

It is now Tuesday, or perhaps even Wednesday, of the crucifixion week. Already the Saviour inwardly feels the turmoil of the coming day of grief. He confesses to being 'troubled'. This is a verb of strong emotion, evoking feelings of deep anxiety and agitation. He gives Himself to prayer. In such circumstances how shall He pray and what shall He say?

It is notable that, while He does approach the hour with holy hesitation and prays, as later in Gethsemane, 'Father, save me from this hour', His final word is not for His own ease, escape or comfort. He does not allow these deep emotions to displace what has been the singular and supreme motivation of His mind, and this is reflected in His request, 'Father, glorify thy name'. The answer to such a request will involve Him in rejection, shame, suffering and ultimately death, but with Him the glory of the Father's name is paramount.

Such an aspiration was not momentary. It was not confined to only this occasion, for it had been the guiding principle of His whole life. This is much more than reluctant resignation. This is beyond a mere passive acquiescence. This is a positive delight in the display of the character of God. Surely this is the only true aspiration of real prayer. Not the imposition of our wills upon God's, but the display of His name.

It is no surprise that this noble request received immediate response from heaven. The Father's delight in the perfect obedience of His Son is seen by this public acknowledgement—one of only three such in the whole of the Saviour's public ministry.

How shall we pray in light of coming crises? Shall we seek our own advancement, or will it be the Father's glory? If we pray like this we must not be surprised if it involves us in what is most distasteful to, and painful for, human nature. It may involve our death, at least the death of earthly ambition, but it will secure the display of His beauty in our lives. We have to confess that many of our prayers are tinged with a form of self-motivation. Today, may we be enabled to follow the pattern of our Lord.

Luke 22. 31-34

SIMON ... SATAN HATH DESIRED TO HAVE YOU ... BUT I HAVE PRAYED FOR THEE

Here is a man in great danger. There will shortly be a severe satanic attack, so severe the Saviour describes it as a 'sifting'. A further aggravation of the whole crisis is that the person who will be the main object of the attack is totally oblivious to the sinister conspiracy. He has been singled out in a special way because he is leader in a group of special men. If he can be overcome the others will soon succumb. This group of men is very important to the Saviour, for He has chosen them to be the carriers of His message after the resurrection. The future of the Christian mission is vested in these men.

It is a great comfort that Christ knows of this attack before it happens. He has already been interceding for Simon. Before this night is over Peter will be acting more like Simon the Galilean than like Peter the apostle. For a while his faith will falter and his identity will be seriously in question, but thanks to the intercession of his Saviour he will have a restoration. Meanwhile the Saviour knows the weakness of His men and is aware that Peter's faith has been weakened by pride and selfish ambition.

How encouraging to know that, due to the advocacy of Christ, failure for the believer is not necessarily final. Peter will shed profusely his bitter tears and his heart will break. These experiences of contrition are part of the answer to the Master's prayer. He will himself be marked by prayerlessness, but the Saviour's prayer interest goes on ceaselessly. Peter has learnt the lesson well, for he later reminds the believers of the 'adversary the devil', and calls them to 'be sober, be vigilant'.

May we commence this day more thankful than ever for the priest who 'ever liveth to make intercession' for us, Heb. 7. 25. Even when we are unaware of our danger He foresees the need and makes prior provision for our defence.

Not only will Peter's failure not be final, it will not be fruitless. He will emerge from the sieve a better man. As a result of the Saviour's prayer he will come out as better grain and will be able to strengthen others. How good to know now that the Saviour is at God's right hand.

John 14. 13-15; 15. 16; 16. 23-26

WHATSOEVER YE SHALL ASK IN MY NAME, THAT WILL I DO

The Saviour is just about to depart. The cross is on the morrow. Shortly the disciples will no longer enjoy direct personal intercourse with the Master which they have known for so long. However, even though He will not be there personally, He will leave behind *His name* and give them permission to use it. What a gracious permission on His part and what a privilege for them.

His is the most influential name in the universe. On earth it is scorned and derided but in heaven it is all-prevailing. It not only bespeaks unlimited power but it tells of unfailing sympathy. There is in this name a blend of authority and tenderness. It will command an audience in the highest court of heaven, and will call the attention of the ear of God. He will delight to hear it mentioned, and will bend to listen to those who reverently breath its precious sound.

How disadvantaged we would be if we had to seek an audience with God in the power of our own name. How could we ever hope to gain His ear. In our sinful infirmity and our human state we must stand back in an embarrassed silence, but we have here the Saviour's granting of His own name, and in its peerless value we come near and have freedom of expression at the throne of grace.

It is not, however, merely a formula of words. It does not merely function as an introduction or conclusion to our prayers. In using this lovely name we must recognize the significance of what it means. If our requests are selfish and carnal, surely these cannot be described as 'asking in the name'. Our requests must be in accordance with all that the name of the Lord Jesus stands for. There must be an agreement between our expressed desires and His character, purpose, word and lordship. When this is true we are really praying 'in His name', and only then can we expect the fulfilment of His promise, 'that will I do'. Whether in the home, in the workplace, in the hospital, in the school or university, let us pray then today, submitting all our petitions to God in the holy, prevailing name of our Lord Jesus Christ.

September 7th
John 14. 16-17

I WILL PRAY THE FATHER, AND HE SHALL GIVE YOU ANOTHER COMFORTER

This is one of those notable New Testament texts where we have the Trinity joined together in one verse. As a result of the request of the Son, the Father will grant the Holy Spirit. There is in evidence a perfect cohesion and equality among the Persons of the Godhead.

The Saviour had Himself been a 'Comforter' to the disciples. They trusted Him for advice, looked to Him for guidance, waited upon His teaching and depended upon Him for defence. However, He is about to leave them but He emphasizes that His departure will be advantageous, since they will receive by His own request a replacement Comforter. This One will stay with them in every situation and be in them. It will not be for a period of three years or a little more, as in the Master's case; His would be a perpetual indwelling.

This is the first of a series of passages in John's gospel where we have the Holy Spirit described as a 'Comforter'. The original word has come into our language as 'Paraclete'. The precise significance of the word is hard to define. Most likely it has legal overtones. The Greeks often used it to describe one who was called to help another in a court, usually as counsel for the defence.

Often the believer finds himself in situations where he is called upon to speak a word in defence of the Saviour, or perhaps the Scriptures, or even the gospel. Wherever this is, be it to the fellow students in the university, or the workmates in the factory, or to the neighbour in the street, we can count upon the help of the invisible Counsellor to supply the necessary wisdom and strength. His services are always available, His information always accurate and of free provision.

The 'Paraclete' engages in a variety of activities. Sometimes He is a remembrancer, at others He is prosecutor; still on other occasions He is teacher and interpreter. He is our guide in perplexity, our light in darkness, our strength in weakness, our consolation in sorrow and our protector in adversity.

May we throughout this day know the gracious help of this Counsellor divine, and appreciate Him as the answer of the giving Father to the request of His beloved Son.

September 8th

John 17

FATHER, THE HOUR IS COME

This beautiful chapter preserves for us the longest recorded prayer of the Lord Jesus. Beginning with request for Himself, vv. 1-5, and moving onward through the apostles, vv. 6-19, to the whole company of future believers, vv. 20-24, the prayer is all-embracive in its scope.

In its outlook this great prayer fills eternity and history. The Saviour recalls the glory He enjoyed with the Father 'before the world was', and, moving into time by way of His incarnation, via the cross, His mind travels on to the glorious future when His own shall be with Him where He is.

The subjects of this prayer are just as grand as its scope. Whether we consider the revelation of His word, or the unification of His own, or the preservation of His servants, or the sanctification of His people, or the glorification of all who believe, the thoughts expressed here are an unfolding of the deepest counsels of God. To be allowed the favour of hearing one Person of the Godhead speak so intimately to another Person of the Godhead, and so be introduced into heavenly secrets is to stand upon the plateau of highest privilege.

Did we not know the historical setting of this great prayer we would imagine that it followed the cross. Chronologically, it precedes Calvary. Theologically, it follows Calvary. The Saviour speaks in the full good of His completed work upon the cross and He anticipates His resurrection and exaltation. What noble thoughts to fill His soul on the darkest evening in history. Death is on the morrow, but His mind is full of eternal life. Tomorrow is a day of shame but eight times here He speaks of 'glory' or 'glorify'. Sorrows unfathomable will be His portion shortly, but here He speaks of 'my joy fulfilled'.

We can detect in the atmosphere of this intercession a longing for home. The Saviour is going back to His Father's place and the anticipation fills His heart with gladness. It is our privilege, as we engage in prayer, to breathe deeply our native air. Amid the unhealthy atmosphere of earth, we can hereby inhale the pure atmosphere of heaven.

September 9th

Luke 22. 39-46

HE PRAYED MORE EARNESTLY

His prayers were always earnest. By common confession we admit that very often our prayers fall short of full sincerity. This was never so with His prayers. Therefore, when we read of Him praying 'more earnestly' we are compelled to take a second look.

There was a mixture of strange emotions in this garden setting which all combined to increase its intensity. We observe an anticipation encompassed by astonishment, anxiety, and alarm. Together these produced what the text describes as the 'agony'. This had dimensions that were spiritual, mental and physical. The prostration, perspiration and prayer were all remarkable.

Notably, it was in a garden setting that we have the first mention of sweat in the Scriptures. On that occasion the first man, in effect, lifted up his voice to God and said, 'Not thy will, but mine be done'. The consequences of such rebellion are with us still. Similar language is the motto of the age. Now, amid the olive trees of the garden of Gethsemane there is a perfect man, who with complete submission speaks to heaven and says, 'Not my will, but thine be done'. The world has yet to see the full effects of His obedience.

The agony was intense. The conflict was real. For the sinless One to be 'made sin', and for the holy One to endure the judgement of God upon sin, was horrific for Him to contemplate, and so affected the perfect emotions of the Lord Jesus. His submission, however, was perfect and His obedience total. The fierce struggle was between what was emotionally pleasing to a perfect human being and the fulfilment of God's redemptive purpose. The Lord Jesus, in Gethsemane, did not act on impulse but in conscious obedience He deliberately chose the Father's will. For such a choice we are eternally grateful. It involved Him in indescribable suffering, but it has secured for us equally indescribable blessing and at the same time brought infinite glory to God, whose will has been accomplished.

Today may bring to us conflicts which, while they are infinitely smaller in significance, will be the same in principle. May the triumph of our Saviour spur us on to do the will of God.

THEN SAID JESUS, FATHER, FORGIVE THEM

The site had been reached; the nails had been fixed; the cross had been upraised; the soldiers had done their gruesome task. It was *then* that Jesus prayed, 'Father, forgive them'. Without a single trace of bitterness or the slightest recrimination the Saviour prayed for His executioners.

It must have taken these men by surprise. The normal reaction was one of rancour and vilest cursing. Not so on this occasion. Here was a person with a difference. He was just as distinct in His death as He had been in His life.

His relationship with God was different. Dying as a condemned criminal, His companions in crucifixion are robbers. This man, however, can speak to God as His Father. The Son of God upon a Roman cross is a miracle of grace which still melts our hearts. His request was also different. He prays, not for vengeance, but for forgiveness. It is pardon for others, not pity for Himself, which is the burden of His heart.

The Saviour fulfils the prophetic word of centuries past, 'He was numbered with the transgressors; and he bare the sin of many, and made intercession for the transgressors', Isa. 53. 12. Likewise, He was practising what He himself had taught His disciples. Earlier He had said, 'Love your enemies, bless them that curse you, do good to them that hate you, and pray for them which despitefully use you, and persecute you', Matt. 5. 44.

His intercession recognizes not only human sin, but human ignorance. He presents it as a consideration in forgiveness. 'they know not what they do.' There is an element of ignorance in all sin. Those who commit it know not its real character, or its full consequences. This ignorance does not remove culpability, else there would be no need for pardon. Rather, it increases the demand for it. The crucified Saviour prays for the forgiveness of His foes and then He dies to make the granting of His request a righteous and glorious possibility.

How do we react to the pain wrongfully inflicted upon us by others? Let us resort to prayer. Such a reaction may bring repentance in our critics and healing to our own wounded spirits.

September 11th

Matthew 27. 45-49

MY GOD, MY GOD, WHY HAST THOU FORSAKEN ME?

The words of this cry, as spoken by the Saviour, constitute the most desperate cry ever uttered in all the earth. Here we sense a darkness that is inscrutable, a depth that is unfathomable, a desolation that is incomprehensible.

These words bespeak an awful sense of loneliness. Loneliness is a common feeling of the human race. There is the loneliness of the orphan, the widow, the unemployed, the individual, the isolated student, the refugee, the rejected poor.

Loneliness is not the absence of people only. It can be experienced in a crowd. It is rather the feeling that no one cares. It is the awful absence of love, compassion and help.

There was never such a situation of loneliness as Calvary. The crowd was there, cold, and bitter. The hosts of darkness were there, malicious and violent. He has been abandoned by His friends and now is surrounded by His enemies. Worse than all there was no help forthcoming from heaven. No voice, either angelic or divine, responds to the enquiry of that penetrating 'why?'. Meditation upon this cry made MARTIN LUTHER exclaim, 'God forsaken of God! Who can understand it?'.

Being forsaken is more than a feeling. It is reality. This is Christ becoming a curse for us. This is the sinless Saviour 'made sin'. This is the heart of the atonement. This is the final dealing with sin and the beginning of true righteousness.

The life of the Saviour had always been lonely. The babe in the manger, the boy in the temple, the praying man in the desert, the agonizer in Gethsemane, the defenceless prisoner in the trials—these had all been scenes of solitude. Loneliness was not a new experience for Him, but nothing previous was to be compared with the desolation of Golgotha.

There is comfort in this cry here for us, as well as salvation. Many will face situations of silence and solitude this day. There is consolation in knowing that upon the throne of heaven now there is sitting One who has known such pain of loneliness. His sympathy is true for all who trust Him, and, further we have His faithful promise, 'I will never leave thee nor forsake thee'. He who Himself was forsaken will never forsake His own.

FATHER, INTO THY HANDS I COMMEND MY SPIRIT

It is peace at last. The work is done. The pain is all but over. The victory has been gained. With a calm confidence the Saviour dies. He concludes His words upon the cross just as He had begun, by speaking to His Father. It is similar with His ministry as a whole. In this gospel His opening words had made reference to His 'Father's business', and this remained His sole priority to the end.

This prayer, like the previous one, is also a quotation from the Scriptures—Psalm 31. 5. In that psalm we discover references that are very pertinent to this situation. How relevant are the words, 'I was a reproach among all mine enemies', v. 11, 'I have heard the slander of many', v. 13; in the same chapter the writer acknowledges, 'My times are in thy hand, v. 15. In His suffering the Lord Jesus not only meditated upon Scripture, but using its language, He employed those very portions which were closely parallel to His own position.

The limits of his suffering had been reached, and the Lord commends His spirit into the caring hands of His Father. Death for Him was entirely voluntary. It was not a matter of 'yielding to the inevitable', as it is with other men when overcome by death; rather it was a case of deliberately relinquishing by One who in death was the conqueror of death.

This word of serene trust has provided many with a cushion of comfort in the day of death. The death of the Saviour has 'softened' death for all who believe on Him. It was a modification of these words which was upon the lips of Stephen, the first martyr, 'Lord Jesus, receive my spirit', Acts 7. 59. They were also reputedly the final words by which the great reformer, MARTIN LUTHER, left this world for glory.

Might we not say these words provide for us the secret of a happy life as well as the secret of a happy death? As we embark upon the hours of another day should not this be our approach to all the demands and duties we may encounter? Let us commit everything into the hands of a heavenly Father who cares for every detail. Our life, health, family, employment are all the objects of His interest. Let us commend every concern to Him.

September 13th

Acts 1. 12-14

WITH ONE ACCORD IN PRAYER AND SUPPLICATION

What an historic occasion this was! Here is the first reference to prayer since our Lord's ascension to the heavens, and here also is the last mention of Mary, the virgin mother of the Lord Jesus. From Olivet, with all its memories of the Saviour, the disciples had returned to Jerusalem. On the Mount of Olives Jesus had taught them and communed with them. He had wept on this mount. He had preached and prophesied here and now from here, near to Bethany, He had gone home to glory. His own had witnessed His ascension, and it seemed so fitting that they should now meet to pray.

They gathered in an upper room, above the level of the noisy street, morally elevated above the bustle of the world which had crucified their Lord. What a variety of men they were, but yet with kindred spirits and a unity of purpose. As in all the listings of their names, Peter is first mentioned, impetuous, impulsive, lovable Peter. Then there were the beloved and faithful brothers John and James. There was the quiet Andrew, who seemed to be always bringing men to Christ, John 1. 40-41; 6. 8; 12. 22. Philip was there also, the evangelist who was later to lead the treasurer of Ethiopia to the Saviour. Thomas was with them, the cautious, sometimes melancholy Thomas. Then there was Bartholomew, better known as the guileless Nathanael of Cana. Matthew the former tax collector, and James the son of Alphaeus were there, with Simon, the erstwhile zealot, and Jude who asked an interesting question in the upper room, John 14. 22. It is touching also to see that the Lord's earthly brethren were there. This is the first indication that they were now believers. These all continued with one accord. The different personalities and temperaments of these men and women were all melted into a common purpose, and in this lovely unity they continued together in prayer.

How important and necessary is this unity, and how beautiful the example left for us in this first recorded prayer meeting. May we emulate their togetherness and their continuance, for in a little while their upper room was to the filled with glory. God grant us the same unity and perseverance in intercession.

Acts 1. 15-26

THOU, LORD, WHICH KNOWEST THE HEARTS OF ALL MEN

How delightful it is to read of Peter that he 'stood up in the midst of them', just as in Acts 2. 14 he would stand with them in bold testimony. This is the same Peter of whom we read in an earlier chapter that he 'stood *with them*', warming himself at their fire who were abusing his Lord, John 18. 18, 25. But Peter is restored now, and courageous for Christ.

Note how these early disciples acknowledge the authority of the Scriptures and the sovereignty of God. In the Scriptures God will speak to them; in their prayers they will speak to God. Psalm 41, Peter says, is the word of the Spirit through the mouth of David, concerning Judas. This wretched man had companied with them and with the Saviour for three years and more, and had come to an ignominious end. A suicidal death, a broken cord or branch, a fall headlong, and his body had burst asunder at Aceldama just beyond the south wall of the city. All Jerusalem heard of it, and the Psalms had predicted not only the treachery but the necessity of filling the apostolic vacancy, Pss. 69. 25; 109. 8. In accordance with these psalms Peter directed that they should now find another to complete their number, but there were certain prerequisites. Such an one must be a witness with them to the life and ministry of the Lord Jesus, and a witness, too, of His resurrection. Two men are marked out as suitable men, Joseph called Barsabas, and Matthias. And now they pray.

It is important to remember that all this is happening prior to the day of Pentecost. They are about to cast lots. This was a Jewish mode of seeking divine direction. There is no casting of lots after Pentecost, but at this time the guiding Spirit had not yet been given. Their prayer is brief but it is a pointed and sincere appeal, directed to a sovereign Lord who knows the hearts of all. 'Show whether of these two thou hast chosen'. Matthias is chosen, but note that it is God's choice, not theirs.

There are important principles for us in this brief narrative, such as the sovereignty of God, the authority of the word of God, sincerity in prayer, and the willingness to accept God's choice. These ensure guidance and blessing.

Acts 2. 41-47

THEY CONTINUED STEADFASTLY ... IN PRAYERS

Peter's powerful address to the nation had pricked the consciences of many who now asked, 'What shall we do?'. The apostles' reply was that they should repent and be baptized in acknowledgement both of their sin and of the Messiahship of Jesus. This would bring forgiveness. Three thousand souls responded to the preaching and although the actual word 'church' (*ekklesia*) does not appear in the best Greek texts until chapter 5 verse 11, nevertheless a church had come into being. What a contrast this was to those three thousand who were slain at the time of the giving of the law, Exod. 32. 28.

Four features characterized this assembly of believers. Firstly there was the teaching ('**the apostles' doctrine**'). How necessary this was in these early days of church testimony. Then there was the **fellowship**, and how necessary, too, was this holy companionship in a hostile world, when so many must have lost former friends and associates. Baptism had separated them. The **breaking of bread** would be to them a hallowed occasion of remembrance, calling to mind Him whom the nation had rejected and slain. And then there were the '**prayers**'.

Jewish minds would not, of course, be strangers to prayers. Their Scriptures were full of prayers, as were their temple services. But prayers would be different now. The New Testament assembly had been born in prayer, 1. 14, and it would seem that a continuing, consistent spirit of prayer prevailed among them in those momentous days. But what prayer now! It was no longer a form of words or a mindless repetition. God was now their Father, and in a holy intimacy they could now approach Him in the name of the Lord Jesus. There was no longer any need for human intervention or priestly mediation. They could come boldly and personally to God, in a child-like converse. And this they did, in happy fellowship together in the exercise. They **continued** in the prayers. If these four features characterized these early believers, there were four results from their steadfast continuance. There was great fear. There were signs and wonders. There was a happy harmony. There was a daily furtherance of the cause of Christ.

Acts 3. 1-11

TOGETHER ... AT THE HOUR OF PRAYER

Peter and John ... together! How often do we find these two men together. Together the Master had sent them to prepare the passover in the upper room, and together they had been in the palace of the high priest later that evening, Luke 22. 8; John 18. 15-16. Together they had hurried to the empty tomb on that memorable first day of the week. Now they are together again at the hour of prayer. What close friends they were in the cause of Christ.

Note that they are going up 'into the temple'. One has said of them that they were now better Jews for being Christians! The upper room was not now a convenient meeting place. There were, after all, more than three thousand of them now, and although the temple would soon have no place for them, nevertheless, there was space in its courts and porches for these believers in the Lord Jesus to congregate and converse.

It was the ninth hour. It was at another ninth hour that the Saviour had cried, 'It is finished'. His offering of Himself at Calvary had made the temple sacrifices obsolete, but still, the temple courts would, at least for now, provide a place for them to meet.

As Peter and John went to pray they were noticed. A man in great need, lame for a lifetime, observed them. What a lesson for us! Perhaps the world observes us too as we go to pray. This man lay at the gate of the temple called 'Beautiful'. But in forty years the temple ritual had done nothing for him, except to throw him alms. Had he now abandoned hope of a cure for his infirmity? Peter fixed his gaze upon the beggar and said, 'Look on us'. Expectantly, the man looked for alms but the apostles had something better than silver and gold. 'In the name of Jesus Christ of Nazareth rise up and walk'. Peter took him by the right hand, lifted him up, and the people watched and wondered as the man stood up, and, walking and leaping and praising God, accompanied Peter and John into the temple.

O that it might be our experience too, that in answer to our supplications we might see the lame walk, and in the joy of their new walk, join us at the hour of prayer to intercede for others.

Acts 4. 23-31

WHEN THEY HAD PRAYED THE PLACE WAS SHAKEN

Peter and John had been apprehended and imprisoned for their bold preaching of the gospel. The next day they were arraigned before the rulers, among whom were Annas and Caiaphas. What memories this would evoke! Some seven weeks earlier their Lord Himself had stood to be judged before these same men. After their powerful defence, Peter and John were commanded and threatened and subsequently released. They go to their own company. How beautiful! They are a new people, these believers, with a greater High Priest than either Annas or Caiaphas, with a greater sanctuary than the Jerusalem temple, and with a fellowship of saints which they never knew in Judaism.

Their report to the brethren results in spontaneous prayer and the Spirit has recorded the substance of their prayer for us. With one accord they lift up their voice to One whom they address as 'Lord'. It is not the usual word for Lord that they use, but the word *despotes*, which means 'master, controller, supreme and absolute owner and proprietor of all things'. He is the God of creation, who has become the God of prophecy, speaking to men through His servants, as David. They quote from the second psalm. Kings and rulers, peoples and nations, would be against the Lord and His anointed. The apostles interpret this with reference to Pilate and Herod, and an unholy alliance of Jew and Gentile, united in opposition to Messiah.

But the sovereignty of God is over all. These kings and rulers are but fulfilling the counsel of the Almighty. All that they were doing was only in accord with His decree. The apostles and their brethren see the over-ruling hand of God in it all. They pray for continuing boldness to testify and preach the word in spite of threatenings. They ask for signs and wonders, a testimony to the name of Jesus to Israel.

These early disciples prayed as Jesus had taught them to pray, Matt. 6. 6-13. They prayed with simplicity and sincerity, with brevity and beauty, with reverence and intelligence, with dependence and confidence. The place was shaken. There was unity, great power and great grace. May it be so today.

September 18th

Acts 6. 1-7

WE WILL GIVE OURSELVES CONTINUALLY TO PRAYER

It was hardly to be expected that Satan could contemplate such a fair scene as those early days of church testimony and not determine to mar it. He had tarnished the beauty of that first creation in Eden, and he would now disturb the beauty of this new creation also. How often in times of blessing does trouble arise among the saints?

Many of those early believers were Grecian or Hellenistic, Greek-speaking Jews from outside Jerusalem and Judea. Others, of course, were Hebrew-speaking Jews from the land itself. There arose a murmuring that in the daily distribution of the relief-funds for the poor, the Grecian widows were being neglected. Whether true or not, there was the ugly suspicion of partiality, and the problem must be addressed. The apostles call the multitude and put a proposition. It was not reason that the twelve should be burdened further with the administration of funds when already they carried the burden of a spiritual ministration to the saints. Should they neglect prayer and ministry in the cause of distributing relief?

They direct that seven reputable men should be chosen. They must be men of integrity, spiritual, wise, and honest; men who could command the confidence of the saints, as Stephen and Philip. It is interesting to note that the names of the seven whom they chose are all of Greek origin. How gracious this was, to recognize that there was indeed a grievance, whether founded or not, and then do the utmost to allay all and any fears of partiality or impropriety. The proposal pleased all, and the apostles, with prayer, laid hands on the chosen seven, in identification with them and approval of them.

With this happy arrangement the dispute was resolved and the apostles were relieved of the burden of a practical ministry, to give themselves to the ministry of the word. Effective ministry however, is effective only because it is ever linked with prayer. So, they say, 'We will give ourselves continually to prayer and to the ministry of the word'. They have left us an apostolic example of wisdom and grace, and the constant need for prayer.

STEPHEN, CALLING UPON GOD

Perhaps it was inevitable that martyrdoms should come. The first martyr is that same Stephen of whom we have read in chapter 6. He was one of those seven men of good report, a man full of faith and of the Holy Spirit, a man of power who wrought miracles among them. His spiritual ability in dispute angered the men of the synagogue. They could not resist his wisdom and so they resorted to false accusations of blasphemy, and brought him to the council. Those who fixed their gaze on him that day saw his face as it had been the face of an angel, as the high priest asked him, 'Are these things so?'.

Stephen addressed the council courteously, 'Men, brethren, and fathers', and first called their attention to 'the God of glory' who had appeared to their father Abraham. Beginning with the patriarch, and passing on to Jacob and Joseph and Moses, he proceeds with a masterly rehearsal of the history of the nation in its unbelief and rejection of the prophets. It is the longest sermon in the Acts of the Apostles. This unbelief of their fathers, he accuses them, has culminated in their betrayal and murder of Jesus the Just One. At this point they gnashed upon him with their teeth, cast him out of the city, and took up stones to stone him.

Under the shower of stones that rained upon him, Stephen kneeled down—but he looked up. He saw the glory of God and Jesus standing to receive him. As he committed his spirit to the Lord Jesus, the life of this beloved, earliest martyr was closed in prayer. And how like his Lord he was! In a loud voice he prayed for forgiveness for those who stoned him, 'Lord, lay not this sin to their charge'. Stephen's last words were an intercession for others. His death was as a falling asleep, as the clothes of his murderers lay at the feet of the young man who was to become the apostle of the Gentiles. It has been so aptly said that 'out of Stephen came Paul'. It has also been so often said that, 'God buries His workmen, but carries on His work'.

May we too learn to pray in the most difficult and adverse circumstances, knowing that there is One who always hears and delights to answer.

Acts 8. 5-8, 14-17

THAT THEY MIGHT RECEIVE THE HOLY GHOST

Yet once again do we find Peter and John together. The circumstances are these. Following the death of Stephen there had been a great persecution of the church at Jerusalem and the believers had been scattered abroad. In the dispersion Philip had gone to Samaria. Philip had been a companion of the martyred Stephen. He was one of the seven chosen for that ministration of relief to the poor in chapter 6. He will later be known as Philip the evangelist, 21. 8. Philip preached Christ in Samaria and as the people heard his preaching and saw the miracles which he did, many believed and there was great joy in the city. How interesting it is to remember that but a few years earlier a woman had brought to them the message of the same Christ and many had believed then also, John 4. 28-30, 39.

When the apostles heard in Jerusalem that Samaria had received the word of God, they then sent Peter and John who immediately recognized that these Samaritan believers had not yet received the Holy Spirit. They prayed for them, laid hands on them, and they received the Spirit. Why was the gift of the Spirit delayed until the coming of the apostles?

We must remember that the Samaritans were not true Jews. They were a half-caste race, part Jewish, part Gentile, see 2 Kgs. 17. 24. They had their own temple on Mount Gerizim and their own system of worship, and the Jews had no dealings with them, John 4. 9. Had they received the Holy Spirit as Philip was preaching to them they might well have been tempted to think that this was their own distinctive form of Christianity, as different to that of Jerusalem as their Samaritan religion was different to Judaism. There was a potential danger of an early division in the work, almost like two churches being established.

The coming of Peter and John from Jerusalem to pray for them demonstrated that the work was all one. This was an identification of believing Samaritans with believing Jews, and a sharing in unity of the blessing of Pentecost. God is never out of time in the working out of His purpose, and those who pray in His will, as did the apostles, are privileged to work with Him in His dealings with men.

Acts 8. 18-25

PRAY ... THAT NONE OF THESE THINGS COME UPON ME

The story of Simon is a tragic story with no ending. We do not know if the prayer for which he asked was ever offered or answered. The apostles had urged him to pray for himself but this he apparently could not do. 'Pray ye for me', he asks, but he had behaved wickedly and Peter could only say, with very little assurance, that if he could repent and pray, perhaps there might be forgiveness. But notice the 'perhaps', with no certain promise.

Simon had been a sorcerer. He had bewitched both small and great in Samaria for a long time so that they called him, 'the great power of God'. But when he saw the miracles and signs which were accompanying the preaching of Philip he seemed to see his own reputation and status being threatened. With the others, he professed to believe and was baptized. Doubtless he had decided that in being part of this new movement which was sweeping Samaria he could retain his influence within it and still hold sway as formerly. But his profession of belief was a falsehood, a deception. His heart was not right in the sight of God.

When Peter and John arrived, and when, by the laying on of their hands, the believing Samaritans received the Holy Spirit, Simon's true condition was revealed. He coveted this power to impart the Holy Spirit to others and offered money to the apostles, wanting to buy it. Was this blasphemy against the Holy Spirit, such as the Lord Jesus had spoken of in Matthew 12. 31? Did Peter see it like this and was this the reason that so little assurance was being given to Simon?

Money could not buy the gift of God. Simon was poisoned and in bondage—in the gall of bitterness and the bond of iniquity. His profession of Christ and salvation had not been real. Peter denounced him and urged him to repent and pray, though forgiveness could not be assured. 'Pray ye for me', he pleads, but there the story ends and we never read of Simon again.

Is it possible still, in our own day, that some profession may not be real? In a sincere and genuine way may such professors, too, say to others, 'Pray for me ...'.

September 22nd
Acts 9. 1-9

LORD, WHAT WILT THOU HAVE ME TO DO?

Here is the first prayer of a new convert. It has been said that Paul settled the matter of his life-service at the same time as he settled the question of the salvation of his soul.

His conversion had been remarkable. Since the death of Stephen he had been the arch-persecutor of the Christians, but he had also been struggling with a troubled conscience, kicking against the goads of conviction. Both outwardly and inwardly this was a restless, unhappy man until the light of the glory of a risen Christ dawned upon him on the Damascus road. It was a moment of revelation and recognition of the Jesus whom he had been persecuting. Saul had thought Him to be dead, but not so. He was alive and in the glory, and He had marked out this persecutor and blasphemer to be a chosen vessel for His service. In Saul's brief prayer there are enshrined some important principles for guidance.

'Lord', he exclaims. We must acknowledge the lordship of a Saviour who must be Lord of all! If we are sincere in our quest for guidance then it is imperative that we are asking for His glory, and that we are fully yielded to Him as Lord of our lives.

'Lord, what ... ?' We must accept His choice. God's plans for us may not always be what we would have chosen but when we ask 'What?' we must be willing to accept His answer. We can, of course, rest assured that His choice is always best.

'Lord, what wilt thou ... ?' We must abandon selfish motives. Those who ask sincerely will not consider any personal ambitions or desires. Saul is bowed down and humbled, blind and broken, desiring only the will of God.

'Lord, what wilt thou have me to do?' We must attempt whatever He asks. There must be a willingness to try. We may sometimes feel that He desires more from us than we are able to do, but in His strength we must trust and act when He shows us the way.

May we then sincerely acknowledge His lordship, accept His choice, abandon selfish motives, and attempt whatever He asks. This is Saul's first prayer.

Acts 9. 10-19

ONE CALLED SAUL, OF TARSUS ... BEHOLD HE PRAYETH

It is now three days since Saul's experience on the Damascus road. The light of the glory of Christ had blinded him and he is now a broken man. The proud and arrogant persecutor is now a humble believer in the Lord Jesus. He has been led by the hand to a house in the city to which he had been travelling. His murderous intention had been to apprehend any who were Christians there, to bring them to Jerusalem, to judgement, and perhaps indeed to death. But now, suddenly, miraculously, he himself was a believer, waiting for further guidance, and fasting, without food or drink while he waited.

The Lord speaks to a disciple in Damascus called Ananias. We have not heard of Ananias before and we shall not hear of him again, but he is a man in the right place at the right time and God will use him. He is directed to the house of one Judas in the street called Straight, which no doubt he knew well. He would find Saul of Tarsus there, and, 'Behold, he prayeth'. Ananias was naturally anxious. He had heard of Saul, enemy of the saints and of the gospel. He had heard what evil this infamous man had done to the church in Jerusalem. Saul's name must have been well known to the believers as a blasphemer and persecutor, an avowed adversary of Jesus and His followers. But things were different now, 'Behold, he prayeth'. It must have been with some trepidation that Ananias set out to find him.

To Ananias is given the privilege of baptizing Saul. 'Brother Saul', he so tenderly addressed him. Saul's sight was restored. He was a chosen vessel. God had great things in mind for this man of whom it is said, 'Behold, he prayeth'.

We remember how Saul had prayed at the very moment of his conversion. In years to come how often he would write to the saints urging them to continue in prayer, to pray without ceasing, and indeed he would write, 'Pray for me'. How early did this new convert learn the value of intercession! Like an infant, as it were, he had learned to say, 'Abba'. His life as a Christian was born in prayer, and doubtless on many subsequent occasions it might again have been said of him, 'Behold, he prayeth'.

Acts 9. 36-43

PETER ... KNEELED DOWN, AND PRAYED

Following the conversion of Saul the churches enjoyed a period of rest. Throughout all Judea, Samaria, and Galilee the work continued to grow. Souls were saved, saints were edified, all were encouraged and comforted, and journeying became easier and safer for the apostles. In these conditions Peter travelled westward to the Mediterranean coast and eventually arrived at Lydda, some ten miles from Joppa, towns which are perhaps better known today as Lod and Tel Aviv.

It was while he was there that two men arrived from Joppa with an urgent request from the believers there. A highly respected and much loved sister in Christ named Dorcas (or, in Aramaic, Tabitha) had fallen sick and had died. Would Peter come without delay? He did. He went with the messengers to Joppa. The body had been washed and prepared for burial and was laid in an upper chamber. So many women were there, in tears, widows weeping, and anxious to show the garments which the beloved Dorcas had made for them while she was alive. She had been full of good works. How they would miss her!

As the Saviour had done at the house of Jairus, Peter asked them all to leave. He had been at the house of Jairus, and with John and James had been allowed to stay in the room when the others were sent out. Now, in the loneliness of the death chamber, Peter kneeled down. He would confront 'the last enemy' and he must pray. It would not be in the apostle's power to raise the dead, but, with trust in the God who was the living God, Peter would command Dorcas, 'Tabitha, arise'. She opened her eyes, saw Peter, and sat up. He gave her his hand, lifted her up, and presented her alive to the saints and widows.

It is a lovely story, of which our text is a central part, 'Peter kneeled down, and prayed'. TENNYSON said, 'More things are wrought by prayer than this world dreams of'. As news of the miracle spread rapidly throughout Joppa and the surrounding area, it is scarcely to be wondered at that many believed. And Peter tarried among them in Joppa for many days.

September 25th
Acts 10. 1-4, 30-33

FEARED GOD ... GAVE MUCH AND PRAYED TO GOD ALWAY

It has often been pointed out that in chapters 8, 9, and 10 of the Acts, three representative men were brought to know the Saviour. It is interesting to remember that at that time only three of our five continents were known to be in existence and these three men were actually natives and representatives of those three known continents. The Ethiopian of chapter 8 was African. Saul of chapter 9 was from Tarsus in Asia, and Cornelius of chapter 10 was from Rome, in Europe. It is as if God, in His sovereignty and in His grace, was confirming that, just as the Saviour had commanded, the gospel was not only for Jerusalem and Judea and Samaria. It must eventually reach out to the uttermost parts of the earth, Acts 1. 8.

Cornelius was a centurion and lived in Caesarea, and with his household he feared God. He devoutly engaged in almsgiving and in prayer. He obviously had certain light, but not the full light of the glorious gospel. God, who is no respecter of persons, takes notice of the man's sincerity and will give him the further light that he needs. By an angelic visitation God commands him to send to Joppa for Simon whom we know as Peter. Peter is lodging by the seaside with another Simon, and while God is speaking to Cornelius about Peter He is also speaking to Peter about Cornelius. The divine arrangement brings Peter to Caesarea where Cornelius and his kinsmen and near friends are gathered. Peter brings to the gathered company the message of salvation through faith in the Lord Jesus.

He speaks of the impartiality of God. He speaks of the lordship of Christ through whom peace was even then being preached to Israel. He rehearses the story of the life and ministry of the Saviour. He tells them of the cross and of the resurrection, and the subsequent appearings of the risen Christ to chosen witnesses. He explains how all the prophets had predicted these things and that forgiveness of sins was now offered to whosoever would believe. The grand result was that these Gentiles believed. They were baptized and God was magnified. It is significant that it could be said of Cornelius that he 'prayed to God alway'!

September 26th

Acts 10. 9-22

PETER WENT UP ... TO PRAY ABOUT THE SIXTH HOUR

God has a solemn lesson to teach Peter and He will choose this hour of prayer to do so. Is there a principle here: that while we would speak to God He would also speak to us, in the stillness of the hour of prayer? Does He not often reveal Himself and His purposes to those who listen while they pray?

With hindsight and from our vantage point we might wonder why Peter needed this special vision to encourage him to take the gospel to Gentiles. Had not the risen Saviour commanded, 'all nations', Matt. 28. 19, 'all the world' and 'every creature', Mark 16. 15? Had He not intimated that Jerusalem and Judea were but the beginning, and that they must also be witnesses in Samaria and unto the uttermost part of the earth, Acts 1. 8? But then, Simon Peter was a Jew, a proud Jew engrained in all the prejudices of old Judaism.

Peter falls into a trance. God is preparing him for the vision. A great sheet descends from heaven to earth containing all kinds of animals, reptiles, and birds. Then the voice is heard, 'Rise up, Peter; kill, and eat'. But by the laws of Judaism these things were unclean. Peter resists and, as often pointed out, his reply is self-contradictory. 'Not so, Lord', he says. But we cannot say 'Lord,' and also say, 'Not so'. Rather, we should comply, and then say, 'Lord'. We must choose. It is the one or the other.

The apostle has to learn that what God has cleansed cannot be called unclean. Three times he is instructed so, until the sheet is taken up to heaven again, leaving Peter wondering. What he did not know, was that God had already spoken to Cornelius in Caesarea, and even now, while he thought about the meaning of the vision, three of the centurion's servants stood at the very doorway of the house. They deliver their message, but the return journey of some thirty miles is perhaps too much for that day. Peter invites them to stay overnight in Joppa, and on the morrow they travel together to Caesarea accompanied by six of the brethren, 11. 12, witnesses to this great occasion.

It is worthy of note that the message of God came to both Peter and Cornelius while they prayed.

286

Acts 12. 1-5, 12-17

PRAYER WAS MADE WITHOUT CEASING

Our chapter begins with the death of James, and ends with the death of that Herod who had killed him. This is the third Herod to be mentioned in the New Testament. They were cruel men. The first, the grandfather of this Herod, was responsible for 'the slaughter of the innocents', Matt. 2. 16. The second had beheaded John the Baptist, Matt. 14. 3-11. This Herod had martyred James and had now imprisoned Peter, with murderous intent towards him also. For how long and how often Peter, James, and John had been together. What close friends they had been, and co-workers in the cause of Christ, but Herod was now responsible for the breaking up of this delightful apostolic trio. It was a serious and solemn thing that he had done.

Peter was no stranger to prisons, see 2. 1-3 and 5. 17-18. Did Herod know this, and did he know also of the remarkable escape from custody in chapter 5 verses 19-23? This time he would ensure the safe-keeping of Peter, giving him into the charge of sixteen soldiers, and intending after Passover to bring him to trial and a public humiliation. Herod, of course, is ignorant of the power of prayer.

The church gathers to pray specifically for the imprisoned Peter. It was prayer without ceasing. It was constant continual intercession which was so soon to have a remarkable answer from God. 'Before they call, I will answer; and while they are yet speaking, I will hear', Isa. 65. 24. It is a promise for a restored Israel of a future millennial day, but it would be fulfilled so literally now for these Jerusalem saints.

Peter sleeps calmly in the prison, chained between two soldiers. Indeed, he sleeps so soundly that the angel of the Lord has to smite him on the side to awaken him. The angel provides a light, bids Peter put on his robe and sandals and follow, and as his chains fall off the soldiers sleep! The gates yield to Peter and the angel. Only when he is in the familiar city street does the angel depart and leave him to make his way to the house of Mary, mother of John Mark, where the believers are praying. Their prayer is answered before the final 'Amen'!

September 28th

Acts 13. 1-3

WHEN THEY HAD ... PRAYED ...
THEY SENT THEM AWAY

When that good man, Barnabas, had come from Jerusalem to Antioch to see what the grace of God had wrought in that city, his heart was gladdened to see the condition of things among the believers there. Barnabas soon recognized that there was a need in Antioch too great for him to meet alone, and so he travelled to Tarsus to find Saul and bring him to assist in the work. For a whole year they continued with the church in Antioch, and indeed it was there that the disciples were first called Christians.

Five prophets and teachers are named as being in the church in Antioch, and it is interesting to see the happy blending of personalities. As we have seen already in chapters 8, 9, and 10, racial, national, and social distinctions are of no account when God is working. Between the names of Barnabas and Saul there are the names of two brethren of African origin, and also the name of one, Manaen, who was actually a foster-brother of Herod the Tetrach. With what measure had the grace of God wrought in Antioch!

It was the ministry of prophets to convey the mind of God where there was no prior revelation. The teacher's ministry was to explain and expound what had been revealed and written. It was while they communed with God in prayer, and fasted, that the Holy Spirit spoke to these prophets and teachers. Saul, of course, was a chosen vessel. He and Barnabas were now to be separated for a particular work for which God was calling them. When they had fasted and prayed, they laid their hands on Barnabas and Saul. This was an act of identification with them. It was an expression of fellowship, and a recognition of the divine call.

They then 'sent them away'. It is generally agreed that a better rendering is, 'they let them go'. Perhaps there was almost a tender reluctance to part with these men. There is an example and a principle here, that those who are commended for a work further afield should be those with whom we really do not want to part. The men whom we let go are the men whom we would fain keep with us. But the great decision is shrouded in prayer, and they must go.

Acts 14. 23-28

THEY COMMENDED THEM TO THE LORD

With the commendation of the saints in Antioch, Paul and Barnabas had departed for Cyprus, accompanied by John Mark. From Cyprus they sailed for Turkey, then known as Asia Minor. They testified in such cities as Iconium, Derbe, Lystra, Perga, and the other Antioch in Pisidia, before eventually sailing from Attalia back to Antioch in Syria. Now, all this was not without persecution. Indeed, it was in Lystra that they stoned Paul and drew him out of the city supposing him to be dead. Many think that it is to this experience that Paul refers in 2 Corinthians 12. 2-3; caught up into paradise, whether in the body or out of the body he could not tell.

During these journeys the apostles preached, as opportunity was afforded them, in the synagogues. Great multitudes of Jews believed, as did many Greeks also, v. 1. Assemblies were formed and it soon became evident that there was a need for elders; men to carry responsibility in the churches.

Paul and Barnabas continued in a ministry of confirmation, exhortation, encouragement, and comfort, and then, with prayer and fasting, ordained elders in every church. Now the word 'ordained' could be misleading. To some it will convey the idea of an official ordination, but this is not so. The word simply means that they 'pointed out', or 'marked out' the brethren suitable for this ministry of leading and shepherding in the assemblies, and there was obviously a plurality of such men in each church.

Such apostolic guidance is not with us today, nor is it necessary. These early saints did not have the New Testament Scriptures that we have. Today we are privileged to have a completed Bible and the appropriate Scriptures, as 1 Timothy chapter 3, Titus chapter 1, 1 Peter chapter 5, will direct us to a recognition of our elders. It has been aptly said that the risen Christ gives the men, the Holy Spirit equips the men, and the spiritual among the saints will recognize them. However, we still need that spirit of prayer in which these first elders were marked out by the apostles.

September 30th

Acts 16. 12-15

BY A RIVERSIDE, WHERE PRAYER WAS WONT TO BE MADE

These words are clarified in the Revised Version: 'by a riverside, where we supposed there was a place of prayer'. Such a place was usually found in a city where no synagogue had been built, due to the absence of ten men to form a congregation. It was usually a modest structure, sometimes consisting of a circle enclosed by a wall without a roof, and sometimes having no outward sign of enclosure whatever.

Our passage refutes the suggestion that only Christians can pray. So does the story of Cornelius of Caesarea, Acts 10. 2. If Lydia and her praying friends had heard something about the good news which was advancing towards Europe, they may well have been praying that it would soon reach Philippi. It is hard to believe that there was no connection between their prayers and the arrival of God's messengers. Church history, including records of the planting and growth of assemblies, is not lacking in examples of divine blessing being poured out in answer to the earnest prayers of unknown women.

But Lydia had already learnt, before Paul and his colleagues arrived in the city, that prayer involved more than making known her requests to God. She was a worshipper, v. 14, a word hard to define but surely involving both abasement and adoration. God had been preparing Lydia for the gospel long before it reached Philippi. Her response was prompt and unreserved. Not that she received the message because she deserved God's favour, for she was a guilty sinner like the rest of us, and needed a little divine 'open-heart surgery' in order to receive the gospel, v. 14. But evidence of her new birth was unmistakable, not least in her hospitality to God's servants. And we can be sure that her prayer life blossomed out in the succeeding days, as she began to feed on the precious truths of the gospel.

The call to prayer comes to all Christians at conversion. Each of us needs a place of prayer, a sanctuary to which we may retreat each day to have dealings with almighty God. We can scarcely conceive of a more vital activity. To neglect it will undermine everything else we do. To fail here is to fail everywhere.

October 1st

Acts 16. 16-18

IT CAME TO PASS, AS WE WENT TO PRAYER

As in yesterday's passage, the RV renders 'prayer' as 'the place of prayer', the venue where Lydia and her friends used to meet before the apostles arrived. Paul and his colleagues saw no reason to abandon that place. It had two advantages: (i) it was outside the city and so offered a degree of seclusion, and (ii) it was by a river and so was probably suitable for baptisms, 16. 13. Moreover, Lydia's conversion would encourage Paul to keep returning to the place of prayer in order to continue preaching to the other women who gathered there. Souls who meet often to pray are more likely to find the Lord than those who never give God a thought, other things being equal.

The pronoun 'we' indicates that Luke was at this time travelling with Paul. The author of the third gospel, with its unique portrait of the praying Christ, quickly saw the importance of such sessions of prayer, as he implies here.

Taking the AV as it stands, Luke's language is very arresting, for he does not write, 'Now Paul and his co-workers held regular prayer meetings by the riverside'. He simply mentions the matter in passing—'it came to pass as we went to prayer'. He takes it for granted, he treats it as the 'norm'. He and his co-workers were well aware of the centrality of prayer. The apostles and preachers of the first century scarcely needed to be exhorted about this. They would no more have contemplated evangelism without frequent prayer than they would have thought of trying to live without breathing. They did not plan and publicize their prayer meetings. They simply cast themselves and their ministry upon God in ongoing and heart-felt prayer.

Perhaps the healing of the demon-possessed damsel flowed from Paul's intercessory instinct. For many days he tolerated her unwanted publicity and waited to act in God's time. When that time arrived, his action was decisive and the damsel was set free. Meanwhile God had doubtless been preparing the jailor for his own encounter with the apostles. Only God can synchronize events to such perfection. We must keep close to Him if we desire to be involved in His work. Hence the need for unceasing prayer.

October 2nd
Acts 16. 19-34

AT MIDNIGHT PAUL AND SILAS PRAYED, AND SANG PRAISES TO GOD

How ought Christians to respond to such dreadful sufferings as those experienced in Philippi by Paul and Silas? The dishonesty of the masters of the demon-possessed damsel, vv. 20-21; the hostility of the multitude, v. 22; the injustice and violence of the magistrates, vv. 22-23; and the cruelty of the jailor, v. 24; these would have been sufficient to reduce lesser men to back-sliding and despair. How did Paul and Silas react? 'At midnight (they) prayed ... .' Would we have done that?

Perhaps we would. Prayer is usually our first response to suffering, and our first request is likely to be that the suffering will be removed! If that is not granted, we will ask for the grace of endurance. David and Peter give us closely-related advice, 'Cast thy burden upon the Lord, and he shall sustain thee', Ps. 55. 22; 'Casting all your care upon him; for he careth for you', 1 Pet. 5. 7. Our burdens and cares are no problem to the Lord. Rather they are among the instruments He uses to fashion us increasingly into His likeness. We should neither resent nor despise them.

But our text goes on '... and sang praises to God ...'. Here is the measure of these men. They did not stoically resolve to put up with their sufferings. Instead they found cause for praise in them. This must have pleased their Master, who in His sermon on the mount had urged His followers, 'Rejoice, and be exceeding glad: for great is your reward in heaven: for so persecuted they the prophets which were before you', Matt. 5. 12. Paul taught that it was a privilege to suffer for Christ, 'For unto you it is given in the behalf of Christ, not only to believe on him, but also to suffer for his sake', Phil. 1. 29.

'And the prisoners heard them.' Probably with mixed feelings! But lasting impressions must have been made on some of those men. When the earthquake came, Paul and Silas apparently persuaded them all to stay where they were, rather than to hazard their lives in the darkness of a damaged building. And Paul's compassion in saving the jailor from suicide was surely the vital factor in his conversion. He had never encountered such love before.

October 3rd

Acts 20. 17-38

HE KNEELED DOWN,
AND PRAYED WITH THEM ALL

This was how Paul brought to a conclusion his meeting with the elders of the church at Ephesus. He had sent a message to them from Miletus urging them to join him there, v. 17. When they arrived, he reminded them in moving terms about his ministry among them, vv. 18-21, 26-27, 31, 33-35. He unfolded to them his personal expectations of suffering and his willingness to face martyrdom for the sake of Christ, vv. 22-24. He told them that he would never meet them again, v. 25. He warned them about his fears for the future of the assembly, and in particular about his certainty that false teachers would become active among them, drawn from their own number as well as from outside, vv. 29-30.

That discourse must have solemnized the Ephesian elders. They felt most keenly his prediction 'that they should see his face no more', v. 38. They were reduced to tears, and fell on his neck and kissed him, v. 37. These are remarkable words, and surely refute the suggestion sometimes made that Paul was a hard and legal man and an authoritarian teacher. He had won the hearts of the Ephesians and cared about them intensely.

But where could Paul find comfort at a time like this? Our text supplies the answer, 'He kneeled down, and prayed with them all'. To kneel helps us to remember our littleness in God's sight, though other postures are acceptable to Him: (i) 'And when ye **stand** praying, forgive', Mark 11. 25; 'Then went king David in, and **sat** before the Lord', 2 Sam. 7. 18; 'And he went a little farther, and **fell on his face**, and prayed', Matt. 26. 39. Reverence is clearly possible irrespective of posture, though we should definitely shun being casual and careless in our approach to God.

Paul 'prayed with them all'. This went beyond praying **for** them all, though the apostle certainly did that. We might envy those elders the joy of hearing Paul's prayers for them, but he wanted to hear their prayers for him. This was no one-man prayer meeting! The content of the prayers remains unknown but we cannot doubt their earnestness. We would do well to borrow more often the disciples' cry, 'Lord, teach us to pray', Luke 11. 1.

October 4th

Acts 27. 21-36

HE TOOK BREAD, AND GAVE THANKS TO GOD

Luke's account of Paul's sea journey from Caesarea to Rome, in Acts chapter 27, reveals the apostle's spiritual stature in a remarkable way. As the dangers increased, so did his moral authority. It is easy to forget, as we read the story, that he was a prisoner rather than a ship's officer! Four times he made significant statements of warning or encouragement, vv. 10, 21-26, 31 and 33-34. Our text describes his behaviour immediately after his fourth utterance. He was concerned that his fellow travellers had gone without food for fourteen days. This was understandable in that they had been living at the stretch as they made what seemed like increasingly futile attempts to bring the ship safely ashore at some place.

It is easy for men, for whom death seems imminent, to panic as they fight for their lives. But Paul had already assured everyone on board that 'there shall be no loss of any man's life among you', v. 22. The only danger now was that of unbelief, so in his final utterance he urged them all to take food, and repeated the promise of deliverance—'there shall not an hair fall from the head of any of you', v. 34.

Then he practised what he preached. He took bread and gave thanks to God. This was no formality with Paul, no hurried repetition of a few well-worn words. He regarded his food as a timely provision from his Father in heaven. He knew who was his great Provider. So his thanksgiving flowed from a lively sense of gratitude; but it also flowed from a life of habitual communion. It was an act of worship, spontaneous and heart-felt.

It was also an act of witness, for he gave thanks 'in presence of them all'. This was not done, of course, with the intention of parading his piety to gain approval. He was simply encouraging them to follow his example. They were weakened by their lengthy abstinence from food and it was urgent for them to renew their strength. So Paul ignored the storm and began his meal. And there must have been something contagious about his calm and buoyant attitude, for we read, 'Then were they all of good cheer, and they also took some meat', v. 36.

October 5th

Acts 28. 7-10

PAUL ... PRAYED, AND LAID HIS HANDS ON HIM, AND HEALED HIM

Paul's God-given prediction of the safety of everyone involved in the storm was vindicated by events. The shipwreck was terrifying but not a life was lost, 27. 40-44. They found refuge on Malta (AV Melita), an island in the centre of the Mediterranean, 100 km south of Sicily. It had been under Roman control since 218 BC. The natives are called barbarians, vv. 2 and 4, but this merely means that they did not speak Greek. They were far from barbarous in their treatment of the survivors of the storm. The weather was cold and rainy so they began by kindling a fire.

Paul, who was never on his dignity when there was work to be done, helped by gathering sticks and gathered a viper as well. It fastened on his hand, convincing the islanders that he was a murderer; but when he calmly shook it into the fire and was unharmed, they decided that he was a god!

The chief official on Malta was Publius, who owned property there and who extended hospitality to his unexpected visitors. He never had cause to regret it. His father was suffering acutely from fever and dysentery. Paul learned about this and promptly visited the sick man.

He began with prayer. This does not surprise us for he knew better than most about the power of prayer. It brought God right into the circumstances. It also turned the sick man's thoughts upward to the living God rather than to Paul, His servant. This reflects the apostle's selfless humility and his desire to exalt the Lord. Next, he laid his hands on the patient, as though to identify with his sufferings and to calm his restlessness. Then he healed him, bringing sweet relief, not only to the sufferer but also to Publius and to the other members of his household.

The blessing did not end there, for 'others also, which had diseases in the island, came and were healed', v. 9. Moreover, we can be sure that Paul seized every opportunity during his three months in Malta to tell out the gospel among the islanders. He knew the limited value of healing the sick without leading them to Christ. A healthy body is of great value on earth but a saved soul is an eternal asset which endures in heaven throughout eternity.

October 6th

Romans 1. 8-17

I MAKE MENTION OF YOU ALWAYS IN MY PRAYERS

Paul had not yet visited Rome at the time of his sending this letter to the church there. F F BRUCE writes that 'although he was a Roman citizen by birth, Acts 22. 28, he had never seen the city whose freeman he was'. He had often planned to go there but had been prevented from doing so, 1. 13. He was not so much interested in seeing the sights of Rome as he was in meeting the saints of Rome. He knew that their faith was being spoken of throughout the whole world, and he heartily thanked God for it, 1. 8. But he had lofty ambitions for them, and he longed to enrich them, to establish them and to comfort them, 1. 11-12.

Until he was able to visit them, he knew that there was one crucial way in which he could prosper their spiritual lives. He could pray for them. Our text reveals the extent of his commitment to this task in remarkable words: 'without ceasing I make mention of you always in my prayers', v. 9. Clearly, this was no light undertaking for Paul. It was no fringe activity which he resorted to when he had nothing better to do. His praying was never sporadic or casual, never half-hearted or lethargic. It was unceasing and persistent, heart-felt and earnest.

This is all the more remarkable when we remember Paul's life-style after his conversion. He knew little of the comforts of a well-ordered home life. His days were not peaceful and predictable. He did not work a five-day week, with the benefits of modern flexi-time! He was an incessant traveller and he trod a pathway of recurring suffering and danger at the hands of violent and ruthless men. He could never set aside specific parts of each day for quiet prayer and Bible study. A careful reading of 2 Corinthians 11. 23-28 alone is sufficient to prove this, and the closing words say it all, 'Beside those things which are without, that which cometh upon me daily, **the care of all the churches**'. Only as Paul habitually and constantly poured out his heart to God in prayer could he find relief from this burden of care. His New Testament letters reveal the scope and depth of his ministry of intercession. Do they not reveal also the paucity of much of our own praying?

October 7th
Romans 8. 14-16

THE SPIRIT OF ADOPTION, WHEREBY WE CRY, ABBA, FATHER

The word 'Spirit' appears twice in our verse and scholars are divided as to whether the capital 'S' should be used in both instances (in which case the Holy Spirit is meant), or whether, as DARBY prefers, the small 's' should be used (in which case it means simply a temper, mood or state). LEON MORRIS, in his *IVP Commentary,* concludes that 'Paul is here saying two things about the Spirit: first, negatively, that the Spirit believers received is not one of bondage; second, positively, He is a Spirit of sonship ... the Spirit does not make people slaves but sons'.

The Newberry Bible replaces the phrase 'the Spirit of adoption' by 'the Spirit of sonship'. Adoption was common in the first century among both Romans and Greeks, though not among Jews. Indeed, among first-century Romans an adopted son was deliberately chosen by his adoptive father to perpetuate his name and inherit his estates. He was not inferior in status to a son by birth. This sense of 'adoption' seems close to biblical usage; in Galatians 4. 5 and Ephesians 1. 5 'adoption' implies 'son-placing', the placing of all believers as mature, adult sons of God with all the privileges and responsibilities of sonship.

The Spirit inspires us to cry, 'Abba, Father'. These two titles are also on the lips of Christ in Gethsemane, see Mark 14. 36, 'Abba, Father, all things are possible unto thee'; and Paul quotes them in Galatians 4. 6, 'And because ye are sons, God hath sent forth the Spirit of his Son into your hearts, crying, Abba, Father'. 'Abba' is an Aramaic word meaning 'Father'. VINE writes that 'it is the cry of an infant, the simple, helpless utterance of unreasoning trust, the effect of feeling rather than knowledge (cf English 'Papa') ... 'Father' is another mode of address. It is relationship intelligently realized by the one who utters it, and the two expressions together indicate the love and intelligent trust of the child'.

The fact that 'we **cry,** Abba, Father' implies the intensity of our feelings. The Spirit will never encourage us to be casual as we draw near to the Father. We may confide in Him as in no one else. Let us ever do so, without reserve.

Romans 8. 26-27

WE KNOW NOT WHAT WE SHOULD PRAY FOR AS WE OUGHT

This phrase describes the dilemma which often confronts us as we start praying. There are circumstances or persons about which we want to pray but we do not know what to ask for. We may lack some of the relevant facts, or we may be unsure as to what would be the best outcome for those involved. For example, if someone contracts a terminal illness involving severe pain and requiring constant attention, ought we to pray for a full recovery or for a speedy home-call with its final relief of all suffering?

The RV translators interpret the phrase differently: 'We know not how we should pray as we ought'. This implies that our problem is not what we should ask for, but how we should ask for it. It is the manner of our praying, rather than its matter, about which we feel uncertain. Sometimes diffidence seems more appropriate than confidence. *The Amplified New Testament* combines the two ideas in this way, 'we do not know what prayer to offer nor how to offer it worthily as we ought'. In the light of this statement, our ignorance about acceptable prayer is total.

Our dilemma is solved in the preceding and succeeding passages, where the intercessory work of the Holy Spirit is explained. 'Likewise the Spirit also helpeth our infirmities ... .' Notice that Paul does not isolate himself from his fellow believers here, as though his prayers are more fitting than theirs. He too needs the Spirit's help, and so do all of us. MORRIS: 'we who are Christians are not the spiritual giants we would like to be (and sometimes imagine we are) ... we are weak, and left to ourselves we will always be in trouble'.

The Spirit Himself 'maketh intercession for us with groanings which cannot be uttered'. Whose groans are these, the believer's or the Spirit's? The Spirit is not said to groan, but to intercede with groans, and these may well be those of the believer. When we cannot find words in which to express our prayer and can only groan, the Spirit takes our groans and makes them into effective intercession. Here is encouragement for those who find praying difficult. Is not this true of us all at times?

October 9th
Romans 10. 1-13
MY HEART'S DESIRE AND PRAYER TO GOD

These words reveal Paul's great longing for the salvation of his fellow-nationals. Earlier in the epistle he shows the intensity of that longing, 'I have great heaviness and continual sorrow in my heart. For I could wish that myself were accursed from Christ for my brethren, my kinsmen according to the flesh', 9. 2-3. So distressed was he by the unbelief of Israel, that he felt ready to forfeit his salvation if only they would receive it. He knew this was impossible, of course, having just unfolded the truth of the believer's security, 8. 35-39. But he meant what he said. He never indulged in exaggeration, and he never mouthed empty claims. Christ had indeed died for Israel, and Paul felt ready to do the same if only it would bring them to Christ. But he knew that only the sacrifice of Christ had atoning value. If that sacrifice failed to awaken them, nothing else could.

How did Paul find relief from the burden of Israel's unbelief? Chiefly by prayer, as our text shows. His prayer flowed from his desire. His desire drove him to prayer. He agonized over Israel, and wrestled with God on their behalf. He could not ease himself of his constant concern at their plight. He often turned away from them in order to preach the gospel to the Gentiles, as his missionary journey make clear. But his heart constantly went out to them.

But what of us? How does our concern for our fellow-nationals compare with Paul's? It is tempting to complain about the appalling evils in our land. It is tempting to denounce the wickedness of those around us. But we need to remember our own pre-conversion misconduct. We may have been hedged about by Christian families and so restrained from the excesses of our pagan contemporaries. But our actions, thoughts and motives could never have borne close inspection in our unregenerate days.

And how many praying Christians pleaded for us at the throne of grace until we were saved? They deserve our undying gratitude, and we should cultivate their example. Our nation desperately needs such intercession today.

299

Romans 12. 9-21

CONTINUING INSTANT IN PRAYER

This phrase is the eleventh of nearly thirty short exhortations which form our passage, and by which Paul appeals for distinctively Christian conduct. His preceding eleven chapters, with the opening verses of chapter 12, laid the doctrinal foundation on which his ethical instructions were built. These instructions do not require the exercise of gifts (he has dealt with those in verses 3 to 8) but the development of good behaviour. We do not all possess the same spiritual gifts, but we are all intended to manifest the same moral features.

Obedience is not easy. We are required to be consistently loving and kind, giving preference to the interests of others, to whom we are to be generous and hospitable. We are to bless our persecutors and to share the joys and sorrows of those around us. We are to be peaceable towards everyone and are never to avenge ourselves. We are not to be overcome by evil, but are to overcome evil with good. And we are not meant, merely, to attempt to meet some of these requirements some of the time, but to achieve them all, all the time! How is it possible?

The answer lies in our text, 'continuing instant in prayer'. The RV renders it 'continuing steadfastly in prayer'. If we want to live as Paul instructs us to live, we must pray as Paul instructs us to pray. Only in this way can we draw constantly upon the divine resources in order to become increasingly what the Lord wants us to be. If we fail in this we shall fall back upon our own resources and prove them to be non-existent. We shall attempt to please the Lord by our own efforts and discover, as we have so often discovered in the past, that it can't be done. The most serious result of such failure will be that we displease the Lord and dishonour Him by our conduct. That alone should bring us to our knees in contrition. But for us, the result will be a sickening sense of defeat and a resultant decline into depression and frustration, until by His grace we resume the path of prayer. He never abandons us, of course, and He is always willing to welcome us back into His presence day by day.

October 11th

Romans 15. 30-33

STRIVE TOGETHER WITH ME IN YOUR PRAYERS TO GOD FOR ME

Paul regularly asked his readers to pray for him. These requests were never casual or formal. They were detailed and earnest. Examples include those recorded in 2 Corinthians 1. 11; Ephesians 6. 19; Colossians 4. 3; 1 Thessalonians 5. 25; 2 Thessalonians 3. 1. The Ephesian example is especially impressive, 'that utterance may be given unto me, that I may open my mouth boldly, to make known the mystery of the gospel'. His concern was not for the opening of the prison door, but for the opening of his mouth in witness! Mighty apostle though he was, he never felt that he could manage without the prayers of his fellow saints.

Our passage begins, 'Now I beseech you, brethren', which can be rendered, 'I implore you'. He strengthens his appeal by adding, 'for the Lord Jesus Christ's sake'. He wants the Lord to be glorified through the answers to the Romans' prayers. He goes on, 'and for the love of the Spirit', which probably means the love the Spirit kindles in believers, cf., 'But the fruit of the Spirit is love', Gal. 5. 22. Such love motivates prayer for others.

In our text Paul urges his readers to 'strive together with me in your prayers to God for me'. He wants them to join him in his struggle. This is the language of conflict. LEON MORRIS quotes E STAUFFER, 'The form of the battle is prayer. In prayer there is achieved unity between the will of God and that of man, between human struggling and action and effective divine operation ... In prayer one man becomes the representative of the other, so that there is here opened up the possibility of one standing in the breach for all, and all for one', *Theological Dictionary of the New Testament*.

Paul knew that in approaching Jerusalem he was likely to encounter many Jewish enemies. He gave his readers three vital prayer topics: (i) deliverance form his unbelieving enemies in Judaea; (ii) acceptance by the saints of the financial gift he brought from the Gentile believers; and (iii) an unimpeded journey to Rome with the opportunity for fellowship with the Roman believers. These prayers were granted ultimately, though the answers were not all predictable. They rarely are!

301

October 12th

1 Corinthians 1. 1-9

I THANK MY GOD ALWAYS ON YOUR BEHALF

The writing of this letter from Ephesus, probably in AD 55-56, was difficult for Paul. He had planted the church at Corinth during at least eighteen months of evangelism among Jews and Gentiles, Acts 18. 1-18. He had persisted in his ministry in the teeth of fierce opposition. When he finally left Corinth, the church was in a healthy spiritual condition, but eventually it lost ground. A careful reading of 1st Corinthians makes it clear that a formidable list of faults and sins had invaded the life of the church.

Paul dealt faithfully with these problems, but it grieved him intensely to have to do so. In a later letter he wrote, 'For out of much affliction and anguish of heart I wrote unto you with many tears', 2 Cor. 2. 4. Some scholars believe that Paul refers here to another stern letter which he had written to Corinth previously. Others are satisfied that he means what our New Testament calls his first epistle. Either way, it is clear that those believers were very dear to Paul. He was no heartless autocrat. Anyone who represents him in such terms does him a grave injustice.

And how striking it is that our text is part of an introductory passage, 1. 4-8, in which Paul expresses his heart-felt appreciation of the Corinthian saints! He thanks God unfeignedly for the grace given them by Jesus Christ. He thanks God that they are enriched by Him in all utterance and in all knowledge, and that they come behind in no gift. Now there was no subtlety in Paul, no use of mere diplomacy to soften the blows which were coming as the letter unfolded. But he wanted the saints at Corinth to know that he still valued them highly, and that he appreciated their gifts and graces.

We sometimes hear assemblies being maligned today because of faults much less substantial than those at Corinth. Deviations from scriptural teaching are always sad, but we should be ever ready to express our appreciation of whatever is of Christ in an assembly's life and witness. If strictures are needed they should be addressed kindly to the elders or believers concerned, and to no one else. Gossip should never be countenanced among believers.

October 13th
1 Corinthians 7. 1-9
GIVE YOURSELVES TO FASTING AND PRAYER

This instruction can only be understood in the light of its context in verses 1-9 of the chapter. W E VINE points out in his commentary that 'the most authentic manuscripts do not contain here any mention of fasting'. Hence it is omitted from the RV and other versions. Paul is concerned about times of prayer in the lives of husbands and wives. He deals with the matter with delicacy but makes clear how his married readers should treat their partners.

He emphasizes that it is wrong for either partner in marriage to persistently deprive the other of physical fulfilment. Commenting on verses 3 to 5, LEON MORRIS writes, 'Each (partner) owes duties to the other. Paul does not stress the duty of either partner at the expense of the other, but puts them on a level, a noteworthy position in the male-dominated society of the time. His verb (in verse 3) is the present imperative, which indicates the habitual duty … (wives and husbands) have obligations to one another'.

Now to our text. In verse 5 Paul recognizes that a Christian couple may agree to abstain from union for a time in order to give themselves to prayer. It is not that the apostle strongly insists on this practice; much less does he teach that all married couples should adopt it. VINE emphasizes the three conditions which should control such abstention: '(i) there must be mutual consent, (ii) it must be temporary, and (iii) it must have the purpose of prayer in view'. It is noteworthy that, so far as God is concerned, married partners belong to each other so fully that persistent abstinence by one against the wishes of the other amounts to an act of fraud, v. 5.

The words 'that you may give yourselves to prayer' mean literally 'that you may have leisure for prayer'. Most of us in the western world find that the pace of life is the enemy of leisurely prayer, yet this is a crucial activity. We have seen that Paul sanctions in this passage one way in which married Christians may achieve greater concentration on prayer. But the attendant dangers he mentions were very real then, and they remain so in our corrupt society today.

October 14th

1 Corinthians 11. 4

EVERY MAN PRAYING OR PROPHESYING

Chapters 11 to 14 of this epistle deal with the conduct of believers in a local church. Chapter 11 is concerned with women's head coverings, vv. 1-16, and with the Lord's Supper, vv. 17-34. Prophesying was a gift available only during the apostolic period, before the New Testament was completed. Since then the prophet has been superseded by the teacher, as implied in 2 Pet. 2. 1. For present purposes, therefore, our text is concerned with the conduct of men as they pray publicly. They are to do so with their heads uncovered. A man's physical head is the symbol of the headship of Christ over the man. For a man to cover his head as he prays publicly would be, therefore, a dishonour to Christ.

But there is more to be said about public prayer than that! Such prayer has this in common with secret prayer, that it is addressed to God. Brethren should remember this. It will discourage them from parading their knowledge of the Scriptures by expounding them as they pray. They will avoid using public prayer to criticize believers or elders, or to send coded messages to the gathered company. The brother who prays publicly is exercising a lofty privilege. It demands a lowly mind and a sensitive heart. As he prays, he should be articulating the praises of the company, and should be expressing their Godward desires and longings. Only the indwelling Holy Spirit can enable him to do this. The prayers of a Spirit-filled man may well prompt his fellow-believers to say silently to the Lord, 'Yes, Lord, that is exactly what I had in mind, that is precisely what I long for. Amen, Lord!'.

Public prayers should also be short. The brother who rambles on at length, week after week, using the same well-worn phrases to utter the same well-worn requests, will certainly weary the saints and discourage others who desire to pray. Nothing is more refreshing than the brief but fervent prayers of a young convert, and the equally brief but fervent prayers of an old warrior for Christ who knows what prayer is about! 'God is in heaven, and thou upon earth: **therefore let thy words be few**', Eccles. 5. 2.

October 15th

1 Corinthians 11. 5, 13

EVERY WOMAN THAT PRAYETH OR PROPHESIETH

Some scholars teach that verse 5 of our chapter implies that women are free to pray or prophesy audibly in church gatherings provided that their heads are covered. But that ignores Paul's insistence on the silence of women in such gatherings, in 14. 34 and 1 Timothy 2. 11, 12. Women are required both to cover their heads and to remain silent in the church. This interpretation is not confined to our assemblies; thus, HODGE writes, 'It was Paul's manner to attend to one thing at a time. He is here dealing with the propriety of women speaking in public unveiled, and therefore he says nothing about the propriety of their speaking in public in itself. When that subject comes up, he expresses his judgement in the clearest terms'. LEON MORRIS seems wide of the mark when he writes that 'in the first century women were uneducated ... The Corinthian women should keep quiet in church if for no other reason than because they could have had little or nothing worthwhile to say', *TNT Commentary*. Where then did Mary and Martha, Priscilla and Phoebe and the devoted women mentioned in Romans 16 acquire their spiritual wisdom?

Many of our assemblies depend crucially for their survival on the fervent prayers of devoted women who, as it happens, form the majority of those in fellowship, at least in the UK. The fact that their public prayers are silent does not diminish their value. We would be impoverished without our sisters. They exercise a sanctifying, and at times a restraining, influence on the conduct of less spiritual men.

Moreover we owe a great deal to the writings of godly women such as AMY CARMICHAEL, ISOBEL KUHN, CORRIE TEN BOOM, and MRS. HOWARD TAYLOR. A glance at the indices of our hymn books will tell us that women wrote many of our favourite hymns. And those who use the *Daily Prayer Guide* and who read *Echoes* monthly and *Look on the Field*s will know that it is sisters rather than brethren who are responding to the call of Christ today for service overseas. Brethren ought not to be reluctant to acknowledge their indebtedness to sisters for the great contribution they make to assembly life. They deserve our sincere appreciation.

October 16th
1 Corinthians 12. 1-3

SAY THAT JESUS IS THE LORD

As Paul turns to this new topic in his Corinthian writings, he underlines the fact that no believer is intended to stay ignorant of spiritual matters. God is not the God of secrecy but of revelation and spiritual education. Furthermore, in terming his readers 'brethren' he reaffirms the bond existing between all believers, that bond being forged through Calvary's work.

However, as a preface to the great subject of gift, he reminds the Corinthians of the privation of their past as opposed to the privilege of their present. They 'were Gentiles', whereas now they were still Gentiles but Gentile believers. 'Carried away'—they had no say in the matter, they were prisoners to their culture and its idolatry and associated immorality, whereas now they were subject to the leading of the Spirit of God in their lives, the divine Teacher, who revealed the things of Christ to their hearts. 'Unto dumb idols' indicates that no communication could ever have been given to them, for the idols had nothing to say nor the capability to say it, whereas now they could receive communication from the vocal God and from His Spirit-empowered servants. What they had failed to recognize in their pre-conversion days was that behind these dumb idols were the satanic forces that enslaved them.

Thus, Paul gives the Corinthians specific guidelines for both prayer and witness based on their spiritual understanding rather than guesswork. None, claiming to be a believer, will ever be able to call Jesus accursed (*anathema*). This militates against the activities of the Spirit whose major work is to glorify Jesus. Contrariwise, only the person indwelt by the Spirit of God will be able to say 'Jesus is Lord'.

What a privilege to take this holy, potent name on our lips. It is the name that speaks of His humanity, the name which caused the spirit world to tremble and acknowledge impotency, Mark 5. 12: it is the name which prevails both with men and God. But He is also Lord-Sovereign, Despotic Lord—the One who bought us, owns us and wants our communication with Him daily to learn and work out His will.

October 17th

1 Corinthians 14. 8-17

WITH THE SPIRIT, AND ... THE UNDERSTANDING

This passage commences with the emphasis on instant communication or else all will suffer from confusion. We are in a battle, and prayer is one facet of this warfare. Communication between the divine Leader and His troops needs to be instantly clear if victory is to be assured.

As the passage unfolds, the continued emphasis is on clarity of communication, particularly so that the listener can enter into the content of the dialogue. Consequently, for the brother who exhibited the gift of tongues in prayer, he needed to be equally zealous for the gift of interpretation so that all could enjoy and enter into his exercise as he led the assembly.

Paul states clearly that praying in tongues means that not only are the listeners excommunicado, but so too is the person engaged in prayer. Thus, whilst an atmosphere of prayer may be exhibited and prayer may be taking place, there can be no sense of fellowship or concern because no one is aware of the matters in hand, be they prayer, praise, supplication or thanksgiving.

Hence the desire of the Spirit-inspired Paul that when the holy exercise of prayer takes place, not only will the spirit of the believer be engaged but so too the mind, which gives understanding. As great as the exercise of tongues must have been, there was implicit in its exercise a barrier to the understanding and therefore to the communication of the burden of the person so occupied. It could even be misconstrued, as was Hannah's godly exercise in 1 Samuel 1. 13.

Prayer, as intercourse between the believer and his God, is a precious occupation. If it is public prayer, then others are entitled to acknowledge its content, particularly unbelievers. They need to be able to hear, understand, and stand in awe at the use of this beautiful and unique channel of communication between the creature and his Creator so that they can join in with an 'Amen'. A sobering question is posed, 'Are all able to give an 'Amen' to my prayers, or are they just so many meaningless words even if in a known tongue?'! Let us pray coherently and with purpose.

307

October 18th

1 Corinthians 15. 54-58

GOD WHICH GIVETH US THE VICTORY

Our reading today opens with a wonderful and positive assertion—'so when'—**not** 'so if'! What a note Paul strikes as he
brings this treatise on the resurrection to its glorious climax. No
note of doubt; no room for error; no thought of failure—everything spoken of is in the assured future tense. We are dealing
with an omnipotent God who has given His wonderful Son a
work to do, and this has been completed to His entire satisfaction.

Consequently, those who have gone before will be robed
with **incorruptibility**. Those of us who remain at His coming
will don **immortality**. Why are these robes available? Great as
death is, there is One who is even greater—He has overwhelmed
this formidable foe.

As a result every blood-bought believer is able to stare death
in the face because its sting has been removed. The One who
bruised the serpent's head in fulfilment of prophecy simultaneously removed the sting of death. Again, the saint with the
aching heart is able to look at the cold grave and challenge its apparent victory. Our faith is in the One who rose from the dead
and is able, with unrivalled authority, to walk the soil of resurrection. Even in life, no grave could withstand His power. In
resurrection, He has publicly and eternally nullified its power,
and rendered it a temporary resting place for the body of both
believer and unbeliever alike. We remember, however, that for
the believer it will be a glorious vacating whereas for the unbeliever it will be the prelude to eternal punishment.

Whilst Paul brings this song of triumph to a thrilling climax,
in prayer he thanks God for the victory which He gives us
through our Lord Jesus Christ. Sometimes we feel down, depressed, even defeated. In such circumstances read again this
chapter—slowly at first, then pick up the momentum as you are
gripped with its contents. You too, with me, will be able to thank
God ever and always for a victory given us, a victory we could
never have obtained. We can enter into the thrill of the watching
Israelites as David felled Goliath with one stone. Our Lord has
overthrown an even greater foe, and in prayer we return Him
our grateful thanks.

October 19th

2 Corinthians 1. 1-4

THE FATHER OF MERCIES

Having spent eighteen months at Corinth, and having brought this church to the faith, is it any wonder such a bond existed between Paul and these believers, even though they had strayed, causing him heartache as their spiritual father?

So, again, he takes to writing a letter, in harness with Timothy, whom he describes as being likeminded.What an encouragement to think that each believer can be helped and sustained by such fellowship.

How often in the Scriptures do we find two working together, particularly an older servant with a younger, as the baton of faith and experience is passed on with future service in mind.

He opens this letter with one of three similar New Testament benedictions, cf. Eph. 1. 3; 1 Pet. 1. 3. It calls to mind the undeserved favour that God bestows upon us and the resultant peace, that precious commodity which 'garrisons our hearts and minds by Christ Jesus'. How precious that these two virtues are made available to us from the One who is our Father and so **cares for us**, and from the One who is our Saviour and **treasures us**. Grace is the source of our blessing, and peace is the river flowing from it. I trust, dear reader, you are experiencing peace as a torrent, or has it slowed to a trickle? Take up this thought in prayer again today—'Grace is still flowing as a river, millions there have been supplied: still it flows as fresh as ever, from the Saviour's wounded side'.

In verse 3, God is introduced to us in a threefold way—'He is the Father of our Lord Jesus Christ', 'the Father of mercies', and 'the God of all comfort'. In our present meditation we shall focus on the second, for all mercies issue from Him. Trace this river too, as it flows right through Scripture, ever protecting us from that which we rightfully deserved. 'As a father pitieth his children' is how He deals with us—He draws right alongside so that He can provide full support at all times, see Ps. 103. 13.

We can thank God for this revelation of His character. We too, in the proportion we receive comfort, will be able to dispense it to our fellow believers. This is how He deals with us, so let us pray to God today that we shall be able to deal with others similarly.

October 20th

2 Corinthians 1. 8-11

YE ALSO HELPING TOGETHER BY PRAYER FOR US

In this little cameo of personal experience, Paul allows us to appreciate a difficulty through which he passed for the cause of Christ, and the prayer-fellowship entered into on his behalf by these Corinthian believers. Could this be an encouragement and source of strength to me today? Is there trouble anywhere?—take it to the Lord in prayer!

His time at Ephesus, undoubtedly referred to here, had climaxed with his life placed in peril. He had known the very depth of despair as unprecedented pressure was brought to bear on him for the sake of the gospel.

However, one of the purposes of this weight being brought to bear on him was so that he would look away from himself and his frailty, to the God who not only had the power to save but also to keep. God's power massively demonstrated in resurrection was that power which moved to protect and preserve him. O that Elisha's prayer for his servant might be realized in us—that our eyes might be opened to see the power of heaven available to preserve us!, see 2 Kgs. 6. 17.

Paul reflects with gratitude on the threefold deliverance effected by God—the One who 'delivers' in the past, 'doth deliver' in the present, and will 'yet deliver' in the future. The word on which his experience hinges is 'trust'. This was no mere theory with Paul, but rather, a daily experiential matter. It enabled him to face every situation with utmost confidence. **When we fear, we do not trust; when we trust, we do not fear!**

But why tell the Corinthians all this? Simply because they had a part in his deliverance, 'ye also helping together by prayer for us'. What a wonderful sense of responsibility and reciprocation. They owed him a debt in their salvation. Now they prayed for him in his troubles. Fellowship in prayer knows no barriers, no distance problem, no cultural or language obstacles. Nothing and no one can thwart that appeal of prayer which wings its way to our Father. Do you know of someone in difficulty, from whatever source? Pray for them today. It may be that in days to come they will recount their story, and you can share in their triumph because you helped together in praying for them.

October 21st

2 Corinthians 8. 16-24

CARE IN THE HEART OF TITUS

Chapters 8 and 9 of 2 Corinthians make for thrilling reading as we are confronted with the practical reality of fellowship between believers. This fellowship touches the hearts as well as the pockets. But the underlying feature is 'they first gave their own selves to the Lord'. If this exists then every facet of fellowship can be explored thereafter.

The Macedonian churches were to be commended for their concern for the poor in Jerusalem. Although having little themselves, they felt an exercise. Having realized this exercise, and given to the Lord, who were they going to entrust with their gift? This is where today's prayer comes in. Paul is able to thank God for a man called Titus; a man also designated 'mine own son after the common faith', Titus 1. 4. As with Timothy, a strong bond existed between these two. Furthermore, as a son, he had learned from his spiritual father. Consequently, there is praise to God in prayer for one who shared the same care in his heart for this matter as the great apostle and the Macedonian saints.

As we peruse today's reading, we find exuding from the heart of the apostle praise to God for one who cared and whose caring was known to all. His conduct in the gospel was known and acknowledged by all. He was the unanimous choice of the local churches, so he was obviously well known and well respected in his labours for the Lord in that area. He is Paul's fellow helper, so that wherever work is to be done, there is Titus, at hand, ready to support Paul.

How vital it is today, especially in monetary matters, that we have brethren in whom we can have confidence; brethren we know to be praying with regard to the disposing of the Lord's money, and, after prayer, are of one mind as to its distribution. Such care and concern is never going to be the result of rationale, or committee meetings, but through exercise of heart. So, the focus we can have today in prayer is firstly about our personal giving, and secondly our stewardship in an assembly context; that those who have the awesome responsibility of distribution may do it as from, and as before, the Lord. Let's pray that we may be sensitive to the Lord's people and this work to know how best to help.

October 22nd

2 Corinthians 9. 6-15

WHICH CAUSETH ... THANKSGIVING TO GOD

Today's reading commences with the agricultural metaphor frequently used in Scripture, that of the sower and his seed. The principle always remains the same—the more I sow the more I reap. This extends to monetary matters and our associated sense of responsibility. These Macedonian believers gave from their 'deep poverty' which 'abounded unto the riches of their liberality', 2 Cor. 8. 2.

To such believers, God's love is particularly directed, for He 'loves a cheerful giver'. Not only is the amount given noted by God, but the spirit in which it is given. But notice in verse 8 of our reading that 'God is'—the reality of God; 'God is able'—the ability of God; 'God is able to make all grace abound'—the liberality of God. We have a mighty God, and He will never be any man's debtor. Thus, as we give, from resources meagre or great, He will always be sure to meet our needs over and above.

Therefore we are encouraged to enter into this God-glorifying sequence of events—we give to Him; He meets the needs of others; our needs are also met—all of which gives us much cause to render praise and worship to our omniscient God! He doesn't provide only for our material needs in this sequence, but our spiritual lives are enrched beyond measure. To begin with, we have an exercise before God; God directs us in this; we share in meeting the needs of others; we hear of how the Lord met their needs; we praise God for our part in this! What a remarkable spiritual experience this is, all emanating from a life of prayer which enables us to be prompted by the Spirit of God and causes praise to be offered to Him.

But as we think of all this, the apostle moves our thoughts on in prayerful thanksgiving, 'Thanks be unto God for His unspeakable gift'. God's giving will always exceed ours, for here is a gift which can never be fully told out. His Son is the greatest gift ever to be bestowed. We can never exhaust our thanks, for the gift itself is inexhaustible. Here, then, is the principle which should support our giving: only the best for Him. So, our worship will be enhanced, and our prayer life enriched, in such response to His bountifulness towards us.

October 23rd

2 Corinthians 12. 1-10

I BESOUGHT THE LORD THRICE

Today's reading gives a rare insight into Paul's personal life and experience of God. It also deals with that difficult subject— apparently unanswered prayer (i.e., prayer not answered the way we would like!).

Paul admits to an experience of being 'caught up'. It gave him an insight into the glories and counsels of God which never left him. His being 'caught up' was illustrative of the rapture of the church.

Having had this experience, which might have caused even a man of Paul's spiritual stature to boast, God intervened. It is amazing how God seems to deal hardest with those who are nearest to Him. What responsibilities privileges bring! Hence, to Paul was given 'a thorn in the flesh'—**physical**; 'the messenger of Satan'—**mental**; 'I besought the Lord thrice'—**spiritual**. Experiences in every realm of his being, which militated against what he would naturally desire. The Lord was working to keep this great man humble and dependent on Him.

How significant that the Lord had a crown of thorns, and that Satan attacked Him constantly; and that in the Garden He prayed three times, each time accepting 'not my will but thine be done'. His experiences will always supersede ours, which makes Him our ideal Great High Priest.

But Paul knew what it was to pray for relief from obvious physical discomfort, and he knew what it was for God to over-rule that prayer. He didn't accept this negatively; rather, he appreciated the positive consequence that God's grace was more than sufficient to enable him to cope with the situation. The flood-tide of God's grace took him above the problem of the thorn that must remain with him. He was prepared to accept God's strength in his weakness: more, he was prepared to 'glory in my infirmities that the power of Christ may rest upon me'. Prayer enables us to enter into God's ways with us and see how He wants to work His purpose through us to His glory and our blessing. Hence, submission to His will helps us prove, 'when I am weak, then am I strong'.

October 24th

2 Corinthians 13. 5-8

NOW I PRAY TO GOD THAT YE DO NO EVIL

A characteristic of teenage children is that invariably they feel they know far more than their parents—in fact they know it all! Often they even consider parents as inferiors who have never stood where they stand. Spiritually this is how the Corinthians were now viewing Paul. They were even casting doubt on the authority of his apostleship, and on his right to come among them in a disciplinary, corrective manner. They were almost challenging him as to the derivation and proof of his authority.

He gives them a threefold test in verse 5—'examine yourselves'; 'prove your own selves'; 'know ye not your own selves?'. In the medical world self-examination is encouraged for certain problems before a visit to the doctor. Often in the spiritual realm there is need for this before we can apply for the remedy of the divine Physician. Often our problems are connected with ourselves, and we have the capacity to remedy them before appealing to the Lord. How often is my attitude towards other believers a wrong one? How often do I feel superior to others—even those who may have been on the road long before me, yet, for some reason I find myself despising them? Such feelings can be real and they need immediate treatment.

I examine myself. Am I in Christ? Have I been saved? Has the Lord kept me? Have I enjoyed His company, and that of fellow believers over the years? If the answer to the foregoing is in the affirmative then there can be no doubt I am the Lord's. But if I am the Lord's then my attitude towards other believers should not be scornful and condescending, but full of grace and love.

Prayerful exercise before God is the answer here. We should pray for one another, but particularly for ourselves that we might think, say or do nothing towards others of which we shall be ashamed, whether now or in a coming day. 'Deliver us from evil' still applies and we need to pray it regularly, for we never can tell the full potential of what lies within. Significantly, we need to be sure that we all 'do good especially to the household of faith'. So as we pray, let's have in mind to 'do good' and 'do no evil'.

October 25th
Galatians 1. 10-17

I CONFERRED NOT WITH FLESH AND BLOOD

Paul's purpose in writing this letter was the defence of the gospel he had brought to the Galatians, whilst at the same time reminding them of the liberty into which, as believers, they had been brought. Accordingly, he reminds them that in his time amongst them he didn't seek to gain followers by currying favour. Neither was the gospel he presented his or any other person's concoction. He didn't receive it second-hand, either orally or academically—rather it was through divine revelation, v. 12. Only such a gospel can liberate from sin, then and today, because, just as the need remains the same, so too does the divine remedy.

He illustrates the life-changing effect of this gospel from his own experience as he indicates his past life and his activities directed against Christ, as well as his status amongst his own people. In both areas this small man was a colossus. Yet, in both these areas, he was sincere, though he was sincerely wrong in motive.

As Paul cites details of his conversion, he does so in uniquely appreciative language: 'it pleased God'—saved at God's pleasure; 'who separated me from my mother's womb'—separated even before birth; 'called me by his grace'—sanctified through unmerited favour. What a conversion! Have you yet been saved, trusting the Saviour? The purpose of Paul's conversion was that God, who revealed Christ to him on the Damascus road, might firstly reveal Him now in Paul, and then through Paul to others through the preaching of the gospel.

That this might be achieved meant unique communion with God; 'I conferred not with flesh and blood'. Rather than go to Damascus, Jerusalem, or to the other apostles, Paul spent time alone with the Lord in prayer and instruction. This vital period prepared him for his unique future ministry. Whatever ministry God has called you and me to (and each of us has a work) it can only be effectively revealed to us as we spend time alone with God in prayer. Have you a secret place where you have dealings with God? He may be waiting for you today—He may have a work for you to do. Time in prayer is where you will receive the guidance you need.

October 26th

Galatians 4. 1-7

BECAUSE YE ARE SONS ... CRYING ABBA FATHER

DEAN FARRAR states that 'Galatians is the rough sketch of which Romans is the finished picture'. What a rough sketch!

Today's verses bring to our attention the contrasts and similarities between the servant under **the law** and the son under **grace**. Paul skilfully paints his picture, using the home background where a 'minor' is no better off than the servant. He occupies a position of dependency and servility until the time decreed by his well-intentioned father. Until that time the father cares for, and provides his every need through the use of tutors and governors.

Such was God's dealing with the Jew in particular. But there arrived an appointed time when the Sent One came. Note the manner of His coming—'made of a woman', stressing His **humanity**; 'made under the law', stressing His **morality**; 'God sent forth His Son', stressing His **eternality**. Because we are now sons and have One to whom we can cry, we have also One from whom we can expect an answer.

The purpose of His coming was to effect His people's redemption from the law which condemned, and for their adoption into God's family. God gave us a place in His family—the position of **sons**—a position to which we really had no right.

Contemplate the outcome of this and the miracle of God's dealings with us. When we became sons, God sent forth the Spirit of His Son into our hearts. Natural parents who 'adopt' can give status but not their spirit to the chosen child. God adopts and gives His Spirit! In consequence, He can expect that first stammering word from His son—Abba, Father. What a thrill for natural parents when an infant first articulates the word 'father' or 'mother'. This is just the beginning of a life-long relationship, cemented by dialogue between parent and offspring. This is what our Father is looking for.

He loves the first words of the newly adopted son in prayer, but He looks for development in thought, appreciation and vocabulary in an ongoing relationship with His heir. Are there long periods of silence or do I give the Father such daily pleasure? Pray today, even if only uttering a couple of words—He loves to hear, and to respond to our cries.

October 27th

Ephesians 1. 15-23

MAKING MENTION OF YOU IN MY PRAYERS

Today's reading is one of the two prayer sections of this letter that provide examples of Paul's prayers on behalf of God's people. How good it is to have specific reasons for prayer. Here, it is to give thanks, one of the primary reasons for prayer. There is always something for which we can give God thanks, even in our darkest hours. Look searchingly and we will find it.

Here, Paul is grateful for their daily faith worked out Godward and their practical living worked out manward. The former always needs to precede the latter. The latter can only be effective if based on the former. Consequently, as he remembers with deep affection these believers, he is able to give God thanks for them in prayer. He had spent two years with them, Acts 19. 10, and in that time a church had been founded in the darkest of circumstances. Wonderful bonds had been forged as these believers were led on to spiritual heights by Paul. Consequently they had a deep place in his affections. Do I have that close relationship with my fellow believers? If so, then it will draw me to them naturally at the throne of grace. If that relationship is absent then it gives me another reason to pray for them.

In a very real sense, this little phrase for today is one of the most humbling in Paul's writings. As busy as he was, as occupied as he was, he was never too busy to pray and to make mention of believers in his prayers. The puzzle in this letter is, that familiar as he would have been with the Ephesians, only the name of Tychicus appears in the letter. Yet his prayers would have been personal for them.

Such a need today should establish such a pattern in my prayers. Do I pray for believers in my assembly by name? Am I aware of their needs and circumstances so that I can pray intelligently? Am I able to give God thanks, or more pertinently, can my fellow believers give thanks for me? If we prayed more for one another, rather than talked about one another, our fellowship would be the sweeter and our testimony the more effective. Let's go on to make mention of one another in prayer. How often have the words 'I am praying for you' been an encouragement to needy believers?

October 28th

Ephesians 2. 11-18

ACCESS ... UNTO THE FATHER

In this passage, a wonderful contrast is drawn, comparing what we were as lost, hell-deserving Gentiles with the position into which we have been brought through faith in the Saviour. Always, it is good to remember what we were—it is the best antidote to pride!

Skilfully, Paul says, 'But now' and continues with a torrent of truth based on the wonderful Person of Christ and His work, past, present and future. 'Ye are made nigh'—enmity has been abolished; reconciliation between Jew and Gentile has been effected; He has preached peace; we are now fellow saints; we are built upon a foundation; 'ye also are builded together for a habitation of God through the Spirit'. Such a catalogue of blessing almost leaves us breathless, as does the whole letter, as we muse upon the wonder and effectiveness of the work of Christ.

Tucked away in the middle of all this is today's verse— 'through him we both (Jew and Gentile) have access by one Spirit unto the Father'. The mediatorial role of the Son is emphasized here in the setting of prayer. Indeed the Trinity is incorporated, for it is the Spirit who facilitates this access through the Son to the Father.

Had the Lord not come, there would have been no Calvary, no salvation, no reconciliation, and no access to the Father for the believer to enjoy today. The word 'access' is used here of one who secures the privilege of an interview with a sovereign! The wonder is that the One to whom we come in prayer is the Sovereign, the great Creator God, but here, 'unto the Father'! How encouraging to appreciate this for, as a Father, God cares for us, watches over us, guides us and with awareness is able to meet our every need. For this access we don't have to make an appointment. It is available and open to us every moment of every day. The question is, How often do I enter in and use this access? 'The veil is rent, our souls draw near'—through Him let's do it today, and every day.

But think again of the 'we'. As we bow before our Father, we join with myriads around the world. We all come together, yet are heard as individuals. What a Father!

October 29th

Ephesians 3. 1-12

BOLDNESS AND ACCESS WITH CONFIDENCE

As Paul opens a new paragraph in his letter, in typically Pauline fashion he builds on the glorious statements of what he has just brought to our attention. Reaching the word 'Gentile' sends him off on another tangent, enabling him to wax eloquent concerning his ministry on behalf of the Gentiles, and God's revelation of the church as the body of Christ, uniting within its compass Jew and Gentile. This mystery was hid from the world, but known always to our great God.

This subject excites Paul as it should us, and so again we see him rising to greater heights as he revels in what God wanted to make men see 'which from the beginning of the world had been hid in God'. The church, asserts Paul, is the greatest masterpiece conceived by God, revealing to 'principalities and powers in heavenly places the manifold wisdom of God'. Thus, WUEST says, 'The church becomes the university for angels and each saint a professor'. God has so much to reveal and every revelation enhances the glory of God. Yet, He has unveiled each revelation in His own set-time and for His own set purpose.

God's restraint in this timetable is remarkable in view of the fact that each revelation unfolds more of the eternal purpose of God. Left to us, we would have revealed all simultaneously. With God, however, it is as if He wanted to 'unwrap these presents' of revelation in His own, ordered time.

Inevitably these revelations are through Christ, who gives not only access, but also boldness to enjoy and utilize this access. There is no reason why we should be reluctant and timorous entering God's presence. 'Boldness' implies the right of every citizen in a national setting. We have this through 'the faith of him'. If this is true, then how much more should we **enter** and how much more **boldly** should we enter. Avail yourself of this again and again. Prayer was never meant to be a single exercise. It provides us with unlimited access to God's presence and we need never think we will wear Him down with constant approach. The door is always open, and He wants us to enter as often as possible.

October 30th
Ephesians 3. 13-21

FOR THIS CAUSE I BOW MY KNEES

For the second time in this letter we enter Paul's prayer life, based on the truth of chapter 2 verses 11 to 22, this being the cause for this wonderful prayer. Note his reverence in prayer, seen probably in physical posture, but certainly regarding his attitude of heart, without which effective prayer is impossible. Today we want to note the wonderful points of Paul's prayer to see if they characterize our attempts at prayer. Let us never be too proud to learn from others!

He wants God to 'grant you ... to be strengthened with his might'. Isn't this what each of us needs for daily, effective living for God? **His might** flowing through us in all our weakness. This strength comes from 'the riches of His glory'. If only we would ask for, and be dependent upon, His strength.

He wants Christ 'to dwell in your hearts by faith'. He indwells every believer, but the word 'dwell' implies 'to settle down and feel completely at home' in one's heart. He won't do this if sin is entertained there, so confession is needed for Him to be comfortable.

He wants me to be 'able to comprehend' and 'to know the love of Christ which passeth knowledge'. The idea of understanding the incomprehensible and knowing that which passes knowledge, seems an absurd paradox. Yet, as I enter into God's presence regularly and dependently in prayer, it becomes an increasing and attainable possibility. He wants revelation to take place—this is only possible when I spend time with Him.

He wants me to know the One who 'is able (has the power—*dunamis*) ... according to the power that worketh in us'. It is amazing to realize that, frail and insignificant as I know myself to be, the power of God can be at work in me and through me as a consequence of my yielding to the able One. I have no ability, no strength, no power—He possesses it all, and, as I hand myself over to Him, He can work through me in a manner I never expected. All this can be known as I bow my knees and enter into His divine presence. Dare I stay outside? I must enter today and prove all this. Prove Him as the One 'able to do exceeding abundantly', today!

October 31st
Ephesians 5. 6-20

GIVING THANKS ALWAYS FOR ALL THINGS

The first half of this letter stresses the wealth of the believer. Then, from chapter 4 verse 1 to chapter 6 verse 9, we have the walk of the believer. Finally from chapter 6 verse 10 to the end we have the warfare of the believer. In the chapter before us today are three exhortations as to 'walk'—'walk in love', v. 2; 'walk as children of light', v. 8; 'walk circumspectly' (accurately, carefully), v. 15.

Walking in the light will mean I am at one with my God and at one with my fellow believer, for I am not walking in the dark. Walking circumspectly will mean I am taking care exactly where my feet go and into whose company they take me. If I practice this, then I am deemed as wise—surely a virtue to embrace. Furthermore, such a walk allows an understanding of the will of the Lord, something for which hopefully we all crave. Surely this should be our sole aim in life—to know and do His will.

The consequence of such a life is that, instead of being intoxicated by the things of the world, I shall be daily filled with the Spirit of God. This should be the norm for my life and is God's desire for me, but it can only and ever be the result of walking as He wants me to walk.

Another consequence of such a walk is an inward communion with God which results in spiritual melody and harmony (attainable even by the tone deaf!) becoming my daily portion. This enables me to rise above even the most adverse circumstances of life. Unbelievable you may say. Not so, says Paul—'give thanks always for all things unto God'. Even in Philippi's cell he sang praises and prayed. Even when surrounded by the beasts of Ephesus he was able to give thanks. Paul wasn't a fair-weather believer. Through communion with his God he was able to accept (if not always appreciate) the 'all things' and so was able to give thanks. Enoch walked habitually with God, and we should aspire to the same, and in so doing we shall be able to enter God's presence always, with a note of thanks. As believers we are not called to walk alone, we are yoked with Christ. He goes through every experience with us and this realization will enable me to pray as Paul prayed.

November 1st
Ephesians 6. 10-20
PRAYING ALWAYS ... IN THE SPIRIT

For the believer who is walking as God intended there will be resultant warfare. Two metaphors, equally familiar to the Ephesians, are employed in today's reading—those of wrestler and soldier. If the wrestler in the games was defeated then his eyes would be gouged out! If a soldier of Caesar was defeated it meant unspeakable shame. Consequently both went into combat determined to stand, determined not to incur shame, determined to be undefeated. This should be my attitude as a good soldier of Jesus Christ. How then can this be achieved?

Daily I have to don 'the whole armour of God'. Neglect of one item will allow my canny foe, the devil, to penetrate and inflict certain defeat. Probably we have all proved this to our cost, so, today, as we start the day, let's pray that with His strength and the armour He has provided we shall stand, to His glory and honour.

Each part of the body has its own appropriate piece of armour, not meant to be admired and talked about, but put on. The items of weaponry cover defence and offence, and victory has been assured us in the name of the Lord Jesus Christ.

However, the final item in our armoury may well be the least used—'praying always with all prayer and supplication in the Spirit' and 'watching', confirming the injunction of the Lord, 'to watch and pray'. It is significant that prayer is the seventh weapon in our list confirming that without it we are less than perfectly equipped. Yet it needs to be wielded. It is a weapon feared by the enemy and can be used to maximum effect if we choose to wield it.

Paul speaks of 'praying always with all prayer', reminding of the need for constancy in praying, and for prayers that are comprehensive to include all our thought and desires. 'And supplication' introduces the idea of a specific targeting of persons or matters, as we beseech God for help in the field of conflict. Whatever obstacles or barriers Satan puts in our way, there is nothing he can do to overcome prayer 'in the spirit'. Let's see to it that as an army of spiritual soldiers we all stand together in prayer and so secure the victory.

Philippians 1. 1-7

MAKING REQUEST WITH JOY

It is noticeable how well the apostle knew his God. He is able to speak of God as 'my God', and the closeness of this relationship is seen again in chapter 4 verse 19. It is surely every believer's objective to know God for himself in an increasing way. Paul's intimacy with his God never manifested itself in over-familiarity. His forms of approach in the prayers of the epistles are always in ways of utmost respect and befitting reverence. The greater our appreciation of God's greatness, His grandeur, and His glory, the greater should be our attitude of reverence and awe.

This prayer, direct to God, is for *all* the saints, v. 4. There was obviously a problem in Philippi, 4. 2. However, we see the wisdom of Paul, who is constantly concerned with the unity and harmony of the assembly. He writes to them *all*, v. 1, he prays for them *all*, v. 4, he thinks of them *all*, v. 7, he longs after them *all*, v. 8, desiring eventually to joy and rejoice with them *all*, 2. 17. This great intercessor embraces *all* saints in his daily care for all the churches, 2 Cor. 11. 28. May our prayer lives mirror that of Paul in showing no partiality. We should not only pray for those who agree with us, but also 'pray for them that despitefully use you', Luke 6. 28.

The apostle indicates that when engaged in prayer for the assembly, he is moved to thanksgiving on every occasion as he brings them to mind and to God. Thanksgiving should be an essential ingredient of every prayer, Phil. 4. 6.

It is a good principle to commend what is praiseworthy, and in this prayer Paul commends the Philippians for their continuous fellowship in the Gospel, v. 5. The Revised Version margin gives an alternative reading for verse 7 as, 'ye have me in your heart', in which case the apostle is praising them also for their love and large heartedness towards him.

The apostle is confident that God who began a good work in them would continue to work in them until the day of Jesus Christ. Then faith will give place to sight, for we shall be with Him, and be like Him, for evermore.

Philippians 1. 8-11

THAT YOUR LOVE MAY ABOUND ... IN KNOWLEDGE, AND ... JUDGEMENT

Paul, having informed the Philippian believers that he is filled with joy and moved to thanksgiving when he thinks of them, now reveals the content of his prayer.

It is good to be able to call God for a witness on all that we say and do, and this he does here as on other occasions, Rom. 1. 9; 2 Cor. 1. 23; 1 Thess. 2. 5, 10. Fervent affection for these saints prompted his supplication for them. He longed after them greatly in the tender mercies and affections that find their source in Christ Jesus. So he prays, 'that your love may abound yet more and more', v. 8. This love is not mere sentiment or emotion directed by impulse, but should be scripturally regulated. Love, we learn, requires to be instructed. Love is to abound more and more in knowledge. As we focus on the object of our love, whether it be God or our fellow man, our understanding needs to be enlightened. Something more than knowledge though is needed if love is to abound more and more, even though our knowledge is of the word of God. The other ingredient is said to be 'judgement'. So Paul is here praying that they will continue to display love, and that their love will be exercised by what they know to be true, and in intelligent discernment.

Such enlightenment will enable them to discern things that are more excellent, and to avoid that which is unworthy.

Paul would have them sincere, pure, and transparent in view of the day of Christ. This day of review follows the rapture, and is mentioned more than once in these early chapters. Salvation will be perfected in that day, 1. 6; the saints should be without offence until that day, 1. 10; he hoped to rejoice because of them in that day, 2. 16. In that day everything will be seen in its true light, when we appear before the righteous Judge at the judgement seat of Christ and are rewarded accordingly, 1 Cor. 4. 5.

With such a prospect before us, may we be 'filled with the fruits of righteousness which are by Jesus Christ', v. 11. May we not be ashamed before Him at His coming, 1 John 2. 28.

November 4th

Philippians 4. 5-7

BE CAREFUL FOR NOTHING ... LET YOUR REQUESTS BE KNOWN UNTO GOD

This Philippian letter is lovely to read and is full of Christ, but in the final chapter it is the Lord and His lordship that is the prominent theme. An acknowledgement of His lordship together with the realization of His presence with us, v. 5, are coupled with exhortations to rejoice. The saints at Philippi were to let their 'moderation' or 'yieldedness' be known unto all men, v. 5. This is an attitude of mind that promotes harmony and unity amongst God's people and seemed to be lacking at Philippi, see 2. 3; 4. 2. We are exhorted to be careful for nothing, and not be over-anxious about the cares of this life, but to be prayerful about everything. The word 'nothing' is in marked contrast to the word 'everything'. We should take all matters to the Lord; nothing is too great or small. The Lord Jesus said, 'Take no thought for your life', Matt. 6. 25, and we should remember the words of Peter, 'Casting all your care upon him; for he careth for you', 1 Pet. 5. 7.

In verse 6 we are encouraged to approach God, and differing aspects of approach are mentioned such as prayers, supplications, thanksgivings and requests.

'Prayer' is the more general word; we should live our lives in the atmosphere of prayer. 'Supplications' would be the more specific requests, and all requests should be made to God with thanksgivings.

If these things characterize our prayer lives, then we will experience 'the peace of God', which is that complete rest which floods the soul of the believer wholly resting in God. Anxiety is replaced by the 'peace that passeth all understanding', that which garrisons the heart; that inner strength that only the Christian knows and experiences, particularly in times of adversity.

We should then be anxious for nothing, be prayerful for everything, and be thankful for anything.

November 5th

Colossians 1. 1-8

WE GIVE THANKS ... PRAYING ALWAYS FOR YOU

This letter is addressed to the saints and faithful brethren in Christ in Colosse. As saints they were separated to God from the world, and as a result lived sanctified lives as faithful brethren. This causes the apostle to commence his prayer with thanksgiving and praise, a practice we would do well to follow. His prayer is addressed to God. Contemplate the fact that the God of the universe can be approached. This is a tremendous privilege. When we approach 'in the name of the Lord Jesus', 3. 17, the One who is infinitely **high**, becomes infinitely **nigh**.

Paul prays for these saints that he has never seen; but he has heard of their faith, love, and hope, the three cardinal virtues of the Christian life mentioned in 1 Corinthians 13. 23, and 1 Thessalonians 1. 3; 5. 8. He looks back with a thankful heart to their initial faith in Christ Jesus. He rejoices in their present love for all saints, and future hope of entering into eternal inheritance.

The gospel of God's grace had reached the Colossians and brought blessings, not least this glorious hope, all of which had been bestowed by the grace of God in truth. In this place, and wherever the gospel was preached in the known world of the day, it bore fruit. The gospel bore fruit in the salvation of souls and the building up of the believers. This should be our prayer for the local assembly in our locality, and beyond.

Epaphras who brought the message to them is commended as a dear fellow servant and a faithful minister of Christ to them. Servants of God in our day are faithfully and fervently seeking to reach others with this same life-giving message, and it is our privilege and duty to uphold them before the throne of grace.

Paul's example of 'praying always' is one to be followed, for it is essential that we maintain with regularity our prayer support for other Christians. What encouragement must have been given to those Colossians by Paul's assurance that daily they figured in his prayers! The God of the universe is always available to respond to the urgent, incessant prayers of the people—He takes delight in their thanksgiving.

What love to Thee we owe, our God, for all Thy grace! Our hearts may well o'erflow in everlasting praise.

Colossians 1. 9-14

FILLED WITH THE KNOWLEDGE OF HIS WILL

The first part of this prayer was in the form of thanksgiving; now the apostle makes specific intercession for these saints. So he prays that they might be filled with the knowledge of God's will. This should be a prime consideration in our lives. The knowledge of God's will as revealed in God's word is to be applied with spiritual wisdom and discernment in everything we do.

The life that is lived in this way, is a life that is worthy of the Lord. Surely, the supreme objective in this scene is to seek to please Him. Again, the apostle would have these believers to be fruitful in every good work. Fruit bearing is external evidence of an internal work of grace. While we are not saved **by** good works we should certainly not forget that we are saved **for** good works. As we are occupied with the *will of God*, the *word of God*, and the *work of God*, we will surely enter into a greater knowledge of God. Now Paul prays that they might be strengthened with all might, for we cannot live for God in our own strength. This God-given strength he prays for is not that they may perform spectacular feats or great miracles, but that it may result in endurance and long-suffering with joy.

Knowing God's will, v. 9, walking worthily of Him, v. 10, bearing fruit for Him, v. 10, finding strength in Him, v. 11, should be the concern of all, finding expression in our personal prayers.

The apostle now prays that they may give thanks to the Father from whom comes every good and perfect gift, Jas. 1. 17. When God saves us He makes us fit for heaven, 'hath made us meet to be partakers of the inheritance of the saints in light'. In doing so He also delivers us from darkness and translates us into the kingdom of His dear Son.

Let us ever be thankful to our kinsman Redeemer who by His rights, readiness, and riches, paid the ransom price by His own precious blood, v. 13.

Colossians 2. 1-7

STABLISHED IN THE FAITH ... WITH THANKSGIVING

In these early days there were false teachers who sought to infiltrate the people of God with their error. Gnosticism prided itself on superior knowledge and mysticism. Asceticism advocated a system of self-denial to obtain a higher spiritual state, Col. 2. 21.

The letter contains warnings against the philosophy of men, worshipping of angels, and matters regarding foods, festivals, and sabbaths. All these things undermine the work of Christ. We need to pay particular attention to this in our day when there are still those who use enticing words and fair speech to deceive God's people.

The apostle counteracts these errors in a masterful way by displaying in this epistle the fullness and supremacy of Christ, and the sufficiency of His work upon the cross. So the apostle exercises 'great conflict' in prayer for these saints whom he has never met. His desire is that they might not be drawn away, but their hearts may be strengthened, knit together in love to present a united stance against the false teachers and their error.

Paul is convinced that the only safeguard against such is the understanding of 'the mystery', which is Christ Himself, 1. 27.

The Gnostics boasted in knowledge beyond that of divine revelation, but here Paul is saying that nothing additional is needed because all the treasures of wisdom and knowledge are hidden in Christ. For this reason, they should not allow persuasive words and clever argument to delude them.

The apostle challenges the Colossians to live in Him, to be rooted in Him as a tree is rooted in the ground, and to be built up as a building is constructed on a firm foundation. An ungrateful heart is open to delusion and deception, but the thankful believer will be established in the faith, walking in Christ Jesus the Lord.

Colossians 3. 12-17

AND BE YE THANKFUL

How grateful we should be that we are the elect of God, holy and beloved. In His sovereignty God chose us to be holy, sanctified and set apart to Himself. We should be **practically** what we are **positionally**; our **state** should correspond with our **standing**. As beloved of God we should in return desire to please Him.

Paul calls upon the Colossians to put on various Christian graces as they would put on a garment, and to have a right attitude towards themselves and their brethren. To bear with one another, and to forgive freely, is to be Christ-like. When such an attitude prevails, it engenders unity and warmth of fellowship.

Love is that essential unifying ingredient that should be found permeating all that is said and done, and the peace of God will arbitrate in our hearts. Our words and actions should make for peace and harmony with others. This passage is teaching that if we are in doubt about any course of action that we are considering, we should ask ourselves the question as to whether we will have peace in our heart and mind if we continue.

As we 'let the word of Christ dwell ... richly', as the word of God is allowed to permeate the mind and find expression in an obedient life, then the 'word of Christ' will be at home in our hearts. Ephesians 5. 18-19 stresses the necessity of being filled with the Spirit, while this section here teaches the importance of being filled with God's word.

The guiding principle by which we may live for God is to be thankful, and to do and say all 'in the name of the Lord', v. 17. This equally applies to our prayer life. We should be able to pray for every activity in which we are engaged.

To pray to the Father, in the name of the Lord Jesus Christ, and also in the Spirit, Phil. 3. 3, is a privilege which is extended to us at any time, anywhere, about anything.

CONTINUE IN PRAYER, AND WATCH ... WITH THANKSGIVING

Exhortations to be diligent and to continue in prayer are timely reminders for every Christian in every age. We should be earnest, vigilant and regular in prayer. The disciples in the Garden of Gethsemane were neither watchful nor prayerful. We need to make time for this essential activity, otherwise we might not find time in an increasingly busy world. Paul never tires of emphasizing that thanksgiving should accompany every prayer. The apostle asks the Colossians to pray for him, and for those who were with him in Rome. It is notable that Paul does not desire that they should pray that God would open the door of the prison for him, but rather that a door of opportunity might be opened for the preaching of the Gospel.

He desires to speak the mystery of Christ; this is the truth concerning Christ and the Church. This mystery which in other ages was not made known has now been revealed, Eph. 3. 5. The fact that Paul taught that Jew and Gentile had been brought together in one body, and that the Gentiles had been made fellow-heirs, was the reason that the apostle was imprisoned.

His thoughts turn now from what he ought to speak, v. 4, to how they ought to live, v. 5. Our talk should correspond with our walk; we are being watched by unbelievers in every aspect of our lives.

In Acts chapter 1 verse 1 we are asked to consider 'all that Jesus began both to do and to teach'. Beautifully we see in Him the perfect correlation of life and lip. We need to pray constantly that all we say and do will be supported in personal testimony of life. We are reminded that the time is short and that we should buy up every opportunity. False teachers came to Colosse just as they present themselves at our doors today. Pray that we may be able to answer in a gracious manner and in words of wisdom and truth.

November 10th

Colossians 4. 12-13

ALWAYS LABOURING FERVENTLY FOR YOU IN PRAYERS

Epaphras now sends his own personal greetings to these believers who were obviously near and dear to his heart. His great sphere of service was fervently labouring in prayer for the assembly. His concern went to the point of agonizing and 'combating earnestly ... in prayer', Col. 4. 12, JND, not only for the saints in Colosse, but also for those in the neighbouring assemblies of the Lycus valley, namely Laodicea and Hierapolis.

He prays for them constantly, fervently and specifically. It is a good exercise to follow the noble example of Epaphras, to pray for each saint in the assembly, and those in the surrounding area. The object of his prayer was that they might stand perfect and complete in *all* the will of God. How important to know and do *all* the will of God, and to make this a matter of prayer. Gnosticism would deny the absolute deity and the perfect manhood of Christ, and undermine the sufficiency of the once-for-all sacrifice to perfect for ever those that are sanctified, Heb. 10. 14. Epaphras was concerned about the spiritual well-being of the Colossians. The danger and errors mentioned in the second chapter were a real threat. The saints at Colosse would need to make a firm stand. They would also need strength to resist the false teachers and the attack upon the testimony, and so stability and maturity in spiritual things was necessary.

We need to be vigilant; requirements regarding abstinence from foods at certain times, invoking the mediation of the saints, and the practice of Mariology, are all with us today. Some come to our doors claiming that Christ was less that the Son of God. We in our day equally need to pray that we 'may stand perfect and complete in *all* the will of God', Col. 4. 12.

If the *constancy* of our prayer is in some doubt today, there is also much to suggest a lack of *fervency* in the way we pray. Perhaps we no longer feel deep concerns regarding the Lord's work so that we pray with passion for its furtherance. Perhaps we have reached a state of unawareness of our own needs, and have become oblivious to the needs of others. Perhaps we feel confident that we can cope with problems without God's help. Acknowledging our shortcomings, let us pray fervently.

1 Thessalonians 1. 1-4

WE GIVE THANKS ... REMEMBERING YOUR WORK ... LABOUR ... AND PATIENCE

As Paul prays for the church at Thessalonica, three attitudes are displayed in intercession; 'giving thanks ... always', 'making mention ... in prayer', and 'remembering without ceasing', v. 3.

This is very instructive, and teaches us that if we follow the apostolic pattern, then we should be **thankful**, **specific**, and **constant** in our prayers.

There are three cardinal graces, **faith**, **love**, and **hope**, that are seen in the Thessalonian believers, and are the subject of Paul's thankfulness in prayer. However, thanksgiving is not for these virtues alone, but also for what they produce in the life, in terms of work, labour, and patience.

'Faith' rests on what is past, 'love' is working itself out in the present, while 'hope' looks to the future. The 'work of faith' may refer to their conversion to God, and also to that work that motivates and inspires the whole of the Christian life. The 'labour of love' suggests something that is arduous and strenuous, motivated by love, supremely expressed at Calvary. 'Patience of hope' points to endurance while anticipating the glorious unseen future.

The 'work of faith' was seen in that they turned to God from idols, 1. 9; the 'labour of love' was displayed as they served the living and true God, 1. 9; and the 'patience of hope' manifested itself in how they waited for His Son from heaven, 1. 10.

We need to pray that faith, love, and hope will find expression in our lives. The saints in Thessalonica were working these things out by witnessing, v. 8, working, v. 9, and waiting, v. 10.

Thanksgiving for these beloved believers was not only prompted by their Christian virtues, v. 3, but also by the glorious fact of divine election. Well may we ask why we were called to hear His voice, while thousands make the wretched choice and rather starve than come! How deeply grateful we should be for God's sovereign grace and God's sovereign choice, demonstrated in our favour!

1 Thessalonians 2. 10-14

FOR THIS CAUSE ALSO THANK WE GOD WITHOUT CEASING

Paul had a deep affection for the Thessalonian believers. He speaks of himself as a gentle nurse and mother, v. 7, and also a devoted father, v. 11.

The apostle and his missionary companions displayed tenderness and care towards these saints, while at the same time he acted as a responsible father in their training and discipline.

Paul lived an exemplary life of dedication and consecration. He could confidently call the Thessalonian believers to testify to these facts and he could call upon God for a witness.

How good to be able to live with a clear conscience before God, moving before an open heaven. May this cause us to prayerfully consider the importance of what we **are**, as well as what we **say**.

Paul's prayer was that they might walk worthy of the Lord, v. 10. The apostle behaved himself holily, justly, and without blame before them, and this nobody could deny. The power of this ministry is that Paul could teach by example. He had the moral right to teach and exhort these things. How important for us to remember that we need to have the moral right to speak to others.

Paul was ceaselessly thanking God for the way they received the word of God. They believed that it did not originate from men, but they received it as truly the word of God. They did not just receive it with the hearing of the ear, but with the appropriation of the heart, deepening their spiritual experience.

The word of God had not only brought salvation to them but it enabled them to stand firm in the face of persecution. Paul links himself with their suffering by addressing them as 'brethren', v. 14. The assemblies in Judaea were being persecuted by their fellow Jews, and the Thessalonians were likewise suffering at the hands of Gentiles, but their steadfast endurance proved the reality of their salvation.

Our aim should be to allow the word of God to work effectively in our lives, developing spiritual growth. For this, let us pray without ceasing!

1 Thessalonians 3. 9-13

NIGHT AND DAY PRAYING EXCEEDINGLY

The Thessalonian believers showed much patience and endurance in trials. It seems that Paul could not thank God enough for all the joy that this brought to his heart. We are given a glimpse into Paul's private prayer life. He prayed by night and by day most earnestly that he would see their faces again. He yearned to see his dear fellow saints whom he admired for their faithfulness in adversity, and longed to instruct further in the things of the Lord.

His regularity and earnestness in prayer, together with intense love for the saints, are things that all would do well to emulate.

Paul prays that their faith might mature, v. 10, their love might abound, v. 12, their hearts might be stablished, and their lives be sanctified, v. 13.

Their faith had proved strong under persecution, yet Paul yearned to return to Thessalonica and deal with their deficiencies, and teach them the truth of God more fully. Satan may have hindered him, but he prays that 'God himself and our Father, and our Lord Jesus Christ, direct our way unto you', v. 11. It is important not to miss that while Paul seeks divine guidance, the verse teaches the lordship and Deity of Christ, and His equality with the Father.

The Thessalonians had already been commended for their love, but he prays for their further development and increase, so teaching us that there is no room for complacency in spiritual things and always room for improvement. Their abounding love should embrace not only fellow believers, but all men. Powerfully, the apostle appeals to them using himself as the pattern, reminding them of his unstinting love toward them.

Finally, Paul prays that these saints might stand blameless and holy before God at the return of the Lord. May it be that when we stand at the judgement seat of Christ, 2 Cor. 5. 10, and when all our lives will be reviewed by the Lord 'the righteous judge', 2 Tim. 4. 8, that we will not be ashamed before Him at His coming, 1 John 2. 28.

November 14th

1 Thessalonians 5. 5-17

PRAY WITHOUT CEASING

In the absolute sense it is not possible for us to pray without ceasing, because we need to engage our minds on activities that are necessary in day-to-day living. What we can say, however, is that the believer should cultivate a continual sensitivity to and consciousness of the presence of God, and live continually in an atmosphere of communion and prayer. Christians, as 'sons of the day', are called to a life of moral uprightness, and consistent living in keeping with such a high calling. It will necessitate putting on the Christian armour of **faith**, **love**, and **hope**.

God has 'not appointed us to wrath' since we are 'of the day'. We shall be delivered from the wrath which God will pour out during the Tribulation period, 1 Thess. 1. 10, and we are appointed to obtain ultimate salvation and future deliverance from the very presence of sin.

The redeemed soul will ever be thankful for the tremendous price paid to secure these things for us, and a remembrance of what we have been delivered from will keep us humble before God.

Whether we are spiritually alert or indifferent, we are to be caught away 'to live together with him', v. 10. Such a great prospect should comfort us and build us up in the faith.

The apostle states a number of things that we should make a matter of prayer. We should:

(i) Pray for elders who labour amongst us, and respect and obey them because they 'are over you in the Lord', v. 12.

(ii) Pray for the unity of the assembly, v. 14.

(iii) Pray that the fainthearted will be comforted and the weak supported, v. 14.

(iv) Pray that grace and patience is shown to all, and that retaliation never crosses the mind, v. 15.

Joy should be the constant experience of every believer, whatever the circumstances, because Christ is the subject and source of all that brings joy.

With all these 'promptings' in mind, we should 'pray without ceasing', thus pursuing a **life of prayer**.

1 Thessalonians 5. 18

IN EVERYTHING GIVE THANKS: FOR THIS IS THE WILL OF GOD

Exhortations follow one another in staccato fashion in this section. The individual believer's responsibility is expressed in terms of **joyfulness**, v. 16, **prayerfulness**, v. 17, and **thankfulness**, v. 18.

This is not merely wise counsel that the apostle Paul gives, but indeed the 'will of God' for every believer. It is true that we should be thankful '**for**' everything, recognizing that God is the source and supplier of 'every good gift and every perfect gift', Jas. 1. 17.

However, we are instructed in this verse to give thanks '**in**' everything, suggesting every circumstance of life. Since it is true 'that all things work together for good to them that love God', Rom. 8. 28, then we should be able to praise and give thanks to God at all times, for all things, in all circumstances.

We may sometimes wonder what good can come out of our disappointment, sorrow, and trial. However, the word of God teaches that God permits things to come into our lives in a process of **refinement**, that Christ-like features might become evident in us—that we might be 'conformed to the image of his Son', Rom. 8. 29.

So, 'In everything give thanks', v. 18, takes on a different perspective when we realize that our lives are not affected by chance, or fate, or luck, but that behind the scenes God is ordering our lives—we must be willing to submit to His control.

Faith lays hold on the fact that our God is too loving to be unkind, and too wise to make a mistake. This is the apostle who praised God at midnight in prison at Philippi, and who was content and rejoiced in prison at Rome. His joy, contentment, and thankfulness were independent of circumstances.

It may not always be easy to give thanks for everything, especially when sickness and heartbreak devastates our lives, but when we are able to look back over life's history, the revelation of the divine plan will cause us to praise Him as we ought.

How good is the God we adore!

1 Thessalonians 5. 19-23

I PRAY GOD YOUR WHOLE SPIRIT AND SOUL AND BODY BE PRESERVED BLAMELESS

Man is a tripartite being of spirit, soul, and body. Each part of us is susceptible to the attacks of the Adversary, and this prayer asks that each part be preserved blameless until the Lord comes. In simple terms it has been said that the *spirit* is our God-consciousness, the *soul* our self-consciousness, and the *body* our earth-consciousness.

The Lord Jesus in His perfect manhood was spirit, soul, and body. He committed His spirit to God, Luke 23. 46, He spoke of His soul being exceedingly sorrowful unto death, Mark 14. 34, and the Epistle to the Hebrews speaks of the body prepared for Him, Heb. 10. 5.

If we succumb to attack in the realm of the spirit, then communion and worship will be marred. If we pander to the fleshly emotions, then we defile the soul, the seat of our thoughts and emotions. Sadly, there are many examples in the world around us of those who abuse their bodies. Our prayer should be that no accusing finger can be pointed at us.

At the time beyond the rapture, when believers appear before the righteous Judge, our lives and service will be reviewed, and rewarded accordingly. How important it is to finish our course with joy, 2 Tim. 4. 7, to be ready to depart this scene, 2 Tim. 4. 6, and not to be ashamed at His coming, 1 John 2. 28.

In the Christian life it is good to start well, but it is better to go on well. The apostle Paul not only fought a good fight, and kept the faith, but he finished his course, 2 Tim. 4. 7.

There are examples of men in the word of God like Gideon and king Uzziah who started well and did that which was right in the eyes of the Lord, but eventually, because of pride, their hearts were lifted up so that they failed in later life. It is sad that even in our day saints of God who have run well for many years and have been a help to other believers, should fall at the last hurdle and sometimes spend their last days outside the fellowship of the assembly of God's people.

May we pray that we will 'be preserved blameless' until that coming, glorious day. 'Maranatha!', 1 Cor. 16. 22.

1 Thessalonians 5. 25-28

BRETHREN, PRAY FOR US

At the outset of the Thessalonian letter Paul prays for them, but now at the close of the epistle the apostle requests prayer for himself and his missionary companions.

In spite of his ability and gifts, Paul was ever conscious of his utter dependency on God. The term 'brethren' is placed at the beginning of the sentence, thus making an emphatic appeal to the affectionate ties of brotherhood. It seems that the request 'pray for us' could include private prayer, as well as the corporate prayers of the assembly. Whatever spiritual heights the apostle was able to scale, he still needed the prayers of others. He says elsewhere, 'Not that we are sufficient of ourselves ... but our sufficiency is of God', 2 Cor. 3. 5.

In the closing section of this epistle, mention is made of three key elements in a fruitful spiritual life. There is prayer, 5. 25, the fellowship of believers, 5. 26, and Bible reading, 5. 27.

'Greet all ... with an holy kiss', 5. 26, in the custom of Macedonia in the first century this was an acceptable way of displaying friendliness and brotherly kindness. Perhaps in the western world in the twentieth century we show affection without undue familiarity to those of like precious faith, offering a hearty handshake coupled with some kindly greeting.

Warm Christian fellowship, together with intercessory prayer, is an important part of the believer's life.

Before the apostle concludes with a brief benediction, a solemn charge is made that this epistle be publicly read to all in the assembly. There were those in the company who were causing concern and Paul is anxious that all are present for the word of God to reach their hearts and consciences.

Praying for God's people, having fellowship with God's people, and reading and heeding God's word are healthy spiritual exercises. We have a duty to pray for others. At the same time, we need their prayers on our behalf.

If the work of the Lord today depended solely on my prayers, could I expect it to prosper?

2 Thessalonians 1. 1-10

WE ARE BOUND TO THANK GOD ALWAYS FOR YOU, BRETHREN

How often do we pray, the Lord in His goodness answers our prayers, and we fail to thank Him for doing so? Paul, Silvanus and Timothy did not forget to do so! In 1 Thessalonians 3. 9-13 they make reference to their prayers for the spiritual growth of the believers at Thessalonica and, in particular, their desire that they would 'increase and abound in love one toward another'. Clearly, the Lord answered these prayers, v. 3. The Thessalonians' faith was making real progress and their love toward each other was increasing continually. Paul and his companions were unable to refrain from giving thanks to the Lord. Indeed, they say, 'we are bound to thank God'; i.e. they count it as a duty and an obligation to do so. However, this is not intended to convey any reluctance on their part. On the contrary, in verse 4, they make it clear that they take genuine pride and delight in the progress of the Thessalonians, in spite of the persecutions and tribulations they endure. The Lord's servants join together in unity to give humble thanks to God. The progress of the Thessalonians and the answer to their prayers are due to Him alone.

Genuine and gracious praise has a positive effect upon fellow believers, particularly those who are passing through difficult times. To assure them that we have also thanked the Lord for them will lift their spirits even higher. What an encouragement it must have been to the Thessalonians to know that Paul and his companions had spoken so highly of them, both to the Lord and to other believers! Our fellow saints would benefit if we followed this example in prayer.

The Thessalonians' hope has begun to waver in the face of persecution. That hope is rekindled by reminding them of: *Righteousness*, v. 5—God's judgements are always right; *Reward*, v. 5—they are suffering now but they will be rewarded in the future; *Recompense*, vv. 6-9—their enemies will be recompensed with judgement; *Rest*, v. 7—relief and release will come, when the Lord comes; *Revelation*, vv. 7-10—the Lord Jesus will be revealed, He will come with His mighty angels and with His saints; He will be the centre of admiration and adoration!

2 Thessalonians 1. 11-12

WE PRAY ALWAYS ... THAT OUR GOD WOULD COUNT YOU WORTHY

We often pray for the salvation of others, but when God calls them and saves them by His grace we act as if they have no further need of our prayers. It is true that only the power of God working in the life of an individual can produce lasting results in them, but prayer is still a vital and necessary link in the chain of their spiritual growth. Paul had prayed for the salvation of the Thessalonians and God had been pleased to call them by the gospel. However, this was not the end of the process as far as Paul was concerned. The glorious future before them was assured but there was no room for 'resting on their laurels'. Far from diminishing, Paul's prayers for them increased in their intensity. He prayed constantly for them, v. 11, and linked himself to them in a very personal way—'*our* God', vv. 11, 12 (his God has become their God). His desire for them in his prayers was:

that God 'may count (account) you worthy of this (His) calling', v. 11. Whether this calling refers to the call of the gospel, or the kingdom of God in its future manifestation, or both, the main thrust of Paul's prayers was that God would work in them in such a way that their lives would be a vibrant testimony to His calling;

that God would 'fulfil all the good pleasure of (his) goodness, and work of faith with power', v. 11. It is not God's goodness, but their delight in goodness and every work undertaken in faith, which is in view. However, these things would not be possible apart from the power which comes from God. Paul, therefore, has a vision for the spiritual progress of the Thessalonian believers which led him to fervent prayer on their behalf. He appreciated that much was at stake spiritually. He prays that:

'the name (character; authority) of our Lord Jesus Christ' would be glorified in them (present), v. 12;

and they 'in him' (future) v. 12—this probably refers to the time when He comes for believers (the rapture).

What a glorious hope, and it is all 'according to the grace of our God and the Lord Jesus Christ', v. 12.

November 20th

2 Thessalonians 2. 13-17

WE ... GIVE THANKS ... BECAUSE GOD HATH ... CHOSEN YOU

If we had a greater appreciation of how precious and special the Lord's people are, we would, like Paul and his companions, feel 'bound to give thanks always to God' for them, v. 13. This prayer is like a jewel set against the darkest of backgrounds. The Thessalonians have been comforted and encouraged by Paul's teaching in 1 Thessalonians about the Lord's return for believers, but the persecution they are facing leads them to believe that the day of the Lord has begun. They have lost the vision of how special they are to the Lord; He would never take them through that day! In verses 1-10 Paul outlines for them the fearful conditions leading up to, and during, that time. He speaks in verse 10 about those who 'received not the love of the truth, that they might be saved'. Such people will 'perish', v. 10; 'believe a lie', v. 11; 'be damned', v. 12. There is nothing here for which to give thanks to the Lord.

It is always a comfort to turn our attention from those for whom there is no hope and to consider 'brethren beloved of the Lord', v. 13. Their persecutors may hate and abuse the Thessalonian saints, but the Lord loves them. If we turn our attention away from the hostility of men against us and dwell upon what God has done and will even yet do for us, we will find much for which to give thanks to the Lord. Paul reminds his readers of their election, v. 13: *The source of it*—God: it is His personal choice (*haireomai*—to choose for yourself—only used three times in the New Testament); *the time of it*—'from the beginning' i.e. from eternity; *the purpose of it*—'to salvation', from the coming wrath but also salvation in its fullest sense; *the ground of it*—'through sanctification of the (Holy) Spirit and belief of the truth'; *the goal of it*—'to the obtaining of the glory of our Lord Jesus Christ': they were called by the gospel in 'time' but this takes them into 'eternity', John 17.22-23.

Like Paul, we should thank the Lord for those He has chosen, but they need our continuing prayers that they might 'stand fast', v. 15; 'hold the traditions' (teachings of God's word), v. 15; be comforted (encouraged) in their hearts, v. 17; established (strengthened) in every good word and work, v. 17.

341

2 Thessalonians 3. 1-5

FINALLY, BRETHREN, PRAY FOR US

Are you conscious of the need of others' prayers on your behalf? It is possible for us to become so busy in our service and even in our prayers for others that we become self-sufficient. We know what they need but we have no sense of dependency in our own lives. Arguably the mightiest of the Lord's servants, the apostle Paul, never reached that point. The more active he was, the more conscious he became of his reliance upon the prayers of the saints. He has prayed for the Thessalonian believers constantly but now, in deep humility, he says to them, 'Finally, brethren, pray for us', v. 1. He not only believed in prayer, but in the power of prayer—he knew that it produced results!

When did you last pray for one of the Lord's servants, e.g., an elder; an evangelist; a missionary; a teacher of the word? If you cannot remember the last occasion, why not rectify it today? Do you appreciate how vital your prayers are? They are needed:

'that the word of the Lord may have free course (run rapidly and unhindered—the analogy of an athlete in a race) and be glorified (honoured; admired by the results achieved) as it is with you' (it led to saving faith), v. 1;

'that we (the Lord's servants) may be delivered from unreasonable (harmful; perverse; outrageous) and wicked (actively malicious; vile) men', v. 2. Clearly, Paul had a specific group of people in mind (the Jews of Acts 18.12) but the principles remain the same today. As then, so it is now, 'all men have not faith (probably used in the sense of belief or trust)'. The Lord's servants need our prayers! If the saints do not pray for them, there is no one else to do so.

Inevitably, the servant who recognizes the need for personal prayer support, is soon found praying again for his readers. Paul has confidence in the Lord's faithfulness to establish and protect them from all evil, v. 3, and in their obedience, v. 4. However, he continues to pray that the Lord will direct (open up the way by removing obstacles) their hearts into a fuller appreciation of God's love for them, v. 5, and into the patience of Christ. He waits patiently to return for them; whatever their circumstances, they must be patient as they wait for Him.

1 Timothy 1. 12-17

I THANK CHRIST JESUS OUR LORD, WHO HATH ENABLED ME

When was the last occasion you turned to the Lord in prayer and thanked Him for your salvation? Have you ever become so thrilled about what God has done for you in Christ that, like Paul, your prayer has flowed into a spontaneous act of praise and worship to Him, v. 17? Sadly, our salvation often becomes so commonplace to us that we lose the sense of wonder associated with it. Paul demonstrates to us the attitude of heart which will lead to thanksgiving to God. Our voices will rise in thanksgiving if we:

Reaffirm that salvation is of the Lord: 'I thank Christ Jesus our Lord, who hath enabled (put strength in) me ... putting me into the ministry (service)', v. 12. He saved us and anything we do for Him is a result of His enabling power.

Remember what we were before He saved us: Paul was a blasphemer, a persecutor and injurious (insolent and outrageous), v. 13. He may have been acting in ignorance but this did not excuse him. It is always good to remember the distance we have been brought by the grace of God.

Refuse to glory in self: '... to save sinners; of whom I am (not was) chief', v. 15. Any feelings of merit in ourselves will silence thanksgiving. Paul's life for the Lord was always marked by deep humility; e.g., 'the least of all the apostles', 1 Cor. 15. 9; 'less than the least of all saints', Eph. 3. 8.

Recognise that we owe everything to the grace and mercy of the Lord: 'I obtained mercy', vv. 13, 16; 'And the grace of our Lord was exceeding abundant', v. 14. Paul may have been acting in ignorance, honestly believing that he was doing God's will, but he regarded himself as the worst of all sinners and therefore acknowledges that it took exceedingly abundant grace to save him! He was the undeserving recipient of God's love. 'But by the grace of God I am what I am', 1 Cor. 15. 10.

Realize the wider plan. Paul appreciated that his salvation reached beyond him—it allowed God to display His longsuffering. In addition, it was a pattern (sketch; illustration) for the salvation of others.

Render praise to God, v. 17. The honour belongs to Him.

November 23rd

1 Timothy 2. 1-7

SUPPLICATIONS, PRAYERS, INTERCESSIONS, GIVING OF THANKS

Many Christians admit to the fact that prayer is one of the weakest aspects of their spiritual lives. We should not be surprised therefore to discover that it is arguably the most ineffective area of our local church gatherings. Our absence from, or reluctance to attend, the meetings convened for prayer, demonstrates how low it is on our spiritual agenda and yet Paul places it on the very top of his agenda when he writes to Timothy. If there is no public prayer, then we cannot expect blessing! Clearly, it is not possible to command or force people to pray; it must stem from an inner conviction and desire. This is why Paul exhorts (encourages) us to do so. A prayerful consideration of his appeal will stir us up to a greater exercise in this matter. We have an obligation to make supplications (requests from a sense of need); prayers (reverential approach to God with our requests); intercessions (personal, confident and intimate conversation with God); giving of thanks, v. 1.

Why then is public prayer so vitally important?

Because men need our prayers—they will not pray for themselves, so we must do so on their behalf—'be (continuously) made for all men; For kings and for all in authority', vv. 1-2.

Because it affects us—it will enable us to 'lead a quiet (external calm) and peaceable (internal calm) life in all godliness and honesty', v. 2. Public prayer does bring results!

Because it brings us in line with the desires of God our Saviour—it is 'good and acceptable in his sight', v. 3. His desire is for 'all men to be saved and to come unto the knowledge of the truth', v. 4. Public prayer is a vital link in the chain of God's salvation.

Because it is based on the work of Christ, vv. 5-6. If we are to pray effectively for all men, there must be a 'mediator ... who gave himself a ransom for all', vv. 5-6. That Mediator between the one God and men is 'the man Christ Jesus', v. 5. If we fail to pray publicly for all men, we are ignoring the work of the Mediator. He has made it possible for all to be saved.

November 24th

1 Timothy 2. 8-10

MEN PRAY EVERYWHERE, LIFTING UP HOLY HANDS

Yesterday's reading introduced us to the importance of the public prayer meeting. Today's passage emphasizes to us the equally important matter of the atmosphere of such occasions. There is little point in believers gathering together for prayer if the atmosphere engendered destroys the potential for spiritual good. It is possible for us to develop a wrong spirit within, which evidences itself in wrong actions and words. Indeed, this danger is open to those who do not take part publicly (the women, vv. 9-10), as well as those who do (the males, v. 8).

Paul directs his opening remarks on this matter to the men:

'I will therefore that men (males, as opposed to mankind in general) pray (present tense—habitual prayer) everywhere (in all places where you meet)', v. 8. Paul expects all men to pray! Prayer has nothing to do with gift—it is the responsibility and privilege of all men to pray. The tone of the prayer meetings will suffer if they do not.

'lifting up holy hands', v. 8. The emphasis in this passage is on the inner life. If men wish to lead others in prayer, they must be morally suited so to do.

'without wrath (ill-will and resentment which leads to a loss of temper) and doubting (inner argument which leads to disputes). Such a spirit will stifle any possibility of effective prayer.

Then, Paul turns his attention to the women, vv. 9-10. They do not take part audibly in public prayer but their contribution is vital! Their outward manner of dress speaks volumes about their character. A woman 'professing (proclaiming) godliness', v. 10, who is 'in modest apparel', v. 9, and adorned with 'good works', v. 10, will enhance the tone of gatherings for prayer. Her 'shamefacedness (modesty which abhors what is unseemly) and sobriety (control over the inner-self; sound judgement)', v. 9, will ensure that she does nothing to attract attention to herself, thereby distracting other worshippers. Her manner is in total contrast to the woman 'with braided hair, or gold, or pearls, or costly array', v. 9. We must be exercised about building up the right atmosphere at the prayer meeting.

1 Timothy 4. 1-6

IT IS SANCTIFIED BY THE WORD OF GOD AND PRAYER

Many of the ordinary everyday things which we do habitually are elevated to a high status in the word of God. One of these, the giving of thanks for our food at meals and on other occasions, is dealt with in today's reading.

When Paul wrote to the Galatians, he encouraged them to 'stand fast therefore in the liberty wherewith Christ hath made us free', Gal. 5. 1. There are always those who will seek to rob believers of their liberty and joy. They surround us with unscriptural restrictions and we find ourselves under the bondage of the wisdom of men. The Holy Spirit, probably through the New Testament prophets, warned of those in latter times (i.e. beyond the time of the writer) who would 'depart (fall away) from the faith', v. 1. They are apostates; i.e., those who deliberately abandon the faith they once professed to believe—they are not Christians but they parade as if they are. Notice how dangerous they are: they are energized by seducing spirits and demons (Satan's agents) v. 1; they speak lies; they are hypocrites; their consciences are seared (cauterized—insensitive to feeling) by their constant rejection of the truth, v. 2. Inevitably, their teaching is negative: 'Forbidding to marry, and commanding to abstain from meats', v. 3. Such ascetic teaching is contrary to the word of God and robs Christians of their liberty in Christ.

The pathway God has shown us leads to praise and thanksgiving:

He created marriage and food—'to be received (shared in) with thanksgiving of them which believe and know the truth', v. 3.

'Every creature (creation) of God is good (excellent), and nothing to be refused, if it be received with thanksgiving', v. 4.

Marriage (Gen. 3. 24; Heb. 13. 4) and food (Gen. 9. 3; Acts 10. 15; 1 Cor. 10. 25-26) are 'sanctified (set apart) by the word of God', v. 5.

They are 'sanctified by ... prayer', v. 5. Prayer is not a magic formula which changes their nature, but as we give thanks, we set them apart as gifts from God. We cannot forbid what God in His creatorial power has set apart!

1 Timothy 5. 1-7

AND CONTINUE IN ... PRAYERS NIGHT AND DAY

Have you ever discovered that some of the most deeply spiritual Christians you meet are widows and, in particular, those who are described in this passage as 'widows indeed (actually; really)'? There are some who have not only suffered the loss of their husbands but have no family to support them, vv. 3, 5. Paul describes them as 'desolate (alone and forsaken)', v. 5. Very few of us ever experience what it is like to be totally alone in this life. There are those widows who can turn to their families and expect to find support there, v. 4. But the 'widow indeed' is conscious of her total dependence upon God. She 'trusteth in (directs her hope towards) God'. We are not surprised therefore, to discover that her private prayers are the mainstay of her spiritual life. She 'continueth in supplications (requests from a sense of need) and prayers (reverent approach to God) night and day', v. 5. This is not meant to convey that there is no break in her prayers, but that prayer is the constant exercise of her heart; she enjoys unbroken fellowship with her Lord. She stands in stark contrast to the widow who spends her time in riotous and luxurious living, who may appear to be alive but is spiritually dead, v. 6. The 'widow indeed' has a meaningful personal prayer life and therefore becomes a real influence for good within the local church prayer meeting, even though she does not take part publicly. She contributes to the spiritual atmosphere of such gatherings. She may be bereft of earthly family support but she has a Father she can cast herself upon in her time of need. She can teach us much about **dependence** upon Him!

The Lord uses the local church as one of the main channels through which He supplies her needs. The children and grandchildren (AV nephews) of widows must recognize their responsibilities in this respect, exercising practical godliness, but we are commanded to 'Honour (respect and support—including financially) widows that are widows indeed', v. 3. The entire passage emphasizes the need for respect and care to be shown, particularly by young men, towards others, vv. 1-2.

November 27th

2 Timothy 1. 1-7

REMEMBRANCE OF THEE IN MY PRAYERS NIGHT AND DAY

Our prayer life tends to be weak at the best of times but when circumstances turn against us it becomes either self-centred or non-existent. Paul's example lifts us on to a higher plane altogether. At this time he is facing his darkest hour. He is in prison, v. 8; he is in chains, v. 16; all have forsaken him, v. 15; only Luke is with him, 4. 11. His journey on earth is drawing to its close and he is shortly to face execution. He may be 'an apostle of Christ Jesus by the will of God', v. 1, but this does not shield him from persecutions and afflictions. Indeed, it guarantees that he will suffer them, but the knowledge that it is the will of God enables him to endure.

We might well ask what could possibly be achieved in adverse circumstances like these? Some amazing things are happening in this prison cell:

God is 'breathing'—a letter is being written which is 'inspired' (God-breathed), 3. 16.

Paul is thanking God—'I thank God, whom I serve', v. 3. There is much to thank the Lord for in prayer, even in the darkest hours of our lives. An elderly, imprisoned apostle thanks Him for a young man, Timothy—for the 'unfeigned (unhypocritical; genuine) faith' that was in his grandmother and mother, and also in him, v. 5.

Paul is praying—'with pure conscience, that without ceasing I have remembrance of thee in my prayers (supplications—needs expressed with fervent desire) night and day', v. 3. Paul's prayers abound with practical lessons. They are from a pure conscience; continuous; unwearied; entirely for others. His aching desires are towards the young man who will carry on the work after his departure. He encourages him to 'stir up (keep in full flame) the gift of God, which is in thee', v. 6—this is not a rebuke but a spiritual father appealing for Timothy's zeal to continue. He reminds him that God has not given us the spirit of cowardice but of power, love and a sound mind (discipline), v. 7. Paul's prison cell might be cold, damp and dark but it is filled with thanksgiving, prayer, grace, mercy, peace and joy!

2 Timothy 1. 8-18

THE LORD GIVE MERCY UNTO THE HOUSE OF ONESIPHORUS

We pray for the Lord's servants, but how often do we pray for their families? We forget sometimes the sacrifices which they make to enable the Lord's work to progress. Perhaps we could make it a priority in our prayers today to remember specific families known to us. Paul had positive memories of Onesiphorus and his service, but he knew that his contribution could not have been made without a highly supportive family behind him. Paul remembered them in prayer as he sat in the darkness of his prison cell.

Onesiphorus was, indeed, a remarkable man. His name means 'profit or advantage bearer'. Clearly, his service was of great profit to Paul. He travelled from Ephesus to Rome at great cost both to himself and his family. When he arrived he would not be deflected from his desire to see Paul, the servant others had forsaken, v. 15. It was dangerous to be associated with Paul, but this did not deter Onesiphorus. Even though he proved difficult to find, Paul says, 'he sought me out very diligently and found me', v. 17. Others were ashamed of Paul's witness to the Lord and of the fact that he was a prisoner of the Lord, v. 8, but Onesiphorus was not 'ashamed of my (Paul's) chain', v. 16. He was prepared to be 'partaker of (to take his share of) the afflictions of the gospel', v. 8. Any servant with an exercise like this was bound to suffer persecution during the early days of the Christian church. Onesiphorus undoubtedly suffered; some believe these verses imply that he was dead at the time of writing and may even have suffered martyrdom for his faithful service. Whatever had befallen him, Paul remembered the cost to his family and prayed, 'The Lord give mercy (the outward manifestation of pity) unto the house of Onesiphorus', v. 16.

Paul also desired that Onesiphorus would gain his just reward at the judgement seat of Christ, v. 18. He had 'refreshed (made cool) ... sought out ... found' Paul, v. 16, not once, but on many occasions. Many others had also benefited from his ministry ('unto me', v. 18, is omitted in many manuscripts). He and his family may have suffered much, but their reward would come.

2 Timothy 4. 9-18

I PRAY GOD THAT IT MAY NOT BE LAID TO THEIR CHARGE

Two factors which are guaranteed to destroy our prayer life are a vindictive spirit against those who persecute us, and bitter feelings towards fellow believers who let us down when the going gets tough. Paul faced both of these pressures at the end of his life, but he was not found wanting and his prayer life remained intact.

Of Alexander the coppersmith he wrote, 'Alexander ... did me much evil ... he hath greatly withstood our words'. Clearly this man did a great deal of harm to Paul at his trial. He opposed everything Paul stood for; he was an enemy of the gospel. However, there was nothing vindictive about Paul's response when he concluded that, '... the Lord (will) reward him according to his works', v. 14. He did not need to seek personal vengeance; he left everything to the Lord.

It is distressing enough to experience opposition from our enemies but it is even more disturbing when we are abandoned by those we thought would stand with us in our hour of greatest need. It is impossible to read this passage without sensing the intense loneliness of Paul at this time. As he sat in the inhospitable surroundings of his prison cell, he felt the loss of his cloak, the books and the parchments, but he longed also for the fellowship of those he loved—Timothy, v. 9; Mark, v. 11. Some had left him to spread the gospel—Crescens, Titus, Tychicus, vv. 10, 12. However, there were others who literally abandoned him. They were once fellow workers and companions but the cost of standing by Paul proved too great for them. He wrote, 'Demas hath forsaken *me* ... and is departed ... At my first answer no man stood with (came alongside to help) *me* ... all men forsook *me*', vv. 10, 16. Paul refused to allow these disappointments to fester within him and disturb his prayers. On the contrary, he prays that their failures 'may not be laid to their charge (account)', v. 16. If he had been overcome with feelings of resentment, he would not have experienced the joy of knowing that 'the Lord stood with me, and strengthened me', v. 17. It was the glory of the Lord, not the failures of men, which filled his heart, v. 18.

Philemon 1-7

MAKING MENTION OF THEE ALWAYS IN MY PRAYERS

Love runs like a golden thread throughout this letter; e.g. 'our dearly beloved', v. 1; 'our beloved Apphia', v. 2; 'Grace to you', v. 3; 'thy love and faith', v. 5; 'consolation in thy love', v. 9; 'brother beloved', v. 16. The letter reveals to us the tenderness of Paul's heart for others. From the very moment we tread upon its threshold, vv. 1-3, we sense the 'family atmosphere'. Paul appeals to the heart of Philemon and writes, not as an apostle, but as 'a prisoner of Jesus Christ', v. 1. He refers to Philemon as ' our dearly beloved and fellow labourer', v. 1. It is not surprising therefore to discover that prayer occupies a prominent place, v. 4. If we truly love our fellow believers, they will always be in our prayers. Paul has genuine affection for Philemon; it appears as if he had led him to faith in the Lord Jesus, v. 19. He is one of the many saints who were constantly in the prayers of the apostle.

Philemon was, of course, a delight to pray for. There was so much to give thanks to the Lord for:

His 'love and faith towards the Lord Jesus', v. 5—this is the basis from which everything else flows. If we love the Lord, we will love others.

His 'love and faith ... towards all saints', v. 5. His love embraces the difficult as well as the easy saints!

His ability to refresh the saints, v. 7. Paul valued those who were able to do this (1 Cor. 16. 17-18; 2 Cor. 7. 13; 2 Tim. 1. 16).

Philemon's personal testimony could not be faulted; he was held in the highest regard by others. He is a real challenge to us! Is our standing among fellow believers so high that they find much for which to give thanks to the Lord?

Philemon stood in special need of Paul's prayers at this time since his remarkable testimony was to be put to a severe test. His former runaway criminal slave, Onesimus, has been saved by the grace of God. Paul now commends him back to Philemon as a 'brother beloved', v. 16. Will he show 'love and faith' towards him and 'refresh' him as he does other saints? Paul's prayer is that he will.

I TRUST THAT THROUGH YOUR PRAYERS I SHALL BE GIVEN UNTO YOU

Paul believed not only in prayer but also in the power of prayer. He was very conscious of the prayers of the saints at Colosse ('you', v. 22, is in the plural) on his behalf. He was in prison and yet he was confident that their prayers would bring about his release. It is good to be aware of our dependence on the prayers of others. It will keep us from feeling self-sufficient and complacent. We thank the Lord for those who prayed for our salvation and for those who pray now for our spiritual welfare. Paul had the faith to believe, and so must we, that the prayers of the saints in a local area can bring results!

This reference to prayer is not an irrelevant postscript. It is part of Paul's plan to ensure a successful outcome to his appeal. Onesimus, Philemon's servant, has wronged his master, v. 18, and has run away to Rome. He is brought into contact with ' Paul the aged, and now also a prisoner of Jesus Christ', v. 9. He is saved by the grace of God—a **bondservant** once to sin, v. 16, is **begotten** by the power of the gospel, v. 10, and becomes a '**brother beloved** in the Lord', v. 16. We should never forget how great a distance the grace of God has brought us. We were sinners for a season, but are saints for ever, v. 5. Paul has the difficult task of commending Onesimus back to Philemon. He does so in a tender and compassionate way:

He does not command or use apostolic authority, but appeals to Philemon's heart. 'Yet for love's sake I rather beseech thee', v. 9.

He links himself on to Onesimus. '... my son' (child), v. 10; 'a brother beloved', v. 16.

He intercedes for him. 'receive (take to yourself) him, that is mine own bowels', v. 12; 'receive (receive in full) him for ever', v. 15; 'receive (as in v. 12) him as myself', v. 17; 'I will repay', v. 19. He intercedes on the grounds of what God has done for us in Christ—He has paid the debt in full; He has received us. That is how Philemon must receive Onesimus—Paul is confident that he will, v. 21. However, Paul hopes to see him soon. What shame there would be on his face then should Onesimus not be with him!

December 2nd

Hebrews 4. 14-16

BOLDLY TO THE THRONE

What we do have, v. 14a. Doubtless, the unbelieving Jews claimed that Christianity was inferior to Judaism in that it had no visible High Priest. 'But', the writer responds, 'we have something far better, something which Judaism has never had—we have a **Great** High Priest'. The Jews of the day had upwards of 100,000 ordinary priests and many chief priests. And, over their history, Israel had known over eighty High Priests. Yet they had never had one single Great High Priest. But that is precisely what Christians have! Israel's High Priest had been privileged to 'pass through' the various compartments of an earthly tabernacle into the symbolic presence of God. But our Great High Priest has 'passed through' (lit) an expanse far greater—'the heavens'—into the immediate and real presence of God; cf. 9. 7, 11-12, 24. Rejoice today that the Son of God once passed upwards through the very heavens His own hands had made, 1. 10.

What we do not have, v. 15. The writer meets an objection. If our Great High Priest is in fact 'the Son of God', and if He now occupies such an exalted position beyond 'the heavens', is He far too distant and remote from us to be able to sympathize with us or in any way to relate to us? 'But', the writer counters, 'we must consider not only **where He now is** but **where He once was**. He has been here—and when here He experienced every kind of testing, trial and temptation to which we are exposed'. He is, therefore, 'able to sympathize with our weaknesses' (lit).

The readers were tempted to turn aside from God's will so as to avoid suffering. But their Great High Priest knew all about that; He had been tempted to do the self-same thing. Yet He had overcome. He had remained 'without sin' and was qualified therefore both to be their Example, 12. 1-4, and to sympathize with them in their trials.

What we have to do, vv. 14b, 16. First, to hold to our confession of faith in the Lord Jesus, v. 14b. Second, to approach 'the throne of grace'—and that 'boldly'. Because our Great High Priest, whose experiences here enable Him to sympathize with our many weaknesses, is now at the right hand of God's throne, 8. 1; 12. 2, we can—and should—draw near to it with complete confidence. Do it today. There you receive mercy for failures in the past and grace to avoid failures in the future.

December 3rd

Hebrews 5. 1-10

WITH STRONG CRYING AND TEARS

Every High Priest has at least three essential characteristics, vv. 1-4. As to his *appointment*, he must be **called by God**, v. 4; as to his *work*, he must **offer sacrifice**, v. 1; and, as to his *nature*, he must be **a man** himself ('taken from among men'), v. 1.

Because the Lord Jesus possesses all three qualifications, the fact that He is not descended from Aaron, 7.14, in no way debars Him from being High Priest. The writer draws attention first to **His divine call**, 5. 5-6. Note the double,'Thou art'; God has appointed no less than His own Son to be our High Priest. The writer comes back later to consider **the great sacrifice which He offered**, 8. 3 to 10. 18. Today's title comes from the brief section concerned with **the reality of our Lord's manhood**, 5. 7-10.

It is the true humanity of the Lord Jesus, emphasized in verses 7 and 8, which enables Him to show concern and understanding for us. *We* are called on to 'offer' up prayer and praise, 13. 15; 'in the days of His flesh' He did just that. *We* look to One who 'is able ... to save', 7. 25; so did He. *We* are exhorted to show 'reverence' (holy and reverent fear towards God), 12. 28; He did just that (translated 'in that he feared'—the only other place in the New Testament where the same noun occurs). *We* are required to pay the price of obedience, 5. 9; He 'learned obedience' and paid its price in suffering. *We* suffer because we are the sons of God, 12. 5-11; He suffered in spite of being the Son of God ('Although he was Son', 5. 8 lit).

No doubt Gethsemane is principally in view. 'Because we are sons, God has sent his Spirit into our hearts, crying, Abba', Gal. 4. 6. Verse 7 tells us of the Son's strong 'crying' (same word), when He addressed God as 'Abba', Mark 14. 36. The ground in the Garden of the Olive Press was moistened by tears as well as by blood-like sweat!

The Lord Jesus entreated the One who was able to save Him 'out of' death (lit). And God **did** save Him. His resurrection was God's answer; the God of peace brought Him 'out of' the dead, 13. 20. He 'was heard'; perhaps a reference to the turning point of Psalm 22—'thou hast heard me', v. 21b. Thereafter the *pleading Sufferer* of verses 1-21a becomes the *praising Saviour*, declaring God's name among His brethren, v. 22—a point picked up earlier by our writer, 2. 11-12.

December 4th

Hebrews 7. 23-28

HE EVER LIVETH TO MAKE INTERCESSION

The writer had spoken of our Lord's **unending life**, v. 16; now he speaks of His **unchangeable priesthood**, v. 24, and His **unfailing intercession**, v. 25.

'**But this man**' is the hinge of a short section in which the Lord Jesus is contrasted with the priests under the Old Covenant, 7. 23-25. The same is true of a later passage, 10. 11-12. In that passage, however, the emphasis is upon **the sacrifice which He offered**. The Jewish priests offered 'oftentimes the same' sacrifices; He offered 'one' sacrifice. Their many sacrifices could 'never' take away sins; His single sacrifice was offered for sins 'for ever'. They 'stood' daily to minister and offer; He 'sat down' because His work of offering was over and complete. In chapter 7, the emphasis rather is upon **the priestly office which He fills**. No Jewish priests could 'continue' indefinitely because in due course they all died; He 'continues for ever' because 'he ever lives'. When those priests 'passed on', so too did their priesthood—to others; because He lives for ever, His priesthood will never be passed on to anyone else.

The writer had recently appealed to God's oath to Messiah, 'Thou are a priest **for ever**', v. 21, and the chapter concludes by assuring us that He is therefore perfectly equipped '**for ever**' (same expression) for His office of High Priest, v. 28. In between, the writer observes that, because He continues '**for ever**' (same expression again), He has no successors, v. 24.

Because our High Priest never has to hand over His priesthood to someone else, He is able Himself to save us 'to the uttermost'—whether 'completely' in terms of *degree* or 'for all time' in terms of *duration*, v. 25. He who is 'able to succour', 2. 18, and able to 'sympathize', 4. 15 (lit), is 'able also to save'. He who loved His own 'to the end', John 13. 1, saves them 'to the uttermost'! How 'great' a salvation is ours, 2. 3. In one sense, we have been saved by His **finished** work—for He 'once' died, v. 27. In another sense, we are being saved by His **unfinished** work—for He 'always' lives, v. 25 (lit). He who once died to 'make propitiation' for our sins, 2. 17 (lit), now lives to 'make intercession' for us, v. 25. In the Lord Jesus, we have a far greater Intercessor than even Moses or Samuel, who were proverbial for their intercessory prayers, Jer. 15. 1.

December 5th

Hebrews 10. 19-20

TO ENTER INTO THE HOLIEST

We have confidence to enter 'through (by means of) the blood of Jesus'. How thrilling to know that we enter the **same place** and by the **same route** as the Lord Jesus Himself; it was 'through his own blood' that He entered once for all into the holy place, 9. 12.

'Since Christ has entered by His blood the holiest on high;
By that *same* hallowed, blood-stained track
Thou welcomest the wanderer back,
And biddest me draw nigh.'

The blood of Jesus stands in marked contrast to the blood of the animal sacrifices which were offered repeatedly under the Old Covenant. Those sacrifices were offered 'day by day', 7. 27; 10. 11, or 'year by year', 9. 25; 10. 1; but His sacrifice was offered once for all, 7. 27; 10. 12. At no time and in no way could those sacrifices 'take away sins', 10. 4, 11. But this He did by the single offering of Himself. In those sacrifices there was a 'remembrance' of sins, 10. 3; the blood of the sacrifices offered on the Day of Atonement served to call the people's sins to account and raised the whole question of the penalty which those sins deserved. But, on the basis of Christ's blood of the New Covenant, God no longer remembers our sins against us, 10. 17.

The Old Covenant ritual illustrated that 'the way into the holiest' had not then been revealed, 9. 8; the 'way' which Jesus has opened for us is therefore said to be 'new' (ie recent, fresh). The 'way' by which we enter the holiest exists only because Christ died for us. In one sense, therefore, it could have been described as a way of death. Yet, because God brought Him from the dead and He now lives, 7. 25, it is described correctly as a 'living' way.

The way into God's symbolic presence (whether in tabernacle or temple) was barred by the (second) veil, 9. 3. For any to have free access it would have required that the veil be rent asunder. Consequent upon the Lord's death, the veil in the temple of Herod was in fact rent in two, Mark 15. 38. By the rending of that veil God set His seal of approval upon Jesus' death and finished work, just as earlier He had set His seal of approval on Jesus' life and unique Person by rending the heavens, 1. 10. The writer now speaks of the Lord's 'flesh' as a 'veil' to stress that only by the rending asunder of His flesh in death could we have access into God's real and immediate presence.

December 6th

Hebrews 10. 22

LET US DRAW NEAR

We are encouraged to **'draw near'**, and this by the very same God who once **'drove out'** the man because of his sin, Gen. 3. 24.

The writer describes believers as those who have had their 'hearts sprinkled' and their 'bodies washed' (bathed, lit). The language is figurative, referring back to the consecration of the priests, the details of which are recorded in Exodus 29 and Leviticus 8. The priests of old ('the sons of Aaron') were both sprinkled with the blood of animal sacrifices, Exod. 29. 21, and bathed in water, v. 4.

Metaphorically speaking, our hearts have been sprinkled with the blood of Christ; we have come to 'the blood of sprinkling', Heb. 12. 24. It is that blood which has cleansed our consciences, 9. 14. Although still **conscious** of the presence of sins in our lives, we no longer have a **'conscience** of sins', 10. 2; the blood of Jesus has removed the burden of our guilt and has silenced the voice of condemnation. All Christians experience the sprinkling of the blood of Jesus Christ at their conversion, 1 Pet. 1. 2.

At our conversion we are also 'bathed'. The Lord Jesus explained to Peter, 'he that is bathed does not need to wash, except his feet, but he is clean all over', John 13. 10 lit. It is very important to distinguish the once-for-all bathing from the regular and repeated washing of the feet. The Greek Old Testament observes the same distinction; the priests were 'bathed' only once, Exod. 29. 4, but they needed to 'wash' their hands and feet every time they entered the tabernacle, 30. 18-20. In our case, according to His mercy, God has saved us, 'by the bathing of regeneration', Tit. 3. 5 lit.

At no time does the writer actually give the title 'priests' to believers, reserving the title throughout for the Lord Himself. Yet, he clearly does view Christians as priests; see 13. 10, 15-16. Under the Old Covenant, the stranger that **'drew near'** to God's symbolic presence was to be put to death, Num. 18. 7. Even Uzziah, the king of Judah, was visited in severe judgement when he intruded into the province of the priesthood and entered into the sanctuary to offer incense, 2 Chron. 26. 16-21. How privileged we are, that, though once 'Gentiles in the flesh', we can now, as Christian priests, **draw near** into God's real and immediate presence. See that you do it today.

December 7th

Hebrews 11. 5-6

THE GOD WHO IS AND WHO REWARDS

Enoch is the writer's second example of the power and effectiveness of faith. He asserts that Enoch was 'translated' to heaven 'by faith' and then explains his reasons for making this claim.

First, God translated Enoch because he 'pleased' Him. This is the equivalent of saying that Enoch walked in fellowship with God, cf. Gen. 5. 22, 24. *Second*, it is not possible to walk with God (and so to please Him) without faith. Such a walk requires faith, Heb. 10. 38. *Third*, the person who 'comes to God' must have faith in both God's existence (that He is) and His character (that He rewards those who seek Him out). Only by such faith can somebody live a life of communion with God as Enoch did. (The 'one who comes to God' is the worshipper, the one who lives a life of communion with God; the word used is the same as that in 4. 16; 7. 25 and 10. 22 ('draw near')).

The chapter begins with a description of 'faith'. There we are told that faith both provides us with the evidence of that which we cannot see and makes real to us that which lies in the future. Both were true in the case of Enoch and, indeed, both are true of all who 'come to God'. **First, we believe in God**—who cannot be seen, v. 27; 1 Tim. 1. 17. Yet, although God Himself cannot be seen, His handiwork most certainly can, Ps. 19. 1-4. As we lift our eyes to the heavens we are compelled to ask, 'Who has created these things?', Isa. 40. 26. Surely, these are not the product of blind, mindless forces! Since the creation of the world, 'the invisible things' of Him (His eternal power and divinity) are clearly seen, being understood from 'the things that are made', Rom. 1. 20.

Second, we believe that we will be rewarded (be paid wages, lit) by Him if we seek Him. Those who seek Him out initially are never disappointed; He amply rewards them, both with the blessings of salvation and with Himself, Gen. 15. 1. This reward is partly enjoyed in the present world but mainly in the world to come. How relevant this was to the readers of the letter, who were called on to endure the afflictions of the present before receiving the 'recompense of reward' which God has promised, 10. 35-36.

Pray with renewed confidence today. You do not speak to the air, for God 'is', and you do not speak to One who is unresponsive, for He 'is the rewarder' of all those who seek Him out.

358

Hebrews 13. 9-16

THE SACRIFICE OF PRAISE

The priests of Israel enjoyed two great privileges. They were **appointed by God to offer sacrifices to Him**. They were also **authorized to be partakers with the altar**, 1 Cor. 9. 13; that is, they had the right to feed on many of the Levitical offerings. Today's reading shows we do not come behind them.

First, we enjoy and appropriate both Christ and His sacrifice, v. 10. The priests of Israel had no right to feed at this 'altar'—not even in picture and type. For, on the Day of Atonement, no part of the sin offering was given to the priests. After the High Priest had sprinkled the blood upon and before the mercy seat, the bodies of both bullock and goat were carried outside the camp and burned there, Lev. 16. 27. This foreshadowed the sufferings of the Lord Jesus outside the gate of Jerusalem, vv. 11-12.

The fact that the camp of Israel had no part in the sin offering symbolized the truth that those who remained in 'the camp' of Judaism had no share in the benefits which come from the true Sin Offering, our Lord Jesus Christ. The writer therefore exhorts his readers to disassociate themselves from 'the camp' and to identify themselves with the Lord Jesus in the place of rejection and reproach, cf. 10. 33.

Second, we are able to offer up our own sacrifices, v. 15. For not only is it said, 'Let us go out **to Him**', v. 13, but also, 'Let us offer up **through Him**'. In the same way, therefore, that we come to God only 'through Him', 7. 25, so also our spiritual sacrifices are acceptable to God only 'through Him', 1 Pet. 2. 5. We do not offer our praises through the medium of saints, angels or Old Testament ordinances, and certainly our feeble, and unworthy praises are not acceptable in themselves. We offer them only on the ground of our Lord's perfect sacrifice and in His name.

The expression 'sacrifice of praise' is quoted from the Greek Old Testament, where it is used to describe one form of peace offering, Lev. 7. 12. Although, therefore, we had absolutely no part in the sacrifice to God of the true **Sin Offering**, v. 11, we are privileged to sacrifice to God our **'peace offerings'**, v. 15. Through Christ, who **once offered Himself to God as a sacrifice of propitiation**, we may, and should, **continually offer to God the sacrifice of praise**. We owe Him this much at least.

WORKING IN YOU

Although it is wrong to covet the **possessions** of others, v. 5, it is not wrong to covet a place in their **prayers**, v. 18. The writer provided his readers with two good reasons why they should pray for him. First, his integrity, v. 18. Second, his example, vv. 20-21. The man who requested their prayers could assure them of his.

His prayer was concerned with their relationship to God. He wanted them to be obedient to 'His' will and pleasing in 'His' sight. He recognized that this could be achieved only as a result of **His** work in them; 'May he prepare you ... to *do* his will, *doing* in you that which is well-pleasing before him', v. 21 lit. Paradoxically, therefore, the work would be both theirs and God's, cf. Phil. 2. 13.

The writer's teaching throughout his letter has been largely concerned with what God has done *for* His people; here his prayer is concerned with what He does *in* them. We should note the way in which he speaks of the One to whom he addresses this particular request. The writer is immersed in his Old Testament scriptures and, as we would expect, the background to his description of God comes from that source. Two verses are especially relevant, 'Where is he that brought **out of** the sea **the shepherd of the sheep** (Moses)', Isa. 63. 11 LXX, and 'Moses took the blood and sprinkled it upon the people, and said, Behold **the blood of the covenant'**, Exod. 24. 8 LXX. That is, in Moses, Israel had a 'shepherd of the sheep' who had been brought 'out of' the Red Sea, and who had ratified with animal blood a covenant between God and themselves, cf. 9. 18-21. That covenant had proved to be 'faulty' because it did not carry in it the power to comply with its requirements, 8. 7-9. That covenant, with all its attendant ritual, proved to be **temporary** and vanished away, 8. 13; 9. 1.

By way of contrast, we have in 'our Lord Jesus', **'the great shepherd of the sheep'**, who has been brought **'out of'**, not the Red Sea but 'the dead', v. 20 lit. He has inaugurated **a new covenant by means of His own blood**, 12. 24; Matt. 26. 28. This covenant is **eternal.** It will never vanish away for under its terms God writes His laws in the very hearts and minds of His people, 10. 16.

Appropriately, the writer looks to the One who deals with His peoples' hearts to 'do **in** you that which is well-pleasing before Him', v. 21.

December 10th

James 1. 1-8

THE GIVING GOD

James was concerned about believers who did not know how to face their many trials and troubles. If any lacked the necessary wisdom to bear and make proper use of their afflictions, he said they were to 'ask of God'. By way of encouragement James described Him as the One who gives without **reservation** (liberally) or **reproach** (upbraideth not).

God gives unreservedly. He gives 'richly', 1 Tim. 6. 16, 'freely', Rom. 8. 32 and 'liberally' (with singleness of heart, lit). God's resources are not simply great; they are infinite. In response to my requests, He gives and I receive. Yet, although thereby I am so much richer, He is not one whit poorer. Usually, when I receive something good (cf. verse 17) from somebody else, I end up with more and they with less. But not so with answered prayer. Notwithstanding all God's bountiful giving, His store is not in the least diminished. If I come to Him for help or strength or whatever, I need never fear that my taking is going to impoverish Him. His vast reservoir of power, grace and wisdom never runs dry!

God never reproaches us for coming too often. He gives ungrudgingly. He never wearies of hearing our requests. Men often excuse themselves from giving to others by pointing to that which they have given in the past. In contrast, even though God gives so generously, He still leaves His door open wide for us to come again ... and again ... and again. God loves a cheerful giver, 2 Cor. 9. 7, for He is one Himself!

Quoting the words of the Lord Jesus, James held out the welcome promise, 'ask ... and it shall be given', v. 5; Matt. 7. 7. And yet it is possible, he added, to ask from 'the giving God' and to receive **absolutely nothing**, v. 7. Why then is this? Because, James explained, effective prayer requires faith. Whereas God *withholds nothing* from faith, Mark 11. 24, He *gives nothing* to doubt and unbelief. **When God spoke to Abraham by way of promise**, Abraham 'wavered not ... through unbelief', Rom. 4. 20 lit. Similarly, **when we speak to God by way of petition**, we should not 'waver' through unbelief. We must learn that, in God's reckoning, whereas nothing is too good for faith, anything is too good for doubt. God gives 'with singleness of heart', v. 5 lit, but not if we are of 'a double mind', v. 8.

December 11th

James 4. 1-5

ASKING AND RECEIVING

Do we experience the joy of answered prayer? If not, the one thing which is certain is that this our fault and not God's. In to-day's reading, James offers us two possible reasons why we are strangers to that joy.

First, often we simply do not ask. We try everything else before we go to God. Although we profess to believe that God has unlimited resources available which He is waiting to bestow on us, we fail to pray—and so we do not receive. O that our hearts and wills were gripped by the firm conviction that **God really does hear and answer prayer!**

If we truly believe that: (i) prayer links our helplessness with God's almightiness; (ii) prayer can do anything which God can do, and He can do anything; (iii) prayer causes more havoc among the unseen forces of darkness than does any other weapon we possess; (iv) prayer changes, not only us when we pray, but actual events and situations; and (v) prayer is the answer to every problem which exists ... **then we will 'ask'.**

Second, when we do ask, we often ask for the wrong things and for the wrong reason. When at last we rouse ourselves to pray, our petitions can be self-centred and concerned with the gratification of our own desires. Yesterday we learnt that we can make known our requests to God yet receive nothing because of the **manner** in which we ask—*in doubt and unbelief*, 1. 6-7. Today we learn that we can make known our requests to God yet receive nothing because of the **motive** with which we ask—*that we might 'spend it in our own pleasures'*, 4. 3 lit. It is possible for us to ask for prosperity, for influence, for a position of leadership, for great knowledge, or for the gift of effective communication, and all solely to gratify our own pride and vanity. We need constantly to examine our hearts as to whether our aim in prayer is really God's glory and not our own.

God looks at the intention behind our prayers. If our goal is our own pleasure and self-gratification, this proves that we have secretly set our heart on, not Him but the world, 4. 4. If we ask God for something which we mean to take and lavish on His rival, are we really surprised that He refuses our request?

December 12th

James 5. 13-18

THE POWER OF PRAYER

We have a God for all circumstances. In times of affliction, we should pray to Him; in times of cheerfulness, we should sing to Him. Do times of trouble drive us **to prayer,** and times of joy **to praise**?

To encourage us to pray, James draws attention to the powerful combination formed by **the right kind of prayer** prayed **by the right kind of man**. The fervent supplication of a righteous man, he assures us, is of 'great strength', v. 16 lit.

James loves to illustrate his points by reference to examples from the Old Testament. Previously, he had cited Abraham and Rahab as evidence of true faith which expresses itself in works, 2. 20-26, and Job as evidence of patient endurance in the face of affliction, 5. 10-11. Now he introduces Elijah as an example of one whose prayer was of 'great strength', 5. 17-18.

Although James was fully aware of the normal weather cycle, v. 7, he was also aware of one occasion when God interfered with that cycle in response to a man's prayers. For, by his prayers, Elijah had both shut and opened heaven. James is not suggesting that we attempt to imitate Elijah's prayers in detail; they accomplished exceptional things in exceptional circumstances. Nevertheless, James insists, the powerful effects of Elijah's prayers really do encourage us—because, if Elijah received such momentous answers, we cannot doubt that prayer is able to achieve great things for us too.

But what kind of prayers proved to be of such 'great strength'? We find that Elijah prayed:

(i) **earnestly,** Jas. 5. 17. We cannot expect God to hear 'prayers' which are cold, lifeless and formal. Do we pray 'fervently'?

(ii) **humbly,** 1 Kgs. 18. 42. Do we pray with due reverence?

(iii) **intelligently.** Elijah prayed in accord with God's will and purpose as revealed by His word, Deut. 11. 16-17; 1 Kgs. 18. 1.

(iv) **specifically.** There was nothing vague or imprecise about Elijah's supplications. Are our requests clear and definite?

(v) **expectantly.** 'Go up now, look ...', he instructed his servant, 18. 42. Are we on the lookout for the answers to our prayers?

(vi) **persistently.** Elijah told his servant to look seven times while he continued to pray, 18. 43-44. Do we give in too soon?

December 13th

1 Peter 3. 1-7

HINDRANCES TO PRAYER

The Christian husband is to show consideration and understanding for his wife. Failure to do so will 'hinder' their prayers, both jointly and individual.

The basic meaning of the word translated 'hindered' is 'to block the way'. Many indeed are the obstacles which bar the way between us and prayer. Alas, so often our experience attests the truth of William Cowper's words,

> 'What various hindrances we meet
> In coming to the mercy seat!'

Today we select five of the most common roadblocks which we encounter on the highway to the throne of grace and offer suggestions for removing them:

'I can't afford the time'. **But** prayer is important; I cannot afford not to pray. I need to *make* the time. Daniel handled top level affairs of State yet made the time to pray three times every day, Dan. 6. 1-3, 10. Perhaps I would accomplish more if I attempted less and spent more time praying about it.

'I don't honestly see a need for it'. **But**, my self-sufficient heart, the Lord Jesus has explicitly said, 'without me you can do nothing', John 15. 5. Do I know better than Him? And have others no needs for which I can pray? What of Christian leaders, other saints, non-Christian contacts? Dare I 'cease to pray' for such?, 1 Sam. 12. 23.

'I don't think that my prayers will accomplish much'. **But** our God is known as, 'Thou that hearest prayer', Ps. 65. 2. I suspect that neither God nor the devil share my low valuation of my prayers. COWPER'S hymn opined that, 'Satan trembles when he sees the weakest saint upon his knees'. Don't underestimate prayer's potential.

'I prayed before and nothing happened'. **But** I must not confuse delays with denials. I know only too well that past 'failures' haunt and discourage me but I 'ought always to pray, and not to faint', Luke 18.1. I give in too soon. 'Persevere' is the word, Rom. 12. 12.

'I don't feel like praying'. **But** it is just when my heart is out of tune with God that I need most to pray. Perhaps some unconfessed sin accounts for my lack of desire for God. Yet, in spite of all, He says to me, 'If from thence thou shalt seek the Lord thy God, thou shalt find him, if thou seek him with all thy heart', Deut. 4. 29.

December 14th

1 Peter 3. 8-17

GOD'S OPEN EARS

Throughout today's reading, Peter lays great stress upon separation from evil in its many forms. Christians are not to return evil for evil, v. 9. In speech they are to refrain from it, v. 10, and in conduct to turn away from it, v. 11. If they suffer, let it be for doing good and not for doing evil, v. 17. 'The Lord's eyes are upon the righteous and His ears open to their prayer', v. 12 lit.

The Lord's promise of 'open ears' can be claimed only if two conditions are met. **First, the supplicant must be 'righteous'.** Measured by God's standard of absolute perfection, we are 'the unrighteous' for whom 'the Righteous One' suffered to bring us to God, v. 18. Nevertheless, having been reconciled to God, we should now be characterized by righteousness in our conduct, 2. 24; 3. 14. Of ungodly and unrighteous men, God has said, 'though they cry in mine ears with a loud voice, yet will I not hear them', Ezek. 8. 18.

Second, our petitions must be made in reality. Mere words are not enough. We need to be particularly careful when praying publicly. It is very easy to fall into the trap of 'praying' to (rather than for) other believers.

The story is told of the young lawyer who had just opened up a brand new office. He was seated behind his shiny new desk, eagerly awaiting his first client. He heard footsteps in the hall and saw the doorknob turn. Wishing to look important, he pretended to be busy, picked up the phone and carried on a fake conversation. 'Yes, I'll have my secretary attend to that. I have a very heavy schedule. You'll need to call me back in a few days'. As the door opened, he motioned as if to say, 'Come in, come in'. A stranger entered the office, listening to one end of the weighty conversation. Finally, putting the receiver down, the lawyer turned to his potential client—'Now, what may I do for you?'. Quietly the man answered, 'I'm from the telephone company. I've come to connect your phone'.

Much of our public praying is like that. We are praying to be heard by the saints, and **there is no one on the other end of the line**. But if we pray with sincerity, we can be sure that God's ears are always open. **We will never get an engaged tone!** Take advantage today of your direct line to the Throne.

December 15th

1 Peter 4. 7-11

PRAYING IN THE LIGHT OF ETERNITY

Peter had been present when the Lord had spoken of another, an eternal, realm. For example, Peter had heard Him speak of 'treasure in heaven, which does not fail', Luke 12. 33, 41. The point registered with Peter and he developed it in his letters.

He wrote of 'an inheritance' which is incorruptible, undefiled and unfading, 'reserved in heaven for you', 1 Pet. 1. 4, of an 'unfading' crown of glory, 5. 4, and of the eternal kingdom of our Lord and Saviour Jesus Christ, 2 Pet. 1. 11. By way of contrast, he taught that the present world and all in it will be destroyed and dissolved with fire, 3. 7, 10-12. The things of earth will not continue for ever. And neither will the adverse circumstances of the present life. When viewed against the eternal glory to which we are called, the various trials and the sufferings of the present are only 'for a little (time)', 1 Pet. 1. 6; 5. 10 lit.

We are not here for ever; we are only sojourners and pilgrims in this world, 2. 11. Peter believed that this should affect our whole outlook on life. We must not be 'short-sighted', 2 Pet. 1. 9; we must assess everything in the light of eternity. Nowhere is this more important than in the matter of prayer. Hence today's text : **'The end of all things has drawn near. Therefore be of sound mind and sober with a view to (your) prayers'**, 1 Pet. 4. 7 lit. Peter's words can be paraphrased, 'This world will not last for ever. Considered in the light of eternity, its end is near. Understanding this, we are able to form a sound judgement of all events and situations around us. We can determine what really matters and what does not. We can be 'free from intoxication' ('watch', AV); not allowing our minds to be muddled and our visions blurred by the seeming importance of this present world. Preparation for the Lord's coming kingdom is far more important. Our prayers should reflect this outlook'.

We need to review seriously the things we pray for. Our prayers are often coloured by the values and priorities of the world around. Our comfort, safety and physical well-being often matter more than does our preparation for our Lord's eternal kingdom. Yet, for example, Peter saw it more important to have one's faith refined by suffering than to avoid that suffering, 1. 7. Ask yourself today which world matters most—and pray accordingly.

December 16th

1 Peter 5. 5-11

ALL ANXIETIES CAST ON HIM

'Casting all your care upon him; for he careth for you' is a golden text in every way. God would not have us **careless**, vv. 8-9; the constant prowling of our adversary calls for constant vigilance on our part. But God would have us **carefree**, v. 7.

Peter's readers had every cause for anxiety. They had more than their fair share of trials. In the present, they suffered simply because they were Christians, 4. 16. Prospects for the future were even worse; in rather ominous words, Peter warned them that the time had come 'that judgement must begin at the house of God', 4. 17. The storm clouds were gathering.

Recognizing that his readers had every reason to be alarmed, Peter alludes to the Greek Old Testament translation of Psalm 55. 22, 'Cast your care upon the Lord'. To stifle any remaining doubts on their part, however, he adds the precious word, 'all'. They need shoulder no anxieties themselves; 'all' could be cast on Him.

Peter had concluded chapter 2 with a reference to the words of Isaiah 53. 6, 'All we like sheep have gone astray ... and the Lord hath laid on him the iniquity of us all'. He now invites his persecuted readers **to cast their cares where God once laid their sins**—on Him! Enjoy today the fact that He who once carried the load of your sins is surely able to carry the load of your cares.

Finally, Peter provides his readers with the reason that they can confidently cast their anxieties on the Lord: 'for it matters to him about you', v. 7b lit. The Lord Jesus once spoke of the hireling to whom it did not 'matter about' the sheep, John 10. 12 (the same Greek expression). But Peter is able to assure his readers that it matters to their Shepherd, 2. 25; 5. 4, about them.

Peter had once been in a great storm and, in doubt and fear, had called out to Jesus, 'Teacher, doesn't it matter to you that we are perishing', Mark 4. 38. Peter has learnt his lesson. Confronted now with a different, but no less fierce, storm, in words reminiscent of his previous experience, he vouches for the fact that the sufferings of his readers are of great concern to the Saviour—'it matters to him about you'. What a thrilling assurance for us to take into the presence of God today. Bring all your cares to Him now, and leave them with Him. **The throne of grace is the place where our burdens change shoulders!**

December 17th

1 John 1. 6-2. 2

IF WE CONFESS … HE IS FAITHFUL … TO FORGIVE

Three important tests of profession are in these verses: they are introduced with the words 'If we say'. The *first* is in verse 6. It tests the profession of *salvation*. The *ongoing* walk of a true child of God must be in the light for he has been delivered from darkness.

The *second* is in verse 8 and tests the profession of a person's *nature*. To claim that there is no sin within is not truthful. The most spiritual believer is conscious of the ever present inner desires of the flesh, with the result of the committing of various sins. What then is the way for a Christian to gain forgiveness? It is to pray; but this is not the normal prayer of communion; it involves confession of sin.

'Confess' is an interesting word; it means to 'agree with', to 'speak the same thing'. Thus when we confess we are telling God about our sin, and agreeing with His verdict on our conduct. When David sinned with Bathsheba there was an initial period when he 'kept silence', he did not admit to God what he had done. When we do not confess sin, we experience the barrenness which was his at that time, Ps. 32. 3-4. It all changed when he said, 'I will confess my transgressions unto the Lord; and thou forgavest the iniquity of my sin'.

John shows that He who *forgives* our guilt when we confess it does so on an entirely righteous basis. He is *faithful* to His promises, and is also *just* in relation to His own character. The forgiveness is also accompanied by *cleansing* from the defilement we incurred when we sinned; what wonderful grace!

The *third test* is of the profession of *behaviour*, v. 10. To say we have not sinned when we have, is to reject God's own testimony thus making Him a liar. Some have made such claims but we truly know that the most spiritual Christian is still susceptible to sin. When we do sin the Holy Spirit convicts us, He is the indwelling '*paraclete*', and it is because of His work within that we make confession and this enables the restoration of **communion**. But there is another '*paraclete*', this is our Lord Jesus Christ whose work of advocacy in the presence of the Father is invoked immediately we sin. This work is based upon His propitiation which is always before the eye of God. This is why our **union and security** are maintained.

1 John 3. 18-24

WE ASK … WE RECEIVE … BECAUSE WE KEEP HIS COMMANDMENTS

Four aspects of the children of God are described in this chapter. First our future *resemblance* to Him, 'we shall be like him', vv. 1-3. Then the thought of *righteousness*, teaching that the life that practises righteousness is proof that new birth has taken place, vv. 4-9. This is followed by *relationship*, 'In this the children of God are manifest, and the children of the devil: whosoever doeth not righteousness is not of God, neither he that loveth not his brother', 1 John 3. 10. Our section deals with the children of God and *reality*.

There is at times a sad lack of reality in all our lives, and here we will see it can also have an effect upon our prayer life. But John first speaks of the reality of our love and uses parallelism to emphasize its importance. In verse 18 'word' should be set against 'deed' and 'tongue' against 'truth'. We so easily speak of loving a brother but often there is little evidence; it really all has to do with the heart. When the apostle speaks of the 'assured heart', v. 19, he is referring to that inward confidence we enjoy when we know that we are enjoying personal uninterrupted fellowship with God. In such condition we are right both with the Lord and with His people. When all is not as well as it should be in the matter of our communion with the Lord, the same heart that formerly was in enjoyment now condemns us. It is here the apostle adds that God is greater than our heart, that is, His judgement of this matter is far greater than any judgement our own heart can make. He knows what has happened with both the reasons and remedy; yes, He 'knoweth all things', v. 20.

These facts have an important part to play in the reality and effectiveness of a believer's prayer life. Such prayer is seen here to spring from a heart which is in true fellowship with God and living in obedience to the commandments of God. This is someone who, in the daily path of life, is practising those things which are pleasing to God from the genuine desire of his heart. The more we love and obey His commandments, the more our requests will reflect the very thoughts and will of God, and as the answer is received the assured heart is satisfied.

December 19th
1 John 5. 9-15

IF WE ASK ... ACCORDING TO HIS WILL ... HE HEARETH US

There is consistency in the way that John speaks of witness when dealing with the person and work of the Lord Jesus Christ. In his Gospel he records the Lord's own comparison, 'But I have greater witness than that of John', John 5.36; so it is here. What God has to say on a topic is always more important than the words of men; thus John speaks of the testimony which God has given concerning His Son. All who have been saved have believed and received it, they actually have the witness within, they are the possessors of eternal life.

Gospel doctrine should always have a practical effect upon our lives. These verses speak not only of the blessings we have within, but also make mention of those who do not have it. They believe not the record, they make God a liar, they have not life. Our knowledge of this should stimulate us to bring God's testimony to bear upon them as often as we can. But not only this, we must be before God in prayer for them.

The great object of this part of the epistle is stated in verse 13, 'These things have I written unto you that believe on the name of the Son of God; that ye may know that ye have eternal life, and that ye may believe on the name of the Son of God'. Assurance of the possession of salvation is a matter which has worried many, yet here is a clear statement of divine fact, 'that ye may know'. How good it is to rest in simple faith upon what God has said.

But this is not all; such trust gives confident boldness in Him. The heart which has fully trusted Him for salvation, and knows that it has eternal life, can also trust Him in the path of life and knows that He will hear when we pray. As our believing is on the name of the Son of God, so our prayer would also be in that same name, John 16. 23-24. But we must ask 'according to his will'. The requests of those who are living in fellowship with Him will not be selfish, nor for carnal gratification. This was how the Lord Jesus prayed in the garden of Gethsemane, 'saying, Father, if thou be willing, remove this cup from me; nevertheless not my will, but thine, be done', Luke 22. 41-42. It is good for us to know that 'he heareth us', and knowing this we know also that there is an answer.

1 John 5. 16-21

HE SHALL ASK, AND HE SHALL GIVE HIM LIFE

We have seen in this epistle that John has important things to teach about prayer. It is therefore fitting that this closing section of the letter should again deal with further aspects.

It has been noted that when prayer is according to His will it will be heard, v. 14, and if heard then the petitions will be granted, v. 15. Now we are led into a well known problem verse where first the apostle shows that we should pray about the spiritual condition of our fellow believers. This is something we often neglect, and when we see failure in others it is wiser to pray on their behalf rather than to criticize them to one and another.

When praying about sin in the life of another believer, we should remember that earlier John has taught that it is not the will of God for His people to commit sin; also that if the believer does sin there is provision made to be forgiven and cleansed from the defilement incurred.

This is the concluding passage in the epistle on the topic of sin in relation to a believer. Here it is clearly taught that when sin is discernible in a brother then we should ask (pray for) on behalf of the person in question. The apostle now points out that there is a sin which is unto (tends towards) death, and spiritual inquiry before God is not therefore suitable; it is not a matter we can pray about. Various views have been expressed regarding the nature of this sin, and each of us must be convinced in his own mind. In the general context of this and other New Testament epistles it is most likely that it is the sin of apostasy, which involves denial of the Person and work of our Lord Jesus Christ. Such an offender would be a brother in name only, but not in fact (see 3. 15). The passages in Hebrews chapters 6 and 10 are interesting parallels here, showing the impossibility of such a person being truly saved, and therefore fitting the terms of the passage.

The chief point of this section is often lost by concentrating on what we are not to pray about. Rather, it is written to encourage us to pray for those we see committing sins which are not to death; we have a responsibility to pray about these and as we intercede according to the will of God we shall with confidence look to the Lord for His answer.

371

3 John 1-4

I WISH ... THOU ... BE IN HEALTH ... AS THY SOUL PROSPERETH

The ministry of this short letter revolves around three men, Gaius, Diotrephes and Demetrius, and the apostle John has important things to say about each. It is clear that Gaius was a truly spiritual man as was Demetrius, but Diotrephes was different. It is also clear that both Gaius and Diotrephes were associated with the same assembly and therefore would know each other well; it is not clear whether Demetrius was known to the assembly spoken of here. Diotrephes was there and took a great place of self importance. It was an assembly where this one brother was not only prominent but wanted to be pre-eminent.

In the opening verses of the letter three particular things are said of Gaius. First, he was marked by **prosperity of soul**, v. 2. Whatever the state of his body, or surrounding circumstances, he had continued to make spiritual progress. He was living in personal communion with the Lord and was in good spiritual condition; how important this is at all times and particularly when times of difficulty come. No doubt this maintained Gaius when confronted with such carnality in his home assembly. Secondly, he was marked by **personal faithfulness**. This brought great joy to the apostle when news of it was brought to him by certain brethren who had seen it firsthand. The truth was not only in him; he walked in it, and as he walked he was following and practising its precepts. Thirdly, he was marked by **practical fellowship** both to his own brethren and to strangers. This was both impartial and affectionate, and the whole assembly knew of his love for those who needed such hospitality. How it must have hurt him when he saw the very brethren he loved and sought to help treated so badly.

Such was Gaius, the man for whom John the apostle is praying. The very request could imply that his physical illness was the consequence of the weight of care he carried for the assembly and its problems. Many of God's choicest saints have suffered physically whilst prospering spiritually. Here John's prayer to God, the very desire of his heart, was that his friend's spiritual prosperity would be matched by physical prosperity also.

Jude 17-25

PRAYING IN THE HOLY GHOST

This letter commences with a section on *contending for the faith*, vv. 1-3, and then continues by showing, through three Old Testament examples, the *condemnation of God on unbelief and evil*, vv. 4-7. This is followed in verses 8-13 by a remarkable description of the *character of evil men*, and a shorter part dealing with the *coming judgement*, vv. 14-16.

The foregoing reveals the serious nature of the content of this short epistle, and the hearts of the most spiritual will be grieved and alarmed in reading it. How is the believer to live in the presence of such opposing evil? What resource will be available? It is with much relief that we turn to this closing section of the epistle which now gives to us the *counsel of God* for such circumstances.

First, there is the **warning** of the word of God, vv. 17-19. Here we are exhorted to remember the words which had been spoken by the apostles of the Lord Jesus Christ. It is always good to know that, however dark the day in which we live, it was known in advance by God, and had already been forecast in the holy Scriptures. We are encouraged that the God who knows it has allowed it, and will maintain His own through it. Next, we have the **warmth** of communion, vv. 20-21. Here is a vital resource for any child of God; it is presented in four ways. First, we are to *build up* ourselves on our most holy faith. This involves constant application of the word of God to our lives; we cannot develop apart from this and through it we will hear His voice. Secondly, there is *praying in the Holy Ghost*; thus we speak to God. This is more than saying our prayers—it is the practice of true comunion, as in the power of the Holy Spirit we both pray and enjoy God's presence. Thirdly, we must *keep ourselves in His love*, enjoying the warmth of it; and fourth, we are to *look for* the mercy of our Lord Jesus Christ. Here is the prospect of His coming.

In verses 22-23 we have our **witness** to others; some near us will need our pity, whilst others require to be snatched away from evil. To be occupied with others will maintain the believer in such evil days. Finally, there is in verses 24-25 the **wisdom** and preservation of God; our trust is in the One who is able to present us faultless in that coming day.

December 23rd
Revelation 4. 1-11

THOU ART WORTHY O LORD

The overall analysis of the book of Revelation is given in chapter 1. 19. The third and final division is 'the things which shall be hereafter'. John is taken up and then invited to see and hear those things which will take place when the church age is ended. At the rapture we too will be taken up, to both see and enjoy what John saw.

First he saw a *door*, heard a *voice* of invitation and saw the *throne*. The *door* and *voice* encourage us that we are going in as soon as the present age is complete, and the *throne* that divine government will remain in control until and beyond then. He then saw who was sitting on the throne. The *jasper stone* on the High Priest's breastplate stood for Reuben (behold a son), and the *sardine* for Benjamin (son of the right hand). Thus he quickly learned that there was a man on the throne and that man is the Son. The *rainbow* was not just a bow, it was round about the throne; the whole scene indicating the completeness of divine purpose. Also around the throne were *twenty-four enthroned elders* showing that the church will be associated with Him in glory.

Next he heard fearful sounds emanating from the throne, teaching that judgements from God, meted out on earth, must follow the rapture. The *seven lamps* tell of the presence of the Holy Spirit, in heaven again following the day of grace, and the *sea of glass* that no more cleansing will be needed and all trouble will be over. The *four beasts* (living creatures) and their service is then described. The *six wings, many eyes* and *constant movement* in the presence of God, reveal that He has ever had in His presence those who are active both physically and mentally, in lauding His holiness (see Isa. 6. 1-4).

And now in the closing verses we learn that in heaven there will be prayer in its highest form. We know both here and in Isaiah 6. 3 that in His presence, and before the throne, ceaseless praise to the Lord is ever given by the living creatures in tribute to His holiness. But now we see that their thanksgivings will be joined by those who, though also enthroned, will constantly fall down before Him to cry, 'Thou art worthy, O Lord'. What a future is ours.

Revelation 5. 1-10

GOLDEN VIALS FULL OF ODOURS ...
THE PRAYERS OF THE SAINTS

John saw that the One 'who sat upon the throne' had a seven-sealed book in His right hand. He then saw, and heard the voice of, a **strong angel**. The words of this mighty being challenged the whole universe to find one who could open the book by loosing its seals. This now turns our attention to the **sobbing seer** who wept because the challenge could not be met. It is of little wonder that John wept at the thought of no one being able to execute those judgements.

Comfort is assured to John by one of the elders, who drew attention to the **springing Lion** of the tribe of Judah who had the needed ability to open the book. The first mention of a lion in Scripture is by Jacob, predicting that the future ruler of the earth would come from the tribe of Judah, the lion tribe, Gen. 49. 9. Here we see the glorious fulfilment of that promise. But when John turns to see that Lion, he sees instead the **slain Lamb**. Here we have cause to think of the great focal point of all history, and the secret of the victory in which He prevailed. It is the sacrifice of Calvary. This is how the Lion from Judah has prevailed; by being the Lamb of God, and through death defeating him that had the power of death. Thus He can, and will, execute the judgements of God against every form of evil. The Lamb has the perfect power and prerogative of a king as seen in the seven horns (see Dan 7. 24; Rev. 13. 1). In the seven eyes we learn He also has that all-seeing perception, which is in the power of the sevenfold Spirit of God.

And now we learn why there are songs of praise to replace the tears which had formerly been shed. He 'took the book out of the right hand of him that sat upon the throne'. This brings us to the **singing saints**. What praise will arise then to Him from all who are in heaven! But then we will have in our hands not only harps, but vials full of incense, the prayers of the saints. Those many prayers we have poured out, both in days of joy and of sorrow, have been stored up. But then they will be released to us again, and as we present our perfected praises, those very prayers will be as a sweet–smelling savour for Him to appreciate.

Revelation 6. 1-2, 9-11

THEY CRIED WITH A LOUD VOICE, SAYING, HOW LONG, O LORD?

The overall programme of judgement on earth at the end time is described under seven seals, seven trumpets and seven vials. These collectively reveal events which will take place after the church has been removed from earth at the rapture. This period is coincident with the seventieth week of Daniel chapter 9 which has not yet been fulfilled. We know, from a comparison of Dan. 9. 27 and Matt. 24. 15, that this final week of years will be interrupted by a very serious happening in the middle of it, thus dividing it into two equal parts. The seven seals of this chapter describe events largely within the first three and a half year period.

Once the Lamb had opened the first seal, John heard a noise as of thunder, speaking of the coming storms of divine judgement. The rider he then saw on the white horse had a bow and wore a crown and went forth as a conqueror. This is not the Lord Jesus; He will not come to earth at this early stage. It is Satan's counterfeit deliverer; the Antichrist, the man of sin. He will be an important figure at the beginning of that week, and sadly, Israel who refused the true Messiah, will accept the false one.

These, and the following verses, have a striking similarity to the early part of Matthew 24. Both passages describe the difficulties which the nation of Israel, and the world in general, will experience in this fearful period. The second seal shows there will be wars and rumours of wars, the third famines and the fourth pestilences and earthquakes.

It is as the fifth seal is broken that again we are brought to consider the subject of prayer. John now learns that the souls of those who had been 'slain for the word of God, and for the testimony which they held' were under the altar. We derive great comfort to know that those departed ones we knew and loved in Christ are safe in His immediate presence. And not only safe, but consciously aware. There is no 'soul sleep' for them. They know and understand. But more! They can pray and commune with the Lord, as here, crying 'with a loud voice, saying, How long, O Lord, holy and true'. And so we learn again there will be prayer in heaven and that direct answers, and reasons for the answers, will be given.

Revelation 7. 9-17

BLESSING ... BE UNTO OUR GOD FOR EVER AND EVER. AMEN

We now come to an interlude in the unfolding programme revealed to John. The content of the previous chapter has been turbulent, but here a calm atmosphere pervades the scene, and John sees four angels who have been given the task of restraining all forces of hurt until the seal of God has been given. In this parenthesis John learns that before the predicted times of trouble and tribulation, God will reserve a remnant from the nation of Israel to be His witness through the dark days to follow. The Church will be in heaven but there will be at least 144,000 true Jehovah's witnesses on earth in those days, each will have been given 'the seal of the living God' upon the forehead. This is the seal of divine ownership to protect and empower them.

But another company is also identified which is so large that it cannot be numbered and is drawn from 'all nations, and kindreds, and people, and tongues' and is distinct from other companies spoken of in the previous chapters. Doubtless this immense multitude is the result of the greatest work of evangelistic effort that the world has ever known. In the midst of the intense persecution of the days of tribulation, the 144.000 sealed servants of God will witness throughout the world telling of the blood of the Lamb, and those who comprise the great multitude spoken of here will have responded to the message.

The conversation between one of the elders and John reveals that these came 'out of' great tribulation. Unlike those who had been sealed, and brought 'through' the period, many of these would have suffered in it, some hungry and thirsty, others praying with tears and many put to death, but here they are being fed by the Lamb who is leading them to fountains of living waters, and God is wiping all tears from their eyes. It is as this remarkable company stands at the throne and before the Lamb that we hear another prayer of deep thanksgiving and rich praise; it comes from the angels, and clearly is a prayer of worship. We will be filled with worshipful praise as we surround that throne and see what grace has done, not only in bringing us there but in seeing them there also.

MUCH INCENSE ... WITH THE PRAYERS OF ALL SAINTS

The parenthesis of the previous chapter is complete; the Lamb has opened the seventh seal and John notes that the whole of heaven has become silent as it quietly anticipates the impending judgements; how solemn to experience this waiting atmosphere. We also note that this period may indicate divine reticence to execute judgement, which is God's strange work; He does not delight in it. John then sees seven angels standing before God and trumpets are given to them. John is thus reminded that all of these judgements are divine in origin. The trumpet judgements describe events to take place within the second half of the seventieth week of Daniel chapter 9. The most momentous years of judgement in the history of earth are about to take place.

And now he sees another angel standing at the altar; some feel that this is Christ. He stands at the brazen altar, the place of sacrifice with its coals of fire, and in his hand there is a golden censer. Here we may pause to remember that the parts of the tabernacle in the wilderness were only types or pictures of the real thing which is in heaven. John is not looking here at typical things. He is looking at the original. In the Old Testament the priest functioned at both the brazen and the golden altar, and so it is here.

At this vital part of the narrative we learn the importance and value of the prayers of many saints down the ages. At the brazen altar much incense is given to the angel, where it is exposed to the fire of the altar thus releasing its fragrance. He then offers it at the golden altar, 'which is before the throne', and with it a new addition, for we see there is added to the incense 'the prayers of all saints'. Both ascend together, and are appreciated by God.

But why are these things introduced at this stage of the book? And why does the angel now take that same censer, and fill it with fire from the brazen altar and cast it upon the earth? The many prayers of imprecation calling for judgement against evil are now to be answered. They have ascended as sweet incense to God, but now the implication of God's answer is to be felt upon earth. He is rich in mercy, but is fearful in holiness and righteous in all His ways.

December 28th

Revelation 11. 15-19

WE GIVE THEE THANKS, O LORD GOD ALMIGHTY

Our chapter commences with the continuation after a second parenthesis, which commenced at chapter 10. 1 and concluded at chapter 11. 14. And now in our opening verse the seventh trumpet is sounded. This should never be confused with the 'last trump' of 1 Corinthians 15. 52, which is the 'trump of God', and will sound at the rapture of the saints of the church age, 1 Thess. 4. 16. Here it is an angelic trumpet, sounded to announce the time of the public manifestation of the kingly glory of our Lord Jesus Christ on earth; it associates with the words of Matthew 24. 31, gathering the elect of Israel to come into the kingdom.

Because a detailed description of the manifestation of Christ is given in Revelation 19, some have taught that this passage teaches a mid-tribulation rapture. It is important to understand that the full period of prophecy from the rapture to the manifestation is dealt with in two cycles between chapters 6 and 19. The first cycle emphasizes **events** which will take place; it concludes with our section today. The second cycle emphasizes **personages** involved and commences at chapter 12. 1 and concludes in chapter 19.

When the worst of judgements have descended upon earth from the hand of God, we have the encouraging reminder that there is a king who in the purpose of God will reign for ever and ever. This is not announced by one single voice, 'there were great voices in heaven'; all are in agreement that the Lord and His Christ would be in control. It is this that raises great prayers of thanksgiving from the lips of the four and twenty elders. Here we are again reminded that in heaven we will for so many causes engage in prayer, but the greatest will always be to raise our hearts in deepest thanksgiving to God upon the throne.

The kingdoms, which God had sovereignly allowed to be in the hands of men, will then be eternally under the control of God and His Son. He will be praised for His eternal being and glory, and for His true position of control. But these great facts will have antagonized the evil hearts of angry men who will be the objects of divine judgement and punishment. But the godly of all ages will enjoy reward.

December 29th
Revelation 15. 1-4

GREAT AND MARVELLOUS ARE THY WORKS, LORD GOD ALMIGHTY

John has been viewing some of the main personages who will figure during the days of great tribulation. Such figures when viewed
in addition to the devastation in the previous chapters bring
thoughts of the tremendous **powers of evil** which Satan will produce in his final efforts. But following such evil there has been the
evidence of **divine power**. He has seen the Lamb and the 144,000
singers on mount Sion. They had been sealed before the days of
trial commenced, but here are singing their unique song of praise
when it is all over. There has been also much mention of angels and
their service. One has been sent into the earth to preach the
everlasting gospel, and others have given special public announce-
ments concerning the various judgements which have yet to fall.

Our section today has the **sign**, the **sea**, and the **song**. The
sign John has to consider is described as 'great and marvellous'
and involves seven angels having seven plagues which are yet to
be poured out. This is a most momentous scene to behold; it is
the time for the seven vial judgements to be revealed. We learn
that in these plagues the wrath of God is 'filled up'. This term
has been translated 'is finished', and it indicates that the great
period of tribulation is nearing its climax.

Before the angels sound their trumpets John sees a sea of
glass, this time mingled with fire showing the vast reservoir of
just and righteous judgements ready to be poured out in divine
wrath upon evil. But upon that same sea many saints are standing. These are they who have been through persecution and
have known the fierceness of the Beast, but here we listen to
them singing songs. Both Exodus 15 and Deuteronomy 32 record
songs of Moses; this song no doubt recalls the themes of praise
from people redeemed and being brought into the land. But here
there is much more—they sing also of the Lamb. What praise
will be upon the lips of those who have been so near to satanic
power, but have been delivered and brought into His presence?
But the praise is not restricted to the deliverance; it expands
upon the greatness of His works, His ways, His name and His
holiness. What themes to thank Him for!

December 30th

Revelation 19. 1-4

AMEN; ALLELUIA

These great bursts of joyful praise and acclamation sounded throughout heaven form a wonderful bridge in this part of the narrative presented by John. First, he has recorded the overthrow of the might and system of evil employed by Satan during the dark days of the seventieth week of Daniel 9. This paeon of praise celebrates victory over the powers of darkness, but also introduces the great event of the public manifestation of our Lord Jesus upon earth at the second advent. Both will be the subject of prayer upon earth, but here we learn that all heaven also will engage in it.

The vial judgements of God have been poured out by the seven angels upon earth and, following the final one, the ultimate overthrow of Babylon has been described. The system of evil which has had such great religious, political and commercial effects upon the world under the control of the Beast will have been completely destroyed. These events are known in heaven, and thanksgivings are now expressed.

This is one of the greatest expressions of prayerful praise in heaven. With 'a great voice' and from 'much people'. All are saying 'Alleluia; Salvation, and glory, and honour, and power, unto the Lord our God'. 'Hallelujah' is composed of two words meaning 'praise Jehovah'. In this passage it is found four times; these are the only uses of the term in the New Testament. This will be heaven's great Hallelujah chorus of praise for the delivering power of God.

The multitude cries 'true and righteous are his judgments'; they have not only seen what has been done, but are aware of the character of the One who has done it. They see as God sees, and are thankful that the great whore has been fully, righteously and eternally judged. Thus, they pray in complete harmony and fellowship with God. They rejoice that the blood of the servants of God has been avenged. They repeat their Alleluia at the ascent of the smoke of burning from this evil system.

This prayerful praise is a stimulus to the living creatures and the four and twenty elders, who cry 'Amen; Alleluia'. We are encouraged to know that in heaven we will be able to engage in such joyful spiritual exercises.

December 31st
Revelation 22. 13-21

THE SPIRIT AND THE BRIDE SAY, COME

This last prayer in the Bible is in response to a promise which has cheered the hearts of so many since it was made. The promise 'I come quickly' is made three times in this chapter; each has unique meaning and will always cause the devoted heart to exclaim, 'Even so, come, Lord Jesus'.

The person who is coming. This promise is made by our Lord Jesus Christ who is both God and man. He is described here under titles which emphasize this. He is Alpha and Omega, v. 13, the One who encompasses eternity, yet speaks of Himself as, 'I Jesus', v. 16. Again, as 'the root' of David, He is both David's Lord and originator, (see Matt. 22. 41-45), yet as His 'offspring' He became his human descendant. These titles cause us to honour and worship Him, but how precious to note that He reminds John of the name He had known so well when He was down here in humiliation, 'I Jesus'; we will never forget what He became and what it involved on our behalf, v. 16.

The promise He has made. At the time of the upper-room ministry the Saviour spoke to His disciples on this subject. He explained that He was not only going away, but would come to receive them to Himself. This is expounded doctrinally in 1 Thessalanians 4. 13-18 where the apostle Paul gives details of the particular revelation which he had received from the Lord on this subject. There we learn that when He comes, the dead in Christ will be raised, and the living saints of this present age will be caught up to meet the Lord Jesus Christ in the air. This is quite distinct from the coming of Christ to earth, described in Revelation 19. 11-16, which will be public when the glory of Christ will be made manifest. This will be private and the Lord Jesus will not come to earth but to the air, to take His people into the Father's house.

The prospect which is ours. The first mention of the promise offers a blessing for keeping the word of God, v. 7. The second refers to the reward which will come from Him when He comes, v. 12, and the third simply but eloquently tells us He is coming, v. 20. In verse 17 the Spirit and the bride are saying, 'Come', for then the Holy Spirit will ascend with the glorified bride into heaven and the longing heart of the bride will be satisfied.

Cover Pictures

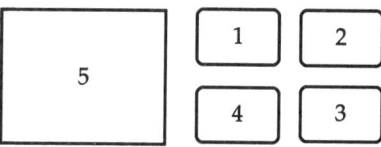

These pictures have been chosen to illustrate the theme of Prayer and have been supplied by Professor Alan Linton of Bristol who has also written these captions.

1. Mount Hermon from the Golan Heights. One of the possible sites of the transfiguration of our Lord. The Hermon range is not far from Caesarea Phillipi (modern Banias) where Jesus was ministering a week before the transfiguration took place. Luke records, '(Jesus) went onto a mountain to pray'.

2. The Valley of Dothan, located among the Mountains of Samaria, where Joseph went in search of his brothers. Jesus often went into **a solitary place** like this to pray to His Father.

3. It was beneath the olive trees in the **Garden of Gethsemane** that Jesus prayed, 'O my Father, if this cup may not pass away from me, except I drink it, thy will be done'. It is possible that the few ancient olive trees growing there today, one of which is shown, derived from the original ones in the olive grove, (Gethsemane means the 'olive oil press').

4. Skull Hill, located outside the city walls north of the old city of Jerusalem. Without doubt, Roman executions were carried out here. Most probably this is the site of Calvary. It was here that Jesus prayed, 'Father, forgive them for they know not what they do'.

5. This symmetrical mountain, **Mount Tabor,** is viewed from the hill where the Jews took Jesus from Nazareth with the intent of casting Him down headlong. It stands on its own at the eastern end of the extensive Plain of Jezreel, which continues west as far as the Mediterranean and is considered to be the site of the future Battle of Armageddon. Traditionally, Mount Tabor is a second possible site of the transfiguration.